THE BRITISH GENERAL ELE...

Other books in this series

THE BRITISH GENERAL ELECTION OF 1945
R. B. McCallum and Alison Readman
*THE BRITISH GENERAL ELECTION OF 1950
H. G. Nicholas
*THE BRITISH GENERAL ELECTION OF 1951
David Butler
*THE BRITISH GENERAL ELECTION OF 1955
David Butler
*THE BRITISH GENERAL ELECTION OF 1959
David Butler and Richard Rose
*THE BRITISH GENERAL ELECTION OF 1964
David Butler and Anthony King
*THE BRITISH GENERAL ELECTION OF 1966
David Butler and Anthony King
*THE BRITISH GENERAL ELECTION OF 1970
David Butler and Michael Pinto-Duschinsky
*THE BRITISH GENERAL ELECTION OF FEBRUARY 1974
David Butler and Dennis Kavanagh
*THE BRITISH GENERAL ELECTION OF OCTOBER 1974
David Butler and Dennis Kavanagh
*THE 1975 REFERENDUM
David Butler and Uwe Kitzinger
*THE BRITISH GENERAL ELECTION OF 1979
David Butler and Dennis Kavanagh
 EUROPEAN ELECTIONS AND BRITISH POLITICS
David Butler and David Marquand
*THE BRITISH GENERAL ELECTION OF 1983
David Butler and Dennis Kavanagh
*PARTY STRATEGIES IN BRITAIN
David Butler and Paul Jowett

*Also published by Macmillan

Series Standing Order

If you would like to receive future titles in this series as they
are published, you can make use of our standing order
facility. To place a standing order please contact your
bookseller or, in case of difficulty, write to us at the address
below with your name and address and the name of the
series. Please state with which title you wish to begin your
standing order. (If you live outside the UK we may not have
the rights for your area, in which case we will forward your
order to the publisher concerned.)

Standing Order Service, Macmillan Distribution Ltd,
Houndmills, Basingstoke, Hampshire, RG21 2XS, England.

The British General Election of 1987

David Butler
Fellow of Nuffield College, Oxford

Dennis Kavanagh
Professor of Politics, University of Nottingham

MACMILLAN
PRESS

First published 1988

Published by
THE MACMILLAN PRESS LTD
Houndmills, Basingstoke, Hampshire RG21 2XS
and London
Companies and representatives
throughout the world

Typeset by Wessex Typesetters
(Division of The Eastern Press Ltd)
Frome, Somerset

Printed in Great Britain by
Camelot Press Ltd, Southampton

British Library Cataloguing in Publication Data
Butler, David, *1924–*
The British general election of 1987.
1. Great Britain. *Parliament*—Elections,
1987
I. Title   II. Kavanagh, Dennis
324.941′0858   JN956
ISBN 0–333–44612–7 (hardcover)
ISBN 0–333–46793–0 (paperback)

Contents

List of Tables

viii *List of Tables*

Illustrations

PHOTOGRAPHS

1. (a) Launching the 1983 manifesto (May 1983)
    Willie Whitelaw   Margaret Thatcher   Cecil Parkinson

   (b) Labour elects its leaders (1 October 1983)
    Roy Hattersley   Neil Kinnock

   (c) The Brighton bomb (12 October 1984)

   (d) Arthur Scargill arrested at Orgreave (29 May 1984)

   (e) Michael Heseltine resigns (6 January 1986)

   (f) The Anglo–Irish Agreement
    Garret Fitzgerald   Margaret Thatcher   Sir Geoffrey Howe
    (15 November 1985)

2. (a) David Frost interviews the Prime Minister (7 June 1987)

   (b) Labour's Press Conference
    Neil Kinnock   Bryan Gould (7 June 1987)

   (c) Campaigning in Islwyn (24 May 1987)
    Glenys and Neil Kinnock

   (d) The Nationalist Accord (20 May 1987)
    Dafydd Wigley (Plaid Cymru)   Gordon Wilson (SNP)

   (e) A Conservative poster (16 May 1987)
    Norman Tebbit

   (f) Lord Young at a press conference (1 June 1987)

3. (a) Launching the Conservative Manifesto (19 May 1987)
    George Younger   Nigel Lawson   Willie Whitelaw
    Margaret Thatcher   Norman Tebbit   Sir Geoffrey Howe
    Douglas Hurd   Norman Fowler

   (b) Launching the Labour Manifesto (19 May 1987)
    Roy Hattersley   Neil Kinnock

   (c) An Alliance press conference (25 May 1987)

   (d) A photo-opportunity: Mrs Thatcher (30 May 1987)

   (e) A photo-opportunity: Neil Kinnock (14 May 1987)

4. (a) A television election (26 May 1987)

   (b) The two Davids at Richmond (7 June 1987)

   (c) The Kinnocks vote (11 June 1987)

   (d) The Thatchers vote (11 June 1987)

   (e) Spitting Image

Preface

The British General Election of 1987 is the thirteenth in a series starting in 1945 and is the fifth study written jointly by the present authors. We have tried to follow a format which has evolved over the years. The book covers the salient events of the parliament, the planning of the parties' campaign strategies, the election campaign itself and the treatment of the campaign by the mass media and opinion polling agencies; it also provides an extensive and analytical statistical appendix. To the best of our knowledge, no other country has managed to establish such a series of election studies, or to provide a comparable set of election data and analyses.

Writing a work in a series imposes constraints since data has to be presented in a form that allows long-term comparison. Yet each election campaign has its own distinctive character, arising from the mix of personalities, issues, events and immediate past history. 'No man can jump twice into the same river. Both the man and the river change'.

Some analyses of election campaigns may err in seeing the decisions and manoeuvres of the winning party and those of the defeated party as contributing, almost inevitably, to the eventual outcome. *Post hoc propter hoc*. 1987 is not quite like that: the majority verdict has been that the Conservatives fought a poor campaign and won, and yet Labour a good campaign and was heavily defeated. The historian also has to avoid being wise after the event. Mrs Thatcher and the Conservatives gained an historic third successive election victory in 1987. The party and its leader have dominated British politics in the 1980s. Yet it is worth remembering that for much of 1986 Labour led in the opinion polls and informed talk was on the likelihood of an election outcome in which no party would have a clear majority.

There are dangers in abstracting an election campaign from the events and trends that occur in earlier years.* For example, the panic in Downing Street on so-called 'Wobbly Thursday', in which the

---

* Two works of virtually 'instant' history on the election were published in July 1987. Des Wilson's *Battle for Power* described the Alliance campaign and Rodney Tyler's *Campaign* portrayed the Conservative effort. Both books added to post-election controversies in the Alliance and Conservative parties respectively. The authors were close to some events of the campaign and wrote from an inside and probably inevitably one-sided perspective.

different teams of ministers and advertising agencies competed for control of the final stages of the Conservative campaign, is described on pp. 106–12. But the disagreements over strategy and advertising, and the tensions between Mrs Thatcher and Mr Tebbit, cannot be properly understood in isolation from the flow of events over the previous 18 months. We explore the background in Chapters 1 and 2. The seeds of the Alliance differences over the dual leadership, as well as over defence and strategy, were laid in the months before the election, particularly in David Owen's deep-seated reluctance to engage in anything but the most minimal form of co-operation with the Liberals. Labour's problems over taxation and economic policy did not just surface in the last week of the election. The party's plans were, in the words of one participant, 'half baked to begin with' and Mr Kinnock and Mr Hattersley never saw eye to eye on the policies. An election campaign is not merely a matter of media hype, photo-opportunities and advertising slogans. The intense focus of the campaign does serve to highlight potential weaknesses in policies and personalities, as well as in party images and organisation.

As usual we have drawn on a wide range of sources, but mainly on the comprehensive press and broadcasting coverage, and on our interviews with key participants which started in early 1984. During these conversations we were reminded again of the many-sided nature of truth and of how events are subject to differences of recall, interpretation and evaluation. To a greater extent than in any previous Nuffield election study we have been assisted by participants providing us with access to relevant documentation – particularly strategy papers, memoranda and private opinion polls. Candidates from all parties kindly found time to reply to our post-election questionnaires about the campaign in the constituencies. On the public mood we have relied on the record number of surveys conducted by opinion pollsters. For a more detailed assessment of the electorate's attitudes we await the results of the British Election Study under Anthony Heath. We have also been helped by comments on earlier versions of our manuscript from some of those most closely involved. We are deeply grateful for all this assistance, some of it necessarily anonymous.

There can never be a final word on this or any other election. Though this book was swiftly written, it is intended for a long-term readership. We have tried to capture some of the essentials of this particular exercise in democratic decision-making, but in the words of R. B. McCallum, who conceived and wrote the 1945 Nuffield study, we are content to 'seek immortality in the footnotes of other authors'.

We are indebted to many institutions and individuals for help in bringing this study to fruition. We thank Byron Criddle, John Curtice, Martin Harrison, Martin Harrop and Michael Steed for their contributions; our colleagues in Nuffield College and the Politics Department at the University of Nottingham for much tolerance and advice; the Economic and Social Research Council for financial assistance; the indefatigable Audrey Skeats and April Gibbon for typing; Clive Payne, Martin Range and others for producing the statistics; our conscientious research assistant Peter Wells, and Kevin Swaddle, Peter Cozens, Helen Fawcett, Roger Mortimore, Susan Scarrow and Jane Kavanagh for other help; Vernon Bogdanor, Michael Pinto-Duschinsky and Peter Morris for commenting on our manuscript; and finally our wives and our children who showed much forbearance throughout the enterprise.

DAVID BUTLER
DENNIS KAVANAGH

3 September 1987

I

1983–1987

1 Background

At the outset, the 1980s did not promise to be the Thatcher decade. But events developed in a way that made the period a ripe seed-bed for the values and the style of government that Margaret Thatcher represented. The Falklands war established in the public mind her strength and her patriotic drive, and the turn-around of the economy suggested a general picture of Conservative competence. Her party's ascendancy was enormously aided by the division of the opposition between a Labour party, dragged down electorally by its unpopular left wing, and a new-born Alliance, full of drive and middle-class idealism, but never quite able to establish itself as the real alternative to the Conservatives. In a world of three-party politics, 42% of the votes were enough to give Mrs Thatcher a comfortable hold on power.

In retrospect her 1983 victory seemed easy. The triumphant war leader could transcend the awkward facts of unemployment and inner-city deprivation and riots. Success in dealing with inflation and the improvement in most people's living standards more than cancelled disappointments in other fields. And the Labour party, under Michael Foot, failed to offer a remotely plausible alternative government: its performance was so unconvincing that its natural second place was closely threatened by the coalition between its own breakaway group, the Social Democrats, and the Liberals.

But there was no reason to suppose that what had happened in 1983 could readily be repeated. The Conservatives were well aware how circumstances had favoured them. The Labour party quickly showed it had learned the lesson from its follies before and during the election. The Alliance, buoyed by a 26% share of the vote, believed that one more heave could really give them substantial parliamentary representation or even a share of power.

Britain had a genuine three-party system for the first time in over 50 years. The electorate was trifurcated, even though the representation in the House of Commons was still overwhelmingly Conservative or Labour. This situation imposed new rules of the game for the political parties. For two out of three Conservative Members of Parliament, the Alliance provided the main opponent in their constituency, although Labour was clearly the chief opposition party at Westminster. Labour faced the dilemma of wanting the

Alliance to fall in the opinion polls so that it would be the only credible alternative to the Conservatives, yet also needing the Alliance to do well enough to damage the Conservatives in the South of Britain. Some people had voted tactically in past elections, but the 1983 parliament saw much more discussion about getting third-placed Alliance and Labour voters to use their ballots to unseat sitting Conservative MPs. The simplicity of the old two-party system had gone.

Mrs Thatcher was the main beneficiary of important social changes. Britain was becoming increasingly a nation of owner-occupiers and shareholders, and decreasingly one of the propertyless and of council tenants, belonging to trade unions and working in nationalised industries. A MORI (Market and Opinion Research International) survey showed that between 1979 and 1987 home-ownership increased from 52% to 66%, and share-ownership from 7% to 19%. The proportion of council tenants declined from 45% to 27%, trade union membership from 30% to 22% of the work force. Each of these trends encouraged pro-Conservative tendencies in some voters. Despite the pockets of impoverishment, Britain was turning into an ever more middle-class society.

The Thatcher years were also a period in which 'popular capitalism' as government ministers liked to call it, spread. The sale of state undertakings provoked a remarkable response. There were 2.3 million applications for the British Telecom shares, 1.1 million for British Airways, 2.1 million for Rolls-Royce and 2.4 million for the British Airports Authority. The Chancellor introduced schemes to encourage private pensions and the purchasers of shares and the new share-owners were fortunate in that they profited from the stock market boom.

Mrs Thatcher lent her name to a new style of politics. Thatcherism mainly reflected her own beliefs, particularly in individual self-reliance, personal responsibility and traditional moral values. Some people were misled into identifying it with a commitment to liberalism or even libertarianism. In fact Mrs Thatcher believed in free-market economics but also in a strong state for defence and law and order. She was not permissive on social questions. Hence the paradox of a government which believed in rolling back the state in some areas yet ruthlessly extended its control in others. It privatised a number of public enterprises; it removed exchange controls; it abandoned prices and incomes policies; it reduced the high marginal tax rates (from 80% to 60%) as well as the basic level (from 33% to 26%);

and it encouraged deregulation in the area of minimum wages. Yet in other areas, notably education, the health service and local government, the Thatcher administration proved vigorously interventionist.

There was much talk that Mrs Thatcher had broken the post-war consensus on domestic politics. In some respects that consensus had already crumbled. In 1976 the Labour government received help from the IMF only after agreeing to make public spending cuts, to impose monetary controls and to continue pay restraint. By 1979 disillusion with trade unions and parts of the public sector, and a sense of the failure of Keynesianism, were widespread. But what was distinctive about Mrs Thatcher was that she was the first leader who did not try to make the consensus work. She frequently expressed her dissatisfaction with the status quo in diverse fields and she equated consensus politics with weak compromise and an absence of political conviction. Her free market critics complained that she did not go far enough in cutting taxes and public spending, in introducing vouchers or extending charges for users of education and health services, or in curbing middle-class 'perks' like tax relief on private pensions or house mortgages. Little was done to trim the rising burden of state expenditure on welfare or the NHS, for ministers knew how popular these were. Monetarism, the hallmark of the 1979 government, was laid to rest under Nigel Lawson.

One does not have to accept all the claims made for or against the Thatcher government: advocates and critics may have exaggerated what the government could achieve, for good or for ill. Mrs Thatcher, like her post-war predecessors, was hemmed in by international constraints, slow economic growth and recalcitrant interests at home. Her governments, however, differed radically not only from Labour but also from previous Conservative governments, notably reducing the autonomy of local government, the size of the public sector and the number of nationalised industries, and abandoning the conciliation of trade unions, the corporatist style of running the economy, and the pursuit of full employment. The years since 1979 saw significant changes in British politics. The style and rhetoric were also more abrasive and challenging, as was shown dramatically in the miners' strike. Both Mr Heath and the late Lord Stockton expressed unease about the direction of Conservative politics and what they regarded as Mrs Thatcher's repudiation of their 'One Nation' legacy.

The public mood was complex. Mrs Thatcher was not liked but she was respected as a leader who stood up for Britain and spoke her mind. There was much public dissatisfaction with the education and health services, which were the responsibility of central and local government. But in each year since 1981 there was a steady rise in the living standards of those in work. Surveys regularly showed large majorities expressing the wish for more money to be spent on welfare services, even if this entailed an increase in taxation. Yet when asked what mattered to themselves and their families, more public spending or tax cuts, a majority preferred the tax cuts (Marplan, March 1987). If one regards the statement in Table 1.1 as expressing important Thatcherite values, then surveys suggest that the electorate was only half-hearted in its support for Thatcherism and actually became less enamoured of it after 1983. But no other party managed to mobilise a large enough coalition of those voters and interests which had lost out since 1979.

Table 1.1   Support for Thatcherite beliefs about politics in 1983 and 1987

Statement agreement	1983 (May) Agree (%)	1983 (May) Disagree (%)	1987 (May) Agree (%)	1987 (May) Disagree (%)	Balance of approval 1983 (%)	Balance of approval 1987 (%)
When dealing with political opponents, one should stick firmly to one's beliefs [one should meet halfway][2]	50	39	45	48	+11	−3
Governments can't do much to create prosperity; it is up to people to help themselves	48	38	39	48	+10	−9
In difficult economics times, the Government should be tough [should be caring][2]	46	35	36	50	+11	−14
In dealing with the rest of the world, it is better for Britain to stick resolutely to its own position [it is better to meet other countries halfway][2]	29	59	28	63	−30	−35
When governments make economic policy, it is better to keep unions and business at arms length [it is better to involve them][2]	27	62	22	69	−33	−47
Average	40	47	36	55	−7	−21

Notes:
1. Excludes responses which are mixed or 'don't know'.
2. Words in square brackets show alternatives in the survey: agreement with statement indicates support for Mrs Thatcher's belief.

Sources: BBC Gallup survey, June 1983; Gallup survey, June 1987.

CHRONOLOGY I (1983–87)

1983

9 Jun.	Conservative Government re-elected (Con. 397, Lab. 209, Alln 23)
11 Jun.	Cabinet reshuffle; Sir G. Howe to Foreign Office; N. Lawson to Treasury; F. Pym dropped
13 Jun.	D. Owen takes over SDP Leadership
16 Jun.	Central Policy Review staff to be abolished
7 Jul.	D. Steel takes three months leave as Lib. leader
13 Jul.	Commons votes 368–145 against capital punishment
19 Jul.	Government defeated as MPs vote pay increase
11 Sept.	SDP conference rejects any merger with Liberals before next election; D. Owen recommends 'social markets'
14 Sept.	S. Gummer succeeds C. Parkinson as Con. Chairman
2 Oct.	Lab. electoral college elects N. Kinnock, Leader, and R. Hattersley, Deputy Leader
11 Oct.	C. Parkinson resigns from Cabinet
25 Oct.	US forces invade Grenada without consulting Britain
14 Nov.	First Cruise missiles arrive at Greenham Common; mass protests.
21 Nov.	Unionists withdraw from Northern Ireland Assembly
	Violent labour dispute at E. Shah's Warrington printing works
17 Dec.	Six die in IRA bombing at Harrods

1984

17 Jan.	Rate capping Bill gets second reading
25 Jan.	Government ban on Trade Unions at Government Communications Headquarters (GCHQ)
1 Mar.	T. Benn returned in Chesterfield by-election
8 Mar.	Miners' year-long strike begins; Notts miners work on
13 Mar.	N. Lawson's first budget raises income tax thresholds
23 Mar.	Sarah Tisdall jailed for leaking plans for Cruise arrival to the *Guardian*
11 Apr.	Second Reading for Bill paving way for GLC abolition (39 Con. rebels)
17 Apr.	Libya embassy siege following shooting of police constable
14 Jun.	Euro-elections (Con. 45, Lab. 32, Others 4)
14 Jun.	SDP wins Portsmouth South by-election
25 Jun.	Fontainebleau agreement on European Economic Community finance, including UK contribution to EEC budget
28 Jun.	Lords defeat Paving Bill for Greater London Council abolition
31 Aug.	TUC General Council backs NUM strike
4 Sept.	N. Willis succeeds L. Murray as Gen. Sec. of TUC
10 Sept.	Government reshuffle. Hurd succeeds Prior in N. Ireland. Lord Young enters Cabinet
20 Sept.	Lib. Assembly defies D. Steel by demanding withdrawal of Cruise
12 Oct.	Con. Conference hotel at Brighton blown up by IRA. Five killed
6 Nov.	President Reagan re-elected
20 Nov.	Br. Telecom privatised – shares four times oversubscribed.

1 Dec.   Receiver takes control of NUM funds
19 Dec. Britain and China agree Hong Kong's return to China in 1997

1985
25 Jan. Televising of House of Lords begins
20 Jan. L. Whitty chosen as Lab. Gen. Sec.
11 Feb. C. Ponting acquitted of breaking Official Secrets Act
3 Mar.   Miners vote to end strike
19 Mar. Budget makes few major changes
23 Apr. Teachers' unions reject pay settlement and begin protracted
         industrial dispute
2 May   Local elections produce 24 hung councils out of 39 English counties
3 Jun.   Green Paper on Social Security suggests end to income-related
         pensions
16 Jun. R. Todd elected TGWU Gen. Sec.
4 Jul.   Liberals win Brecon & Radnor by-election
18 Jul. 'Top peoples' pay increase of up to 48% provokes Con. revolt
2 Aug.   Breakaway Union of Democratic Mineworkers (UDM) established
6 Aug.   TUC–Labour party document *A New Partnership – A New Britain*
2 Sept. Government reshuffle. D. Hurd to Home Office; L. Brittan to
         Trade & Industry
3 Sept. N. Tebbit and J. Archer as Con. Chairman and Deputy Chairman
9 Sept. Rioting in Handsworth
1 Oct.   N. Kinnock attacks Militant members of Liverpool Council, and
         black sections at Lab. Conference
6 Oct.   Tottenham rioting and murder of policeman
15 Nov. Anglo-Irish agreement signed at Hillsborough
1 Dec.   C. of E. '*Faith in the Cities*' report on urban deprivation
3 Dec.   Luxembourg summit agrees Common European Act

1986
9 Jan.   M. Heseltine resigns from Cabinet over Westland sale
23 Jan. N. Ireland by-elections. Unionists lose Newry to SDLP
24 Jan. L. Brittan resigns over Westland affair
25 Jan. Start of printworkers' strike at Wapping (ends 5 Feb. 1987)
7 Feb.   Austin Rover sale abandoned
12 Feb. Channel Tunnel approved by Britain and France
18 Feb. Single European Act signed
26 Feb. Lab. NEC accepts report on Militant
4 Mar.   *Today* newspaper launch
5 Mar.   High Court endorse surcharge on Lambeth and Liverpool Councils
18 Mar. Budget
28 Mar. Victory for last of 37 unions in vote on keeping Political Fund
10 Apr. Lab. win Fulham by-election. SDP comes third
14 Apr. Sunday trading bill defeated 296–282 on Second Reading
15 Apr. British bases used for US bombing of Libya
22 Apr. Lab. launches 'Freedom and Fairness' campaign
28 Apr. Chernobyl nuclear explosion
3 May   Major violence in Wapping printworkers' dispute

8 May   Liberals win Ryedale by-election, almost win W. Derbyshire
8 May   Council elections show some Con. gains
21 May   K. Baker replaces Sir K. Joseph at Education
5 Jun.   Alliance Defence Commission reports; is snubbed by D. Owen
12 Jun.   D. Hatton expelled from Lab. party
12 Jun.   N. Ireland Assembly dissolved
3 Jul.   Peacock report on BBC
18 Jul.   Lab. narrowly retain Newcastle-under-Lyme in by-election
3 Aug.   Mrs Thatcher isolated at Commonwealth heads meeting over S. Africa. Rumours of Queen's displeasure
23 Sept.   Liberal Assembly votes for non-nuclear defence in defiance of D. Steel
26 Oct.   J. Archer resigns as Con. Deputy Chairman
27 Oct.   Big Bang in City
27 Oct.   *Independent* newspaper launch
6 Nov.   N. Lawson announces £5bn increase in public spending
17 Nov.   P. Wright *Spycatcher* case begins in Australia
8 Dec.   British Gas share sale oversubscribed

1987
26 Jan.   Relaunch of SDP/Liberal Alliance
5 Feb.   End of Wapping printworkers' dispute
26 Feb.   SDP wins Greenwich by-election
1 Mar.   Gorbachev offer to cut intermediate missiles
12 Mar.   Government approves Sizewell nuclear plant
17 Mar.   Budget takes 2p off income tax
28 Mar.   Mrs Thatcher visits Moscow
28 Mar.   N. Kinnock visits Washington
8 May   *News on Sunday* launched
8 May   Local elections
11 May   Election announced

The other parties tried to cope with the impact of Thatcherism on the public. Leaders of the parties recognised a greater public approval for the ideas of thrift, enterprise and self-reliance and hostility to restrictive practices. The government also appeared to have shaped decisively the agenda on such issues as the role of trade unions, the sale of council houses to sitting tenants, and the transfer of state services and enterprises to the private sector. Dr Owen admired Mrs Thatcher's vigorous 'no nonsense' style of leadership and, like her, believed in a strong nuclear defence and a social market approach to the economy. The Labour party moderated some policy stands, and Mr Kinnock was also determined to provide strong leadership to his party. Trade union leaders adopted a lower profile and the defeat of Mr Scargill in 1985 demonstrated that they were no longer the power in the land that they had been in the mid-1970s.

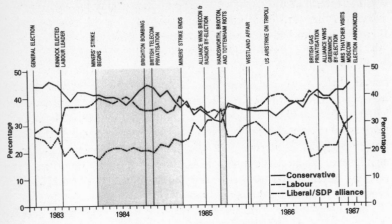

Figure 1.1   Party support 1983–87

The 1983–7 parliament was more tranquil than its predecessor. Party fortunes fluctuated – but never as violently as in the previous four years. Mrs Thatcher and her colleagues encountered rough patches – and so did her opponents – but the government never hit points as low as the Crosby by-election in 1981, or as high as during the Falklands triumph in 1982. The Conservative party was defeated in by-elections, and trailed at times in the opinion polls, but it never lost the confidence engendered by its 146-seat majority in the House of Commons.

Figure 1.1 makes plain that the electorate had become less volatile than in recent parliaments. In a mere 18 months in 1980–82 opinion poll support for each of the three parties fluctuated between the high 40s and the mid-20s. But during the four years from 1983 the movements were smaller. The Conservatives rarely dipped below 30% and Labour effectively remained between 27% and 40%. The Alliance, apart from two jumps, stayed in the 20%–30% bracket.

Certainly there was no doubt about the Prime Minister's dominance in parliament and in the country. Immediately after the election she dismissed Francis Pym from the Cabinet and a year later she accepted the departure of her most vigorous ministerial critic, James Prior. Her recruits, Douglas Hurd, Kenneth Baker and Lord Young, were not hardline 'dries' but, except over the Westland affair, there was no evidence of trouble in the Cabinet, and her Treasury team, under Nigel Lawson, maintained a fairly stern financial discipline.

Yet the limits to her authority were demonstrated three times in the first month of the parliament. The members immediately elected a Speaker, Bernard Weatherill, whom she did not want; they awarded themselves a pay increase of which she disapproved; and they voted, 368–145, against capital punishment, which she supported.

In the early part of the parliament, the Conservatives were of course helped by the disarray of the opposition. David Owen immediately jostled Roy Jenkins out of the leadership of the six SDP MPs, while David Steel took three months' leave from the Liberal leadership to consider his position. David Owen persuaded the SDP not to support a merger and the Liberals somewhat reluctantly acquiesced. The continuance of their separate party identities led, not to violent rows, but to delays and misunderstandings over candidate selection and over policy.

The Labour party, with their lowest vote since 1918, were deeply shaken by the election. Michael Foot soon announced his intention of standing down. Tony Benn's defeat meant that the left had no obvious standard-bearer. The battle between Neil Kinnock on the centre left and Roy Hattersley on the right was conducted with less rancour than had been expected, and Neil Kinnock's decisive win put the party on the road to a slow recovery. But the 209 Labour members were unable to make very much impact in the lop-sided parliament.

The most politically important event was the miners' strike which lasted from March 1984 to March 1985. This clumsily managed protest against pit closures ended in complete defeat for Mr Scargill and the National Union of Mineworkers.[1] It was accompanied by violence at those pitheads where miners defied the picket line. While it lasted the dispute placed great strains on the loyalty that the Labour party and the TUC normally have towards miners. The refusal of Mr Scargill first to hold a national ballot, and then to entertain any thought of compromise or to condemn violence on the picket line, made it difficult for those who sympathised with the miners' cause to give them unequivocal support. Ian MacGregor, the tough Scots-American chairman of British Coal, proved as intransigent as Mr Scargill but, as polls showed, public opinion was on his side. The NUM, having lost the support of a third of their members, mainly in the Nottinghamshire area, could never marshall enough support from dockers, railwaymen and electricity workers to make their strike effective. For a full year the struggle divided Labour and discouraged potential recruits. A few sympathisers were radicalised by the dispute but the failure of the miners to circumvent the legal barriers, or the police lines, and their ultimate humiliation was a profound discouragement to all who sought to challenge the Thatcher government by confrontation.

Apart from the miners' strike, the number of days lost in disputes sank to a record low. Some attributed this to unemployment, and a recognition that strikes cost jobs. Some explained it as the reward for the government's new laws. Certainly recourse to ballots averted strikes on the railways, among post office engineers and at British Leyland, and heavy fines on the miners and the printers warned other unions against illegal action. The two major disputes in the latter part of the parliament hardly affected the national economy. Teachers, uneasy about cuts and falling real salaries, engaged in guerilla warfare from 1984 onwards, though never attempting a full-scale strike. And the print unions became involved in protracted disputes as the new technology threatened their traditional craft and its accompanying restrictive practices.

A provincial publisher of free newspapers, Eddie Shah, provoked violent disturbances in Warrington in November 1983 as he refused to maintain a closed shop in his modernised plant. His successful resistance led him to plan a new national newspaper, *Today*, which had a somewhat unsuccessful launch in March 1986. He also inspired the major national proprietors to be tougher with the unions. Newspapers were in any case moving out of Fleet Street and using dispersed printing arrangements. In the process the *Daily Express* and the *Daily Telegraph* changed hands to more ruthless millionaire owners. At the *Daily Mirror* Robert Maxwell drastically cut jobs. In December 1985 Rupert Murdoch fired all his production staff when they refused to co-operate; he moved his four titles, headed by *The Times* and the *Sun*, to a new plant at Wapping – where he produced them at vastly reduced cost by a new work force of electricians. For a year there were violent scenes at Wapping, especially on Saturday nights, when the print unions, joined by some unwelcome allies from the extreme and anarchist left, tried to block the distribution of the *Sunday Times* and the *News of the World*. But in the end the print unions had to accept defeat.

The trade unions were beleaguered. Their membership was falling more rapidly than the level of employment. They were divided over acceptance of the new union legislation as well as by internal disagreements over the extent of their support first for the miners and then for the printers. Len Murray was replaced by Norman Willis as TUC General Secretary, but the emergence of Ron Todd in the

Transport and General Workers' Union (TGWU) and John Edmonds in the General, Municipal and Boilermakers (GMB), combined with structural changes which favoured white-collar union representation on the General Council, probably made it easier to maintain a moderate stance. And the unions did have one major triumph. The Trade Union Act of 1984 required them to ballot their members on whether they wished to maintain a political fund. Intense lobbying produced on average an 80% 'yes' vote among the 37 unions that had to vote in the winter of 1985–6. This attempt, at least, to block political activity by the unions, a measure which could have cut off the bulk of Labour party funds, came to nothing.

Events overseas made remarkably little impact on British domestic politics. The last major colonial problem facing Britain moved towards solution with the signing, on 19 December 1984, of an agreement to hand Hong Kong back to the Chinese in 1997, but with her capitalist institutions guaranteed for a further 50 years. Despite Tam Dalyell's efforts to continue the argument over the sinking of the *Belgrano*, there was little echo of the Falklands war and little effort at *rapprochement* with Argentina. Famine in Africa excited much sympathy and inspired the remarkable fund-raising efforts of the pop star, Bob Geldof, in 1985. Britain broke off relations with Libya in 1983 following the shooting of a policewoman in London, and with Syria in 1986, following the revelations of the activities of hit-squads in London.

Anglo-American relations came into question in October 1983 when American forces intervened in the troubled island of Grenada, without Mrs Thatcher being informed, and again in April 1986 when the government allowed US aircraft to use bases in Britain for their air raids on Libya. Mrs Thatcher remained unequivocally loyal to the United States and the 'special relationship' in face of Labour critics and some Conservative doubters. She had been equally robust in November 1983 when the first Cruise missiles arrived at the Greenham Common airbase in Berkshire. This development, and the demonstrations which followed, were associated with a sharp increase in CND support and activity, and helped to ensure the Labour party commitment (formally confirmed in the 1984 and 1986 party conferences) to the unilateralist stance, which was to loom so large in the election. But Mrs Thatcher benefited from the moves towards *détente* which followed from Mr Gorbachev's accession to power in the Soviet Union in March 1985 and which continued, despite the failure of his Reykjavik meeting with President Reagan in October 1986.

Three *causes celèbres* were spin-offs from world events. In March 1984 Sarah Tisdall, a Ministry of Defence secretary, was sent to prison for leaking to the *Guardian* details of how the arrival of Cruise missiles was to be handled. In February 1985 Clive Ponting, a senior defence official, was acquitted of leaking to Tam Dalyell the details of how questions about the sinking of the *Belgrano* were to be dealt with in the House; this case brought to a head growing anxieties about the constitutional problems involved in the strains felt in the relations between ministers and their civil servants. In January 1984 the government, perhaps under American pressure, announced that all workers at the Government Communications Headquarters at Cheltenham must renounce their union membership. The TUC offered 'no strike' assurances but, despite prolonged protests, the government was adamant.

Britain's relations with Europe attracted some attention. Mrs Thatcher's obduracy was repeatedly displayed as she secured a new arrangement for Britain's budgetary contributions at the Fontainebleu summit in June 1984 and as she fought at successive summits to modify the Common Agricultural Policy. After the 1983 election the Labour party abandoned its outright hostility to membership of the Community and in the Euro-elections of June 1984, it managed to increase its MEPs from 17 to 32; but the new delegation to Strasbourg remained profoundly anti-Community; in 1985 it displaced its left-wing leader, Barbara Castle, with the even more critical Alf Lomas.

However, despite battles over mutton exports to France, the most 'European' decision of the parliament came in February 1986 when Mrs Thatcher and President Mitterrand signed a Channel Tunnel agreement at Canterbury. And Mrs Thatcher moved sufficiently in her attitude to add her signature, on 18 February 1986 to the Single European Act which significantly increased the central authority of the Community institutions.

The question of how far the country should go in ostracising South Africa caused controversy in the Commonwealth and in Britain. The Commonwealth Heads, meeting in New Delhi in November 1983, set up an 'Eminent Persons Group' to find some line of reconciliation – but when this failed there were attempts to impose mandatory sanctions on trade with South Africa by both the EEC Summit in June 1986 and the meeting of seven Commonwealth leaders in August 1986. Mrs Thatcher was almost alone in resisting sanctions on the grounds that they would not help blacks or promote constructive change. In the summer of 1986 it was widely reported that her position was opposed not only by her Foreign Secretary, Sir Geoffrey Howe, but also by the Queen, who was plainly conscious that she was not only the Queen of England but also Head of the Commonwealth ('I have just seen my hundredth Prime Minister'). An unattributable press briefing (which was later attributed to the Queen's Press Secretary) indicated a degree of royal displeasure at Mrs Thatcher's intransigence.

Northern Ireland remained, as ever, a source of worry. But a bipartisan approach survived. A mass break-out of IRA prisoners from the Maze in September 1983, like the death of six people from an IRA bomb outside Harrods in December 1983 and the continual reports of murder from the province, failed to provoke any serious 'troops out' movement in Britain. In October 1984 the IRA carried out a bomb attack on the Imperial Hotel at Brighton during the Conservative Conference, which cost five lives, and from which Mrs Thatcher had a narrow escape. This had important psychological effects and led to a great increase in security. Mr Tebbit (whose wife was badly injured) and Mr Wakeham (whose wife was killed) were among the badly hurt. But the outrage did not cause any alteration in policies towards Ulster. And when, in November 1985, a laboriously constructed Anglo-Irish agreement was signed at Hillsborough, it received a general welcome in Britain though it was excoriated by the Unionists as a sell-out to Dublin. The 15 Unionist MPs resigned from parliament to fight by-elections as a quasi-referendum against the Agreement and, though one lost his seat, the votes made plain the sentiment of the Province. But Westminster was never aroused and, with Labour support, the government ploughed on with its policy of conciliatory firmness.

The government suffered some embarrassment in October 1983 when Cecil Parkinson had to resign from the Cabinet over revelations about an affair with his secretary. More substantial troubles came from the party's hasty, and for a time unpopular, pledge in 1983 to abolish the Greater London Council (GLC) and the Metropolitan Counties. Under its flamboyant leader, Ken Livingstone, the GLC flaunted slogans on County Hall, across the river from parliament, denouncing the decision to deny Londoners a democratic voice (and also blazoning the level of unemployment). A paving Bill to provide for an interim authority after the GLC's term expired in 1986 was defeated in the Lords. A brilliant and expensive public relations campaign almost led to a similar fate for the main abolition bill. But, once the deed was done, pro-GLC feeling died away (the

Metropolitan authorities never excited much support). Attention switched to the alleged misdeeds of the Militant-dominated council in Liverpool and of the 'loony left' borough councils, such as Brent, Camden and Lambeth.

Their specific policies in support of gays, lesbians and other minority and left-wing groups excited media ridicule. But the most important confrontations came over the setting of acceptable domestic rates. Under the Rates Act of 1984 the government imposed a ceiling on rate increases and, under a complicated formula, a number of local authorities were ratecapped. Some of them defied the government by refusing to curtail expenditure or to authorise a proper budget. Faced with a threat of legal action all except Liverpool and Lambeth caved in; after prolonged court proceedings, a number of councillors in those authorities, including Liverpool's Militant deputy-leader, Derek Hatton, were surcharged and disqualified as councillors. Once again the Labour leadership, though indignant at government policy, was caught in the dilemma of how far to support its own people when they went beyond the law in opposition to Thatcherite policies. Urged on by Neil Kinnock, the National Executive Committee (NEC) expelled, with great difficulty, a few Militants, but it failed to dissociate the party's image completely from that of all of its more strident followers.

A notable example came in October 1985 when, following a riot in Tottenham in which a policeman was hacked to death, Bernie Grant, the black council leader and prospective MP, congratulated the local youths on giving the police 'a bloody good hiding'. A major disturbance in Handsworth, Birmingham in September 1985 also had racial overtones and caused grave concern. The troubles never escalated to the heights reached in Brixton in 1981, but the plight of the inner cities in general, as well as in racial, terms continued to trouble the government and the nation.

The government's attempts to keep welfare state spending under control were felt not only in local government but in the health service and education. The government claimed that National Health Service (NHS) spending was increasing in real terms: the opposition said that it was not keeping up with the demands of an ageing population and the new technology, and quoted stories of lengthening waiting lists for operations and understaffed wards. Nurses' dissatisfaction with their pay were headline news in 1984 and again in early 1987. There were complaints that excessive resources were diverted from routine necessities to heart transplants and even more to the treatment of Aids, the newly-discovered plague which attracted increasing publicity in 1986 and was even the subject of a special Cabinet committee (which Mrs Thatcher declined to chair).

Education was a natural target for some cuts through falling pupil numbers and the government could point to an improving teacher-pupil ratio. But government inspectors reported declining standards of maintenance and shortages of school books. Teachers became increasingly restive about their pay. Sir Keith Joseph's attempts to impose a new contract of service and to get the rival unions to modify the unsatisfactory Burnham committee arrangements for settling salaries only succeeded in provoking a series of one-day strikes and work-to-rules which lasted throughout the second half of the parliament. Higher education had its grievances as university budgets were trimmed and dons were urged to make their universities rather more self-sufficient. Academic indignation with government policy found expression in January 1985 when, by a two-to-one vote, Oxford dons refused to give an honorary degree to the university's most influential graduate, Margaret Thatcher.

The most serious political trouble encountered by the government occurred in the autumn of 1985. That summer they had suffered from the change in oil prices and the insensitive increase in top people's salaries. But the row over the Westland helicopter company was a remarkable self-inflicted wound. The survival of this medium-size firm was in jeopardy. Michael Heseltine, the Defence Secretary, wanted to save it through a deal with a European consortium. Mrs Thatcher and Leon Brittan, the Trade Secretary, thought that Sikorsky, an American company, offered the best lifeline. There was little evidence of collective responsibility as the disagreements between the Prime Minister and her defence minister were freely aired in the mass media. When Mr Heseltine decided that he was being denied a fair chance to put his case to his colleagues, he resigned, walking out in the middle of a Cabinet meeting. Two weeks later Leon Brittan was forced to go because of the 1922 Committee reaction to revelations of how his side of the battle had been conducted through improper leaks (in which Downing Street also was implicated). In the key Commons debate on 15 January Mr Kinnock was thought to have let Mrs Thatcher off the hook – but there is no doubt that for some months she and, in particular, her style of government, were severely shaken. One consequence seems to have been that she accepted defeat in Cabinet a month later over the proposed sale of Austin Rover to an American firm.

Table 1.2   Economic and political indicators, 1983–87

	(1) Real personal disposable income (*1980 = 100*)	(2) Weekly earnings (*Jan. 1980 =100*)	(3) Retail prices (*1975=100*)	(4) Unemploy- ment (*UK*) (%)	(5) Days lost in strikes (*000s*)	(6) Gross Domestic Product (*1980=100*)	(7) Money supply (m³) £m
1983 2	100.0	147.9	247.5	10.7	635	102.8	97 435
3	101.1	150.4	250.7	10.8	690	104.1	98 457
4	102.2	152.5	253.5	10.8	822	105.1	100 791
1984 1	101.7	154.9	255.1	10.9	3 004	105.7	102 812
2	102.3	155.9	260.1	11.0	8 414	105.6	105 581
3	102.4	159.1	262.5	11.1	7 494	106.9	108 101
4	106.9	163.3	265.8	11.3	8 223	110.7	111 123
1985 1	104.5	166.8	269.2	11.2	4 577	109.2	115 082
2	105.8	170.2	278.4	11.3	597	110.6	118 335
3	106.0	173.9	279.1	11.3	498	110.4	123 214
4	108.4	176.1	280.5	11.3	728	110.7	126 230
1986 1	108.9	180.6	282.5	11.5	649	111.9	134 536
2	110.6	183.9	286.1	11.6	603	112.6	141 220
3	111.0	186.8	286.5	11.7	288	113.4	147 105
4	112.2	190.1	290.1	11.4	381	114.5	150 422
1987 1	114.1	193.1	293.7	11.1	2 067	116.4	160 455
2	114.2	198.4	298.2	10.7	750	177.4	168 348

Sources:
1. *Economic Trends* (Real Personal Disposable Income, seasonally adjusted).
2. *Economic Trends* (Weekly Earnings, seasonally adjusted).
3. *Economic Trends*.
4. *Monthly Digest of Statistics*.
5. *Monthly Digest of Statistics*.
6. *Economic Trends* (Gross Domestic Product at factor costs).
7. *Financial Statistics* (Sterling money supply (m³) £m seasonally adjusted).
8. *Economic Trends*.
9. *Financial Statistics* (FT–Actuaries all shareholders index, daily average).
10. *Financial Studies* (Average daily telegraphic transfer rates on London).
11. *Financial Statistics*.
12. *Economic Trends* (London clearing banks, base rates. Figures for median date of each quarter).
13. *Economic Trends* (Average price of new dwellings mortgages approved).
14. MORI (monthly bulletin) *Public Opinion in Great Britain*.
15. *Public Opinion in Great Britain* (unweighted average of published polls).

Economic indicators gave a mixed message. Unemployment remained between 3.1m and 3.3m throughout the parliament. The opposition argued that changes in the method of counting concealed at
least a million further jobless. The government boasted of the positive
increase in the number of people employed and of their increasingly
sophisticated efforts to provide training and to deal specifically with
the young and the long-term jobless. But apart from unemployment
the government could point to other indicators of success. Inflation
stayed at an annual rate 3–5% throughout the parliament, well below
the level of most major democracies. Thanks to North Sea Oil the
balance of payments remained favourable, although the collapse in

(8) Balance of payments (£m)	(9) FT Index (10 April 1962=100)	(10) US $ to £	(11) Sterling Exchange Rate Index (1975=100)	(12) Interest rates (%)	(13) House prices (1980=100)	(14) MORI 'State of the Economy Poll' net optimists	(15) MORI Polls (Voting intention)		
							Con.	Lab.	L/All.
−49	436.17	1.55	84.3	10.0	116	+10.0	43.0	27.0	25.0
1153	449.30	1.51	84.9	9.5	118	−9.0	44.5	29.0	25.5
452	450.53	1.47	83.2	9.0	117	−12.0	42.5	36.5	19.5
1249	499.22	1.44	81.7	9.0	121	+2.5	41.5	38.5	18.5
−343	510.33	1.40	79.8	9.5	125	−9.5	39.5	38.5	20.5
−158	502.57	1.30	78.0	10.5	127	−21.5	39.5	38.5	20.5
534	554.54	1.22	75.1	9.5	125	−22.5	42.5	35.5	20.5
−155	613.81	1.11	72.1	14.0	130	−19.5	39.0	36.5	22.5
1302	625.40	1.26	78.9	13.5	134	−21.0	35.5	36.0	27.0
1147	619.96	1.38	82.1	11.5	137	−17.0	31.5	34.0	32.5
612	668.73	1.44	79.6	11.5	144	−11.5	36.0	35.5	26.0
682	728.99	1.44	75.1	12.5	147	−14.5	35.5	36.5	28.5
−94	800.71	1.51	76.1	10.5	159	−13.5	35.5	39.5	24.5
−931	792.51	1.49	68.3	10.0	165	−16.0	36.0	37.0	25.0
−757	806.81	1.43	68.3	11.0	167	−11.0	39.5	39.5	18.5
667	943.78	1.54	69.9	11.0	173	+4.0	40.5	34.0	23.5
−174	1064.63	1.64	72.7	9.5	181	+17.5	42.5	30.0	26.0

oil revenues (the world price fell from £28 a barrel to £13 between December 1985 and August 1986) caused some anxiety. The bulk of people in Britain benefited from a slow but continued expansion of the economy. For those in work the average wage rose from £140 in June 1983 to £190 in June 1987; allowing for inflation and tax changes, this represented a real addition of 14% to disposable income (see Table 1.2).

The period saw increasing focus on the City. Financial news became more prominent in all the media. Britain's decline as a manufacturing power was compensated by an expansion of financial services. Exchange rates oscillated – from £1.45 to the dollar in March 1984 to £1.05 in February 1985 and back to £1.55 in April 1986. Share prices boomed (the *Financial Times* All-Shares Index rose from 436 in June 1983 to 2134 in May 1987). Mergers and take-overs, actual or attempted, made headlines. Several major newspapers changed hands; so did some major names among High Street stores and, in the biggest and most disputed of these affairs, the giant Guinness absorbed the giant Distillers in April 1986 for the sum of £2.5bn. In a long anticipated move in October 1986 the 'Big Bang' adapted the City to the new world of communications. Bankers and stockbrokers merged to cope with 24-hour world-wide trading as deals moved from the floor of the Stock Exchange to VDU terminals. The press ran stories about the huge salaries which went to the bright young people who could cope with the vastly increased volume of trading.

Some scandals attached to all these developments and the opposition revived Mr Heath's 1973 remarks about 'the unacceptable face of capitalism'. The ruthless financial manoeuvrings during the Distillers take-over led to prosecutions and, in other developments, the probity of some parts of the insurance market at Lloyds came into serious question, and the Bank of England had to take charge of the overstretched merchant bank, Johnson Matthey. But in a bull market relatively few small people got hurt. The 'go, go' climate of the financial world must have advanced the Conservatives' electoral prospects more than it damaged them.

Governments can get stale in office once they have fulfilled their original programme. But in privatisation the Conservatives found an endless set of new opportunities. During the parliament one-third of state-owned industries were sold to the public. These flotations were all widely advertised and pitched at prices which guaranteed profit for investors (see Table 1.3). One result was that the number of

Table 1.3   *Privatisation of state-owned corporations, 1983–87*

Date	Corporation	Value (£)
10 Aug. 1984	Jaguar Cars	294m
3 Dec. 1984	British Telecom	3916m
14 May 1985	British Aerospace	550m
12 Aug. 1985	Britoil	450m
13 Dec. 1985	Cable and Wireless	602m
10 Oct. 1986	Trustee Savings Bank	1360m
8 Dec. 1986	British Gas	5600m
11 Feb. 1987	British Airways	900m
20 May 1987	Rolls-Royce	1360m

private shareholders jumped from under three million to over eight million between 1979 and 1987. The Labour party and the unions objected to privatisation and even Harold Macmillan grumbled charmingly about 'selling off the family silver'. But the policy was, on the whole, popular, and it helped the Chancellor to balance his accounts. It was seen a source of new property-owning Conservatives and as an intellectual stimulus for the party. Sir Keith Joseph, before 1979, had argued that previous Conservative governments had compromised too readily with Labour policies in pursuit of 'the middle ground', yet the Conservative dilemma was that, as Labour moved to the left, so did the policy mid-point. By compromising, Conservatives assisted in the ratchet effect of socialism. Instead of accepting whatever level of state activity had been reached, Conservatives were now rolling back the frontiers of the state, reversing the ratchet, and giving new life to capitalism. The selling-off of water supplies and even of the railways and the mines began to be discussed. And in the NHS and local government the contracting-out of services was steadily, though controversially, extended with Westminster backing.

Yet the government could not escape from intervention in industry. Apart from the Westland affair, it seems that Mr Younger almost resigned as Secretary of State for Scotland in order to stop the closure of Ravenscraig, Scotland's only steel plant. Scotland indeed was a continual worry for the Conservatives. They fared appallingly in the 1985 local elections following a general rates revaluation. In an attempt to rescue the situation, and in response to Mrs Thatcher's aversion to the whole system of local rates, the government decided to switch to a poll tax (or 'community charge') as a source of local funding and this highly controversial policy was being enacted as the election approached.

The government fared less well in electoral than in economic indicators. Their experience in the 16 British by-elections of 1983–7 was uniformly disastrous. They lost four seats and they were pushed into third place in every Labour seat: in their own strongholds their vote fell by an average of 14%. The Alliance, on the other hand, fared extraordinarily well. They received more votes than any other party and, except in Fulham, they always came first or second. Labour, apart from its April 1986 victory in Fulham, found little comfort in any by-election result (see Table 1.4).

Table 1.4   16 Westminster by-elections, Great Britain, 1983–87

	Votes %	% Change	Seats			
			Held	Gained	Lost	3rd place
Conservative	30.4	−14.0	5	—	4	7
Labour	28.4	+0.4	5	1	1	8
Alliance	39.1	+12.3	1	4	—	1

The Euro-elections on 14 June 1984 witnessed a slight setback for the Conservatives – but they still won 45 seats to Labour's 32. The Alliance's 19% of the vote secured no MEPs. However, the outcome was almost overshadowed by the SDP's unexpected triumph on the same day in a Westminster by-election for the safe Conservative seat of Portsmouth South. A year later the Liberals won another Conservative stronghold, Brecon & Radnor, and in May 1986 yet another, Ryedale. And there was the final, deceptive victory in February 1987 in Greenwich, where a seat that had been Labour since 1945 fell to the SDP.

The annual rounds of local elections offered less clear-cut encouragement to the Alliance. In May 1984 there was no major evidence of a shift from 1983 but in 1985 the shire councils, last elected in 1981, showed a marked movement. The Conservative vote dropped 13% from 1983, and the Alliance was able to secure the balance of power in 24 of the 39 County Councils. In 1986, in the London boroughs, and in districts throughout Britain, the Conservatives suffered heavy losses in seats last fought during the Falklands war in May 1982. In 1987 the Conservatives lost seats but the movement to Labour and the Alliance was not on a scale to deter Mrs Thatcher from going to the country. The two tables on the opposite page (1.5 and 1.6) tell the story.

Liberal and SDP candidates made a net gain of over 200 council seats in by-elections during the four years, and the advance was evident in every part of the country. Every week the readers of *Liberal News* and the *Social Democrat*, as well as the Alliance leaders, were getting evidence that they were at least as popular as the Labour and Conservative parties.

The opinion polls ebbed and flowed. The Conservatives fell behind Labour from January 1985 to September 1986, but never by more than 6% or so. The Alliance dropped to 19% in late 1983, but then crept up to the level of the other parties for a while in the summer of 1985. Their rating declined after their defence disputes in September, but still kept around 25%. However, in February 1987, after their extraordinary triumph at Greenwich where their support had jumped from 15% to 53% in the course of a three-week campaign, they experienced a brief burst into the lead nationally.

The Alliance was now bidding to demonstrate that it remained a major political force which could, in a general election, displace Labour from second place in the popular vote. Labour was eager to

Table 1.5   Local election changes, 1983–87

	Gen. El. (GB) 1983	June 1984 (GB) Europe	May 1984 E&W District Council	May 1985 E&W County Council	May 1986 E&W District Council	May 1987 E&W District Council
Con.	43.5	−2.7	−3.0	−12.8	−7.4	−2.2
Lab.	28.3	+8.2	+3.7	+8.6	+2.7	−3.1
Alln.	26.0	−6.5	−0.7	0.0	+4.3	+5.0

Source: *Economist*.

Table 1.6   Local by-elections, 1983–87
(three-cornered fights only)

	1983 (%)	1984 (%)	1985 (%)	1986 (%)	1987 (Jan.–June) (%)
Con.	35.5	35.0	30.4	33.0	39.0
Lab.	32.0	33.2	31.4	29.0	26.4
Alln.	31.1	29.2	35.1	34.8	33.1

Source: Information supplied by David Cowling.

show that the road from 1945 was not at an end, despite the adverse changes in economic and social structures.

The stakes were high for all major political parties. The Conservatives were bidding for a third successive victory under the same party leader. If they gained office for a further five years they would have an opportunity to shape the agenda of British politics for the rest of the century and perhaps to 'kill off Socialism', which Mrs Thatcher had often claimed to be her objective.

There had been a few setbacks in local elections and in opinion polls but, despite the Westland affair, it had been a relatively tranquil parliament for ministers. There were some rebuffs in the House of Lords and some small back-bench revolts, but the government did not feel seriously challenged in debate and John Wakeham, the Chief Whip, had relatively little difficulty in keeping his troops in line. Mrs Thatcher had gone through one or two bad patches but in Cabinet and in parliament she remained overwhelmingly dominant. She had brought on some new talent – only four of her May 1979 Cabinet were still in office in July 1987 – and she was presiding over an economy that, despite three million unemployed, was continuously growing. An expanding economy is the most generally accepted formula for electoral success.

NOTES

1. There are a number of studies of Mrs Thatcher's impact on recent British politics on the nature of Thatcherism. They include:

   The Financial Times, *The Thatcher Years* (London, 1987).
   J. Bulpitt, 'The Thatcher Statecraft', *Political Studies*, 1985.
   D. Kavanagh, *Thatcherism and British Politics: The End of Consensus?* (London, 1986).
   W. Keegan, *Mrs Thatcher's Economic Experiment* (London, 1985).
   A. King, 'Margaret Thatcher, the Style of a Prime Minister', in A. King (ed.), *The British Prime Minister* (London, 1985).
   A. Walters, *Britain's Economic Renaissance* (London, 1985).
   H. Young and A. Sloman, *The Thatcher Phenomenon* (London, 1986).

2. See M. Adeney and J. Lloyd, *The Miners' Strike, 1984–1985* (London, 1986); M. Crick, *Scargill and the Miners* (Harmondsworth, 1985); P. Wilsher *et al.*, *Strike: Thatcher, Scargill and the Miners* (London, 1985); and G. Goodman, *The Miners' Strike* (London, 1985).

2 Conservative

Party organisation has special problems for a party in government. For the Conservatives these were ironically compounded by the comprehensive nature of their victory in 1983. The party could anticipate another four or five years in office and by 1987 would have been continuously in government for eight years. The leadership almost inevitably thought more in governmental than electoral terms. In addition some of the major achievements of the government – notably trade union reform and low inflation – were seen as achievements for the first rather than the second administration.

Getting the right leadership for the party organisation has always given difficulty to Conservative leaders. Cecil Parkinson had greatly improved his standing through his chairmanship of the party, and he was appointed after the 1983 election to be Secretary of State for Trade and Industry. He was replaced as party chairman in September by John Selwyn Gummer, an appointment that was a surprise to Mr Gummer himself and to many observers. Mr Gummer was a junior minister in the Department of Employment and his senior minister, Norman Tebbit, warned him that he was going to a bed of nails. Indeed Mr Tebbit had advised Mrs Thatcher against the appointment, and a number of colleagues regarded this as a case where Mrs Thatcher had not really thought things through. Central Office was short of money and there was some inertia following the 1983 success. But Mr Gummer's lack of political weight with other ministers (unlike Cecil Parkinson and Norman Tebbit, his successor, he was not in the Cabinet) and his lack of managerial skills clouded his chairmanship.

Mr Tebbit, in spite of his lengthy convalescence from the Brighton bombing in October 1984, was reluctant to assume the post. He enjoyed his work at the Department of Trade and Industry; he saw the danger of losing his parliamentary platform when no longer a departmental minister and he did not much relish the weekend party engagements which would keep him away from home. However he yielded to Mrs Thatcher's insistence and took over in September 1985. He was a political heavyweight, had a higher media profile than Mr Gummer, and was much engaged in Cabinet committees.

Inside Central Office Mr Tebbit made a number of personnel changes and he was relieved of some routine work by two appointments. Jeffrey Archer, a former Tory MP and now a best-selling novelist, was appointed as Deputy Chairman (on the initiative of Mrs Thatcher) and spent much of his time speaking in the constituencies. Peter Morrison, a former junior minister at the Department of Trade with Mr Tebbit, was also appointed a Deputy Chairman in October 1986 (on the initiative of Mr Tebbit) and given responsibility for administration and budgeting in Central Office. Peter Cropper who had left the Research Department and returned to the Treasury as a political adviser in April 1985, was replaced as Director by Robin Harris, who had been a political adviser to Leon Brittan at the Home Office and earlier at the Treasury. As his chief of staff, Mr Tebbit had Michael Dobbs, who took leave from the Saatchi firm to work full-time in Central Office. Mr Dobbs had worked with Mr Tebbit since 1979 and been his political adviser when he was Secretary of State for Employment and then for Trade and Industry. Although Mr Dobbs was effectively Mr Tebbit's deputy ('you are me when I'm not here') Mrs Thatcher would not agree to the chairman's proposal that Dobbs be given the title of Deputy Chairman. Mr Tebbit liked to work through committees and was less accessible to staff than Mr Parkinson. Some critics complained that he kept his cards too close to his chest and objected to his liking for large meetings (though, of course, large meetings make it easier for decisions to be taken at the top).

John Lacy was redeployed to the post of Director of Campaigning in 1985 and took over the recruitment and training of agents. The number of full-time agents continued to decline to around 280. On the eve of the election something under half of associations had full-time agents, though all the 'tactical' (or critical) seats had such help. Central Office distinguished two types of tactical seat. There were 59 seats which the government needed to hold to ensure a parliamentary majority of 52; this list included the four seats which the party had lost in by-elections in the 1983 parliament. In addition there were another 13 seats which, although the sitting members had good majorities, might be vulnerable because of local or personal factors. Most tactical seats had computers linked with Central Office through Telecom Gold to ensure direct communication with the centre (see p. 214).

Harvey Thomas, who had worked with Billy Graham in the United States, was first appointed Director of Publicity by John Gummer and then moved to Director of Presentation and Promotions by Mr Tebbit. He had particular responsibility for public events like press and party conferences and election rallies. Fund raising remained, as in 1983, with Lord McAlpine. (The party spent £4.8m centrally in

1982–3 and £8.9m in 1986–7.) Sir Christopher Lawson, who had been Director of Marketing in the 1983 election, was brought back in March 1986 to head a special services unit and had responsibility for computers, direct mail and private polling. Direct mail to potential supporters, which had been tried with limited success in 1983, was resumed in July 1986, initially using the British Telecom shareholders' lists, though alternative lists were used to address young householders and shareholders in other privatised industries. The party was pleased with the 5% response rate (which gained over 25 000 new members and receipts of over £1.5m from donations) but gave up before the dissolution, for fear of infringing election law.

The separate Marketing Department was wound up and absorbed with the Publicity Department. Anthony Shrimsley carried on as Press Director until his death in October 1984. He was then replaced for a year by Sir Gordon Reece, who had been the party's Director of Publicity in the 1979 election. John Desborough, a journalist formerly on the *Daily Mirror*, headed a new information section with special responsibility for the press. Most significant was the failure to appoint a Director of Communications. At one time it was hoped that Sir Gordon Reece would take the job. (In retrospect, since Sir Gordon had been employed as a consultant by Ernest Saunders of Guinness, there was some relief that he had not accepted once the various Guinness scandals were revealed.) After many soundings Mr Tebbit arranged for a person with a background in public relations to be interviewed by Mrs Thatcher in January 1987. She, however, refused to pursue the matter. Mr Tebbit lined up another candidate for interview in February but again there was no follow-up and the post remained unfilled. The Prime Minister and chairman did not agree on the calibre of person required or on the job-specification. The role of Mr Dobbs as a link with Saatchi, and of Mr Thomas on presentation, made the scope of the post too limited for a heavyweight figure; Mr Dobbs was already a director of communications.

The Thatcher and Tebbit partnership was not a harmonious one, and for the first half of 1986, communications between them were poor. During the many discussions over Westland at the end of 1985, Mr Tebbit worked for a compromise, or at least a way of keeping an increasingly exasperated Mr Heseltine on board. Mrs Thatcher, however, had had enough of Mr Heseltine by the time he resigned. Mr Tebbit also doubted the wisdom of the proposed sale to General Motors of Land Rover, a course of action strongly favoured by Mrs Thatcher, though one which found her virtually isolated in Cabinet. Mr Tebbit was more impressed than the Prime Minister by the Chief

Whip's warning that the Government might be defeated on the issue. From early 1986 there were well-publicised rumours of strains between the party chairman and the Prime Minister. It was widely reported in the media that he did not fully support her decision to allow American bomber raids on Libya to set out from British bases, and that he was offended at the decision being taken by a small group of ministers.

At one time Mr Tebbit seems to have entertained hopes of being in charge of manifesto preparations. Mrs Thatcher, however, set up a Strategy Group, called the 'A-team' by the press and No. 10, which consisted of senior Cabinet members, and was charged with responsibility for the manifesto (see p. 31). Some Cabinet colleagues were also disturbed by Mr Tebbit's abrasive style with the opposition parties, and by his brush with the BBC for its coverage of the bombing of Libya. They thought that the attacks were counter-productive, particularly at a time when they were trying to prevent defections to the Alliance. Gradually, Mrs Thatcher seems to have felt that Mr Tebbit was not a good administrator of the party machine. 'A superb player, but no manager' was one judgement. Increasingly she looked back fondly to 1983 when Cecil Parkinson had personally managed her campaign. By contrast Mr Tebbit seemed intent on conducting a separate election operation; one official commented 'he does not understand that Central Office is the instrument of Mrs Thatcher's campaign'. The strained relations between Prime Minister and party chairman were to have unhappy results for the conduct of affairs in June 1987.

To understand the origins of the tensions between the two it is essential to recall how vulnerable Mrs Thatcher felt in the wake of the Westland crisis (see p. 17). In February 1986 she learned that some of her more trusted senior ministers (and their wives) were talking of the need to replace her. Rightly or wrongly, she grew more convinced that Mr Tebbit regarded her as 'finished' and was using Central Office to advance his own claims to the succession. Henceforth she looked with a jaundiced eye at the activities of Mr Tebbit, Central Office, and Saatchi and Saatchi, the party's advertising agency. This was the background to Mrs Thatcher's decision in March 1987 to put Lord Young into Central Office – partly to assist Mr Tebbit, and partly to organise Mrs Thatcher's tours and television appearances – and to the tensions and 'wobbles' over strategy during the election.

In the course of the parliament there was much speculation that

Thatcherism had run out of ideas for extending the free market and cutting state spending. Mrs Thatcher had boasted in the 1983 election campaign of how much her government was spending on services, and claimed that the National Health Service was 'safe' with her. From the right of the political party there were accusations of drift and a lack of radicalism (or free-market policies); some of these criticisms were echoed in editorials in the *Economist* and *The Times*. A group of young right-wing MPs published *No Turning Back* at the end of 1986, in which they called for the extension of free-market principles to the health and education services.

The picture was, in fact, more complex. In the second half of the parliament one could point to many radical initiatives that the government was taking, notably selling British Gas, British Airways and Rolls-Royce to private investors, introducing a core curriculum in schools, abolishing the Burnham pay machinery for teachers, establishing city technology colleges in education, and legislating to introduce a poll tax in Scotland. There were also abortive attempts to liberalise Sunday trading, and sell off Land Rover and parts of British Leyland to American companies. In early 1987 radical proposals to allow state schools to opt out of local authority control and to arrange for council tenants to set up their own housing associations, were being examined by Cabinet committees.

The position of Mrs Thatcher and of the governments was at its weakest in early 1986 in the wake of the Westland affair[1] (see p. 17). There is little doubt that the Heseltine resignation damaged Mrs Thatcher, seeming to confirm the suspicions that she was bossy and high-handed or, alternatively, that she was indecisive. She lost battles in Cabinet and felt that her own position was weak. In May 1986, at a time when the government was languishing in the opinion polls, and following poor local election results, John Biffen, the leader of the House of Commons, recommended in a *Weekend World* television interview that Mrs Thatcher should adopt a 'balanced ticket' for the next election, and a more humble and caring approach to the voters. This was a remarkable piece of frank speaking from a senior member of the Cabinet. It provoked Downing Street sources to give guidance that Mr Biffen should be seen as a 'semi-detached member of the government'.

Mr Tebbit had a straightforward view of the electorate and the forces that moved it. He thought that voters had reasonably well-established expectations of the positive and negative features of the Labour and Conservative parties and would punish a party which performed badly on its so-called 'strong' issues. Labour, for example, was rated highly on 'caring' issues like health and education, but less well on managing the economy and defence and on providing strong and united leadership. The Conservative strengths and weaknesses were the reverse of Labour's and, above all, the Conservatives were expected to provide competent government. The 'Tebbit theory' of why Westland was so damaging for the Conservatives was that is upset established expectations. It showed the leadership to be uncertain and divided, the government floundering on one of its 'strong' issues, namely defence, and Mrs Thatcher fussy and domineering, rather than resolute.

The party was embarrassed by the activities of its so-called 'raving right' although these did not get the adverse publicity which attended Labour's 'loony left'. The member for Billericay, Harvey Proctor, attracted unsavoury support with his vigorous campaign to repatriate coloured immigrants. Another MP, Peter Bruinvels, formed a 'law and order society', and raised over £100 000 for the purposes of bringing a sedition charge against Mr Scargill in 1985. Winston Churchill mobilised some right-wing Conservative back-bench support for his abortive private member's bill to ban 'video nasties'. These campaigns to promote greater authoritarianism and control in the social sphere were countered by libertarian groups who wanted the Conservative government to reduce the role of the state. Such voices were influential in the Federation of Conservative Students (FCS), who regularly shouted down 'wet' ministers at their conferences. After one FCS official called for Lord Stockton to be tried as a war criminal (for his role in repatriating East European prisoners of war), Mr Tebbit disbanded the organisation.

Central Office inevitably came in for attack when the voters turned against the government. Large Conservative majorities were overturned in by-elections, and it was not until 1987 that local elections brought any relief. In April 1986 the party lost Fulham to Labour and, the following month, lost the apparently 'safe' Ryedale seat to the Liberals, and almost lost West Derbyshire. Scotland was a particularly unfavourable territory, following the rating revaluation and doubts over the future of Garscadden steel works and the closure of the Caterpillar plant.

There was a subtle change in the political balance of the Cabinet. After the 1983 election Mrs Thatcher had abruptly sacked Francis Pym from his post as Foreign Secretary. In his place she appointed the faithful Sir Geoffrey Howe and promoted Nigel Lawson to the

Treasury. Although the distinctions between 'wet' and 'dry' ministers ceased to have much meaning after the 1983 election, the Cabinet was one very much to Mrs Thatcher's liking. Ministers like Cecil Parkinson, Norman Tebbit, Leon Brittan, Norman Fowler, Tom King, Nigel Lawson, Nicholas Ridley and Lord Young all owed their advancement to her. Successive reshuffles since 1981 had produced an exodus of many 'wets', and the marginalisation of Jim Prior in Northern Ireland. Michael Heseltine at Defence until 1986 and Peter Walker at Energy remained powerful voices for a different kind of Toryism, but they were not significant in the economic debates in Cabinet. The Treasury's rule on economic matters was unchallenged.

Yet after Westland and the consequent loss of Mr Heseltine and Mr Brittan, the retirement of Sir Keith Joseph from the Cabinet, the promotions of Kenneth Baker (to Education), Kenneth Clarke (to Employment) and Malcolm Rifkind (to Scotland), and the higher profile assumed by Douglas Hurd as Home Secretary, had the effect of giving the Cabinet a less Thatcherite appearance. The political right, variously associated with the Monday Club and the 92 Club, became increasingly unhappy with the reshuffles and the failure of right-wing politicians to be promoted to the Cabinet. Mrs Thatcher shared the unease of the party's right wing, but acquiesced in suggestions that the ministerial talent lay elsewhere in the party. The suggestion that Rhodes Boyson should succeed Sir Keith Joseph as Secretary of State for Education was regarded by senior ministers as 'utterly inconceivable'. On matters of political management she continued to rely on the advice of the Deputy Prime Minister, Lord Whitelaw, and the Chief Whip, John Wakeham. Indeed, with the breakdown of the Thatcher–Tebbit axis she came to trust these two and the right blamed them for its failure to gain more ministerial posts although this seems in fact to have been a reflection of Mrs Thatcher's judgment of the available talent. Lord Young at Employment, Douglas Hurd at the Home Office, and Kenneth Baker at Education, significantly improved their reputations in government.

A key post-Westland development was Mrs Thatcher's decision to set up the Strategy Group. Its regular members, apart from Mrs Thatcher, were Sir Geoffrey Howe, Nigel Lawson, Douglas Hurd, John Wakeham, Lord Whitelaw and Mr Tebbit. Robin Harris, the party's Research Director, acted as secretary. She was not alone in feeling that the Cabinet – a large body, meeting weekly – did not provide adequate opportunity for senior ministers to review political developments and consider new initiatives. Above all, Mrs Thatcher wanted back-benchers to know that a 'team' was actively engaged in thinking about the next election. The group met weekly for the rest of the parliament, dealing with the co-ordination and presentation of government policy and with campaign preparations and strategy. One member dismissed as 'paranoia' Central Office criticism that establishing the body was a vote of no confidence in Central Office, and observed that Cabinet government always relied on committees.

In the House of Commons the majority of over 130 proved troublesome for the whips and there were many small acts of rebellion. Mrs Thatcher was rebuffed, largely by her own back-benchers, over the choice of Speaker in 1983. Further revolts followed over MPs' pay, over proposed housing benefit and rate support grant changes, over Britain's contribution to the European Commission and, most spectacular of all, over Sir Keith Joseph's plans to make major cuts in support for students in higher education. In April 1984, 43 Conservatives voted for an amendment to the Trade Union bill which would have required individual members to 'contract in' when paying the political levy. In July 1985 the government was nearly defeated in the Commons on a motion to reduce the Lord Chancellor's salary, a Labour vote of censure on the government's acceptance of the proposals of the Top Salaries Review Board for large increases in the pay of senior public servants. In April 1986 the government was defeated by 14 votes on the second reading of its Shops Bill, a measure designed to permit easier trading on Sunday. In fact, the number of dissenters would have been higher on these and some other votes had it not been for negotiated compromises between the Chief Whip and potential rebels.

There was some uncertainty about whether Saatchi and Saatchi, the agency which had handled the party's advertising in 1979 and 1983, would retain the account. Although some voices in Central Office and Saatchi were heard to wonder whether another contract was in the interest of their respective organisations, it was generally assumed by both organisations that Saatchi would continue as the agency. In spite of the lobbying of other agencies (see pp. 34–5) it was well placed. Not only was it a known quantity to the party, but many party advisers felt that there was a learning curve for an agency, and that Saatchi had a head start over any rival. In addition, Mr Tebbit strongly objected to transferring the account to an American company like Young and Rubicam, which was rumoured to want the account. Michael Dobbs, the chief assistant to Mr Tebbit, was also a Deputy Chairman at Saatchi.

Qualitative research about the electorate's mood, conducted for Saatchi by BJM Research Associates in October 1985 and updated some months later, was presented to the Prime Minister and the Strategy Group at Chequers on Sunday 13 April 1986. The report presented by Michael Dobbs and John Sharkey was not reassuring. It claimed that the voters' underlying attitudes had hardly changed since similar research in 1982,[2] but that perceptions of the government had. The government was now seen as more 'harsh', 'uncaring' and 'extreme', a consequence largely of a perception that it had lost its sense of direction; it was no longer regarded as resolute and purposeful. Such findings raised delicate questions about the balance between Mrs Thatcher's perceived assets and weaknesses. Many voters did not link her strengths to any obvious sense of purpose; what came across was negative – she was 'bossy', and 'fussy'. Above all, she was not seen as forward-looking. The research also showed that the party was not especially associated with 'freedom of choice'; it scored poorly on leadership; its supporters were particularly critical about its record on health and education; and disaffected Tories were likely to defect to the SDP. The research was conducted in the wake of Westland, a bad time for the party, and was delivered at a time when relations between the Prime Minister and the Chairman were cool.

The Saatchi-Central Office report recommended that SDP supporters should be a prime Tory target, and that positive action on policies and presentation would have to be taken in health and education. The party had to protect itself against the opposition cry 'Its Time for a Change', and convince voters that it was still the party of reform and of the future. At the next party conference, ministers should be forward looking and present the Tory vision of the 1990s. As a Saatchi executive put it: 'People want to know what Maggie wants'.

According to some reports, the advertising agency's suggestion that the government's message was not getting through partly because of her, upset Mrs Thatcher and she sought alternative advice from Young and Rubicam. This agency did research in mid-1985 and in January 1986 on what was called cross-lateral consumer characteristics, concentrating mainly on values and life styles among the electorate. The research relied on lengthy (and expensive) interviews to probe respondents' goals (what they wanted), values (why they wanted it), and benefits (what they got from it). It assumed that for each individual there was one dominant motivation which affected his or her behaviour and attitudes.

Young and Rubicam divided the electorate into three different value groups, which cut across conventional market research social classes; the constrained (for example, old age pensioners) – 26%; the middle majority (for example, 'Mr and Mrs average') – 63%; and the innovators (for example, well-educated groups) – 11%. The most pro-Conservative category in the middle majority were the so-called 'succeeders'; these were ambitious, optimistic, progress-oriented, pro-establishment and pro-authority. They were high-income earners, like businessmen and managers. The largest single category (in the middle majority group) were the 'mainstreamers', at 40%. These people were conservative, patriotic, home-centred, traditional, and voted Tory in 1979 and 1983. In 1985 and 1986, however, they were turning to other parties, particularly the Alliance; they were concerned over education, law and order and the NHS, although less about unemployment, and blamed the government for failures in these areas. According to Young and Rubicam too much of the Conservative message was oriented to (and largely accepted by) the 'succeeders'. The 'mainstreamers' felt neglected and the party's communications effort should henceforth be redirected to them; in particular it should combat their pessimism about the state of the country and their doubts whether there was a plan for its future.

A former Conservative publicity chief, Geoffrey Tucker, was a consultant for Young and Rubicam and had close links to Lord Whitelaw. In November 1984 he made a presentation of the research to Lord Whitelaw, who in turn arranged for John Banks of Y & R to show the work to Stephen Sherbourne, Mrs Thatcher's political secretary, at No. 10. Geoffrey Tucker and Sir Ronald Millar, a speechwriter for Mrs Thatcher, had a number of weekend meetings with Mrs Thatcher, and then with other Cabinet ministers, to explain the research and its consequences for her political strategy. The research was then distributed regularly to a small group of ministers (Whitelaw, Wakeham, Lawson and Hurd) and to Sir Ronald Millar and Sherbourne.

Parts of the Young and Rubicam message were not much different from that offered by Saatchi, but it argued that Mrs Thatcher was a strength, not a weakness, and that the Tories would lose the election without her. It claimed that the main problem for the Government was that it was failing to get its message through (for example, on health), rather than that its policies were wrong. Young and Rubicam also indicated that Westland was only a passing problem for voters, and that defectors from the Tory party still believed in many

Thatcherite values but wanted to see her exercising strong leadership and doing something to meet their concerns over education and the health service. Young and Rubicam were commissioned to carry on with research, using funds raised by the party Treasurer, Lord McAlpine; the findings were regularly distributed to a select group of senior ministers but not to Mr Tebbit who did not want to be shown them. Mrs Thatcher in effect had her own research about public opinion, independent of Central Office. Saatchi and Central Office were not convinced of the merits of the approach and claimed that Young and Rubicam were touting for business. Mrs Thatcher, however, found the work useful; it confirmed her own intuitions; above all, it was important in restoring her self-confidence. The cover story for these meetings was that Geoffrey Tucker and John Banks were helping to write speeches for Mrs Thatcher.

Tim Bell, a former director at Saatchi, had left the agency at the end of 1984 to join Lowe, Howard-Spinks, and Bell. It was an acrimonious departure but he was paid a retainer by Saatchi for political advice in the event of the company wanting to use his services at the next election. Mr Bell had handled the Tory account in 1979 and 1983 and reputedly enjoyed Mrs Thatcher's confidence. He hoped to be used in a freelance role by Saatchi again, and was resentful when he found Mr Tebbit would not entertain the idea. He was close to Lord Young and sought to maintain his personal links with No. 10. The positions and rivalries of all three agencies were selectively leaked to the press in the summer of 1986 – and stories continued to appear up to and during the election.

The October 1986 Conservative conference was effectively the launching pad for the party's recovery. Saatchi played a major role in setting the general style of the conference. They devised the conference theme, suggested some of the contents of ministers' speeches and coordinated the publicity. Ministers were urged to concentrate on future plans in their departments, and to give voters a clear perception of what the party stood for: 'Even when people disagree with our policies, as long as they understand what we are about, some will vote for us', said one strategist. A high profile was urged for Mr Baker, Mr Fowler and Lord Young, heads of large spending departments. The conference theme, *The Next Move Forward*, was an anticipation of the Conservative party's election campaign slogan. The conference was followed by an upsurge in the polls.

In late 1986 there were targeted increases in spending on health and education, and above-average pay settlements for teachers and nurses. The contraction of higher education promised in Sir Keith Joseph's White Paper (Cmnd 9524) was followed by new plans from Kenneth Baker in 1987 which promised expansion. Norman Fowler's plans for a radical reshaping of the State Earnings Pension Scheme (SERPS) were scaled down.

The party's private surveys and reports of door-step reactions showed that the Conservatives remained vulnerable on the issues of education, the National Health Service and unemployment. By January 1987 the party had recovered some ground on these issues compared to the previous spring. But among the skilled workers (the C2 group) the party was still 5% below its 1983 share, and it had also lost ground to Labour among first-time voters, under-35s and in the North. Unemployment appeared to be the major concern of voters, and Labour was seen as the best party to tackle it. The government's message on the benefits of the tax cuts – a central tenet of Thatcherism – found steadily fewer takers.

A close reading of the survey material, however, revealed some positive signs. An important distinction, though one rarely drawn, is between the issues which voters think are *important for the country* and those which are *important for themselves* and which will affect their votes. Young and Rubicam research in May 1986 showed that unemployment was at the top of responses to the first question, but well down on the second. The main concerns affecting voters personally were the NHS, law and order, and the standard of living, and the Conservatives were well ahead of Labour on the last two. A poll by Marplan in March 1987 also went some way to explaining the paradox of why an electorate, although anti-Thatcherite in values, still perferred the Conservatives over other parties. When asked what mattered to them and their families (as opposed to the interest of the country on the Gallup questionnaire) a majority preferred tax cuts to increases in public spending. And by a large majority (59% to 19%) they thought that people would vote according to their own and their families' interests. Indeed the quality research commissioned by Saatchi and Central Office for the party indicated that voters' thinking about the future was concentrated on their families. Voters' concern over the family was linked to worry over unemployment, because they thought this weakened family life, and to unhappiness about law and order which was thought to have deteriorated because of a decline in family values. Voters gave the government credit for firmness, but blamed it for a perceived lack of fairness – although ministers regularly denied that there had been cuts in spending on health and education. Health and education, rather than unemployment, were the key issues for Conservative supporters and likely defectors.

The party's position was strong for much of the parliament, as it clearly benefited from facing two opposition parties. It had a lead in the Gallup opinion polls for 33 of the 47 months of the parliament.[3] But there was a mid-term lull in the government's fortunes. In September 1985 Gallup had the Alliance comfortably in the lead, and there was also a dip in Tory support in the first half of 1986 when Labour moved ahead. At the time of its 1986 annual conference Labour had a 6% Gallup lead. Thereafter, the Tory position steadily recovered after its successful conference in October; in contrast the Alliance suffered from its defence quarrels, and Labour's standing in the polls also fell.

One Conservative strategist interviewed in September 1986 thought that the next election would be the most difficult for the Conservatives: 'In 1979 Labour threw it away, and the same happened in 1983. In a way there was no alternative. This time, we have got to go out and win'. The party was also aware of the problems of Mrs Thatcher's image which, surveys showed, had deteriorated since 1983. Many Conservative defectors (particularly to the SDP) regarded her as authoritarian. However, she still scored high ratings as a decisive leader. A Central Office adviser dismissed suggestions that she might soften her image: 'You don't go into a shop, buy a tin of baked beans and expect them to be transformed into peaches'.

The strategists were also concerned over the amount of good will which, according to the private polls, Tory voters had for the SDP and, particularly, for David Owen. A Conservative difficulty was that the Alliance attracted support in spite of its poor image on leaders and policies, and the electorate's lack of a clear view of what it stood for. 'We can't really attack its leaders or policies. The SDP is a nice warm home for Tories', said one strategist. Conservative voters were less well disposed to the Liberals, and Mr Tebbit therefore felt free to attack them and David Steel. Some Conservative MPs, regarding the Alliance as the main opponents in their own constituencies, wanted Tory fire to be concentrated on the Alliance rather than Labour. Mr Tebbit's line, however, was that Labour was the alternative government and as such had to be attacked. But the party did sponsor surveys of Alliance candidates and showed the deep policy divisions that existed. When the Alliance support climbed in early 1987 he

criticised the Alliance parties for offering Labour a back door to
office.

What was effectively the first formal campaign preparation meeting
took place on 8 January 1987. Norman Tebbit, Michael Dobbs,
Robin Harris, Peter Morrison, Stephen Sherbourne and Margaret
Thatcher met at the house of Lord McAlpine in Great College Street
in Westminster. It was an all-day meeting to consider a 100-page
strategy document which had been written by Michael Dobbs during
December 1986. Throughout the meeting Mrs Thatcher was emphatic
that the next campaign should be positive about the government's
record, and also have radical proposals for the future. The participants
agreed that the next election would largely be fought about which
party could best serve the people's needs in the future. The Conservative party would also have to balance the electorate's desire for
stability and security with its desire for change. The document
recommended that the next manifesto 'should be an essay on the
future as well as a detailed political programme' and should build on
the successful 1986 party conference theme of 'The Next Move
Forward'.

The Labour party was expected to fight on the caring issues, water
down its more left-wing policies, and attack the personalities and
'uncaring' image of the government. Mr Kinnock would fight a
presidential campaign emphasising his youth and his family image
but, it was suggested, he was too insubstantial a figure to fight this
sort of campaign. The document claimed that the party could place

the Labour party, and in particular Mr Kinnock, on the defensive by
pressing them for details of their policies and specific commitments,
particularly on key issues like defence, taxation, trade union
reform.

We must exploit the desire to cover up these details. The Labour
party leadership must be tied in with their extremists. Their long
list of extremist party candidates must be exploited . . . we must
put as much personal pressure as possible on Mr Kinnock.

As for Mrs Thatcher, the document rejected some mass media
advice that she should adopt a softer image: 'While your personal
campaign should emphasise being in touch with ordinary people, we
believe you should play to your strengths, which above all are
leadership, strength and experience' (emphasis in original).

Another important strategy meeting was held on 15 April at Downing Street. Lord Young was present, rather than Michael Dobbs, who had largely written or edited the papers for discussion, but all the other members had been at the 8 January meeting. This group agreed with the recommendation that the Conservatives should polarise issues, and emphasise the differences between Labour and Conservative. The Conservative's key issues would be tax and defence, matters on which the two main parties clearly differed and which it would be difficult for the Alliance to fudge. Labour, according to Saatchi, would not fight on specific policies but on 'The caring romance of Socialism'. It expected, however, that the theme and Mr Kinnock would burn out in the course of the campaign. The strategy paper suggested that the options facing voters at the next election would be between a Conservative victory and a hung parliament, Conservatives should stress the unattractiveness of the latter and argue that it could lead to a Labour government by the back door. The 8 January document had argued for just such a strategy:

> It is vital that we establish a clear contrast between us and the other parties, because we believe that the clearer the choice which is facing the electorate, the more their basically conservative instincts and values will be reflected in Conservative votes. We need clear distance between ourselves and the other parties. Moreover, we believe that the best means of squeezing the Alliance is to concentrate the voters' minds on a clear choice between the two major parties rather than presenting them with a confused 'middle of the road muddle'.

There was a brief discussion about what use the party's central campaign might make of such controversial personalities as Cecil Parkinson, Michael Heseltine, Leon Brittan and Ian Gow, all of whom had resigned from ministerial office during the course of Parliament. It was decided to give a role to the first but to take no action on the other three.

On policy a number of small groups had been set up in July 1986 (to report in December 1986), with a view to suggesting ideas for the party manifesto. Before 1983 Sir Geoffrey Howe had been in charge of a similar operation, but the groups had submitted their reports too late to influence the final document. In 1987 the groups worked to the Strategy Group, with the Prime Minister at its head. The policy groups covered nine areas: managing the economy; working in Britain; Home Office and inner city affairs; national health service; education and training; housing and planning; family and society; young people; and foreign affairs. The groups consisted of a mix of MPs, politically sympathetic academics, and businessmen. The groups managed to submit their reports by December 1986 and Mrs Thatcher read them over the Christmas holidays.

Gradually the organisation of the campaign was taking shape. John Sharkey and Maurice Saatchi presented their advertisements to Mrs Thatcher at Downing Street on 24 April. Mrs Thatcher praised the copy which attacked the other parties but expressed dissatisfaction that there was not more positive material on the government's achievements. She asked that advertising work should maintain a balance of two-thirds positive to one-third negative copy. The advertisers were not convinced, but complied. One week later, on 1 May, the advertising team met the Prime Minister again with more positive advertising copy, most of which was approved. By the weekend of 2–3 May the agency had a complete campaign package, including the first election broadcast, endorsed by Mrs Thatcher. It was also agreed with Mr Tebbit that Lord Young would have a base in Central Office, be responsible for Mrs Thatcher's tours, design and presentation of the manifesto, party election broadcasts and share television work with the chairman. It had already been decided that her itinerary would concentrate on areas of economic success and enterprise. Mrs Thatcher, like Mr Kinnock (see p. 61), was to be seen and filmed in locations associated with progress, in her case ones that reflected the benefits of Thatcherite policies.

Mrs Thatcher was still doubtful about Central Office. She had heard complaints about its unpreparedness, and was uneasy about it handling her own campaign. In 1983 she had leant heavily on her team of Cecil Parkinson, Tim Bell (for some television interviews) and Sir Gordon Reece. All were excellent communicators and personally close to her, but, for various reasons, were under a cloud in 1987. She regretted that they would not be part of the official Conservative campaign. She did not empathise with Mr Dobbs, and relations with Mr Tebbit were never as close as pre-Westland. She found Lord Young personally congenial and respected his communicating and managerial abilities. Clearly, he was expected to fill this gap. Moreover, in the event of an Alliance surge, Lord Young would be more appealing to potential defectors than Mr Tebbit.

There was great momentum behind calling a June election, not least from Central Office and Tory back-benchers. Mrs Thatcher perhaps allowed expectations to go so far that she lost full control of the decision on timing. As in 1983, Mrs Thatcher did not look forward to an election, gave few clues to her thinking, and ostentatiously resisted the attempts of the media to decide for her. She was on record as favouring a term of at least four complete years for a government which had an adequate majority; this ruled out holding the election simultaneously with the local contests on 7 May. Although some advisers still canvassed this date she decided that there was no point in deciding without evidence from 'the biggest poll of all', the local elections. Mr Tebbit was against 7 May, partly because it would mean a longer campaign – extra days would be added because of Easter – which, he thought, might help the Alliance; the government also wanted to get some essential legislation through. October was still a possibility, and was reportedly favoured by Nigel Lawson, Lord Whitelaw and John Moore. It had the advantage that the unemployment figures would fall further, and it would still allow a short campaign. The economic situation gave marvellous political opportunities to choose between spring and autumn, and to combine tax cuts, public spending increases and economic prudence likely to steady the City.

Some ministers wanted the 1987 Budget to concentrate on tax cuts, while others called for increased public spending, particularly to reduce unemployment. In the end the Budget, by providing both, helped to allay divisions within the Cabinet. In the last weeks of parliament there were many signs that the government was clearing the decks for an election; the recommended award by the pay review body for the nurses was approved in full; Mr Baker made reassuring noises about the future of village schools; and the government removed the threat of dumping low-level nuclear waste in a number of key Conservative constituencies.

The positive news from public and private polls and local elections, and the expectations among many party workers, as well as sympathetic newspapers, made it politically difficult to delay a decision. There was no guarantee that electoral prospects would improve later, and indeed they might worsen. Even before the local election results were in and analysed by the party's election expert, Keith Britto, to suggest what would happen in key parliamentary constituencies, June had become inevitable. Even the 'Octobrist' ministers had shifted. The Central Office computer prediction, based on the local elections and private poll findings, nationwide and in marginals, was for a 94-seat Tory majority (compared to the final outcome the prediction was too kind to the Alliance (41) and too harsh to Labour (212)).

Mr Tebbit was widely credited with advocating an early (May or June) election. He had obvious reasons for encouraging the speculation – to create confidence and to put the party organisation on a 'ready to go' footing.[4] Mr Tebbit, however, was more concerned with the party regularly scoring 40% or more in the polls, having a lead of 6 or 7% over the second party, and being reassured that an Alliance upsurge would not threaten too many Tory seats. The local elections on 7 May actually showed some Conservative gains over the good results of May 1983. Further public polls on the following weekend, when Mrs Thatcher met senior ministers at Chequers, showed Tory leads of 11% and 13%. Compared to the position 12 months earlier, the Conservative party's prospects had been transformed.

At Chequers there was little debate over the election date. 4 June was excluded because of problems of clearing essential legislation through parliament and because it was a Jewish holiday. 18 June was also ruled out because the campaign would be too long. 11 June seemed the natural date. It would complete four years in the life of administration, the benefits of the budget tax cuts would be in voters' pockets, house mortgage cuts would have taken effect, and the impression of the Moscow triumph would still be present. There were remarkably few cautionary sounds from MPs or from Central Office. The Chequers meeting also provided an opportunity for some last-minute discussions about the manifesto, and Mrs Thatcher suggested that John Wakeham should have a role in co-ordinating the radio and TV appearances of ministers. She regarded him as another 'safe pair of hands' to have in Central Office along with Lord Young. Mrs Thatcher was aware of Young and Rubicam research, conducted in early April, which showed that more people would be 'happy' with a government led by the Alliance than by any other party; if the Alliance could exploit anti-Tory tactical voting it could threaten the Conservatives. But by May the Alliance danger appeared to have lessened. Ministers departed from Chequers sure that Mrs Thatcher had decided for 11 June. The next day, Monday, 11 May, the Cabinet convened to be told that 11 June was indeed the day, and the announcement was made as soon as Mrs Thatcher had visited the Queen that afternoon.

As in 1983, the government was calling an election against a background of a remarkably favourable set of economic and political indictors. The five national polls (NOP, Gallup, Marplan, Harris Weekend World and Harris TV-am), reporting in early May, before the election date was announced, showed an average Conservative 42%, Labour 30.5% and the Alliance 25.5%. Interest rates were also coming down. On Friday 8 May the bank rate was reduced to 9%, the fourth cut in two months, and there were highly optimistic reports about the economy from the Confederation of British Industry (CBI) and Institute of Directors. Wage settlements averaged 7.5%, compared to inflation at 4%, and represented a substantial increase in living standards for those in work. A MORI survey, in May, of public expectations for the economy over the following 12 months showed a positive balance of 14% expecting it to get better, a figure which matched the previous optimistic peak, reached on the eve of the 1983 election. The Harris private surveys for the party on unemployment were also encouraging. Although most people regarded unemployment as the most important issue, the proportion regarding it as such was declining; there was also a fall in the numbers of voters who thought that unemployment was a 'serious problem' (a) nationally, (b) in their own area, and (c) for themselves and their families. The May unemployment figures reported a fall in the number out of work for the ninth consecutive month.

Yet, offsetting these positive omens, it could be noted that the Conservative lead in the polls was only six months old, and not as large as at the outset of the 1979 and 1983 elections. In both those elections the Conservatives had lost at least 5% of their lead by polling day; Saatchi talked of a 'brickwall campaign' to keep intact the Conservative lead. Mr Tebbit expressed concern about a possible 'Kohl effect'. This was based on the recent general elections in Austria and West Germany that had shown some voters reacting to a likely landslide for one party by supporting a third party. He thought that the prospect of a 'hung' parliament would make voters turn away from the Alliance as they concentrated on the central issue of which party they preferred in government. Saatchi and Mr Tebbit wanted the party to pace their campaign efforts and save much of their advertising and Mrs Thatcher's energies for the last phase of the campaign.

In January 1987 three people were charged with drafting the manifesto. They were Robin Harris, Brian Griffiths, the head of Mrs Thatcher's Policy Unit, and Stephen Sherbourne, her political secretary. The trio felt that they needed a minister who could reconcile disagreements and push things along inside the government machine. Mrs Thatcher was, however, reluctant to give any minister such overall authority. She considered and excluded Nigel Lawson and Norman Tebbit, and did not appear to have anybody else in mind. In February Stephen Sherbourne was commissioned in her name to secure drafts of policy proposals from ministers. Only then did she invite John MacGregor, the Chief Secretary of the Treasury, to supervise the preparation of the manifesto.

On 4 March John O'Sullivan, a writer on *The Times*, joined the group, and his remit included drafting the manifesto. His first draft was completed on 3 April and considered by a manifesto committee on 13 April. A second draft was completed on 16 April and considered at Chequers on 20 April by the Strategy Group. At that meeting Norman Tebbit and Nigel Lawson made useful editorial changes – Mr Tebbit had been a sub-editor earlier in life and Mr Lawson had once been editor of the *Spectator*. The document rarely drew on the work of the policy groups, only turning to them when proposals from departments had been thin. Mrs Thatcher was fully engaged in the process. For example, an early plan to combine material on law and order and national defence in one chapter (on security) was overturned by her insistence that law and order should stand out more boldly and be included in the section on domestic policy.

At an earlier stage it had been planned to list the government's achievements in a concluding section of the manifesto, but because the achievements were so frequently mentioned in the first part, the result was to make the document repetitious. Mrs Thatcher suggested publishing two separate documents, a manifesto and a booklet *The First Eight Years* on the Government's achievements. As a way of distinguishing future proposals from past achievements Lord Young suggested that the proposals be highlighted in a bold blue. The new policies on education and housing were inserted very late in the manifesto and were vigorously pushed by the Prime Minister. One person closely concerned with the development of the manifesto said that Mrs Thatcher was personally responsible for the document's detail and radicalism. After the Chequers weekend Sir Ronald Millar, a speech writer for Mrs Thatcher since 1975, joined John O'Sullivan, and the two men rewrote the draft manifesto over a day and a half to make it more readable.

The Next Moves Forward, at 77 pages, was the bulkiest post-war manifesto produced by any party. It contained radical proposals for state education, local housing and local authorities. The latter would be shorn of most of their functions in education, housing and local planning. Domestic rates would be abolished (a long-time aim of Mrs Thatcher) and replaced by a community charge. The party promised further privatisation, notably in electricity and water, more trade union legislation, an extension of share ownership, and a continuation of tax cuts. Council tenants would be given the right to choose their own landlords, and parents and head teachers more autonomy with the right to choose to opt out of local authority control. Conquest of inflation remained the government's first objective and would be achieved through strict control of public expenditure and reduction of government borrowing. Like Labour's manifesto, the Conservative manifesto bore the signs of a reaction to 1983. That manifesto had been castigated for being bland and showing signs of hurried preparation. This time Mrs Thatcher pushed radical policies and the manifesto was subject to extensive discussion and rewriting (in contrast to Labour's preparation).

Media analysis and speculation had been intense in the weeks preceding the declaration. Since the turn of the year the recovery of the government in the opinion polls, the Greenwich by-election, Mrs Thatcher's triumphant visit to Moscow, Nigel Lawson's budget and then the local election results had all been covered as significant events in themselves and analysed for their implications for the election prospects. Unlike the coming of the election in February 1974 or even 1979, the build-up to the 1987 election lacked drama. On each of those earlier occasions the central planks of the government's anti-inflation strategy had been challenged, indeed destroyed by industrial disruption, and there was a sense that the government could not carry on without a fresh mandate. As in 1983, the government had a commanding majority in the House of Commons; although a year of its term of office remained, and there was no obvious danger on the horizon, it went at a time of its own choosing. It sought endorsement of its record in office and a vote of confidence in its policies for the next Parliament.

NOTES

1. On Westland and its political repercussions see, apart from the parliamentary debates and newspapers of the period; P. Hennessy, 'Helicopter

Crashes into Cabinet: Prime Minister and Constitution Hurt', *Journal of Law and Society*, Autumn 1986; P. Hennessy, 'Michael Heseltine, Mottram's Law and the Efficiency of Cabinet Government', *Political Quarterly*, 1986; Fourth Report From the Defence Committee Session 1985/86, *Westland plc: The Government's Decision-Making*, H.C. 519/985/6.

2. See *The British General Election of 1983*, pp. 35–6.

3. It has been normal for governments to trail in mid-parliament – the Conservatives were only ahead in the Gallup poll for 15 out of the 48 months of the 1979–83 parliament. After October 1974 Labour was ahead for only 14 months out of 54. In 1970–74 the Heath Government led for only 4 months out of 43.

4. On the coming of the election, see P. Kellner, 'All Signs Point to a Hung Parliament', *Independent*, 20 October 1986, 'Falling out with the June Crowd', *Independent*, 23 March 1987 (pieces which impressed Mr Tebbit), 'The Economy says a Summer Election', *Economist*, 3 January 1987, pp. 21–2; R. Oakley, 'Election: Thatcher Options', *The Times*, 19 March 1987.

3 Labour

The Labour party was in a dire position after the 1983 election. It had been reduced to 209 MPs, its lowest post-war figure, and to a mere 28% of the vote, its lowest share since 1918 and lowest percentage vote per candidate since 1900. In parts of South Britain it had been virtually wiped out, and in most Conservative seats it ran a poor third behind the Alliance. The only groups amongst which it had secured over 50% of the votes were council tenants and blacks, and the only areas, the old coalfields and the inner cities. To gain a working parliamentary majority at the next election Labour needed a swing of over 10%, twice as high as had been seen in any post-war general election. Optimists could point to the exceptional circumstances surrounding the 1983 election – the government's Falklands success, Labour's divisions over the changes to its constitution, and the deputy-leadership fight between Denis Healey and Tony Benn, the split which resulted in the formation of the Social Democrats, and the weak leadership of Mr Foot; they could argue that this remarkable conjunction of unfavourable events was unlikely to be repeated.

On the other side pessimists argued that the changing nature of the electorate – particularly the spread of private home-ownership, the decline of manufacturing industry, and the steady reduction in the size of the manual working class – boded ill for the party. Labour had last exceeded 40% of the vote in a general election in 1970.[1]

The new leadership, therefore, faced a major challenge in the 1983 parliament. Under Mr Kinnock the party certainly improved its position, but there were many signs that it was far from a full recovery. In contrast to the position facing Hugh Gaitskell after 1959 when Labour had also suffered its third successive election defeat, the rise of the Alliance meant that Labour was no longer the only significant alternative to the Conservative government.

In retrospect few even of Michael Foot's friends would claim that he had been a good leader of the party. He suffered from hostile media treatment and his authority in the party had been weakened by bitter factionalism. But his unease with modern methods of communication had been manifest during the 1983 campaign, when he preferred to harangue the party faithful at rallies and showed himself unsympathetic to the requirements of the television age. He was bored by the public opinion polls, photo-opportunities and advertising. His opinion poll ratings were disastrous and the great majority of his colleagues regarded him as an electoral liability. Indeed, shortly before the announcement of the 1983 election, there had been discreet moves to get him to stand down.

Within three days of the election defeat, the white-collar union, Association of Scientific, Technical and Managerial Staffs (ASTMS) under Clive Jenkins, announced that it would be nominating Neil Kinnock in the leadership election due at the October party conference – a decision already agreed with Mr Foot. This was the first of many endorsements for Mr Kinnock from trade unions and constituency parties. Roy Hattersley also entered and, in spite of the candidacies of Peter Shore and Eric Heffer, it was clear that this would be a two-horse race between the centre left and centre right. It was something of a generational change as previous contenders like Denis Healey and John Silkin decided not to stand. Neither Mr Kinnock nor Mr Hattersley had previously sought the leadership or deputy-leadership. Tony Benn, being out of the House of Commons, was not eligible.

This was the first time that Labour's new electoral college (adopted at the Wembley conference in 1981) had been used to choose the party leader. Mr Foot had been elected by the Parliamentary Labour Party (PLP) in late 1980 and was not challenged thereafter. The contest had none of the bitterness of the 1981 Benn–Healey fight for the deputy-leadership, partly because there was little doubt that Neil Kinnock would win, and partly because, in understandable reaction to the outcome of the general election, the candidates and many of their active supporters exercised self-restraint. Neil Kinnock's campaign was skilfully managed by Robin Cook and he won decisively. Mr Hattersley easily fought off the challenge of Michael Meacher for the deputy-leadership. The new leader gained 73% of the trade union vote, 91% of the constituency vote and 47% of the PLP vote. For the deputy-leadership Mr Hattersley gained 88% of the union vote, 51% of the constituencies and 56% of the PLP vote. In a fragmented field (Peter Shore and Eric Heffer gained derisory support) it was noteworthy that both Mr Hattersley and Mr Kinnock enjoyed wide backing throughout the three groups in the electoral college.

Mr Kinnock was a member of the Campaign for Nuclear Disarmament (CND), and had risen through an association with the *Tribune* left of the party. But the left wing of the party itself was dissolving into 'soft' and 'hard' groups. The former was largely associated with *Tribune*, the latter with *Campaign*, a group of some 30 MPs with Tony Benn and Eric Heffer as its most prominent members. Mr Kinnock had already demonstrated his independence from factional ties before 1983. As shadow spokesman for education he had resisted pressures in the PLP for a promise to restore all the cuts in education spending made by the Conservatives. In the 1981 deputy-leadership contest he had voted for John Silkin on the first ballot and then abstained, rather than vote for Tony Benn in the run-off. This decision, in which he was joined by some other centre-left MPs, infuriated Mr Benn's backers, who attacked him as a 'Judas'. He had also opposed the Labour government's plans for Welsh devolution in 1976 and 1977. Many of the 'hard' left regarded Mr Kinnock as a political opportunist, but he was the only effective contender for the leadership presented by the left. Like Harold Wilson he rose as a man of the left but once he had become leader he dropped some of his old views.

Neil Kinnock was only 41 and, when elected as leader, was totally inexperienced in government.[2] He had served briefly (and unsatisfactorily) as a parliamentary private secretary to Michael Foot when the latter was Secretary of State for Employment in 1974–5. In the 1979 parliament he had shadowed Education. It was in these years that he emerged as a star of the party conferences and local constituency parties and was regularly elected to the constituency section of the NEC. His critics complained that he was too much a crowd-pleaser and that his oratory was superficial and flashy. Mr Kinnock certainly had self-doubts as a Labour leader, but he gained in confidence the more he travelled abroad and participated in great parliamentary occasions.

Charles Clarke, an ex-President of the National Union of Students (NUS) and Mr Kinnock's parliamentary adviser when he had been shadowing Education, managed his political office and acted as chief of staff. Patricia Hewitt, the Labour candidate in 1983 in Leicester East, and an ex-general secretary of the National Council for Civil Liberties, became his Press Secretary; after the general election she had written to both Neil Kinnock and Roy Hattersley offering her help and it caused some surprise when Mr Kinnock offered her the appointment. Mr Kinnock also took over Dick Clements, a former editor of the *Tribune* who had worked with Michael Foot since 1982.

Advice on economics came from Henry Neuberger (who had also worked for Mr Foot), and John Eatwell, who took leave from his post as a Cambridge economics don.

Neil Kinnock rapidly achieved command of the party machine. At first he tended to ignore the Walworth Road party headquarters which had been deeply discredited by the 1983 election. As long as Jim Mortimer (appointed in 1982) remained General Secretary, it was difficult to tackle the many problems which had been identified in the 1983 campaign.[3] There was not even a formal post mortem on the 1983 election. In advance of the changes in Walworth Road which he considered necessary, Mr Kinnock quickly established a Campaign Strategy Committee (CSC), separate from the NEC, and it soon became a key decision-making body for party broadcasts, opinion polling and campaigns, matters on which the NEC had not taken much interest in the past. It brought together representatives of the NEC, the PLP and Shadow Cabinet, and the trade unions. The group met monthly and was responsible to the NEC for campaign strategy. In fact, to some extent it by-passed the NEC – until Mr Kinnock had an NEC more to his liking.

In 1972 the party had commissioned an Organisation and Management report which recommended the appointment of three directors (for research, organisation, and finance and administration) who, together with the General Secretary, would act as a directorate of the party machine. For a variety of reasons this structure was never created, though many insiders agreed on the need for thorough reforms and for a senior appointment in publicity and communications. Mr Kinnock instigated a review on the organisation of Walworth Road, which was conducted by a sub-committee of the Strategy Committee. The most significant input came from the heads of departments but the report was largely written in Mr Kinnock's office by Charles Clarke.

An opportunity for reorganisation came in 1985 with the appointment of Larry Whitty as the General Secretary. Mr Whitty was 41 and a research officer with the General, Municipal, Boilermakers and Allied Trade Union (GMBATU). It was decided to reduce the number of departments to three and to advertise the key posts, in spite of opposition to the new scheme from Eric Heffer, Dennis Skinner and Tony Benn on the NEC. In organisation, David Hughes, the National Agent, moved sideways to deal with party rules, appeals and mediation, and Joyce Gould, the chief woman officer, was appointed as the new Director of Organisation. Geoff Bish, the long-serving Research Director, was appointed Director of Policy Development. Nick Grant, who had been in charge of publicity in the election, and had come in for much criticism, left the organisation and was replaced in October 1985 by Peter Mandelson who took over a much expanded department called Campaigns and Communications. Mr Mandelson was the only outsider to be appointed to a major departmental post.

As party leader Mr Kinnock worked hard, and front-bench colleagues praised his chairmanship of the Shadow Cabinet, and the way in which he was invariably well-briefed on the issues. He got his way over party appointments and policies, persuading Denis Healey and Roy Hattersley to acquiesce in a defence stance which they had opposed in the past. Although elected leader as the candidate of the left, he soon began to hammer the hard left at the annual Conference and in the NEC, and to ridicule its demands for what he termed 'impossibilism'. Many Labour MPs regarded him as a good leader of the Labour party but still had doubts about how he would shape up as Prime Minister. The judgement of Conservative and Alliance MPs was often scathing, largely because his strengths were seldom demonstrated when they saw him in parliamentary debates.

Mr Kinnock profited from the widespread realisation that many of the disasters of the period from 1979 to 1983 had been self-inflicted. He was determined to produce a change. In a lengthy radio interview with Michael Charlton on 11 December 1985 he explained:

> there's been an immense change in the Labour Party, partly because of my insistence upon different directions, but also because the Party has responded with readiness to a new assertion of what we stand for and the directions in which we should be going.

Neil Kinnock's attempt to distance the party from these memories was set out in his first party conference speech as leader in Brighton in 1983. He reminded delegates of why winning the next election was so important: 'Just remember how you felt on that dreadful morning of June 10th, just remember how you felt then and think to yourselves, June 9th, 1983, never, ever again'. The overriding goal would be electoral victory and his socialist message would be attuned to the hopes and fears of the electorate. The party would have to appeal to the 'haves', as well as the 'have nots', the home-owners as well as council tenants. Mr Kinnock regularly stressed the need for realism and modesty in what the party promised. He prided himself on possessing a keen sense of what the 'ordinary' Labour voter wanted, and was hostile to many of the sectional demands made by groups within the party. In particular he regarded the campaigns by Derek Hatton, the Liverpool Militant, and Arthur Scargill the National Union of Mineworkers' (NUM) leader, as dead ends and likely to alienate existing and potential supporters. They represented challenges to his leadership and his visions of the party which had to be defeated.

In spite of left-wing pressure in the NEC and at Conference, he refused to countenance the reimbursement by a future Labour government of the fines levied on rebel Labour councillors in London and Liverpool and on the NUM. In a powerful speech at the 1985 party conference in Bournemouth, he caused uproar with his attack on the Militants in Liverpool 'the grotesque chaos of a Labour council – a *Labour* council – hiring taxis to travel around a city handing out redundancy notices to its own workers' and Eric Heffer, a Liverpool MP and member of the NEC, walked off the platform in protest.

As far back as 1976 the party's General Secretary and the National Agent had presented their first report on Militant penetration of constituency Labour parties, and in 1982 that Conference upheld the NEC's expulsion of leading members of the editorial board of *Militant*. The national party grew increasingly concerned about the ruling Labour group in Liverpool which appeared to be under the control of the Militant-dominated City Labour Party. An NEC team, after a long-drawn-out inquiry, found that party rules had been infringed, and the 1986 party conference voted to expel from the party 11 leading Militants, including Mr Hatton.

The miners' strike lasted for a full year from March 1984 to March 1985 and Mr Kinnock walked a fine line, supporting the miners, without endorsing Mr Scargill's strategy, and condemning violence by both pickets and police. It was a no-win situation for any Labour leader. He was criticised by those who wanted him to rally behind Mr Scargill as well as by those who wanted him to dissassociate the party from the tactics of the union leadership. Although Mr Kinnock gained high marks from most colleagues for his stance, these internal party problems helped to make his leadership look introverted. Many of his battles were being fought within the Labour party rather than concentrating on the political enemy outside.

A number of factors, however, combined to make the NEC more manageable than it had been in the days of Mr Callaghan, changes in composition helped, particularly the failure of Margaret Beckett and Eric Heffer to be re-elected in 1986, and the choice of more supportive trade union representatives. The general willingness to give the new leadership the benefit of the doubt and a good deal of advance fixing on terms acceptable to Mr Kinnock also made the monthly meetings less fraught. There was still opposition from a hard core led by Tony Benn, Dennis Skinner and Joan Maynard. The last major act of defiance by the left on the NEC was its opposition to his campaign to oust Militant organisers in Liverpool. Presented with an NEC report recommending expulsion, there was a concerted walk-out by Messrs Heffer, Benn, Skinner and others on 26 March 1987, so leaving the NEC without a quorum. Subsequently the rules about an NEC quorum were changed and the expulsions went ahead.

The change of mood was also seen in the NEC's backing in 1986 for the imposition of Mr Kinnock's candidate, George Howarth, in the Knowsley North by-election on Merseyside, and in the 19 to 6 vote in April 1987 to withdraw endorsement from the black activist, Sharon Atkin, as Labour candidate for Nottingham East (see p. 56). But there is no doubt that the management of the NEC proved very demanding on Mr Kinnock's time and energy. Neil Kinnock had constantly to take initiatives, to table amendments and suggest changes in the working of resolutions. In the NEC, as in the PLP, he could take advantage of divisions among the left, and usually he could work with Michael Meacher and David Blunkett (leader of the Sheffield council).

Mr Kinnock was aware that attempts to project him as a credible national leader were doomed until he first established his hold over his party. There was a logic behind Mr Kinnock's actions and their sequence: first appoint a Campaign Strategy Committee and give it authority over election preparations, build up a strong private office, control the PLP, win over the NEC, and then take on the Conference. After three years his leadership was almost unassailable.

In the House of Commons Labour members were greatly outnumbered by the government benches. But attendance was often poor, even for key Labour motions. The party's frustration was that, as an opposition, it could only be influential when a large number of Conservative back-benchers rebelled and then, almost inevitably, dissent on the government side took the headlines. Mr Kinnock was perhaps at his least impressive in the House of Commons. In the eagerly awaited Westland debate he spoke at length, but to little effect, and his performance dismayed many in the PLP.

One of the first Kinnock initiatives was the abolition of all the existing subcommittees of the NEC Home Policy Committee and the appointment of small joint committees, consisting of equal numbers from the PLP and the NEC. There was also a new modesty about policy-making and a greater willingness to trust the PLP leadership. A document from Geoff Bish in September 1985 looked back on the 1983 campaign and commented:

> we encouraged the two competing centres of authority (the NEC and the Shadow Cabinet) to develop policy separately; we had too many policy sub-committees, doing too much detailed policy work – and thus producing too many policy commitments, many of which were disliked or disbelieved by the voters; and the sub-committees were too large with fluctuating memberships and with much too small an input from the very people (Shadow Spokesmen) expected to expound and – implement – the policies themselves. As a result of this it was almost impossible to present clear political strategies for the electorate or to indicate our priorities – or to work together in a united way to defend them.

Geoff Bish, therefore, argued that the party should abstain from the ambitious policy-making exercises of the past. It should aim to agree on the basic outlines of policies and to put off, for as long as possible, any formal work on the party manifesto. Cutting back the number of policy commitments and detail was important in advancing the credibility of the party. Mr Bish observed:

> In this way we will not only avoid giving the impression again of making promises which will not be believed; but we will also avoid making unnecessary enemies. Even more important, we will then be able to keep our message clear and simple – and to project a proper sense of priorities, vision and direction.

In spite of some left-wing complaints, preparation of the manifesto was clearly under Mr Kinnock's control, and proved to be a much less divisive process than it had sometimes been in the past (see p. 71).

On policy the party made some shift from its 1983 programme. It now accepted the sale of council houses to tenants and no longer opposed British membership of the EEC. But there was still the same unilateralist thrust to its defence policy. Although the party's confused stance on this issue had cost it dear in the 1983 election, the PLP and, even more, the conference, had a unilateralist majority. Mr Callaghan was a prominent dissenter from the new line, but most other senior sceptics – notably Denis Healey, Peter Shore, and Roy Hattersley, kept quiet for the sake of party unity. The policy involved the removal of all nuclear weapons from British soil (and therefore decommissioning Polaris and cancelling Trident), but it envisaged continued membership of the North Atlantic Treaty Organization (NATO) and increased spending on conventional forces. On industrial relations Mr Kinnock did not make the ground with the unions he had hoped for; pre-strike and union executive ballots would remain, but the opportunities for the closed shop and secondary picketing would be restored. On social ownership (the new term for public ownership) the party stated that the reversal of the Thatcher government's acts of privatisation was not a high priority, but promised major expansions of state ownership and intervention in the economy.

Mr Kinnock's front-bench team was very different from Michael Foot's, let alone the Labour Cabinets of the 1970s. Only Denis Healey (the self-proclaimed Gromyko of British politics) and Peter Shore remained from the Cabinets of the 1960s. The Shadow team as a whole certainly lacked top-level experience; apart from Healey and Shore, only Hattersley, John Smith, John Morris and Stan Orme had served in the Cabinet. Around Neil Kinnock there was a recognisably influential group of Denis Healey, Roy Hattersley, Gerald Kaufman, John Smith, John Cunningham and, later on, Bryan Gould. In the 1983 Parliament the last two were clearly rising stars. Bryan Gould had replaced Robin Cook as campaign co-ordinator in 1986 when the latter was not re-elected to the PLP Committee, but he also spoke on Treasury matters. The leadership group, like the Shadow Cabinet as a whole, was predominantly a centre-right body, and among the Shadow Cabinet there was no recognisable Kinnock group, or even (apart from Hattersley, Gould, Smith and Cunningham) people with whom Neil Kinnock regularly conferred.

Mr Kinnock worked closely with union leaders, particularly leaders of major unions, not least to get favourable votes at annual conferences. On policy the party and unions co-operated to launch a 'Jobs and Industry' campaign in April 1985, the central plank of which was the pledge to reduce unemployment by one million in the first two years of a Labour government. Mr Kinnock and Mr Hattersley

1983–1987

accepted that there was no point in talking about incomes policy or even wage restraint. But they made clear that a Labour government's plans for public spending, low pay and job creation all depended on responsible wage-bargaining – 'You can't have it out of both pockets', was Mr Kinnock's message.

The difficulties which unions were experiencing affected the politics of the party. In late 1983 NGA members and supporters were involved in often violent picketing scenes at Eddie Shah's publishing plant in Warrington. The lengthy industrial action by the print unions, when Rupert Murdoch's News Ltd moved its papers to the Wapping plant and dismissed all its print workers, was another continuing embarrassment. As a gesture of support Labour leaders boycotted the Murdoch papers. The regular violence on the picket line in Wapping was a problem for them, as it had been during the year-long strike by miners between March 1984 and March 1985. The breakaway Union of Democratic Miners (UDM), largely based in Nottinghamshire, applied for entry to the party and the TUC. But Labour's constitution provided that only unions recognised by the TUC could be affiliated to the party, and the TUC refused recognition.

On the positive side, however, the trade unions continued to finance the Labour party through routine subscriptions – union ballots on retaining a political fund in 1984–5 had all been successful. Trade Unions For Labour (TUFL) raised additional money for the election. The party survived financially with expenditure rising from £3.9m in 1982 to £6.1m in 1986.

Many of the party grew concerned at the 'loony left' activities of some Labour-controlled councils in London. They were also worried about the amount of time which the leadership had to devote to combatting assertive voices in the party pleading for special interests. In addition to Militant, the tabloids played up the anti-police remarks made by the black Haringey leader and Labour candidate, Bernie Grant; the Brent Labour Council's suspension of the headmistress Mrs McGoldrick, on account of unproved allegations of racism; and Sharon Atkin's accusation that the party was racist. Throughout the parliament Labour had to grapple with charges of extremism and groups demanding for special treatment on racial and sexual grounds. The worries came to a head with Labour's disastrous showing in the Greenwich by-election in February 1987, when a safe Labour seat was lost to the Alliance. Patricia Hewitt, Mr Kinnock's press secretary, complained in a letter, later leaked to the *Sun* newspaper, that fears of extremism, combined with the loony left image of Labour in

London (and its handling of issues relating to gays and lesbians) had cost the party dear. Mr Kinnock was furious at the way these issues, and the negative publicity they attracted, handicapped the party's ability to make progress on the bread and butter issues of jobs, pensions, housing and schools. A number of trade union leaders, including Ron Todd, of the Transport Workers' Union (TGWU), and John Edmonds of the General and Municipal, publicly expressed their impatience at the time the leadership was giving to these issues.

Reselection proved much less troublesome than it had in the last parliament and only six sitting MPs were directly ousted in the reselection process. But the hard left made substantial progress in some new selections (see pp. 192–4). On the eve of the election the NEC imposed the sitting members on the Vauxhall and Newham North West parties, the constituency parties' selection procedures having been declared invalid for allowing local black sections' delegates to participate. It did the same to the two St Helens parties where efforts were being made to dismiss the sitting MPs, John Evans and Gerry Bermingham. Elsewhere Robert Kilroy-Silk resigned the safe Knowsley North seat in June 1986, alleging Militant penetration of the local party, and Renee Short in Wolverhampton North East and John Silkin in Deptford, stood down rather than face bitter reselection battles. But Peter Shore in Stepney, and Gerald Kaufman in Manchester Gorton, held on in spite of local opposition. Mr Kinnock was frustrated in two attempts to weaken the influence of the hard left in local parties. He lent his personal support to the 'one member, one vote' campaign for the selection of parliamentary candidates, but this was narrowly defeated at the 1984 conference. In 1985 Mr Kinnock chaired a committee to set out 'the principles of democratic socialism'. Such a statement could have provided a means for party leaders to exclude extremists from party membership, but the committee failed to come up with an agreed statement.

Individual membership of the party rose somewhat from the 1983 figure, (283 000), but following the increase in the rate of subscription (£10) in 1985, numbers fell away again to 297 000 in 1986. The decline in full-time constituency agents was arrested but, at between 60 and 70, it offered limited back up to voluntary efforts.

The tasks of regional organisers were made more difficult in seats where Militant or other groups were active and local parties were divided. This was particularly true in London, the North West and Nottinghamshire. While the party was vastly improving its communications, its regional and constituency organisation remained

a major weakness. Another worry for the leadership was the campaign
TV87 (Tactical Voting 87) launched at the end of 1986 to encourage
tactical voting by third-place Labour and Alliance voters in order
to oust Conservative MPs. The strategy implicitly assumed the
improbability of Labour gaining a majority of seats. Mr Kinnock
went out of his way to dismiss this as 'fruit machine politics', claiming
that Labour was the only alternative government. However, there
were many prominent left-wing supporters of TV87, including Professor Eric Hobsbawm, the Marxist historian, Stuart Weir, the editor
of Labour's *New Socialist* magazine, and the Labour MP Frank Field.
One result of the campaign was the enforced resignation of
Mr Weir. Newspapers like the *Guardian*, *Today* and the *New
Statesman*, although well disposed to Labour, also supported tactical
voting.

Opinion polling remained with Robert Worcester's MORI, as it
had at all general elections since 1970, despite a move by Dennis
Skinner (a long-standing opponent) at the NEC in 1984 to discontinue
the arrangement (see p. 133). In August 1983, before he was
elected leader, Neil Kinnock told Mr Worcester that he wanted the
organisation to carry on polling for the party. At the time it was
conducting surveys on behalf of Roy Hattersley for his leadership
campaign. In its post-1983 election report for Labour, MORI had
stated that it could not serve the party effectively unless it was fully
involved in the preparations for the campaign. Relations improved
greatly during the 1983 parliament. The organisation met the polling
subcommittee of the Campaign Strategy Committee[4] monthly and
reported to the CSC. It also reported periodically to the Shadow
Cabinet and Mr Worcester regularly provided private memoranda
for Mr Kinnock.[5]

In August 1986 Robert Worcester circulated a memorandum
suggesting how Labour might build on its 'natural base' of some
30%. How could it get the extra 10% of votes which would enable it
to win the election? He argued that voting behaviour was a product
of a triangle of factors; issues, party image and leadership. Labour
at the time had a lead over the Conservatives on most of the key
areas, with the exception of law and order and defence. But when
people were asked which party had the best policies generally, the
Conservatives drew level with Labour. On leadership Neil Kinnock
was liked for his personal qualities but seen as lacking in strength. The
memorandum suggested that other Labour spokesmen were not
doing enough in their speeches and media appearances to publicise

Mr Kinnock's assets. Although Labour's image had improved *vis-à-vis* the Tories since 1983, on every single item its position was worse than it had been in September 1974. In particular it was handicapped by policy and personality divisions, by its perceived extremism. He continued: 'people want a party that they can *trust*, that will keep its *promises*, that has a *concern* for the interests of the people and that can *best improve their standard of living*'. Mr Worcester suggested that party spokesmen should hammer home these themes in their speeches and interviews as well as election broadcasts.

MORI also helped strategists to identify Labour's target voters. Obviously Labour had to recover the heavy losses it had suffered among skilled and unskilled workers and trade unionists between 1974 and 1983. But the 100 and more seats Labour needed for a parliamentary majority contained above average numbers of home-owners and white-collar workers.[6] Hopes for further detailed academic analysis of the social and economic characteristics of voters in the marginal seats from academics were not fulfilled. Campaign advisers decided to target 'soft' and ex-Labour voters and weak Liberal/SDP supporters; within these the single largest group were women aged 25–45. Other target voters included pensioners, first-time voters and white-collar trade unionists.

A key appointment was that of Peter Mandelson as the new head of Campaigns and Communications. He was a grandson of the old Labour deputy-leader, Herbert Morrison, and he had been a Lambeth councillor and a producer with London Weekend Television. He used his many contacts with people in television and advertising to strengthen the team of volunteers assisting the party. Like Neil Kinnock, he also took a 'never again' view of the 1983 election. In his presentation to the NEC, when being interviewed for the job, he impressed Mr Kinnock with his detection of a new mood among the electorate. Many people accepted the need for individual enterprise, but they were also looking for a more caring government and a more socially just society – Sweden rather than the United States was the model for many people. Arguing that the Labour party spent too much time talking to itself rather than promoting its values among the general public Mr Mandelson wanted to close the credibility gap which dogged the party on account of its internal divisions, distrust in its own leadership, and public doubts about its economic competence. After his appointment Peter Mandelson worked closely with Mr Kinnock and his private office and proved much more sophisticated than his predecessors in using television and mass communications.

Labour's campaign preparations began in early 1985 when Patricia Hewitt wrote a lengthy memorandum to Mr Kinnock suggesting that the party must begin to plan for the next election; the manifesto, scripts for election broadcasts, campaign schedules, leaflets, advertisements and finance should all be complete by March 1987. Mr Kinnock informally established a staff planning group which was initially given the title of the General Secretary's Committee and then renamed the Campaign Management Team (CMT). It consisted of Larry Whitty, the three Walworth Road directors, Charles Clarke and Pat Hewitt from Kinnock's office, and Robin Cook from the PLP, until he was replaced by Bryan Gould in October 1986. It was not an official group, but an in-house body which reported directly to the leader. It met monthly in 1986 and fortnightly in 1987. Mr Kinnock regarded the Campaign Strategy Committee as too large for effective planning and feared that plans might be leaked. In late 1986 a Leader's Committee was set up.[7] In the past such a committee had come into being after the calling of a general election, but this time Mr Kinnock was determined to iron out differences of emphasis well in advance of the election campaign, saying: 'If there are going to be problems, I want to have them out and resolved before rather than during the election'.

Patricia Hewitt and Peter Mandelson appreciated the importance of continuous television coverage in modern electioneering and wanted to ensure that during the election Labour would have a 'good media day'. In a memorandum addressed to the Campaign Management Team in December 1985 Patricia Hewitt wrote: '1987 will be an ENG [electronic news-gathering] election with news editors demanding – and getting – virtually instant responses to every key speech and statement. We have to be able to cope with the problems this will cause, and exploit the possibilities'.

Immense effort was put into organising photo-opportunities for Mr Kinnock and other key campaigners, and ensuring that the text of a major evening speech would be available by 6.00 p.m., for the main night-time news broadcasts. A particularly important development was the suggestion by the two strategists that Mr Kinnock should hold about half of his daily press conferences in regional centres. There was some discussion over this proposal in the Campaign Strategy Committee in Spring 1986. Patricia Hewitt argued against having Mr Kinnock at all the regular daily London conferences on the grounds that anti-Labour journalists would use them to run hostile stories and distract the party from focusing on its chosen issues. She concluded: 'their useful functions can be fulfilled as well by a less rigid schedule (e.g. some in London, some in other parts of the country; some in Transport House, or wherever, others in more unusual locations)'.

The party turned down the idea of abandoning completely the London morning press conferences, fearing that it would leave too much initiative to the other parties and that Labour leaders would be accused of running away from tough questioning by journalists. In March 1987 the Campaign Management Team agreed to Ms Hewitt's and Mr Mandelson's suggestion that Mr Kinnock should hold regional press conferences; Bryan Gould and occasionally, Roy Hattersley, would meet the London press.

It was also agreed that the schedules of the leader and key campaigners should be geared to the deadlines required by broadcasting media, and that locations for visual coverage, particularly for the leader and the spokespersons at the day's press conference, should be matched as far as possible to the day's theme. The plan was to have the heavyweight speakers – Messrs Kinnock, Healey, Smith and Hattersley – speaking in different parts of the country on the key issue of the day. In early April Charles Clarke and Patricia Hewitt gained Neil Kinnock's approval for the schedule which they had prepared. They persuaded him to open Labour's campaign in Birmingham rather than Scotland, on the grounds that the Midlands had many key marginals and that Scotland would present a less progressive backcloth for the image which Labour wished to project. Charles Clarke also spoke informally to leading Shadow Cabinet members to get their agreement for the draft schedules.

Patricia Hewitt and Peter Mandelson also gave much thought to providing photo-opportunities for Mr Kinnock. Because they found that constituency and regional agents were not skilled at suggesting suitable locations, they asked various TV freelancers to find spots which would associate the party with progress, youth, enterprise and dynamism. In another memorandum, entitled 'Finding the Best Places to Visit', written in early 1986, Patricia Hewitt commented:

locations must reflect the overall themes and style of our campaign. In particular they must be *positive*, we want places that are modern, that show the best of Britain and, in particular, the best of what Labour councils are doing; places that encapsulate Kinnock's Britain. We do NOT want any closed factories, derelict housing

sites, run-down hospitals, industrial wastelands or other wrecks of
Thatcher's Britain. We also want *people* – bright, attractive people
presenting an image of the broader base Labour has to capture –
not people who present an image of old-fashioned Labour die-
hards.

The projection of a positive image of the Labour party and, above
all, of Mr Kinnock, was central to the campaign preparations. In
1983 the party had worked with an advertising agency headed by
Johnny Wright. Labour's disorganisation and mistrust of advertising
at the time meant that it was not a fruitful relationship. The party
was not a good client for an advertising agency. Labour had attacked
the Conservatives for using an advertising agency (Colman, Prentis
and Varley) in the 1959 election; Patrick Gordon-Walker, from the
Labour front bench, complained that it introduced 'the worst sort of
Americanisation' into British democracy. By 1964, however, Labour
recruited its own professional advertising men. But many in the party
remained uneasy with the values and methods of advertising and
market research. After 1983 many Labour party influentials were
again prepared to embrace modern communication techniques.
  Soon after his appointment Peter Mandelson invited Philip Gould,
of Philip Gould Associates, to review the party's communications
efforts and make recommendations for the future. Within a month
(late December 1985) Mr Gould presented his 64-page report which
was distributed to a handful of people. It suggested that the party
communications were uncoordinated, lacked an impact on voters,
and used over-complicated language. The report also complained
that the lines of responsibility between different officers and groups
were not clear. Most of its recommendations were implemented,
including:

● greater concentration on securing publicity through the mass
  media rather than relying on the localised campaigning of the
  party,

● the Director of Campaigns and Communications to be in complete
  charge of communications and implementation,

● a Shadow Communications Agency to be set up with a full-time
  co-ordinator,

● the party's messages to be simplified, repeated and orchestrated,

● opinion polling to remain with MORI (but the qualitative research to be undertaken separately) and the organisation to be better integrated into the campaign planning,

● work on identifying 'target' voters to be carried further,

● a smaller working communications group to be set up, with its membership confined to people involved in campaigns and communications.

There was little chance that the party would appoint a full-time advertising agency; it would not find the money and there was no outstanding agency available. Boase, Massimi, Pollitt (BMP), which had handled the 'Save the GLC' campaign, would not take the party's account because of resistance from some of its board members. But many of the 'save the GLC' and BMP group were prepared to work voluntarily for the party. Mr Mandelson immediately appointed them in early 1986, and asked Mr Gould to co-ordinate their work.

Mr Mandelson then reconstituted the informal 'breakfast group' of public relations volunteers which Robin Cook had built up since November 1984. A new Shadow Communications Agency was established to deal with all aspects of communications – design, speechwriting, research, copywriting and art direction – as well as advertising. A group of volunteers (of whom only Philip Gould and Deborah Mattinson were paid) enabled the party to tap the skills of people from various agencies: it was ratified by the NEC in March 1986 with Philip Gould as its full-time co-ordinator. Gradually its work expanded to include subgroups of journalists, writers (chaired by Ken Follett and including Colin Welland, John Mortimer, Hanif Kuriechi), broadcasters and a by-election team. The agency met monthly and was chaired by Chris Powell or Peter Herd (both of BMP).[8] This Central Management Group worked on the 'Freedom and Fairness' and 'Investing in People' campaigns, and on 'Modern Britain in a Modern World' in December 1986.

Party conferences were more effectively stage managed than before. Conference, television and press addresses by Mr Kinnock and other prominent spokesmen took place against carefully designed backdrops. Mr Kinnock began to wear sober dark suits, white shirts and had his balding hair cut short. Party political broadcasts and leaflets were professionally designed; the party won endorsements from pop and sports stars; leaders appeared on TV chat shows; and Mr Kinnock took part in a pop song video. Authority over party political broadcasts was removed from the NEC and given to a subcommittee of the Campaign Strategy Committee, chaired by Mr Kinnock. John Gau, formerly a BBC current affairs producer, was given control, and also commissioned to make the election broadcasts. There were predictable criticisms from some left-wingers that the party was trying to out-Saatchi Saatchi. Hugh Hudson, producer of the award-winning film *Chariots of Fire*, approached Mr Mandelson in Autumn 1986, offering to work for Labour. He was asked to prepare a video of the leader's speech at the party conference, which was to become part of his election broadcast.

The Shadow Communications Agency's main work for the election was completed during December 1986 and from January 1987 a smaller group of Bryan Gould, Philip Gould, Peter Mandelson, Chris Powell, Peter Herd, Deborah Mattinson and Patricia Hewitt met every Tuesday at 8.30 a.m. to deal with immediate issues. Its suggestions for the campaign strategy were presented in February. It drew on the qualitative research into the mood of the electorate which showed three underlying features:

(i) Dissatisfaction with the quality of life (particularly welfare services and opportunities for children);
(ii) doubts about the strength of the 'real' economy, but
(iii) the widespread feeling of being financially better off.

Labour's task, it suggested, was to exploit the unhappiness with the social condition of the country and to undermine the economic satisfaction by emphasising the industrial decline and unemployment. But it acknowledged that people were not turning to Labour because of the negative features of its image and because of confusion about what the party stood for. The Agency argued that Labour should vigorously attack the Conservatives on social issues and present a clear focus that:

'(i) Makes the contrast between what people feel about the declining quality of life, and what we offer as an alternative. In effect, a contrast between hope and despair.
(ii) Taps the emotion people feel in this area.
(iii) Makes it clear that while the Tories are better for the few we are better for everybody.' (see Figure 3.1)

The team made several presentations on campaign strategy to

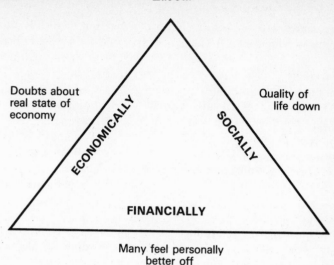

Figure 3.1   Key findings from research – the mood of the people

regional groups of candidates, party workers, and a joint NEC-Shadow Cabinet meeting, advising how Labour could best attack, defend, and generally employ the media to advantage. In February 1987 it recommended a battery of words, phrases and arguments which campaigners should repeat as they attacked the government

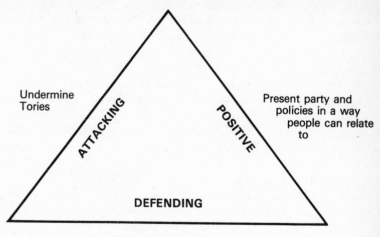

Figure 3.2   Communications objectives

and presented Labour positively on defence, social issues and the economy (see Figure 3.2). This is a sample of the suggested phrases:

Attacking	*Positive*
'Children Have No Future'	'Children'
'The Welfare State is Under Threat'	'Future'
'We are not Paying Our Way'	Investment'
'The Real Economy is in Decline'	'Training'
'Cutting our Real Defences'	'Building for the
'Life Has Got Worse under the Tories'	Future'
	'Strengthening our
	Real Defences'

Mr Mandelson was determined that the main party speakers should appear near television centres, and that leading speakers and candidates should co-ordinate what they were saying on each day of the campaign. The party headquarters would use the British Telecom Gold electronic mail box to communicate speedily with candidates. Neil Kinnock would take at least half of the press conferences in the regions, calculating that television was the most important medium for transmitting the party's message, and that it would cover regional press conferences. Anticipating a May 1987 election, the team launched a modest poster campaign using only 300 sites for that month. By the time the election was called Mr Kinnock had already approved a series of press advertisements as well as plans for election broadcasts and commercials for the cinema. In contrast to the shambles of 1983, a planned communications campaign was being realised.

Mr Kinnock's team wanted him to fight a so-called 'People's Campaign' on the social issues. They were aware of the voters' cynicism about politicians ('they'll promise anything'), distrust of Labour, and rejection of extremism and disunity. Therefore, according to a memorandum from Ms Hewitt:

We should be looking for a campaigning style that addresses these problems. Election campaigning has become extremely stylised and, in many ways, remote from real people. The issues are filtered by the political correspondents; the conflicts between politicians are often indirect (mediated by interviewers or news reporters); contact with the people is visibly stage-managed (walkabouts, Thatcher with calf etc.). Where real people break through into the election – Election Call, Nationwide, the Granada 500 with people questioning politicians – the public laps it up.

By 1987 there was no doubt about Labour's electoral recovery – its morale was much higher than in 1983. It had a more credible and realistic programme, a more professional organisation, a youthful and telegenic leader, and a central command which had clearly showed its determination to root out extremism in the party. The electoral objective was to raise Labour's standing in the polls from 35% to 40%. In the first half of 1986 the government's mishandling of Westland, Labour's success in the Fulham by-election, and its new-look 'Freedom and Fairness' campaign helped. At the end of the year it had 38% support in the polls and, compared with 1983, it had recovered especially strongly in the north, the working class and the 18–24 age group.

But even when Labour had been leading in the opinion polls, through much of 1985 and 1986 its ratings rarely touched 40% and there appeared to be something of a ceiling around 36–37%. Its by-election record was unimpressive and the gains in local elections were not sufficient to suggest a full recovery. The party did particularly badly in seats which it defended or in which it was in third place. The more professional campaign methods were seen to special advantage in Fulham, but they did less well in Greenwich in February 1987 when the left-wing candidate Ms Deidre Wood saw a near 5000 vote lead over the Alliance turned into a 6000 vote deficit. There was also mounting evidence in opinion polls that Labour was not doing as well in the key marginals as it was nationally. The party was still preferred to the Conservatives on education, the National Health Service, and employment, and Mrs Thatcher was not widely liked. Labour, however, was vulnerable to charges that it was unduly influenced by the trade unions and left-wing extremists and the government's overall image was more favourable.

The slippage in Labour's position actually began soon after its successful annual conference in October 1986. The Alliance parties' split on defence, coupled with Mr Kinnock's passionate conference speech repudiating nuclear weapons, increased the salience of the defence issue. In contrast to the successful Conservative conference (with its emphasis on new policies) Labour's 'Investing in People' campaign launched on 15 October fell flat. In December Mr Kinnock's public standing was damaged by revelations of the contacts between his office and Malcolm Turnbull, who was Peter Wright's defending counsel, in an Australian case brought against the former MI5 agent by the British Government. It was even more damaged by his clumsily-managed trip to Washington to explain Labour's defence policy. The opinion poll ratings of Mr Kinnock and the party plummeted. An already fragile position was further weakened in February when the party lost Greenwich. 'We had been knocked down [by the US trip], Greenwich was the knock out punch', said Philip Gould. On the eve of the 1983 election the party had at least held on to the marginal seat of Darlington even though this had proved a false dawn (it was lost three months later).

When MORI reported to the Campaign Strategy Committee in April 1987 it noted that the party had slipped from an average of 40% in the last quarter of 1986 to 35% in the first quarter of 1987. Over the same period the Tories had risen to 41% and the Alliance were up 4% to 23%. A comparison of Gallup findings on public attitudes taken in January and April 1987 showed how Labour's image had deteriorated particularly after Greenwich. The proportions of voters agreeing that Labour was 'too extreme' increased from 53% to 67%, that its leaders were 'poor' from 54% to 69%, that it was 'too split and divided' from 56% to 73%, and that the economy would worsen under Labour from 41% to 55%. Continuing headlines about divisions over defence and about Militant and black sections only added to the perceptions of division and incompetence to govern. Some opinion polls actually had Labour in third place.[9]

In the April Gallup poll Neil Kinnock trailed the other party leaders, with only 26% thinking that he was doing a good job as Labour party leader and 63% thinking he was doing badly, a net negative score of −37% (Thatcher had a net score of −7%, Steel +28% and Owen +31%). The proportions thinking that previous successful opposition leaders were doing a good job on the eve of previous elections were; Wilson (1964) 58%, Ted Heath (1970) 28%, Harold Wilson (1974) 38%, Margaret Thatcher (1979) 43%. Only Michael Foot with 19% in 1983 had had a worse rating than Neil Kinnock among post-war leaders. The halo effect of the leadership election in 1983 had worn off. Voters liked his personality; he outscored Mrs Thatcher on being in touch with ordinary people, personal warmth and uniting the country. But on questions relating more directly to leadership capability – strength of personality, decisiveness and gaining respect for Britain abroad – he lagged far behind. In some respects it was still the one-sided Foot v Thatcher contest. Rows, divisions, challenges to Mr Kinnock by Militant or black sections, and the 'extreme' image of some Labour-controlled London boroughs all contributed damagingly to a perception of weak leadership. His advisers knew that it was important for his image (and Labour's) that he should be seen to be standing up to extremists and to be clearly in charge of the party.

The party decided to tackle this problem directly and run an almost presidential campaign, relying heavily on Mr Kinnock. Members of the communications team were influenced by the campaign film of the former US Vice-President, Hubert Humphrey, *What Manner of Man*. A hint of this was conveyed by Johnny Wright, who had directed the party's advertising in 1983 and was now an observer. On the *Weekend World* television programme on 10 May 1987 he advised how Labour should get across its image:

> Run a Presidential style campaign on Neil Kinnock, focus on the man, focus on his abilities, his youthfulness, his natural appeal to the new voter, where I think the Labour Party will do very well in the next election and make it almost a single-minded pitch for the man, to build him up, because he's undoubtedly the most attractive leader of the four main political figures in the country.

It was possible to identify three broad problems for Labour, each of which remained from 1983. The other parties' charge that it was unilateralist and prepared to leave Britain defenceless was a major electoral liability. A Labour campaign at the end of 1986 tried to emphasise the need for Britain to choose between strong conventional forces or having Trident; it could not have both. Conference and the NEC supported the Kinnock policy but Mr Kinnock never fully persuaded some of the heavyweight figures in the Shadow Cabinet. Mr Kinnock's two visits to the United States in November 1986 and late March 1987, and his attempt to convince the Reagan team of the merits of Labour's defence policies were failures. A number of campaign advisers opposed both visits. After the first visit the party's private polls found that opinion turned against Labour's message that Britain could have a strong defence without nuclear weapons. The rebuff to Mr Kinnock in the White House on 27 March contrasted with Mrs Thatcher's reception in Moscow the following week. James Callaghan's public disagreement with the party's nuclear policy and his subsequent spat with Mr Prescott in the House of Commons tea-rooms kept the issue and the party divisions in the headlines.

In spite of the government's poor record on matters of law and order Labour still ran well behind the Tories on this issue. Mr Kinnock himself took a particularly strong line on the issue, but the party suffered from its association with some of the London Labour authorities which were hostile to the police. Trade union militancy and the well publicised 'loony left' activities of a few Labour authorities tainted the party with being soft on crime and on 'extremism'.

Finally, in spite of Mr Hattersley's determination to limit the spending promises made by the party, particularly by Michael Meacher, the health and social security spokesman, many voters were still worried that the party's programme would raise levels of taxation and inflation to unacceptable levels. An internal document in early 1985 commented on the party's private polls: 'Most people think of Labour as a party that cares . . . but that does not know how to generate wealth and that prints money to solve economic problems. In a word, is Labour "fit to govern"?'

For the government John MacGregor published in March 1987 a costing of the Labour party's programme in terms of how much extra public spending and taxation it would involve, and received extensive publicity for his disputed figure of £34bn. In February and March 1987 the party's plans on jobs, industry and training were launched against the unfavourable background of Greenwich and the 'tea-room row' between James Callaghan and John Prescott. Some Shadow Cabinet members were so concerned about the failure of the party's campaign to get its economic message across that they argued that they should concentrate on its stronger 'social' issues. Labour spokesmen castigated the government's tax cuts 'for the rich', argued that the revenue should have been spent on improving social services and job proposals, and promised to reverse Nigel Lawson's 2p tax reduction in the 1987 budget. Detailed tables were prepared for Mr Hattersley (and shown to Mr Kinnock) concerning the net losers and gainers from Labour's taxation and spending plans. The information was not fully digested, with damaging results in the election (see p. 106).

In past elections the meetings between the NEC and the PLP, required by Clause V of the Party's Constitution to approve the manifesto, have been politically fraught occasions. In 1979 Mr Callaghan angered the left by exercising what was effectively a personal veto on some of its favoured policies. In 1983 the meeting was largely a formality; the left had its way, and the document was immediately christened 'The longest suicide note in history'. It is a measure of Mr Kinnock's dominance that in 1987 so little fuss was made about the manifesto. The joint PLP–NEC policy committees had agreed a series of policy statements, the last one on the economy being issued in January 1987. Mr Kinnock wanted a short manifesto, which would highlight a Labour government's pledges to a £6 billion job creation programme and a £3.6 billion package to attack poverty. Promises of spending in other areas would only be fulfilled if and when the economy grew.

In March a meeting between Neil Kinnock, Tom Sawyer (chairman of the NEC's Home Policy Committee), Tony Clarke (head of the International Committee), Larry Whitty and Geoff Bish commissioned Mr Bish to draft the manifesto. He was told to keep it short and avoid detail by supplying cross-references to the relevant party statements. Mr Kinnock found the draft lacking punch and style and asked Bryan Gould and Gerald Kaufman to rewrite it. Then in April Mr Kinnock and Charles Clarke wrote another version, omitting the cross-references from the Bish draft. Finally, in early May, Charles Clarke and Geoff Bish added the final touches for the Clause V meeting. Mr Kinnock's concern for secrecy meant that only a handful of people were privy to the document, and Mr Hattersley saw it shortly before the Clause V meeting.

The manifesto was agreed at an amiable, two-hour Clause V meeting on 12 May. The general mood of the meeting was, according to one participant: 'If Neil doesn't want it, then we won't have it'. Some left-wingers raised objections on particular items but it was Kinnock supporters who favoured taking votes, both to cut through the discussion and to show the strength of support for the leader. On the defence section, Dennis Skinner and Tony Benn proposed that a future Labour government withdraw from NATO, and that it close down the American bases, but were outvoted 31 to 6 and 29 to 6 respectively. Mr Benn later sought consolation in the new precedent of taking votes at a Clause V meeting, claiming that the left could use it in the future. Although Neil Kinnock had kept close control of the manifesto, left-wingers could be mollified by its proposals for a wealth tax and social ownership of British Gas and British Telecom. But, compared to the 1983 programme, there were no proposals to abolish the House of Lords, to withdraw from the European Community, to close down American nuclear bases in Britain, or to take over private hospitals (though a Labour government would phase out private beds in the NHS).

At the heart of the manifesto was the party's programme for job creation (one million in two years) and greater investment in industry. On defence the party reaffirmed its nuclear policy but readers of the fine print noted a softening of policy. Cruise would now be retained while the Gorbachev–Reagan disarmament talks continued with a good prospect of success. However, Polaris would be decommissioned and Trident cancelled. Labour also proposed a minimum wage and an £8 increase in old age pensions for couples. Mr Kinnock had clearly succeeded in slimming down the manifesto commitments and presenting a set of popular themes with which the party could be associated.

Despite all the apparent improvements, in some respects Labour approached the election in an even worse position than in 1983. There were doubts over the national leadership qualities of Kinnock, and there were internal rows. The upsurge in the strength of the Alliance raised the serious prospect that it might actually beat Labour for second place in votes, and at least one leading member of the Shadow Cabinet regarded it as a make-or-break election for Labour: if the party did badly this time, its decline would be terminal. For Neil Kinnock, who had for three and a half years maintained a single-minded focus on victory, the electoral prospects threatened a cruel judgement. According to one of those close to Mr Kinnock:

> Obviously if we'd gone into the election campaign at 36/38% things would have been very different. What changed everything, of course, was Greenwich and subsequent rows – all of which were peculiarly disastrous because they reawoke the fears which many potential Labour voters still had about Labour extremism, divisions, unfitness for government and Kinnock's own leadership ability.

Yet Mr Kinnock could point to many achievements by the end of 1986, when Labour was still scoring 38% in the polls. It is difficult to think of any post-war leader of the party who had such simultaneous command of the conference, NEC and Shadow Cabinet. He had reorganised the party machine in Walworth Road and down-graded the NEC by giving so much latitude to the Shadow Communications Agency. He had shown resolution in taking on Militant. He had changed the party's policy on council house sales, British membership of the European Community, renationalisation, and he had secured acceptance of a clearer and more unified line on defence than the shambles of 1983. Not since 1964 had a Labour party been so disciplined and single-minded in its pursuit of office.

Labour strategists were confident that they would wage an efficient and professional campaign, and that Kinnock's qualities, so savagely and unfairly attacked by the press, would come through; they believed that they could deny the Conservatives an overall victory. Observers of the Labour party between 1983 and 1987 must have been struck by how many of Kinnock's new men and women – in the party organisation, the shadow advertising agency, and in his private office – were, above all, Kinnock loyalists, people who believed in his abilities and his political future. For them the 1987 election would be a stage in their long march to rebuild the Labour party. They aimed to do well in the election in spite of the many handicaps imposed on them by their party's past and extremists.

NOTES

1. On Labour and the electorate, see: A. Heath *et al.*, *How Britain Votes*, 1985; R. Rose and I. McAllister, *Voters Begin to Choose*, 1986; P. Dunleavy and C. Husbands, *British Democracy at the Crossroads*, 1984; I. Crewe, 'Can Labour Rise Again?', *Social Studies Review*, 1985.
2. On Neil Kinnock, see M. Leapman, *Kinnock* (London, 1987) and R. Harris, *The Making of Neil Kinnock* (London, 1984).
3. See *The British General Election of 1983*, pp. 274–83.
4. The polling committee consisted of Gwyneth Dunwoody (chair), Michael Meacher, Robin Cook (later Bryan Gould), John Cunningham, Jo Richardson, Peter Kellner, Lord McIntosh, Joyce Gould, Geoff Bish, Peter Mandelson, and Rex Osborn from Walworth Road, Nigel Stanley (a political adviser), Brian Gosschalk (from MORI) and Patricia Hewitt from Mr Kinnock's staff. Nearer the election Philip Gould was added to represent the Shadow Communications Agency.
5. The Shadow Communications Agency used the services of many volunteers to carry out qualitative research as to public opinion.
6. For this type of electoral research see I. McAllister and R. Rose, *The Nationwide Competition for Votes*, 1984.
7. The members of the Leader's Committee were: Neil Kinnock, Roy Hattersley, John Cunningham, Denis Healey, Gerald Kaufman, Robin Cook, Bryan Gould and John Smith from PLP; David Blunkett, Tom Sawyer, Betty Boothroyd, Tony Clarke, and Diana Jeuda from the NEC; and Ron Todd and John Edmonds from the unions.
8. The other regular members of the Central Management Group were Peter Mandelson, Robert Worcester and Patricia Hewitt, and, from advertising, public relations and market research, Philip Gould, Richard Faulkner, Colin Fisher, Roddy Glenn, Peter Head and Deborah Mattinson.
9. See P. Kellner, 'Will the real Labour Party Please Stand Up?', *New Statesman*, 8 May 1987.

4 Alliance

The Alliance parties entered the 1983 parliament in a strange position. With the support of more than a quarter of the electorate, there was no doubt that they formed a formidable third party. Three-party politics, at the electoral level at least, had arrived. But with only 23 seats the Alliance was virtually irrelevant in parliamentary terms; it had problems in providing spokesmen for all portfolios and the two leaders complained of the difficulty they found in getting called by the Speaker. A campaign in 1984 for proportional representation attracted little attention.

The Alliance parties enjoyed moments of euphoria in the parliament, notably when their opinion poll ratings surged, usually in the wake of by-election victories. In July 1985 they actually moved into a short-lived lead in the polls. The hard-core Alliance support stayed at 15–20% of the electorate, higher than the Liberals had ever attained in the post-war period. However, the novelty of the SDP in 1981, and of the Alliance in 1983, wore off during the parliament: their newness was a wasting asset and so was the claim of SDP leaders to have had experience of government.

Roy Jenkins was widely judged to have been something of a lacklustre figure first as SDP leader, and then as the Prime Minister-designate of an Alliance government during the 1983 election campaign. Immediately afterwards, David Owen made it known that he would stand for the leadership, but Roy Jenkins resigned without a contest. In spite of the Social Democratic Party's diminished status in the new parliament (6 MPs), the emergence of David Owen dismayed a number of Liberals, who favoured closer relations or even a merger of the parties. Dr Owen was a strong opponent of the convergence of the two parties, let alone any merger.

The hopes of some senior Liberals for a union of the two parties were frustrated, largely because David Owen was determined to preserve the SDP as an independent party. But in the latter half of the parliament the two parties moved closer together, less perhaps than Liberal supporters of merger hoped, but probably more than David Owen would have liked. David Owen favoured a strong line on many issues which distinguished his party from both Labour and from the Liberals. He supported most of the Conservative reforms on industrial relations and indeed claimed that the government had

borrowed many of its ideas from the SDP. He also backed the
government in its determination not to concede to the miners'
demands in their year-long strike. Above all, he made a stand about
Britain's independent nuclear deterrent. In 1986 he disowned his
own senior colleagues, Bill Rodgers and John Roper, when the
parties' joint 'Defence and Disarmament Commission' agreed on a
package maintaining Polaris but recommending that no decision
about a replacement should be taken before a general election.
Finally, he was in favour of what he called the social market,
endorsing competition between firms in a free market as the best
generator of national wealth – the bigger the national cake, the bigger
the share for the less well-off. Over time, however, and particularly
after Roy Jenkins assumed the economic portfolio for the Alliance,
there was some dilution of this economic stance.

It was possible to see David Owen as being on the centre-right of
the political spectrum, particularly on defence, on many economic
issues, and on industrial relations, whilst many Liberals were on the
centre-left. Some of his Alliance critics described him as Thatcherite
and right-wing. In fact he favoured radical egalitarian policies on
health and poverty. He would claim that he saw some good things in
Mrs Thatcher's work which should be built upon but that her approach
to the economy was deeply misguided. It was true, however, that he
appeared more out of sympathy with Labour than most Liberal MPs,
and that he had moved further away from Labour than the other
members of the SDP's founding Gang of Four. Many Liberals
compared Dr Owen unfavourably with the other three – Shirley
Williams, Roy Jenkins, and Bill Rodgers.

There were important changes at the top of the Social Democratic
Party. The Gang of Four which had led the breakaway from Labour
in 1981 ceased to operate as a collective leadership. David Owen's
impatience with Roy Jenkins had never been disguised. Shirley
Williams and Bill Rodgers, although continuing as President and
Vice-President of the party, inevitably took a less prominent role
once they had lost their parliamentary seats in the 1983 election. In
setting up what he called the Co-ordinating Committee, which met
weekly in his private office and was attended by senior party officials,
Dr Owen succeeded in by-passing, to a large extent, the SDP's
National Committee.

David Owen's resistance to a merger of the two parties was based
on his belief that the SDP appealed to a number of people, particularly
ex-Labour voters, who would not support the Liberal party. Being

separate, in his view, helped the Alliance to gain an extra increment in electoral support. Private surveys conducted for the Conservative party showed that Tory defectors after 1983 went to the SDP rather than the Liberals and that Conservatives preferred Owen to Steel while Labour voters preferred the Liberals to the SDP and Steel to Owen (see p. 137). On the other hand, surveys also showed that, in terms of policy preferences and social background, the supporters of the two Liberal and Social Democratic parties were rather similar. In addition, Dr Owen was fundamentally sceptical about the Liberal party's seriousness on a number of political issues; too many Liberals, he felt, were self-indulgent and more interested in articulating protests than in gaining political power. He was also dismissive of Liberal advocates of compromise during the miners' strike. He felt that his suspicions were eventually confirmed when the Liberal Assembly voted against nuclear weapons in September 1986. Some of these feelings about the Liberal party were, of course, shared by David Steel.

Influential voices in both parties deplored the waste of organisational resources involved in maintaining separate party organisations in London and in the constituencies. But the Owen line prevailed – it had, after all, been accepted at the 1983 SDP conference at Salford. He certainly provided more drive and direction than Roy Jenkins, who would have liked to merge the two parties straight away.

The consistency of Dr Owen's position became clearer in some of his remarks after the 1987 election was over. For him the Alliance ought never to have become a 'partnership of principle', but a plain and simple *electoral pact*. In the event, his pro-merger (or at least not anti-Liberal) colleagues caused this position to be fudged. If the relationship was to be only an electoral pact, his dislike of joint spokesmen, joint policy-making, and joint selection, his rejection of a single leader, and his veto over clear organisational links, all can be seen as a perfectly coherent political position. Most Liberals never understood that this was David Owen's basic attitude to the Alliance. On defence they were less enamoured of the maintenance of a British nuclear deterrent in all circumstances than was David Owen. They had difficulty with his style, particularly his belief in the importance of strength and conviction which struck some as Thatcherite. 'I really don't understand his character or politics', 'a bloody difficult man', 'it is like negotiating with the Soviet Union', were remarks made by leading Liberals and SDP members. Dr Owen's view of the negotiations with the Liberals was that a strong stand had to be made, not only to get correct decisions but to preserve the independence of the SDP, which he called 'the great untold story of British politics'.

Yet in some parts of the country where the need to campaign together in local – and parliamentary – elections concentrated the minds of local activists, something akin to a merger actually occurred. There was joint open selection of candidates in 78 cases (see p. 197), and in a further 60 allocated seats to the SDP, Liberals were allowed to share in the selection process. David Owen had opposed this because, since the Liberals had many more members than the SDP, he felt, in some cases, correctly, that there would be strong pressure on SDP candidates to play down distinctive SDP policies in an attempt to court Liberal activists. In his words it would be 'merger by the back door'. After the 1983 election a Joint Leaders' Advisory Committee was established to improve co-ordination between the two parties. It consisted of a dozen influential figures from each party; it met monthly and was chaired alternately by the two leaders. It made little progress in planning the future of the Alliance although its title was changed in the summer of 1985 to the Alliance Strategy Committee. A pointed memorandum in May from the Liberal activist, William Wallace, was circulated to leading Liberals and leaked in September. Mr Wallace caused a stir by urging the leaders to recognise the lack of governmental experience of most of the would-be ministers and begin preparations for government.

The Alliance never got near to electing one single leader (though some senior Liberals, notably David Penhaligon and Richard Holme, an influential adviser of Steel's, pressed for this) but a formula was agreed that the leader of the larger of the two parties in the next parliament would be Prime Minister or Leader of the Opposition. Given that the Liberals would probably capture at least two-thirds of the first 100 Alliance seats, this was certain to be David Steel.

David Owen also resisted the appointment of joint spokesmen and a joint leaders' office until very late in the parliament. He claimed that he wanted to have agreement on policy before the appointment of policy spokesmen, though he procrastinated on joint policy-making as well. In fact, separate party spokesmen were seen as the symbol of SDP autonomy. The joint team was not unveiled until the Barbican 'relaunch' of the Alliance in January 1987.

There had been something of a change in the character of the SDP since its foundation in 1981 and a number of people who had only then entered politics now came to the fore. A good example was Rosie Barnes, who won the Greenwich by-election in February 1987.

It won especially strong support from the academic and professional middle classes. Membership fell between 1982 and 1984 but then recovered. By 1987 the number reached 60 000 and there were a further 30 000 people who made contributions to the party, mainly picked up as a result of its successful direct mail programme. The SDP appeared to be more of a centralised, London-based party, the Liberals more of a regional and participatory party. The SDP drew the bulk of its members from the Home Counties, whereas the Liberals were stronger in the other regions. Some Liberals spread the canard that the SDP had more members in Camden than in all of Yorkshire.

Indeed, the SDP with an income of nearly £0.8 million in 1985–6 (it had been £0.9m in 1982–3), was in better financial shape than the larger Liberal party. Running costs were paid from members' contributions (averaging £13 per annum for renewals and £8 for new members). The party also had a few rich supporters, led by one of the trustees, David Sainsbury, as well as 30 000 national donors whom it could approach regularly with appeals for specific projects. Throughout the parliament Richard Newby remained as National Secretary of the party machine in Cowley Street, with Alec McGivan as National Organiser. In 1985 the party established a special General Election Unit, headed by Richard Newby, with Alec McGivan as deputy. The group selected 60 'target' seats – with 20 in a priority category – and gave grants for local parties to purchase computers and employ full-time agents.

The rationale behind the unit was that it should establish a safety net, in the vain hope that (see p. 212) whatever the Alliance's national level of support, the SDP would get more seats than were due on a uniform national swing. Its responsibilities were exclusively constituency centred. None of its members were given a role in the central planning of the general election strategy – and some of the campaign failures were attributable to this. The unit's establishment owed much to the expensive advice of an American firm of political consultants, Matt Reese and Associates. It was intended to service target constituencies and to promote a new, business-like, campaigning ethos that focused on clear goals, efficient deployment of resources, and systematic measurement of achievements. 'Lots is not a number' became something of a catchphrase. It gave advice on computers and arranged training courses for candidates and agents.[1]

Two of the early Alliance MPs proved to be right-wing mavericks as the election approached. John Horam, a Labour, then an SDP

MP in the North-East until 1983, refused to try for Carshalton, a seat in which he had shown considerable interest. It was known that he was unhappy with the direction of Alliance economic policy and it was little surprise that he announced his conversion to the Conservative party the weekend after the Greenwich by-election success. Neville Sandelson, another ex-MP, urged Alliance supporters to vote for the Conservative party, in seats where only the Conservatives could defeat Labour, arguing that the main task of the Alliance was the destruction of the socialist party, and that this would best be achieved by the return of another large majority for the Conservatives.

David Steel took a three-month sabbatical from politics after the June 1983 election. He had been exhausted by the campaign and was certainly disappointed to have had such slight parliamentary reward after seven years as Liberal leader. His absence reminded many Liberals of how indispensable he had become. Mr Steel's long-term strategy was based upon a realignment which would produce a new centre-left party. The replacement of Roy Jenkins (who agreed with the strategy) by David Owen undermined these plans.

The Liberal party organisation continued to be run on the proverbial shoe-string. Its central expenditure rose from £250 000 in 1983 to £700 000 in 1986. John Spiller became Secretary-General for a short spell until ill-health forced his retirement. His eventual replacement in February 1986 was Andy Ellis, who achieved some fame as a result of his effective operations in by-elections. Mr Ellis interpreted his role more as a campaigner than as a manager of the party machine. In contrast to the SDP's centralised control of its 'target' seats operations, the Liberals allocated the management of 'targets' to their area agents and had little or no funds to distribute.

During the parliament Simon Hughes and Michael Meadowcroft emerged as vigorous radical figures, notably at the party's annual assemblies. Both were firmly on the left-wing of the party and, when it came to defence, were unilateralist. Cyril Smith went into a self-imposed exile after the Harrogate Assembly in 1983 when he complained of David Steel's 'autocratic' style, but then made a much publicised peace treaty with David Steel at the Eastbourne Assembly in 1986. Other figures to emerge in the course of the parliament were Paddy Ashdown and David Alton, the latter as Chief Whip. The death of David Penhaligon in December 1986 removed not only the Alliance chief spokesman on the economy, but also one of the Alliance's most effective communicators in the party, and David Steel's likeliest successor as party leader.

The Liberal party had a complex and somewhat anarchic party structure, which gave David Steel much trouble. His insistence on maintaining a veto over items to be included in the Liberal manifesto, although supported by the 1984 Assembly, outraged a number of Liberal activists who saw him behaving as an Alliance rather than a Liberal leader, whereas David Owen always manoeuvred for his own SDP. Liberal activists insisted that the party's Assembly was making policy for the Liberal party and should not be distracted by calculations of what the SDP might think of their resolutions. They complained that the SDP had had too much influence in drawing up the 1983 election manifesto, and that there had been too much secrecy in policy formation. David Steel not only had to think of what David Owen would accept, but he also had problems with Liberals who thought that their party was making too many concessions to the SDP. A major shock came for Mr Steel in 1986 when the Assembly rejected the Steel–Owen proposal for a new European nuclear deterrent, throwing it out by 27 votes (652 votes to 625). The easy-going arrangements, by which any Liberal member (up to one per 25 constituency members) could register at the Assembly and then be able to vote, amazed onlookers. It took until the end of the year for the policy committees of the two parties to agree a defence policy and override the Assembly decision.

Both parties made progress in local elections, and by 1987 Alliance parties controlled or held the balance of power in over 100 councils. At the parliamentary level in June 1984, the SDP captured Portsmouth South from the Conservatives; in July 1985 the Liberals captured Brecon & Radnor, and in May 1986 Ryedale, again from the Tories. Each party enjoyed a major boost in early 1987. Rosie Barnes captured Greenwich from Labour for the SDP at a by-election, and Matthew Taylor, David Penhaligon's Liberal replacement, held Truro with an increased majority. The Alliance total by-election vote in the parliament was larger than that of either Conservative or Labour (see p. 21).

An Alliance Planning Group met weekly from November 1986 to prepare for the election campaign. Apart from the two party leaders, it also had as members John Pardoe, Des Wilson, and Paul Tyler from the Liberals, and Lord Harris of Greenwich, Roland Freeman and Polly Toynbee from the SDP. It was only at the end of March that the two chief party organisers, Dick Newby of the SDP and Andy Ellis of the Liberals, were added. David Abbot, of Abbot,

Mead, Vickers advertising agency, was given control of the party's advertising. The advertising agency was appointed late, and showed limited understanding of the SDP or the Liberals, or even, some complained, of politics.

The Alliance leaders decided to focus much of their assault on the Conservative record, although Liberals were keener to attack Mrs Thatcher's style. The Alliance leaders ostentatiously wrote off Labour's chances ('unelectable, so why waste time?'). As Labour's standing in the polls declined in March and April, so some Alliance strategists took seriously the goal of overtaking Labour in popular votes. The leaders were also determined to start their campaigns early on to see if they could make a breakthrough to unsettle the other parties. The Planning Group was virtually unanimous about the advantages of the two party leaders campaigning together in their forays through the country. It was clear that the electorate found some difficulty in understanding the idea of a partnership between the parties. Though there was widespread liking for each of the party leaders, the Alliance was still seen to be divided. Advisers argued that the leaders should tackle the problem head on by being seen on television together as often as possible. This would show party co-operation and power-sharing in action. 'It is our u.s.p. [unique selling proposition] and we must go hard on it', said one advertising consultant.

In the run up to the election much of the talk in the Alliance camp was of the prospect of holding the balance of power, either to influence the legislation of a minority government or to form a coalition with Labour or Conservative. David Owen dismissed talk of an Alliance government, or even of overtaking Labour, as unrealistic, and instead advocated the merits of a coalition government. There were extensive discussions in the Strategy Committee about the best Alliance response to a balanced parliament. Few doubted that the Alliance should aim for power-sharing and should spell out the terms well in advance of the election. In an interview with the *Independent* on 2 April, David Owen explicitly stated that the Alliance would vote down any minority government which introduced a Queen's Speech without prior negotiations with, he envisaged, a coalition which would last for at least two or three years. He also advocated the use of referendums to legitimise any far-reaching constitutional changes such as electoral reform (there was general agreement among Alliance leaders about the key policy areas on which they would seek agreement, namely unemployment, strong defence and electoral reform. The leaders had discussed the details of a draft proportional representation bill).

It could be said in defence of a coalition or power-sharing approach, that it would mark another stage in the progress of the Alliance. Its leaders would appear as a more serious political force and be in a position to promote their agreed policies. David Owen and David Steel deliberately spoke about 'a balanced parliament' rather than deadlock or minority government, and about the opportunity it presented for promoting 'good' consensus policies.

Yet there were dangers to the coalition approach, which some strategists were aware of. One was that the public had no enthusiasm for coalition or minority government. According to a MORI poll in the *Economist* on 31 January 1987, only 27% favoured an outcome in which no party had an overall majority – even Alliance voters were equally divided. In the past, notably in the two 1974 elections, deadlock was the prelude to a return to majority government. When Liberals had held the balance in parliament, as in 1924 and 1929, and again in February 1974, they had been squeezed in the following election. The same misfortune followed the Lib–Lab pact of 1977–8. Survey evidence also suggested that Alliance voters split three ways regarding the options in a balanced parliament. Just over half would prefer the Alliance to coalesce with the Conservatives and one-third with Labour, while the rest would not welcome a coalition with either party or said 'don't know'.

Any coalition with the Conservatives would only follow the loss of many Tory seats, largely to the Liberals in the south of Britain. Many such gains would have to come from Alliance success in squeezing third place Labour votes and appealing to anti-Conservative sentiment. Such 'tactical' Alliance voters might not be happy with the Alliance supporting a repudiated Conservative administration, particularly if it was still headed by Mrs Thatcher. It was also well known that most Liberal activists were more anti-Conservative than anti-Labour and intensely disliked the tone and style of Mrs Thatcher. Indeed, David Steel at one time had stated that a precondition for any negotiations with the Conservatives would be the resignation of Mrs Thatcher. Under some pressure from David Owen he withdrew the remark. Such a coalition would also leave Labour as the most effective anti-Conservative party.

Any arrangements with a minority Labour government might also cause difficulties for Alliance leaders, particularly David Owen.

Although there was some convergence between the Alliance parties' programmes on such issues as devolution, an economic recovery package to reduce unemployment, freedom of information, greater spending on health and education, and a preparedness to accept the major trade union legislation of the Thatcher government, the parties clearly disagreed about defence. David Owen, moreover, was particularly sensitive to the Conservative charge that a vote for the Alliance would let in left-wing socialism by the backdoor.

Alliance policy was made in a long series of joint committees in which the parliamentarians, officials and activists played a prominent role. The process was time-consuming, because the two parties first shaped their own positions, then reconciled the two stands at the joint policy discussions, and then took them back for approval to separate party meetings. On many issues agreement was reached without difficulty, though usually after some delay. The defence package was particularly tortuous. David Owen originally proposed the establishment of a joint commission on defence, in order to take discussion of the issue out of the normal channels of the two parties. The SDP and the Liberal members of the commission were chosen by the respective party leaders. In the summer of 1986 it was leaked that the commission would recommend abandoning Trident but would not take a decision on whether or not Polaris should be replaced. Dr Owen regarded this as a fudge and was infuriated by leaks suggesting that David Steel regarded the compromise as a Liberal triumph. Before the report was issued, he unilaterally declared that Britain must retain her nuclear weapons and be prepared to replace Polaris. The defence split dated from the row this produced in July and not from the Liberal Assembly vote in September. The two leaders, after an August visit to France, produced in early September a new compromise under which Britain's nuclear weapons should form part of an Anglo-French deterrent. The SDP conference accepted this, but the Liberal Assembly threw it out in September 1986. After torturous negotiation between the policy committees of the two parties, David Owen managed to re-establish the original scheme in what he regarded as an improvement but then felt that he had to make concessions over nuclear power; his wish to make greater use of nuclear energy was opposed by many Liberals, but his hand was greatly weakened in the wake of the Chernobyl nuclear disaster.

It had been decided long in advance that the two parties would jointly launch their pre-election programme, *Partnership for Progress*, at the Barbican in January 1987. With the two parties having lost so much ground in the wake of the summer and autumn divisions over defence, this relaunch was an opportunity to make a fresh start. The January 1987 policy statement, *The Time has Come*, was regarded as the basis of the manifesto. Originally the joint policy committee (consisting of about 40 people, and chaired alternately by David Owen and Alan Beith) set up a team of 14 people, 7 from each party; however, to cut through such a cumbersome structure, the task of writing the manifesto was given to the Liberal spokesman on foreign affairs, Alan Beith. The final document reflected the compromises in *The Time Has Come*. Two late additions allowed local authorities some discretion over the sale of council houses and offered house-holders up to £60 a week tax free for renting rooms. Some Liberal partisans (and after the election, Dr Owen) felt that the negotiating process had resulted in the omission of radical proposals.

The Alliance was the first of the major parties to reveal its manifesto at a press conference on Monday, 18 May, at the National Liberal Club. The contents of *Britain United: The Time has Come* had been much trailed in advance. At its heart were a web of proposals for constitutional reform – less secrecy in government by the repeal of section 2 of the Official Secrets Act, and the passage of a Freedom of Information Act; decentralisation for stronger local government; fixed terms for parliament; proportional representation; and the incorporation of the European Convention on Human Rights in a British Bill of Rights. There were also proposals for job creation and more spending on education and training. An incomes policy would control inflation through an 'inflation tax' to penalise companies paying excessive wage increases, and a local income tax would replace domestic rates. The Alliance would cancel Trident but maintain and modernise Polaris.

The Alliance entered the election in good heart. On the eve of the dissolution a Gallup poll actually found it ahead of Labour and the average of the last pre-election polls placed it at 25%. In three of the last four general elections the Liberals or the Alliance had steadily improved their standing. In 1983 the Alliance started off with 17% in the opinion polls and ended with 26% of the actual vote. However, there was no iron law that what had happened once would happen again. In particular it was rash to expect that the Labour vote would collapse as drastically as it had in 1983. None the less the Alliance campaigners sometimes spoke almost as if that was inevitable. One bonus came on the eve of the election when the broadcasting companies granted the Alliance parity of time with the two other major parties. In the past the Alliance and Liberal surge had been explained largely in terms of its enhanced media profile. Surely it would happen again.

NOTE

1. The SDP's manual, *Campaigning in the 80s*, was eventually made available to Liberals and was bought by many Liberal candidates at £15 per copy. It also found echoes in the Labour party's manual *Campaign to Win*.

II

The Election Nationally

5 Campaign

The election announcement on Monday, 11 May, came as no surprise. Well before the local council voting on 7 May gave the psephological go-ahead, Mrs Thatcher and her Downing Street spokesmen may have allowed expectations to rise beyond the point of no return (see p. 41).

The Opposition parties made routine complaints about the legislation that would have to be abandoned (notably the Criminal Justice Bill). Parliament had to be dissolved on 18 May, and in four days the government, making quick concessions on detail, hurried through the Finance Bill which endorsed the Budget changes including the 2p tax cut; the Scottish Rates Bill which provided for the first Poll Tax experiment since 1698; and the Bill which authorised the construction of the Channel Tunnel.

All parties had grounds for high morale at this point. The polls were averaging Conservative 43%, Labour 29%, Alliance 26% – though the Conservative lead ranged from 9% (Gallup) to 18% (NOP). But the local elections had given each party grounds for hope in particular constituencies. Labour, recovering from the setback at Greenwich, had faith in its own preparations and in the greater television exposure that the campaign would offer. The Alliance had not only the stimulus of Greenwich, but also the memory of the great surge of support in the final days of 1983. The Conservatives, however, could point to the Stock Exchange's reaction, with a 50 point rise on the announcement, and to the bookmakers, with 5–1 odds on a government victory.

Each of the parties had made detailed plans for the campaign but only the Labour party, with traumatic memories of its disorganisation in 1983, stuck closely to its original intentions, and only the Labour party curbed the inevitable tensions between the party headquarters and the teams around the leaders. The Labour routine started at 7 a.m. when Bryan Gould and Peter Mandelson met leading figures of the Shadow Communications Agency to consider strategy suggestions and approve advertisements. Between 7.20 and 8 a.m. Bryan Gould and Peter Mandelson met with the management team, which consisted of the directors in Walworth Road and, when they were available, Patricia Hewitt and Charles Clarke from Neil Kinnock's office. This meeting received reports from the monitoring groups reporting on polling, the media, and the party's own feedback. Bryan Gould and Peter Mandelson would then move two miles north to Transport House in Smith Square where they would meet Neil Kinnock (when he was available) and other shadow ministers or listen down the line to Neil Kinnock's news conference if he was out of London; in the latter event Bryan Gould, or occasionally Roy Hattersley, would give a briefing at 10.30 a.m. for the London press, without television cameras. The management team would meet again at 1.30 p.m. to review the situation and confirm plans for the next day. Three times a day a briefing to candidates would be sent out on Telecom Gold.

Meanwhile Neil Kinnock would be touring the regions though usually getting back to his Ealing home by 11 p.m. for further speechwriting and a few hours sleep. Mr Kinnock's speeches, described by one aide as 'the high point of our campaign' were very much his own work, though he had drafts from John Eatwell and John Newbiggin. He and Mrs Kinnock would enter the nightly rallies to the music of jazz band and the announcement 'Ladies and Gentlemen, the next occupants of No. 10 Downing Street – Neil and Glenys'. Mr Kinnock would usually approach the platform shaking hands with well-wishers and punching the air, in a generally revivalist atmosphere. The official Campaign Committee met two or three times a week at Walworth Road, with extended discussion at weekends, so that Neil Kinnock could engage in a general review of the situation.

The Alliance day began at 7 a.m. when the Alliance Planning Group met under John Pardoe and Lord Harris of Greenwich[1] to discuss the reports of media and party reactions which Des Wilson and his team had prepared during the night. At 7.45 a.m. the two leaders arrived and were briefed for the press conference for that day. The 8.30 a.m. press conference enabled the leaders to get off in good time to different parts of the country – but David Steel and some of the press corps complained that they were not at their best so early in the day. The two leaders travelled separately by plane or 'battlebus', meeting up again at a provincial 'Ask the Alliance' rally in the early evening. They each averaged about 5 hours' sleep a night (which seems to have been about the ration, too, for Mr Kinnock and Mrs Thatcher, although none of the four leaders ran out of adrenalin by 11 June). The campaign headquarters were at the SDP offices in Cowley Street, but, for reasons of space, the press conferences were held three-quarters of a mile away at the National Liberal Club. The Alliance Planning Group met again at 10.15 a.m.

CHRONOLOGY II (May–June 1987)

May

Mon.	11	Mrs Thatcher announces election
Tue.	12	Mrs Thatcher speaks of going 'on and on'
Wed.	13	Labour agrees manifesto
Thu.	14	Gallup puts Alliance second; Marplan gives Cons. 14% lead
Fri.	15	Jobless down by 36 000. Inflation up by 0.2% to 4.2%; Mrs Thatcher speaks at Perth Con. Conference; Mr Kinnock at Llandudno Lab. Conference; Parliament dissolved
Sat.	16	Healey to Russians 'Labour will lose'
Sun	17	Sunday papers raise scandals about Steel, Proctor
Mon.	18	Alliance launch manifesto
Tue.	19	Conservative and Labour launch manifestos; US warship hit by Exocet in Gulf
Wed.	20	Teachers to increase strikes
Thu.	21	Gallup cuts Alliance from 30% to 23%; Kinnock election broadcast
Fri.	22	Mrs Thatcher's confusion on education; David Steel gets libel damages from the *Daily Star*
Sat.	23	Alliance to cut double act
Sun.	24	Kinnock on Frost Show; Sunday papers on Hattersley
Mon.	25	Bank Holiday; 'Dad's Army' challenge to Labour
Tue.	26	Alliance cites '101 Damnations'
Wed.	27	Mrs Thatcher's Newport rally
Thu.	28	Gallup cut Alliance to 18%; Kinnock replies on defence; British envoy kidnapped
Fri.	29	Kinnock visits Liverpool; Nominations close
Sat.	30	Biffen 'I won't crawl'
Sun.	31	Kinnock calls for end of private schools

June

Mon.	1	CBI buoyant report
Tue.	2	Newsnight poll suggests hung parliament
Wed.	3	Gallup, Con. lead down to 4%
Thu.	4	'Wobbly Thursday' at Con. HQ; Stock Exchange falls Mrs Thatcher on private health
Fri.	5	Mrs Thatcher at Chester
Sat.	6	Powell endorses Labour defence policy
Sun.	7	Challenges on Chiefs of Staff attitudes to Labour; Advertising begins; Powell attacks Con. nuclear policy; Con. Wembley Rally; Lab. Islington Rally
Mon.	8	Tax headlines; Mrs Thatcher to Venice; Civil Service strikes
Tue.	9	Venice summit; Healey row in TV studio
Wed.	10	Final appeals
Thu.	11	Polling day

to consider reports of what had happened at the rival press conferences and again at 6.30 p.m. to consider monitoring reports.

The Conservative daily routine centred around the press conference. Overnight reports from the regions, the polls and the press were collated for a preliminary meeting at 7.45 a.m. before Mrs Thatcher came at about 8.15 a.m. for her briefing meeting. This was initially far too large and had to be cut down in the end, and it usually consisted of about ten, in addition to the ministers who were to appear with Mrs Thatcher at 9.30 a.m.[2] In Smith Square at 7 or 8 p.m. there was a strategy meeting, largely of the heads of Central Office departments, presided over by Mr Tebbit.

Immediately after the press conference Mrs Thatcher would go on her travels, usually taking the train to Gatwick airport in order to fly to a provincial destination where she would proceed in her battlebus to planned walkabouts and small meetings. Unless she had a live broadcast she would get back to Westminster by 7 or 8 p.m. On five occasions she addressed a major rally with a loyal audience bussed in. She would enter to deliver a carefully-crafted 40-minute speech to the strains of 'Jerusalem', or to a tune specially composed by Andrew Lloyd Webber, accompanied by a laser show. Mrs Thatcher relied primarily on Stephen Sherbourne, Sir Ronald Millar and John O'Sullivan for speechwriting suggestions, though ideas also flowed in from sympathetic journalists like Paul Johnson and Woodrow Wyatt.

At the outset of the campaign the economic indicators were favourable. Unemployment was falling – it dropped by 36 000 in April – and there was the prospect (never firmly promised but, in fact, realised) that the May figure, due on 18 June, would drop below three million. On 15 May it was announced that the inflation rate had jumped from 4.0% in March to 4.2% in April – but a future fall was confidently forecast. On 1 June the CBI reported that factory orders were at a 10-year peak. The pound rose against the dollar and the deutschmark as the campaign continued. More buoyant balance of payments figures were revealed on 4 June.

Of course all parties sought to dominate the news with their issues, gimmicks and quotations. Mr Tebbit paraded with a bulldog; Mr Steel was given a black retriever; Mr Kinnock kissed babies; Mrs Thatcher cuddled a toy panda. All were photographed in factories, in hospitals, in shopping centres, wearing safety helmets, sterile overalls or Wellington boots. Helicopters and battlebuses were used as workmanlike transport, and decked out to suggest images of modernity and efficiency. The backdrops at each press conference

IS THIS LABOUR'S IDEA OF A COMPREHENSIVE EDUCATION?

TAKE THE POLITICS OUT OF EDUCATION. VOTE CONSERVATIVE ⊠

were changed to avoid the sense of repetition. When the leaders of all parties were out in their buses or even on walkabouts, their staff were in constant touch with London through portable telephones (except when, as too often happened, they found themselves in black holes in the radio network).

Yet weariness with the campaign was soon voiced. Princess Anne's remark on 20 May ('People are going to be bored to tears by the end') was echoed by some politicians and many of the public. It was a familiar complaint and not a surprising one as only 30% of people claim to be interested in politics. In fact very little happened in the course of the campaign that stood out as a genuine news story. Gaffes were few and the leaders went safely through their pre-packaged routines, as intended.

Ted Heath observed on 2 June, 'This is my twelfth campaign and I think it is the dirtiest of them all'. Some of the popular press reached a new low at the start of the contest with several stories suggesting improper behaviour by leading individuals. Headlines on 17 May about an alleged affair involving David Steel won immediate and large damages for the Liberal leader from the *Daily Star*. On the same day there were stories about the private life of an important Labour official and about the Conservative MP Harvey Proctor. Aspects of Roy Hattersley's life were made a major feature in the *News of the World* on 24 May and developed in other papers. Libel actions are still pending but there is no evidence that these stories affected votes nationally or locally, and senior figures in all parties deplored the personalisation of the campaign.

However, the election was not especially dirty or violent. There were a number of injunctions and pre-emptive libel writs which probably reflected more an increased awareness of legal remedies than an increase in reckless accusation.[3] An ice-cream that hit Mr Heseltine and an egg that missed Mr Steel won publicity for their sheer rarity. An arson attack on the constituency headquarters of the Hackney North Conservative Association was mercifully unique. Heckling was scarce, because open meetings were few, and publicity focused so much on the party leaders who were hemmed in by security precautions. Mrs Thatcher's movements were never announced more than a couple of hours in advance: the reporters accompanying hercomplained that each day was a mystery tour. Walkabouts were rendered meaningless as face-to-face contacts with the electorate, not only by security arranagements, but by the mobs of photographers and by reporters seeking to overhear each informal word. The bomb threats came to nothing and the identity cards issued to reporters by Conservative Central Office were accepted by Labour and the Alliance.

But if it was not a dirty campaign, it was a personalised one. The competence of Mr Kinnock, the compassion of Mrs Thatcher, and the differences between the two Davids excited continuous comment. Mr Kinnock denied that Labour was fighting a presidential campaign yet the Labour story was overwhelmingly projected by him (see pp. 154–5). When Labour's press conferences were held outside London it was Neil Kinnock who took them and he, rather than Roy Hattersley or Bryan Gould, who was seen on TV as the spokesman for his party's policies. As in 1983 Mrs Thatcher had planned to take less of the early limelight – she played little part in the first four of the Conservatives' five election broadcasts. But she chaired the party's press conferences and, except on Saturdays, only missed 4 of the 17 daily gatherings. She always appeared flanked by the ministers appropriate to the allotted theme but she answered most of the questions herself in considerable detail and it was rare for anyone other than herself to top the Conservative segment of the news bulletins. David Owen and David Steel were also together at almost all the Alliance's press conferences and the 'Ask the Alliance' evening meetings. Although they brought in other spokesmen, interest focused overwhelmingly on what each of them said – and on whether they differed in emphasis.

There were background figures, people with name recognition, who were mentioned in the campaign coverage but who never really made news. Denis Thatcher was photographed whenever the Prime Minister was on tour but, apart from one slightly tactless letter about the Ulster situation, he was never quoted. Glenys Kinnock was even more sympathetically visible (only her husband, among Labour personalities, gained more photos in the press), appearing both with her husband on the platform and independently in tours of hospitals and schools, but she was equally discreet.

Three figures from the Conservative past were very energetic campaigners, well-photographed but never stepping out of line in their remarks. Michael Heseltine sturdily supported the government on defence and made some effective jabs at Labour. Ted Heath lamented 'An attempt has been made to obliterate me from the history books and certainly from public life' but he did everything possible for a Conservative victory. Jeffrey Archer addressed the faithful in many parts of the country, without embarrassing the party. These three received more coverage than many leading members of the Cabinet like Lord Whitelaw and Lord Hailsham, and even Sir Geoffrey Howe.

On the Labour side the potential boatrockers were scarcely audible. Tony Benn stayed mainly in his Chesterfield constituency. Arthur Scargill addressed a few rallies but offered no gift quotations to the Conservatives; the day after the result he complained of 'undue pressure from the top to stop me speaking'. Derek Hatton remained unreported. Only Ken Livingstone hit the headlines, first at a Gay Rights conference on 23 May, and then by being, somewhat implausibly, accused of planning a post-election coup against Neil Kinnock, similar to his seizure of the GLC leadership in 1981. On 23 May Mr Kinnock angrily dismissed the possibility:

> People who have a separate manifesto will not at any stage or any time be exercising influence over the leadership, direction, policy or strategy of the Labour party . . . All of Labour's candidates in this election, if elected, will be subject to the requirements of the party's standing orders. If they at any stage give the impression that it is not the case it will be impossible for them to remain in the party.

Except in their own territory the Scottish and Welsh Nationalists and the Ulster campaigners received little national media coverage. The only outsider to make news was Enoch Powell, with his battle for survival in South Down, and with his one sharp incursion into the national scene on 7 June when he advised people to vote Labour

Daily Express, 22 May 1987

1a. Launching the 1983 manifesto (May 1983)
Willie Whitelaw Margaret Thatcher
Cecil Parkinson *The Press Association*

1b. Labour elects its leaders (1 October 1983)
Roy Hattersley Neil Kinnock
The Press Association

1c. The Brighton Bomb (12 October 1984)
The Press Association

1d. Arthur Scargill arrested at Orgreave (29 May 1984)
Neville Pyne, Sheffield

1e. Michael Heseltine resigns (6 January 1986)
The Press Association

1f. The Anglo-Irish Agreement
Garret Fitzgerald Margaret Thatcher
Sir Geoffrey Howe (15 November 1985)
The Press Association

2a. David Frost interviews the Prime Minister (7 June 1987)
The Press Association

2b. Labour's Press Conference
Neil Kinnock   Bryan Gould (7 June 1987)
The Press Association

2c. Campaigning in Islwyn (24 May 1987)
Glenys and Neil Kinnock
The Press Association

2d. The Nationalist Accord (20 May 1987)
Dafydd Wigley (Plaid Cymru)   Gordon Wilson (S
The Press Association

2e. A Conservative poster (16 May 1987)
Norman Tebbit
The Press Association

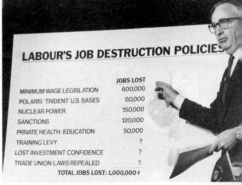

2f. Lord Young at a press conference (1 June 1987)
The Press Association

3a. Launching the Conservative Manifesto (19 May 1987)
George Younger   Nigel Lawson   Willie Whitelaw   Margaret Thatcher   Norman Tebbit
Sir Geoffrey Howe   Douglas Hurd   Norman Fowler   *Financial Times*

3b. Launching the Labour Manifesto (19 May 1987)
Roy Hattersley   Neil Kinnock
The Press Association

3c. An Alliance Press Conference (25 May 1987)
The Press Association

3d. A photo-opportunity: Mrs Thatcher (30 May 1987)
Popperfoto/Reuter

3e. A photo-opportunity: Neil Kinnock (14 May 1987)
Popperfoto/Reuter

4a. A television election (26 May 1987)
John Voos/The Independent

4b. The Two Davids at Richmond (7 June 1987)
The Press Association

4c. The Kinnocks vote (11 June 1987)
Reuter/Popperfoto)

4d. The Thatchers vote (11 June 1987)
Reuter/Popperfoto

4e. Spitting Image
Charlotte Winn, Sunday Times

because of the absurdity of the government's independent nuclear deterrent.

The election had a clear run as far as competing news was concerned. Internationally an Iraqi missile hit a US ship in the Persian Gulf on 17 May; the Lebanese Prime Minister was murdered on 1 June; a British diplomat was kidnapped in Tehran on 28 May and his release after 24 hours coincided with the virtual ending of diplomatic relations with Iran. But, although the last episode showed the government acting firmly, overseas headlines had little impact on the campaign.

One international event of significance was the Venice summit of the leaders of the seven major democracies on 8–9 June. Mrs Thatcher, however, broke off from electioneering only for 24 hours – a brief parade on the international stage which, the opposition complained, was essentially electioneering. Roy Jenkins, veteran of 14 elections, commented 'This is the most insular campaign I have ever fought'.

On the domestic scene, too, there were few distractions. Industrial action by teachers and civil servants in the final week drew few headlines. Richard Branson crossing the Atlantic in a hot air balloon, and a gruesome child cruelty case attracted some attention, as did the Derby on 4 June. The arrests of Keith Best, the Conservative ex-MP who had made multiple share applications, and Ernest Saunders, who had led Guinness in its dubious take-over battles, may have pointed to the unacceptable face of capitalism but, being *sub judice*, were little exploited. Genuine news stories that would provide copy for politicians to develop in their search for votes were in short supply.

Tactical voting had been much discussed in the run-up to the election, but less was heard about it during the campaign itself. Its impact had been spectacularly demonstrated in the Greenwich by-election. No party could openly endorse tactical voting since that would involve, in some cases, advising a vote against its own candidates. But the *New Statesman*, *Today*, and the Bishop of Durham emerged as its advocates. There was a certain amount of private enterprise. An organisation, TV 87, was launched in February to guide electors on the most effective way of casting an anti-Conservative vote in their own constituency. A kindred group, the Centre for Electoral Choice, founded by the ingenious Lord Young of Dartington, published on 20 May a *Consumers' Guide to Tactical Voting*. There were also some small-scale efforts to arrange for the pairing of Labour and Alliance voters in promising and hopeless seats. A number of articles in the serious press gave information about the local situation and about constituency opinion polls, but it is unlikely that any of these activities were as important as the local propaganda that the Alliance, in election addresses and last minute leaflets, used to persuade voters that it was the only party that could oust the incumbent.

The basic difficulty facing those organising tactical voting stemmed from the fact that Alliance voters were as often anti-Labour as anti-Tory. Labour voters, with no hope for their local candidate, might vote Alliance as a second best way of ousting a Conservative MP and his government. But Alliance voters faced with a realistic choice between Conservative and Labour would split almost equally (see p. 82). A further weakness in the tactical voting argument was that its effective goal, a hung parliament, was not popular; polls had shown that only a quarter of the electorate said they would welcome it.

Polls dominated the campaign. The record of the 58 nationwide surveys, each duly reported in every newspaper, is dealt with in the next chapter. But it is important to realise that each party's campaign was shaped by the message of the polls. The Conservatives could afford to take things easily when they had a steady lead of 10%. When, on 4 June, rumours and rogue polls briefly suggested a downswing, the reaction was strong and immediate. The Labour party, which had entered the campaign worrying whether it could keep the Alliance in third place, was alarmed by Gallup's findings on 14 May that the Alliance had overtaken it.[4] It then found comfort in its early surge from 29% to 34% in the average of polls. Thereafter, morale was kept up by the occasional rogue poll and by the evidence from some surveys that the party was faring better in marginals than elsewhere.

For the Alliance the polls were uniformly depressing. No study conducted after 11 May gave the party more than 25%, and for most of the campaign the party struggled to keep above 20%. The late upsurge of previous elections was constantly cited but it was not until the last two days that there was even the slightest evidence of a recovery. Only a few deceptive polls from target seats offered any encouragement.

In the first days there were a few candidate stories: the right-wing Labour MP in Cleveland, James Tinn, stood down in Redcar; Deirdre Wood, the left-wing loser in the Greenwich by-election, was reselected

by one vote; the NEC ended disputes over the reselection of four
MPs, each time in their favour. On the Conservative side the
controversial Harvey Proctor stood down on 16 May just before his
conviction for sex offences, but John Browne, embattled in a law
suit, was readopted in Winchester. When nominations closed on 27
May each side had put up a full slate in the 633 constituencies – with
no significant breakaway independents. The National Front, for the
first time since 1966, put up no challengers, blaming the increased
deposit,[5] but the Greens fielded 133 hopefuls.

The Scottish Nationalists left Orkney and Shetland to a local
separatist, but fought everywhere else in their own territory, as did
Plaid Cymru. A separate set of battles went on between 77 candidates
for the 17 Northern Ireland seats, with the Unionists putting up a
common front almost everywhere, but with several contests between
the SDLP and Sinn Fein for the Catholic vote.

In the last days of the parliament, the usual point-scoring went on
in a desultory fashion. But it was on Friday, 15 May, after the MPs
had departed to their constituencies, that the campaign was really
launched. As in the previous two elections Mrs Thatcher gave her
first rallying cry to the Scottish Conservatives, who greeted her at
their annual conference at Perth with the chant '10 more years, 10
more years'. She attacked Labour's programme as an 'iceberg
manifesto – one-tenth of its socialism visible, nine-tenths below the
surface'; she described a vote for the Alliance as 'not a choice but a
step into the unknown, into a no-man's-land of confusion, uncertainty
and parliamentary chaos'; she boasted that the Conservative achievements of the first two terms were 'spring-boards for even greater
achievements in our third'. At the same time Mr Kinnock was
demonstrating to the Welsh Labour Party gathered at Llandudno his
renewed power of oratory. He spoke of what the welfare state had
done for him 'The first Kinnock in a thousand generations to go to a
university' and he went on,

Labour cares all the time. Care is not a weakness but the very
esence of strength . . . You hear the Tories talking about freedom.
We'll be hearing a great deal of that over the next month from the
same people who have spent the last eight years crushing individual
freedoms under the weight of unemployment and poverty, squeezing individual rights with cuts and means tests and charges.

During this preliminary week the Alliance twice stole headlines by

'Never mind, Denis, you'll only be 108 when I retire'

News of the World, 14 June 1987

anticipating their manifesto. On 12 May they produced a costed version of their spending plans, duly certified by the leading chartered accountants, Coopers and Lybrand. The following day they issued their *Great Reform Charter*, outlining their proposed constitutional changes.

The other parties provided two of the key gaffes of the election in these first days. On 11 May Mrs Thatcher worried even some on her own side when she spoke of going 'on and on' as Prime Minister. On 12 May Denis Healey observed that the Russians 'were praying for a Labour victory'. Each drew back in later remarks, but the original indiscretion continued to be exploited by their opponents.

On the following Monday, 18 May, the routine campaign began with the Alliance launch of their manifesto, *Britain United*, buoyantly presented to a London conference by the two Davids. Mr Owen and Mr Steel spoke of the manifesto as both a programme for what they would do in office, and a negotiating document for what they would insist on, in the event of a hung parliament. Whereas Labour's programme was 'a menu without prices', their's was 'a menu with prices'. The document received a lukewarm press, even from friendly papers like the *Independent* and the *Financial Times*. The latter found it too bland and middle of the road, while the *Independent* claimed 'ALLIANCE RALLYING CRY IS WEAK'.

By mismanagement the Conservative and Labour manifestos, *The Next Move Forward* and *Britain Will Win*, were unveiled almost simultaneously the following morning, sharing space on the bulletins and in the press and inviting direct comparisons. All the manifestos were slickly presented. The Conservative one was the longest and most detailed, even without its separate booklet listing the achievements of the past eight years. It was projected as a radical document and its far-reaching proposals for the reform of education and housing tenure excited surprised comment (see p. 45). 'TORIES OFFER RADICALISM AND TAX CUTS' headlined *The Times*, 'POWER TO THE PEOPLE IS MAGGIE'S WAR CRY', headed the *Sun* on page 2 – but it did not lead the front page in any of the tabloid press.

The Labour manifesto, agreed on 12 May (see p. 71), was presented by Neil Kinnock and Roy Hattersley, who entered the Queen Elizabeth II Conference Hall to soft lights and the strains of Brahms Anthem in D. At 17 pages it was the shortest of the manifestos and was as remarkable for what it left out as for what it included (see p. 71). At the press conference launch Mr Kinnock claimed, 'What you see is what you get'. But critics were quick to fasten on to the omissions. Mr Tebbit made great play with the many left-wing motions which had been passed by the annual party conference but were not included in the manifesto (many of the motions did not have the two-thirds majority of Labour Conference votes which is necessary for a policy to become part of the party programme). Critics also pointed to the manifesto's failure to cost its programme and its lack of a policy for inflation, apart from a reference to the proposed national economic assessment between employers, unions and ministers, which would meet annually. But the *Financial Times*' headline, 'LABOUR ADOPTS CAUTIOUS APPROACH', was kindly, and the document drew praise for its presentation, although *The Times* sourly noted 'The name changes but the strain remains the same'. Mr Heseltine scathingly claimed that 'never had so much been hidden from so many by so few'.

Labour's campaign received its biggest boost at the outset with its first election broadcast on 21 May. The slick presentation of Neil Kinnock as a family man of humble origin, offering caring and effective leadership (see p. 154), put heart into all of his followers and alarmed his opponents. It had a sharp impact on his poll ratings – and it stood in stark contrast to the null first effort by the Alliance and the smooth but routine one of the Conservatives (see p. 156).

The first substantial controversy of the election flowed from the Conservative manifesto's description of the Alliance's policy as 'one-sided disarmament'. When David Owen wrote to Mrs Thatcher to protest, she jumped at the opportunity to highlight the Alliance's difficulties in this area:

> There is only one reason why you are so vague on this crucial defence question. It arises from the need to present a semblance of unity between the SDP and the unilateralists of the Liberal party.

She suggested that the Alliance was 'fellow-travelling' with Labour over defence. Dr Owen exploded on 21 May that this was

> a far more potent libel for me than being accused of having it off with someone . . . Hell's teeth – that is the issue on which I broke with the Labour party . . . It really is sticking in our gullet that only the Tories understand the national interest, only the Tories are patriotic.

In a television interview that day, the Alliance leaders seemed to move to a harder line on defence, suggesting that they would consider preserving a limited Trident programme. David Owen said that, while preferring a non-ballistic system, 'we have left ourselves open to persuasion by the Chiefs of Staff and by intelligence information', and David Steel made it clear that if nuclear deterrence failed he would be ready in the last resort to push the button. From the Conservative side Mr Younger and Mr Heseltine continued to attack the Alliance policy as 'a shabby deal' and to stress the yawning gap between the Liberal and Social Democrat positions. But on the Alliance side, Simon Hughes and one or two others on the unilateralist wing protested at the hardening line, and David Owen plainly felt that David Steel had been intimidated from going further by fear of a more serious revolt among Liberal candidates.

However, this was only a sideshow to the main row over defence which focused entirely on Labour's position. In a TV interview with David Frost on Sunday morning, 24 May, Neil Kinnock trapped himself:

David Frost: 'If you haven't got nuclear weapons, the choice in that situation would be to subject your forces to an unfair battle'.

Neil Kinnock: 'Yes, what you're then suggesting is that the alternatives are between the gesture, the threat, or the use of nuclear weapons – and surrender.

In these circumstances the choice is posed, and this is a classical choice, between exterminating everything you stand for and the flower of your youth, or using all the resources you have to make any occupation totally untenable.

Of course, any effort to occupy Western Europe or certainly occupy the United Kingdom would be untenable. Our potential foes know that very well and are not going to be ready to engage in attempting to dominate conditions that they could not dominate'.

His words were distorted over the next two days to imply that Britain would rely on guerrilla bands or 'Dad's Army' for its defence. Mr Kinnock himself referred to the efficacy of the Mujahadeen forces in Afghanistan. As the popular press developed a crescendo of mocking indignation, Labour sharply dismissed questions on the topic and refused to nominate a spokesman on a Radio 4 discussion.[6] Neil

LABOUR'S POLICY ON ARMS.

CONSERVATIVE ☒
THE NEXT MOVE FORWARD

Kinnock, touring the country, was accused of running away, and so on Thursday, 28 May, he appeared, as planned, in London and exposed himself to a full press conference grilling on the subject. He was felt to have handled questions well and there was no subsequent return to the charge that he was avoiding questioning.

But the defence issue had clearly damaged Labour. The Conservatives were convinced that their most effective advertisement was the one showing a soldier with his hands up labelled, 'Labour's Policy on Arms'. Norman Tebbit observed 'Britain has no ambition to live under the Red Flag of Socialism or the White Flag of surrender'.

While this was going on, General Rogers, NATO's Supreme Commander, was denying reports that he had advocated the withdrawal of US troops from Britain if Labour won, and on 27 May President Reagan gave momentum to the defence issue (and to the Conservative campaign) when he observed that, should Labour come to power, the US administration would have to persuade them of 'the grievous error of nuclear disarmament'.

The issue moved from the forefront of the campaign but echoes continued to be heard. There was some speculation, dismissed by Labour as 'mere Murdoch mischief', that Peter Shore would refuse to serve in a unilateralist Labour Cabinet, and Denis Healey seemed to distance himself slightly from party policy with the suggestion of a period of negotiation before ousting Cruise missiles (Neil Kinnock had, in fact, agreed that Labour 'would not jog anyone's elbow' if arms negotiations were under way). At the same time Mr Healey tried to widen the issue with an attack on Mrs Thatcher's approach to the arms control negotiations going on between Russia and America. 'She rejects the very concept of nuclear disarmament', he wrote in the *Sunday Mirror* on 31 May.

The Conservatives always felt that Labour had three key weaknesses – defence, the 'loony left', and economic competence. As we have seen, the defence theme was effectively exploited in the last week of May. The 'loony left' theme was referred to repeatedly, and a Labour council's appointment of a young gay with a criminal record as a school governor was trumpeted by the *Sun* on 27 May. The second Conservative election broadcast (27 May) deployed all the extreme quotations from Labour spokesmen that could be found (see p. 156). They had, indeed, been anticipated on 26 May by the Alliance release of the names of '101 Damnations', actual or likely Labour MPs with a hard left record (the plausibility of this list was dented by the inclusion of Tam Dalyell whose causes had never included sympathy for the hard left). The theme of the 'Iceberg Manifesto' was revived several times as the campaign advanced.

But the most effective propaganda was probably on tax. On 23 May John MacGregor, the Chief Secretary, gave a new costing of Labour's programme, alleging that it involved £35bn extra spending. Nigel Lawson argued that this would require income tax at 58%, or VAT at 50%. In the final week the onslaught became more vigorous and specific. Labour spokesmen had argued (Mr Kinnock and Mr Hattersley had promised) that Labour's tax increases would not hurt anyone earning less than £500 per week. But under questioning Neil Kinnock admitted that there would be some losers under these tax schemes, after Bryan Gould and Roy Hattersley had seemed to promise there would be none. The *Daily Mail* on 5 June could headline 'LABOUR'S LIES ON TAXATION' with concrete examples of how a £10 000 a year policeman would pay £10 more a week. The *Daily Express* on Saturday, 6 June, under 'EXPOSED: LABOUR'S TAX FIASCO', quoted Nigel Lawson and City analysts agreeing that Labour's policies would be inflationary and that everyone, not just the rich, would be hit by higher taxes. The theme was raised repeatedly, making front-page headlines on the final Sunday, Monday, and Tuesday, although on 8 June Bryan Gould gave unequivocal assurance that only the richest 5% would be worse off if Labour gained power. The argument was technical but Labour spokesmen certainly failed to sound authoritative as they tried to rebut Conservative teasing for muddling their figures.

Convention and prudence made governing parties reluctant to be lured into new commitments in the course of electioneering. One important policy development during the campaign came in a television interview on 4 June when Mrs Thatcher was at last drawn into an explicit promise to resist the European Commission if it insisted on Value Added Tax being imposed on food or childrens' clothing.

The Conservative press conferences saw three conspicuous fumbles by Mrs Thatcher and her colleagues. On 22 May Mrs Thatcher, intervening gratuitously after the conference should have ended, seemed to suggest the possibility of a fee-paying element in state education. 'We have not thought to preclude those schools [which voted to break away from the local education authority] from raising extra sums of money'. After an agitated day of questioning Mr Tebbit inserted a careful rebuttal in his evening speech at Chingford: 'Schools which opt out . . . will still be state schools. We do not, and will not, charge admission fees at state schools'. Mrs Thatcher confirmed this the next day (while at the same time praising grammar schools).

But the opposition had been given the material to play on parents' fears. Giles Radice for Labour suggested that the government wanted to return to 'privileged education for the lucky few and secondary moderns for the rest'. Paddy Ashdown for the Alliance warned that the Conservatives 'must be stopped from doing this terrible damage'.

At the press conference on 27 May, Kenneth Baker was put up to answer questions on education and Mrs Thatcher, uncharacteristically, remained silent. But the defence issue drowned his emollient answers. In the next few days there were some small counter-jabs from the Conservatives pointing to Labour leaders who had once sent their children to fee-paying schools and quoting Merlyn Rees's defence of independent schools. But in the final weeks of the campaign it was the rumbling guerrilla strikes of the teachers that made the main news about education.

A second, less important, fumble at the Conservative press conference came on 2 June when Nicholas Ridley and Mrs Thatcher got into a mild tangle over the infinitely complex questions involved in proposals for the freehold tenure of flats. The changes would affect millions of voters, but the problems proved too complex to be sorted out by an inexpert press conference.

A more serious 'own goal' came on 4 June when a harassed Mrs Thatcher said she used private health facilities because she wanted to go into hospital on the day 'I want at the time I want and with the doctor I want . . . I exercise my right as a free citizen to spend my own money in my own way'.

Perhaps the most curious feature of the election was 'Wobbly Thursday' – a crisis of confidence in the higher echelons – that afflicted the Conservative campaign for 24 hours on Wednesday and Thursday, 3 and 4 June.[7] In the middle of it, Mrs Thatcher sought to overturn Central Office's campaign strategy and radically alter the thrust of the advertising.

The crisis was a product of five features.

1. Mrs Thatcher had long felt dissatisfied with the planning of the campaign (see p. 28) and she was unhappy about Central Office's management to date and the lack of impact of Saatchi's advertisements. Lord Young was in regular touch with Tim Bell and Sir Gordon Reece, a group of so-called 'exiles', and they fed her

misgivings. Another senior minister, John Wakeham, was communicating daily with Reece, Geoffrey Tucker (and Y & R), and Michael Dobbs (and Saatchi).

2. Mrs Thatcher was tired and irritable, and her nervousness was exacerbated by a persistent toothache. Experienced members of the staff recalled similar temperamental outbursts in 1983, but then Cecil Parkinson was available to reassure her.

3. The professionalism of Labour's campaign had surprised Central Office and many commentators. Mr Kinnock and Labour were widely regarded as having outscored Mrs Thatcher and the Conservatives.

4. There were personal tensions and rivalries which were barely controlled. Mrs Thatcher did not want to have a confrontation with Mr Tebbit; her staff always had to take care that Mr Tebbit did not encounter Tim Bell while Mr Wakeham and Lord Whitelaw kept the activities of John Banks and Geoffrey Tucker from Mr Tebbit. 'We were walking on eggshells', said one minister, 'and our nerves were on edge'.

5. On Tuesday night the BBC *Newsnight* poll in marginal seats had held out the possibility of a hung parliament. On Wednesday night it was learned that the Gallup poll due to be published in the next day's *Daily Telegraph*, showed the Conservative lead down to 4%.

Mr Tebbit and Mr Dobbs professed to be unworried by the polls, preferring to wait for Marplan and their own private polls. Mrs Thatcher grew increasingly agitated as the party's lead seemed to slip. She wanted not just to win but to win by a big margin, 'to look right', as she put it in discussions. She was also frustrated with Central Office.

A further gloomy piece of news arrived on Thursday morning in the form of the latest Young and Rubicam tracking research. This was distributed to Lord Whitelaw and Mr Wakeham in 12 Downing Street and to Sir Ronald Millar and Stephen Sherbourne. A seven-page memorandum by John Banks reported how, on many image questions, Labour's position was improving and the government's declining. 'The trend is now dangerous' wrote Mr Banks. He recommended that, to appeal to the 'mainstream' voters (see p. 34), the party should be more positive in its communications, concentrate more on Mrs Thatcher and, above all, show voters what they stood to lose under Labour. The message should be: Don't let Labour ruin it. Mr Sherbourne gave a summary of the memo to Mrs Thatcher.

By now Mrs Thatcher was determined to change the thrust of the party's advertising for the last week of the campaign and the final election broadcast. Tim Bell and Frank Lowe produced some advertising copy which stressed the government's accomplishments on taxes, and health spending, and a slogan, 'Britain is a success again. Don't let Labour ruin it'. Mrs Thatcher liked the positive tone but Mr Tebbit, when he saw the work, was dismissive. Harsh words were exchanged between the party chairman and Lord Young, who knew the proposals were what Mrs Thatcher wanted. At one point Lord Young assailed Mr Tebbit, claiming that his ego was endangering electoral victory. The two men had tried to curb their growing irritation with each other and Mrs Thatcher was not prepared to have a confrontation with Mr Tebbit. He was annoyed because Lord Young had assured him that Mr Bell would not be employed in any way on work affecting the campaign apart from the production of the manifesto. She left Lord Young to resolve the issue over advertising. Mr Tebbit and Saatchi thought the campaign was on course and were relaxed about the polls. Other voices told Mrs Thatcher that the election was slipping and that the strategy (including advertising) must be changed. Under protest, Saatchi's adapted the ideas and modified the slogan; 'Britain Is Great Again: Don't Let Labour Wreck It'. In spite of claims by various agencies to sole authorship it is clear that all three, Bell, Saatchi and Y & R, were independently almost identical slogans. The message strongly echoed Harold Macmillan's pre-1959 slogan 'Life's Better with the Conservatives. Don't Let Labour Ruin It'. That slogan had been created by

BRITAIN IS GREAT AGAIN. DON'T LET LABOUR WRECK IT.

VOTE CONSERVATIVE ☒

Geoffrey Tucker, then with Colman, Prentis and Varley, and now a consultant with Y & R. Lord McAlpine came up with the money to spread the advertisements ('it's better to be a poor party in government than a rich party in opposition') over pages of each national paper on each of the last four days of the campaign. The advertisements (see pp. 110–11) covered a wide range of themes, defensive and offensive, but were always accompanied by the refrain 'Britain's Great Again. Don't Let Labour Wreck it'.

It was also decided that Mrs Thatcher would appear on more television programmes and that her speeches would deal more positively with the government's achievements (for example, taxes, wider share-ownership, trade union ballots and living standards) and the threats posed by a Labour government. Geoffrey Tucker and John Banks wrote passages along these lines for Mrs Thatcher's speechwriters and they were, to some extent, incorporated in the 5 June speech at Chester and at the Sunday rally at Wembley.

DON'T UNDO 8 YEARS WORK IN 3 SECONDS.

CONSERVATIVE X
THE NEXT MOVE FORWARD

WE HAVE MAINTAINED BRITAIN'S DEFENCES AND BROUGHT RUSSIA TO THE NEGOTIATING TABLE.

Labour would abolish our nuclear defence without Russia giving up a single weapon.

BRITAIN IS SECURE. DON'T LET LABOUR WRECK IT.
VOTE CONSERVATIVE X

WE HAVE OUTLAWED SECONDARY PICKETING AND THE VIOLENCE THAT GOES WITH IT.

Labour would bring back secondary picketing.

**BRITAIN IS GREAT AGAIN. DON'T LET LABOUR WRECK IT.
VOTE CONSERVATIVE ⊠**

THE BASIC RATE OF INCOME TAX IS DOWN TO ITS LOWEST FOR NEARLY 50 YEARS.

Labour would put it up again.

**BRITAIN IS GREAT AGAIN. DON'T LET LABOUR WRECK IT.
VOTE CONSERVATIVE ⊠**

1 MILLION COUNCIL HOMES HAVE BEEN SOLD TO THEIR TENANTS.

The Labour Party want to end tenants' automatic right to buy.

**BRITAIN IS GREAT AGAIN. DON'T LET LABOUR WRECK IT.
VOTE CONSERVATIVE ⊠**

THE AVERAGE EARNER'S TAKE HOME PAY IS UP 21% MORE THAN INFLATION.

Under the last Labour Government, it increased by less than 1%.

**BRITAIN IS GREAT AGAIN. DON'T LET LABOUR WRECK IT.
VOTE CONSERVATIVE ⊠**

But the agitations of Wobbly Thursday were in fact ended when Mr Tebbit was able to take advance information of Marplan's poll for Friday's *Guardian* to Mrs Thatcher. It showed a Conservative lead of 10%. After the election, however, what happened in Central Office on 4 June became a major press story (see p. 251).

Every poll showed that the NHS was Labour's strongest, and the Conservatives' weakest, issue. In press advertisements over the last week, Labour's portrayal of hospital waiting lists and an uncaring Mrs Thatcher were plainly more compelling than Conservative statistics about NHS spending (see p. 247). The misfortunes of Mark Burgess, a ten-year-old with a heart condition, awaiting an ever-delayed operation were highlighted by the *Daily Mirror* and at the press conferences. Once again a small counter-attack was made when it was revealed that Mrs Healey had had a private hip operation two years earlier. This led on 9 June to a vehement and much publicised confrontation in the TV-AM studio between Denis Healey and the pregnant presenter Anne Diamond. On election eve this was headlined 'HEALEY THE HYPOCRITE' (*Daily Express*) and 'HEALEY'S GIFT TO THE TORIES' (*Daily Mail*). But it produced a moving defence of the Healeys from Neil Kinnock who said that he would pay for private medical treatment 'in an extreme emergency':

> But what I have always said, and would always say, is that if I had a child in agony, and if it was impossible to secure attention, I would do anything to get attention for them. Anybody who suggests otherwise is not being honest with themselves. Thank God, I have never been faced with such a problem.

Other themes were raised from time to time. At an Alliance Press conference on 22 May Shirley Williams talked about the Conservatives failure to combat crime by demonstrating the lethal objects available on public sale. But Gerald Kaufman used a more effective gimmick at Labour's Leeds press conference on 26 May when, behind his and Neil Kinnock's heads, a 'crimeometer' steadily ticked up new figures for offences committed since 1979.

Unemployment, a strong Labour theme, was repeatedly raised. There was extended argument on how far the government had fiddled the statistics downwards. As for future policy, Labour's promise to cut the figure by one million in two years and the Alliance's to cut by one million in three years were never matched by the Conservatives;

NATIONAL HOSPITAL
FOR POLITICAL GAFFES
AND PUNCH-UPS

PRIVATE WARD

The Times, 10 June 1987

they merely pointed to the solid fact that the numbers were coming down.

An early Labour poster cited an alleged broadcast remark by Norman Tebbit in 1983 'If unemployment is not below three million in five years then I'm not worth re-electing'. On 21 May Mr Tebbit offered £500 to charity if Labour could prove he ever used the words. However, that day a press officer in Labour headquarters unexpectedly dug up the relevant tape which had slightly different words 'If I did not think we could do that [cut unemployment below 3m], I don't think we'd be in a position to win the next election'. Both sides claimed victory from the exchange and suggested that the other should pay up £500. Neither did. The press verdict was that honours were even but Labour strategists felt that it had been worth 'pushing the public's least favourite Tory politician on the Tories' most vulnerable subject into the headlines for 48 hours'.

Although the Conservatives made some acid remarks about Arthur Scargill and the unions, union power did not reach the headlines except when, on ITV's *This Week* (28 May), Neil Kinnock promised to relegalise secondary picketing. This provoked David Owen to suggest that he wanted 'to handcuff the police and turn the streets over to Arthur Scargill's and anyone else's private armies'. Mrs Thatcher in Edinburgh on 29 May said that under Labour:

> Unions would decide which factories would work normally and which would close down whether they were involved in the strike or not . . . Bring back secondary picketing and you bring back violence at the factory gate.

The Labour party did not let itself be drawn further into an area where, whatever the rights of the matter, there were no votes to be won.

Administratively the Alliance campaign went relatively smoothly.[8] But the fact that the party had sunk to third place in the polls meant that it usually sank to third place in the bulletins, and that the stories tended to be not about its policies but about its supplementary thrusts on whatever subject the other main parties had made the issue of the day. 'The polls marginalised us' was the verdict of one of their strategists. It had been envisaged that the joint appearance of David Owen and David Steel at each morning press conference, as well as in the evening 'Ask the Alliance' rallies, and in all major television interviews would prove to be the Alliance's unique selling proposition, a practical demonstration of how two parties could work together in the new politics of co-operation. In practice it proved embarrassing to them both as one tried to maintain a look of rapt attention while the other was speaking, and both hedged their own words to avoid any suggestion of disunity. On 27 May, at the end of the first full week of campaigning, David Steel spoke of cutting down joint appearances in which they looked 'like Tweedledum and Tweedledee', conjuring up memories of TVs satirical *Spitting Image* programmes in which David Steel always appeared as a puppet in Dr Owen's coat, dutifully agreeing with him (see p. 144).

But underlying the blurred image left by a dual leadership, there were real differences. As the election progressed it became plain that the SDP was more dedicated to preserving the nuclear deterrent than the Liberal party. It also became plain that Dr Owen would be much more ready to do business with Mrs Thatcher than would Mr Steel.

On the Robin Day phone-in programme on 3 June David Steel said 'I find it unimaginable . . . that there would be circumstances in which a minority government led by Mrs Thatcher could be sustained in office by us' and the next day he told a student in St Andrews that he wouldn't work with Mrs Thatcher. He later backtracked, referring to possible crises 'I cannot say absolutely in no circumstances, ever in creation, that we would not be in the same government'. On 4 June David Owen seemed to discount the possibility of the Alliance taking part in a Labour-led government ('the one fundamental issue for me is the security of our country . . . and on that test the Labour party fails'); Labour would not ask them – and the Alliance could not join them – unless they repudiated their left-wing and its policies. On his battlebus the same day David Steel indicated to the journalists that he regarded as 'a little weak' the joint Alliance line that they would, if necessary, work with a Conservative government, though 'preferably not' under Mrs Thatcher'.[9]

All in all the two Davids managed to avoid explicitly contradicting each other; despite the cartoonists' portrayal of disarray, they put a good face on their co-operation right to the end of the campaign (which was to make the breakdown in understanding over the merging of the parties in the weeks that followed all the more surprising).

On the final Sunday, 7 June, the Conservative and Labour parties staged their largest media events. Mrs Thatcher addressed a 'family rally' at Wembley. Sixty buses brought the faithful to two hours of songs and jokes, and a host of stars from the worlds of sport and

"Well it was never till death us do part!"

The Times, 5 June 1987

entertainment, including Mrs Thatcher's impersonator, Janet Brown, were introduced. The Prime Minister gave this message:

> I don't know about Dad's Army, but I'm a mum and I'd like to think that those people who believe in keeping Britain strong, free and properly defended belong in Mum's Army.

> Next Thursday when the people go to the polls, I believe Mum's Army will include thousands of traditional Labour supporters who just can't stomach the defence policy or rather, the no-defence policy, of today's Labour Party . . .

> The leader of the Labour Party even talks about occupation. Occupation? Occupation of Britain? After winning two world wars without a single enemy soldier on British soil? We Conservatives will never take risks with Britain's security . . . Let us have lasting peace in Britain so that you can be able to run your own life, spend your own money and make your own choices.

At the same time Neil Kinnock was speaking to 2000 activists at a 'Coming up Roses' rally in Islington, which was also described as a 'family day', with the necessary range of stars in support. In an emotional speech Mr Kinnock promised victory and turned on the uncaring style of Mrs Thatcher and the Conservatives:

> In eight years, their policies have crushed communities and shattered families, put decent housing and regular transport beyond the reach of millions, made school books and hospital equipment dependent on fund-raising, spread poverty at home, cut aid to fight poverty abroad and pushed the tax burden to its highest level in industry.

> After that eight years, there is greater fear on the streets, anxiety is used as an economic weapon, prejudice is given legal force, morality is a mixture of being economical with the truth and worshipping the gods of greed . . .

> Will she understand that mercy is the responsibility of the strong, the greatest privilege of might? I doubt if she will. We know her too well. In eight years, her government has shown no quality of mercy.

The Alliance offered no such climax, but the two Davids went doggedly on, criss-crossing the country and meeting all sorts of questions at the nightly 'Ask the Alliance' rallies and, in the final days, taking what comfort they could from the very slight rise in their poll standing.

In the final days there was an unprecedented volume of press advertising. The Conservatives spent £2m using all the main newspapers except the *Daily Mirror* (Robert Maxwell refused to accept them). The Conservative campaign with its advertising blitz and its assault on Labour's tax policies finished strongly. Labour, in comparison, seemed to run out of steam. Their last thrust, an appeal to their lost supporters 'Come home to Labour' made little impact and they offered no major running stories.

The nervousness on Thursday, 4 June, had not been confined to the Conservative camp. The *Newsnight* poll and the false rumours that the next day's Marplan poll would show the Conservative lead down to 2% produced a panic in the City. £6bn was knocked off share prices. There was much comment about the influence of polls on the market and some suggestions of alleged leaks being used to manipulate prices.

The final movements of the polls did not seriously disturb most people's expectations of a Conservative victory. A MORI marginals poll in *The Times* on the last Monday, as well as the BBC *Newsnight* poll on the Wednesday, gave some slight encouragement to those who thought that the anti-Conservative swing would be highest in the key seats. 'I believe this tilted us towards confidence, even complacency in the final week' wrote one Labour insider. But the nationwide polls were agreed in giving the Conservatives a lead of between 7% and 12%, and on 9 June the stock market surged in anticipation with a record 34 point rise in the FT all share index.

Thursday, 11 June, was generally cool and dry, though there were heavy showers and some thunderstorms in the South-East – London had 0.4in. of rain. There were no significant snags or disturbances. Early reports of a high poll were hardly fulfilled although the turnout of the registered electorate at 75.3% in the UK (75.5% in GB) was 2.6% higher than in 1983. Granted that the register was at least 7% inaccurate at compilation on 10 October 1986 and that eight months had elapsed, it is reasonable to suppose that the actual abstention rate was not more than 15%.[10]

At 10 p.m. when the last votes had been cast, there was a flutter of excitement when an election day survey, prepared by Gallup for the BBC, suggested a Conservative lead of only 5%, giving a majority

of 26. But an exit poll, done by Harris for ITN, pointed to a 9%
Conservative lead and a 68-seat majority.

At 11.01 p.m. Torbay was once again the first seat to declare,
followed quickly by Guildford, Basildon and Cheltenham. It was
plain that the Conservatives were winning comfortably. Out of the
650 seats 597 were counted on the night and by 2.33 a.m. the 326th
Conservative victory (Barrow & Furness) confirmed Mrs Thatcher's
majority.

The final outcome, a clear majority of 102, was slightly more than
the Conservatives might have hoped from a 12% lead in votes – but
the swing was uneven and Labour wasted votes, piling up ever larger
majorities in safe seats. There was a 1.6% swing from Conservative
to Labour, ranging from almost nothing in the South to −3.6% in
the North and −5.8% in Scotland.

In the South of England the Conservatives gained five seats from
Labour (see Figure 5.1) and lost only one (Oxford East). In the West
Midlands they gained one and lost one. They lost four seats in
Nottingham, Leicester and Norwich and four seats in Wales. Labour
had seven gains in the North of England but it failed in some expected
targets like Hyndburn, Darlington and Batley. In Scotland Labour,
with 42% of the vote, got 50 of the 72 seats, the Conservatives being
reduced from 21 MPs to 10. The Scottish Nationalists lost their two
seats to Labour but gained three new ones from the Conservatives.
Plaid Cymru won one more seat (see Figure 5.2).

The Alliance, at 23%, ended with 22 seats (compared to 26% and
23 seats in 1983). They lost three of their five by-election gains as
well as some leading figures – Roy Jenkins, Ian Wrigglesworth and
Clement Freud. However, the Liberals won three new seats but
David Owen was left with only four SDP colleagues, two in London
and two in the North of Scotland.

Apart from Roy Jenkins, the most notable casualty was Enoch
Powell who lost South Down to the SDLP in the only seat to change
hands in Northern Ireland. The Sinn Fein abstentionist, Gerry
Adams, held on in West Belfast.

Neil Kinnock observed on the day of defeat,

What has happened is that there are people who, for reasons best
known to themselves, have voted for maintaining division in our
country . . . [Mrs Thatcher's policies would] deepen the divisions,
worsen the afflictions and increase the loss of trade, the loss of
industry and the loss of jobs. Naturally we will argue against that

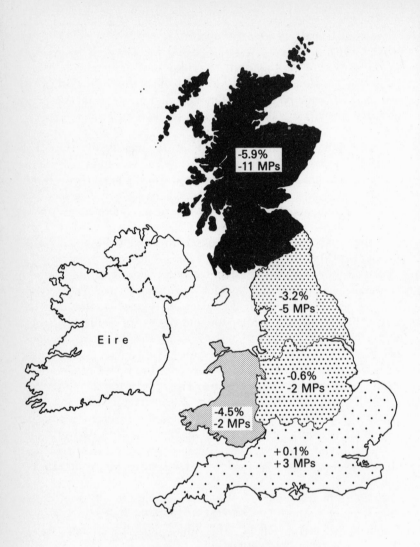

-5.9%
-11 MPs

-3.2%
-5 MPs

Eire

-0.6%
-2 MPs

-4.5%
-2 MPs

+0.1%
+3 MPs

Conservative — Labour Swing 1983-87
Conservative ± MPs 1983-87

Figure 5.1   The regional pattern, 1983–87

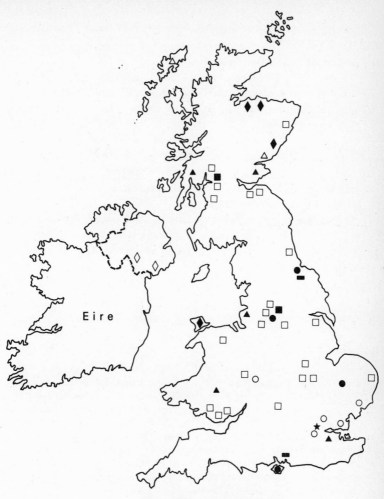

○ Conservative gain from Labour (5)
● Conservative gain from Alliance (4)
□ Labour gain from Conservatives (23)
■ Labour gain from Alliance (2)
△ Labour gain from Scottish Nationalists (2)
▲ Alliance gain (4)
◆ Nationalists gain from Conservatives (4)
◇ SDLP gain from Ulster Unionists (2)
★ Labour by-election gain recovered by Conservatives (1)
▬ Alliance by-election gain recovered by Conservatives (2)

Figure 5.2   Seats changing hands, 1983–87

and resist it wherever possible through the democratic system. But
the best way to resist it was yesterday, through the ballot box.

David Steel's election night reaction was:

> We have to regroup and consolidate. We must undergo our
> internal debate about the future of the Alliance. But my view is
> that we press on.

David Owen's immediate comments, which included references to
the government reaping 'the reward of determined, clear, firm
leadership' focused on the need for preserving the independent
identity of the SDP in the future.

Mrs Thatcher spoke of her 'fantastic triumph and of the hard work
that lay ahead'. Asked by Robin Day if she would go on to the year
2000, she replied, 'You never know, I might be here. I might be
twanging a harp'.

NOTES

1. The others were Dick Newby, Polly Toynbee and Roland Freeman from
   the SDP and Des Wilson, Paul Tyler and Andy Ellis from the Liberals.
2. Those usually present were Norman Tebbit, Lord Young, Peter Morrison, and John Wakeham, as well as David Willetts and Stephen Sherbourne from No. 10 and Robin Harris, Sir Christopher Lawson and
   John Desborough from Central Office.
3. The most important legal actions were a successful suit banning the local
   government union National Association of Local Government Officers
   (NALGO) (which was not affiliated to the Labour party) from publishing
   recruiting advertisements on the decline of public services and another,
   unsuccessful, action against the authors of an anonymous advertisement
   attacking particular left-wingers.
4. Labour strategists, looking back, admitted to a 'nervous Thursday' on
   14 May that could be set against the Conservatives' 'Wobbly Thursday'
   on 4 June (see pp. 109ff.). The Gallup poll of that morning, by placing
   them third, conjured up nightmare memories of 1983.
5. *The Representation of the People Act 1985* increased the candidate's
   deposit from £150 to £500 but lowered the condition of forfeiture from
   one-eighth to one-twentieth of the valid vote. Only one candidate of the
   three main parties failed to get the required 5%.
6. On *Election Call* on 22 May Labour's John Smith, normally a politician

with safe hands, fumbled badly at an ordinary citizen's probing about the adequacy of Labour's defence policy. But at least his performance was not as disastrous as John Wakeham's on the same programme two days earlier, offering Conservative answers to the problems of poverty (see p. 150).

7. 'Wobbly Thursday' became public knowledge in a *Times* editorial on 6 June and a front-page article by Peter Stothard in *The Times* on 13 June. It was given great prominence a month later with the serialisation in the *Sunday Times*, and then the publication of Rodney Tyler's book *Campaign*, which gave a detailed but partial account of the conflict between the Conservatives' advertising agencies.

8. For an insider's view see Des Wilson's *Battle for Power* published three weeks after the election.

9. The Alliance Planning Group 'read the Riot Act' to their leaders for fraternising so freely with the journalists on planes and battlebuses. This was the source of several damaging quotations and stories that distracted from the planned theme of the day.

10. See J. Todd and B. Butcher, *Electoral Registration in 1981* (OPCS 1982) and an updated study by M. and S. Pinto-Duschinsky, *Voter Registration: Problems and Solutions* (Constitutional Reform Centre, 1987); see also J. Todd and J. Eldridge, *Electoral Registration in Inner City Areas 1983–4* (HMSO, 1987).

6 Polls

Between 11 May and 11 June 1987, 73 nationwide surveys on voting intention were reported;[1] almost every major newspaper sponsored its own poll, as well as recording everyone elses. In addition there were 18 survyes of marginal seats which were often adjusted to offer a nationwide picture. There were also at least 100 polls (some of dubious quality) in individual seats, as well as surveys covering particular areas, notably Scotland, the North-West and London. There had been 49 nationwide polls in 1983 but all these extra surveys made 1987, by a considerable margin, the most exhaustively polled election in British history.[2]

Moreover, since it was a carefully packaged election with few strong news stories, the polls tended to take a leading place in election reports. The *Guardian* and the *Independent* carried the latest results in a box high up on every front page. *The Times* made a poll story its main headline in five of the ten issues between 1 June and 11 June (and on four other days carried a smaller front page poll story). Its lead on 4 June ('Wobbly Thursday') was 'POLLS BREATHE NEW LIFE INTO CAMPAIGN'. The popular press was more capricious but all at some time or other splashed a poll report – 'POLL HORROR FOR KINNOCK' (*Daily Express*, 14 May); 'POLL BOOST FOR KINNOCK' (*Daily Mirror*, 19 May); 'ITS UP THE POLL' (*Sun*, 4 June). But the headlines even in the serious press gave a confusing message that helped to develop cynicism about the polls.

The market research industry is large and diverse, with over 300 companies registered, but only a limited number of firms have done much political polling. Five companies stand out:[3]

Firm	Founded	Head	Parent company
Gallup	1937	G. Heald	—
NOP	1957	J. Barter	Associated Newspapers
Marplan	1959	N. Sparrow	Ogilvy and Mather
Harris (formerly ORC)	1967	J. Hanvey	Louis Harris Associates N.Y.
MORI	1969	R. Worcester	—

In February 1987 these five companies announced that they were

Table 6.1 Polls on voting intention, May–June 1987

Dates	Fieldwork sampling	Company (Publication)	C. (%)	Lab. (%)	Aln (%)	Other (%)	Total (%)	C.-L. %	C./Lab. swing (%)
6-11.5	1 735(180)	NOP (Standard)	46	28	25	1	100	+18	−1
7.11.5	1 085(110)	GALLUP (Telegraph)	39	28	30	3	100	+11	+2.5
8-12.5	1 445(103)	MARPLAN (Guardian)	43	29	25	3	100	+14	+1
8-12.5	1 934(178)	MORI (Sunday Times)	44	31	23	2	100	+13	+1.5
11-13.5	1 424(73)	MORI (Times) (Adj)	43	32	23	2	100	+11	+2.5
11-14.5	1 521(65)	MORI (S/T) (Pnl)	44	30	25	1	100	+14	+1
13.5	1 020(50)	MARPLAN (D.Express)	41	30	26	3	100	+11	+2.5
13-15.5	1 040(97)	HARRIS (Observer)	42	33	23	2	100	+9	+3.5
13-15.5	3 164(100)	HARRIS (W/W) (Adj)	40	34	25	1	100	+6	+5
14-17.5	2 410(102)	NEWSNIGHT (Adj)	40	34	24	2	100	+6	+5
16-17.5	1 058(97)	HARRIS (TV-am)	42	32	24	2	100	+10	+3
18.5	1 072(54)	MARPLAN (Today)	41	33	24	2	100	+8	+4
19.5	1 976(52)	NOP (I'dent) (Adj)	42	34	23	1	100	+8	+4
19-20.5	2 640(197)	GALLUP (Telegraph)	42	33	23	2	100	+9	+3.5
18-21.5	1 079(98)	HARRIS (TV-am)	43	36	20	1	100	+7	+4.5
20-21.5	1 328(65)	MORI (S/T) (Pnl)	44	31	24	1	100	+13	+1.5
20-21.5	1 066(97)	HARRIS (Observer)	41	34	22	3	100	+7	+4.5
21.5	1 517(103)	MARPLAN (Guardian)	41	33	21	5	100	+8	+4
20-22.5	1 432(140)	GALLUP (S'graph) (Pnl)	42	33	23	2	100	+9	+3.5
20-22.5	1 386(66)	HARRIS (W/W) (Adj) (Pnl)	42	35	22	1	100	+7	+4.5
22-25.5	1 075(98)	HARRIS (TV-am)	42	37	21	0	100	+5	+5.5
26.5	1 035(69)	MARPLAN (Today)	42	35	20	3	100	+7	+4.5
26.5	1 978(52)	NOP (I'dent) (Adj)	42	35	21	2	100	+7	+4.5
26-27.5	2 506(194)	GALLUP (Telegraph)	44.5	36	18	1.5	100	+8.5	+3.8
27-28.5	1 188(65)	MORI (S/T) (Pnl)	44	32	23	1	100	+12	+2
27-28.5	1 072(98)	HARRIS (Observer)	41	37	21	1	100	+4	+6
27-28.5	1 296(66)	HARRIS (W/W) (Adj) (Pnl)	41	37	21	1	100	+4	+6
26-29.5	1 067(97)	HARRIS (TV-am)	45	32	22	1	100	+13	+1.5
28.5	1 553(103)	MARPLAN (G'dian)	44	32	21	3	100	+12	+2
27-29.5	1 271(140)	GALLUP (S'graph) (Adj)	41.5	34	22.5	2	100	+7.5	+4.3
29.5	1 302(50)	MARPLAN (S.E'ss) (Adj)	45	31	23	1	100	+14	+1
29-30.5	1 420(73)	MORI (Times) (Adj)	44	32	22	2	100	+12	+2
30.5-1.6	2 116(60)	NEWSNIGHT (Adj) (Pnl)	40	36	22	2	100	+4	+6
30.5-2.6	1 573(100)	HARRIS (TV-am)	42	36	20	2	100	+6	+5
1.6	1 063(69)	MARPLAN (Today)	44	33	21	2	100	+11	+2.5
2.6	1 989(52)	NOP (I'dent) (Adj)	43	34	20	3	100	+9	+3.5
2-3.6	2 553(200)	GALLUP (Telegraph)	40.5	36.5	21.5	1.5	100	+4	+6
3-4.6	1 305(65)	MORI (S/T) (Adj) (Pnl)	43	32	24	1	100	+11	+2.5
3-4.6	1 087(98)	HARRIS (Observer)	44	33	21	2	100	+11	+2.5
4.6	1 576(103)	MARPLAN (Guardian)	44	34	20	2	100	+10	+3
3-5.6	1 100(60)	HARRIS (W/W) (Adj)	40	35	24	1	100	+5	+5.5
3-5.6	1 275(145)	GALLUP (S'graph) (Pnl)	41.5	34.5	22.5	1.5	100	+7	+4.5
3-6.6	2 102(98)	HARRIS (TV-am)	43	33	22	2	100	+10	+3
5.6	1 300(23)	MARPLAN (S.E'ss) (Adj)	47	30	21	2	100	+17	−0.5
5.6	1 065(69)	MARPLAN (Today)	43	35	21	1	100	+8	+4
5-6.6	1 443(73)	MORI (Times) (Adj)	43	34	21	2	100	+9	+3.5
7-8.6	2 023(60)	NEWSNIGHT (Adj) (Pnl)	39	36	24	1	100	+3	+6.5
8.6	1 575(103)	MARPLAN (Guardian)	45	32	21	2	100	+13	+1.5
8-9.6	2 122(99)	HARRIS (TV-am)	42	35	21	2	100	+7	+4.5
8-9.6	2 005(195)	GALLUP (Telegraph)	41	34	23.5	1.5	100	+7	+4.5
9.6	1 086(69)	MARPLAN (Today)	43	35	21	1	100	+8	+4
9.6	1 702*	ASL (The Sun)	43	34	21	2	100	+9	+3.5
9-10.6	1 668(165)	MORI (Times)	44	32	22	2	100	+12	+2
10.6	1 633(103)	MARPLAN (Guardian)	42	35	21	2	100	+7	+4.5
10.6	1 668(52)	NOP (I'dent) (Adj)	42	35	21	2	100	+7	+4.5
11 June	**Final Result**		**43**	**32**	**23**	**2**	**100**	**+11**	**+2.5**

Abbreviations: 'Adj' indicates a marginals poll adjusted to reflect the whole country; 'Pnl' indicates a panel survey; W/W – Weekend World; I'dent – The Independent; S/T – Sunday Times; S'graph – Sunday Telegraph; S.Ex'ss – Sunday Express; ASL – Audience Selection Ltd.; * – Telephone poll.

forming an Association of Professional Opinion Polling Organisations (APOPO) to exchange information among themselves and to make it available to others. At the same time the wider Market Research Society, anxious about the popular image of election polling, set up a monitoring panel to collect all poll findings and, with a 'hot-line', to answer questions from journalists and from the wider public and to refer controversial matters to a panel of experts. The pollsters and their client papers generally honoured the agreed code of conduct, by which the main technical details of any survey were made public. But other papers, as they reported their rivals' poll findings, often in summary form, were less scrupulous and a number of their reports had decidedly misleading headlines.

Most of the polls used quota samples of between 1000 and 2000 and most were conducted over a one- or two-day period. Telephone polls, a subject of controversy in 1983, were shunned, except by Audience Selection in the *Sun*; but some experiments were made with this hazardous but increasingly attractive technique. Refusal rates were only occasionally reported, nor even in some cases the number of 'don't knows'. There were complaints at the prominence given to poll findings and the industry had reason to be sensitive. On 24 February, following the Greenwich by-election, a Labour MP's 10-minute rule bill to ban polls had actually secured a first reading by 116 to 103 and with only four Labour MPs voting against it. During and after the election further calls for the banning of polls were voiced – but none of the party leaders lent their support.

Polls had their impact on the stock market, and advance leaks, accurate or invented, of their findings, could wipe millions off the value of shares, as the false rumours on 4 June showed. It is worth considering, however, what might have happened if there had been a ban on polls. Bogus tips about what the parties' private polls were reading – or even about agents' reports from the constituencies – would have made a volatile market far more jumpy than when it was anchored by the relatively stable message of almost daily public polls.

In 1987 polls were not telling a very exciting story. More than half had a Conservative lead in double figures and, after the first week, put the Alliance at least 10% behind Labour. Though there were one or two 'rogue' polls, the average of the polls (and most papers carried a 'poll of polls' report) was very stable and there was no evidence of systematic bias in any direction of any of the polls, although, ironically, the findings of MORI (Labour's private pollster)

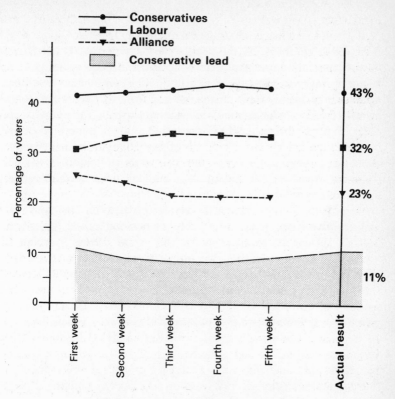

Figure 6.1   Poll of polls, May–June 1987

tended to favour the Conservatives while those of Harris (the Conservative's private pollster) were less good for them.

The 'rogue' polls which caused flutters at party headquarters came mainly from Gallup. On 14 May the *Daily Telegraph* reported the Alliance at 30%, 2% ahead of Labour at 28%, when every other poll put Labour ahead by between 3% and 8%. On 28 May Gallup reported the Alliance down at 18%, 2% less than any other poll during the campaign. And on 3 June Gallup cut the Conservative lead over Labour to 4%; Harris in the *Observer* on 31 May was the only other newspaper poll that ever put Labour as near to the Conservatives. The polls, as the last chapter showed, caused acute worry in some Conservative quarters whilst helping to sustain Labour morale.

But, apart from Labour's first surge, the main encouragement for the opposition parties came from constituency polls (which sometimes suggested breakthroughs far beyond the national tide) and from surveys confined to marginal seats collectively. The latter gave a very mixed message. As early as 18 February, a MORI poll conducted in marginals for *The Times* had suggested that the Conservatives were faring better in seats that might change hands than in the country as a whole. Simultaneously MORI's national poll, translated into seats on a uniform swing from 1983, suggested that the Conservatives would be 12 short of a clear majority, while the results from the marginals pointed to a lead of 94. This may have been a 'rogue' finding, but at the time it was echoed by Gallup and Harris. A repeat of the poll on 7 April indicated only a 10-seat difference from the swing in marginals and the country as a whole. But during the election, special marginals polls (MORI in *The Times*; Marplan in the *Sunday Express*; NOP in the *Independent*; Gallup for the *Daily Telegraph*; Harris for LWT's *Weekend World* each Sunday; and Vincent Hanna's BBC *Newsnight* polls) gave very conflicting stories. Consider the situation in early June as shown in Table 6.2.

Table 6.2   Swing in Conservative–Labour marginal polls

Poll	Swing
Newsnight (*BBC*)	5.9%
Harris (*LWT*)	5.5%
NOP (*Independent*)	1.5%
Gallup (*The Daily Telegraph*)	1.5%
MORI (*The Times*)	1.5%
Average swing in nationwide polls	3.0%

Newsnight and Harris suggested that Labour would do better in marginals than in the rest of the country whilst MORI, NOP and Gallup suggested that it would do worse. The difference between *Newsnight* and MORI would make a difference of over 100 seats to the parliamentary majority. One reason for this contrast seems to be that different groups of marginals yielded different election results; some surveys were focusing on close marginals where the swing turned out to be small, and some covered a much wider band of seats where the swing proved to be greater. Another reason seems to lie in the variation in the types of quota control used by the rival organisations; those who used housing tenure to select their sample consistently over-estimated Labour strength. These surveys made headlines but, in view of the conflict of evidence, mature observers tended to rely simply on the nationwide figures which told a more consistent story.

The polls that made most stir throughout the campaign were the BBC *Newsnight* surveys, flamboyantly presented by Vincent Hanna. This series of polls was an ambitious attempt to look at changes in voting during the campaign. Teams of social science students were recruited from colleges across the country and a 2000-interview panel survey in three waves (the first on May 13–17) was conducted in three types of seats:

(a) Conservative/Labour marginals (a Conservative majority of under 22%)

(b) Conservative/Alliance marginals (under a Conservative majority of under 22%)

(c) Three-way marginals (Conservative marginals but with Labour and Alliance within 5% of each other).

The panel secured a response rate of 87% and 84% response in the second wave (29–31 May) and 81% in the final wave (7–8 June). Each survey correctly spotted that the Alliance would do comparatively well in Conservative–Alliance marginals and that Labour would flourish in the three-way marginals. Unfortunately, in Conservative–Labour marginals where the key to the election lay, the survey consistently overestimated Labour strength; being a panel study an error in the original sample could be expected to persist. The second survey made a particular contribution to the Conservatives' 'Wobbly Thursday' on 4 June (see pp. 109ff.). This suggested that Labour was leading the Conservatives by 3.4% in the seats they might hope to gain and that there had been a 1% swing to them in the previous two weeks. The final poll in these seats suggested a further swing and a 5.9% lead for Labour. This would have represented a 6.7% swing from 1983 and, given a uniform movement across the country, would produce a hung parliament.

Newsnight resolutely put 'health warnings' about their findings with cautions about translating their vote percentages into precise numbers of seats – although not about translating them into 'bad news' for the Conservatives. None the less, the high profile presentation of the

figures and their, often inaccurate, prior leaking had a disproportion-
ate impact. There was much subsequent criticism of the *Newsnight*
poll but it should be pointed out that in the previous week the key
finding on the swing in Conservative–Labour marginals was almost
duplicated by Harris in *Weekend World*. But *Newsnight*, being later
and more publicised, took the blame for being the poll most in error –
and for error in a pro-Labour direction.[4]

The BBC's difficulties were compounded on election night when a
quite separate BBC Gallup poll, taken on election eve and election
day, suggested a Conservative lead of only 5%, while ITN's Harris
exit poll recorded a 10% lead (as against the 11% lead which actually
materialised).

One innovation was the 'rolling poll' used each morning by TV-
am. Harris first interviewed a sample of 1000 and then each day
interviewed a further 250 dropping the oldest 250 from their sample;
in the last week of the campaign the sample was increased to 500 per
day. The four-day moving average proved rather capricious, and
the Conservative lead fluttered between 4% and 13% during the
campaign.

The *Sunday Times* conducted an interesting poll on a panel basis
over four weeks. Behind its very stable findings it revealed a lot of
'churning', of cancelling switches between the three parties and 'don't
knows'. A proportion of respondents are wholly capricious. But on
the *Sunday Times* figures over 7 million electors switched their voting
intentions during the campaign – without making much net difference
to the outcome.

The regional polls did not do very well. For example, a Harris
poll in the *London Daily News* on 10 June, suggested that London
would divide: Conservative 41%, Labour 36%, Alliance 21%. The
outcome was 46%-32%-21% – a 9% underestimate of the Conservative lead. System 3 in the *Glasgow Herald* suggested that Scotland
would divide; Conservative 22%, Labour 48%, Alliance 19%, SNP
19%; the outcome was 24%-42%-19%-14% an 8% overestimate of
the Labour lead.

On 10 June the *Guardian* listed surveys in 28 marginal seats
conducted by the major polling organisations. Five of these indicated
the wrong winner and some of the others were as much as 10% out
in their estimate of the party lead.

There were a few specialist polls. On 29 May the *Times Educational
Supplement* reported a MORI poll showing that Conservative support
among teachers had fallen from 44% to 24% between 1983 and 1987;

Alliance support had jumped from 28% to 46%, while Labour had only moved from 26% to 28%. A survey in *The Times Higher Education Supplement* on 5 June showed university teachers divided Conservative 17%, Labour 39%, Alliance 39%. A mail survey in the *Farmer's Weekly* suggested that Conservative support among farmers had fallen from 85% in 1983 to 69% in 1987.

Polling, as always, focused overwhelmingly on voting intentions and on the possibilities of tactical voting. But the serious press (and notably Gallup in the *Daily Telegraph*) did report polls on issues and personalities as well as on who was running the best campaign. The improvement in Mr Kinnock's rating, and the verdict that Labour was putting on the more impressive campaign, had some impact on party morale. But the findings on issues were hardly striking and, as we show in Chapter 1 they did not change much during the campaign – though education and defence became more salient. Even the evidence on willingness to vote tactically or to welcome a coalition government was little headlined – and did not offer much encouragement to the Alliance.

There was rather less talk about betting on the 1987 election than four years earlier. The odds on the Conservatives getting most seats were lopsided, ranging between 5-1 and 10-1 on. Gambling on majorities flourished with most money going on a 50-seat majority. More sophisticated betting was possible on this occasion through the IG Index, a financial futures concern which invited wagers as bulls or bears from a given number of seats. The break-even points are revealing (see Table 6.3).

Table 6.3   *IG Index break-even points, 1985–87*

Date	Con.	Seats Lab.	Alln.
20 Sept. 1985	285	240	98
9 Dec. 1986	315	271	43
18 Mar. 1987	353	220	58
5 May 1987	360	212	58
8 Jun. 1987	356	242	34
10 Jun. 1987	365	238	28

The betting odds were only reflecting general expectations. Throughout the election over three-quarters of voters told the pollsters that they thought the government would be re-elected.

The final nationwide surveys on voting intention by the major

organisations were all within the accepted margin of error. All but
MORI underestimated the Conservative lead – which might suggest
a late swing to the government and, as in 1983, MORI came out best
(Table 6.4). It made a courageous forecast from a one-off survey,
since it suggested a Conservative lead distinctly higher than that
shown by any of its competitors, and with a full awareness that since
the 1960s the party ahead in the polls had always fared less well than
the final forecasts.

Table 6.4   Record of the final polls: 1987 election

Poll by	For	Con. (%)	Lab. (%)	Alln. (%)	Ave. error (%)	Gap (%)	Error on swing (%)	F/cast (%)	Error on swing (%)
Harris	TV-am	42	35	21	2.0	7	4	4.5	+2.0
Gallup	D.Tel.	41	34	23.5	1.5	7	4	4.5	+2.0
Marplan	Guard.	42	35	21	2.0	7	4	4.5	+2.0
NOP(Adj.)	Indep.	42	35	21	2.0	7	4	4.5	+2.0
ASL(Tele)	Sun	43	34	21	1.3	9	2	3.5	+1.0
MORI	Times	44	32	22	0.7	12	1	2.0	−0.5
Result of vote		43	32	23	—	11	—	2.5	—
Poll average		42	34	22	1.6	8	3	3.5	+1
Difference		−1	+2	−1	—	−3	—	+1	—

It is worth recording that a British Market Research Bureau Survey
six weeks after the election found 60% of its sample recalling the
poll predictions as being 'fairly accurate' or 'very accurate', as against
17% saying 'fairly inaccurate' or 'very inaccurate', with 23% saying
'don't know'.

During the parliament there was a substantial amount of private
polling by the main parties and qualitative as opposed to quantitative
surveys grew in importance. However, during the election private
polling probably counted for less than in the past. The growing
volume of public polling meant that the need for private research
was diminished. All parties devoted considerable efforts to analyse
published surveys and to avoid duplicating research that they could
have for free. However, substantial sums were spent on private polls.
During the parliament the amount spent by the Conservatives
averaged about £100 000 a year, and by Labour about £85 000. During
the campaign the Conservatives and Labour each spent about
£120 000.

The Labour party had used MORI, and its American director, Robert Worcester, for private polling since the 1970 election. The relationship had had its troubles since some left-wing members of the NEC were suspicious both of polling and of Mr Worcester. Before the June 1983 election MORI's contract had not been approved until February and the campaign research programme was only settled at the beginning of May. But the lesson was learnt, and from October 1983 Mr Kinnock and his staff maintained close and continuous relations with the organisation. There is little doubt that the link between pollster and party was the closest and most intelligent that has been achieved in recent British politics (except perhaps for the Conservatives and ORC in 1970).[5] MORI supplied analysis of nationwide published polls, specific surveys of target groups and marginal seats, by-election analyses, and qualitative research. Robert Worcester and Brian Gosschalk made presentations of poll findings to the NEC, the PLP, to various party groups and training courses, to the Shadow Advertising Agency and occasionally to the Campaign Strategy Committee. An atmosphere developed in which the party and its advisers could not be unaware of what the public was thinking and what it would stand. The private polls' importance in this phase lay in the guidance that they gave about the handling of the defence issue (see p. 66) and the identification of target voters (together with the indication that for them education and health were more important than jobs).

Many of the messages that MORI had to bring were depressing. Only for a short while in 1985, and from January to October 1986, was Labour in the lead, while by-elections, national and local, seldom gave much comfort. There was intense frustration as the party seemed unable to lift itself beyond a plateau of around 38%.

During the election MORI conducted 20 routine polls, based on about 650 interviews in 55 Conservative-held marginal seats. It also prepared special reports on trade unionists, young voters and pensioners. The findings were reported partially to the Polls Monitoring Group,[6] which met at 6 p.m., and then occasionally to the Campaign Management Team at 7 p.m. but there was always a report for their early morning meeting with recommended courses of action. Communications between the two groups was improved after the first week when Larry Whitty or Bryan Gould made a point of attending the Polls Monitoring Group, but some complaints were still made about the inadequate contact between the pollsters and those who used their findings.

With memories of past leaks, it had been intended that the voting intention findings should be kept secret from any but the top two or three in the campaign team. Although this proved impracticable, the findings were never leaked from the monitoring. The figures anyway would have added little to the message of the public polls, except when they were 'rogue' findings. There was nothing to be gained from reports of a Conservative lead that fluctuated from 20% (16 May) to 4% (22 May) back to 14% (29 May), then to 5% (31 May) back to 15% (7 June), before ending at 6% (9 June). But these variations, expected from small samples, did not invalidate the general messages from the surveys:

● Labour was weak in defence; its salience as a major talking point rose from 20% on 18 May to 60% on 29 May and in the same period those thinking Labour would handle defence badly rose from 57% to 66% while those thinking Labour would handle defence well fell from 31% to 24%. No other issue changed its ratings so sharply.

● Labour continued to be well regarded for its handling of health, education and unemployment, but more thought Labour would handle the economy, the cost of living, and, above all, inflation, badly. Nothing said in the campaign changed these ratings. On 28 May, 56% said they thought there would be an economic crisis under Labour.

● Labour was seen by 46% as making promises the country couldn't afford as against 18% for the Conservatives and 18% for the Alliance.

● Voters in these 55 marginal seats were expecting a local Conservative victory by a majority of two-to-one.

● When asked if the campaign in the last day or two had made them feel more or less positively towards Labour, around 30% said less and only 15% said more. (The Conservative campaign also evoked a negative verdict but only by 23% to 14% and the Alliance by 15% to 13%).

● Individual comments stressed the worries of electors on defence, on the 'loony left', and on where the money would come from for Labour's programmes.

All this was depressing news, repeated day after day. Yet there was some comfort. Neil Kinnock received a steadily improving rating, especially after his first broadcast. When asked on 6 June to choose the best Prime Minister, Mr Kinnock lost to Mrs Thatcher by only 49% to 41% and, significantly, he had moved into the lead among Alliance supporters. (Bryan Gould misleadingly suggested that he was ahead amongst all voters.) Neil Kinnock's first election broadcast on 21 May produced an overnight jump of 10% in the proportion believing he would do an effective job as Prime Minister. This improvement, reinforced by evidence from the public polls, led to one of the few changes of tactics that could be attributed directly to the private polls on either side. Since only 25% of people had seen Mr Kinnock's broadcast it was decided to repeat it on 4 June as Labour's fourth election broadcast. It also produced a temporary jump in Mr Kinnock's ratings.

The Conservatives continued to rely on the Harris Research Centre under John Hanvey for most of their research, although they did secondary analysis from Gallup's findings. Saatchi and Young and Rubicam, conducted their own qualitative and quantitative research, though it is not clear how fully this was absorbed into Conservative strategy at Smith Square. Harris again conducted a daily 'Fast Feedback' operation, interviewing 100 opinion-formers to monitor progress on the campaign.

The poll findings were reported to Keith Britto, who had monitored polls for Central Office since 1974, and to Sir Christopher Lawson, who had returned to Central Office in an overseeing role. During the campaign the academic Michael Pinto-Duschinsky again helped with the analysis of findings.

In 1983–7 the Conservatives conducted the major tracking surveys each year, with qualitative and quantitative interviews; there were also a few constituency studies and a little research in specific policy areas and among specific groups, such as students, and particular types of marginal seats. There were few by-election surveys because the lawyers were worried about breaches of law on election expenses. In addition, the Conservatives bought monthly from Gallup the cumulative figures of all their nationwide surveys, published and unpublished, which gave them regular access to a very large sample of voters (8000–9000) so that they had detailed regional and social breakdowns at their disposal.

Mrs Thatcher and some senior ministers, though not Central Office, were also provided with survey findings by Young and Rubicam (see

p. 108). This research had been presented during 1986 and 'tracking' studies were continued during the campaign. The Young and Rubicam reports given to Downing Street on 3 June pointed to a worrying decline in the Conservative performance on issues, and a rise for Labour. In a post-election report Young and Rubicam argued that the Conservative victory rested on the massive support of the 'succeeders' (80% Conservative) and 'mainstreamers' (50% Conservative).

Less polling was done by the Conservatives during the campaign than on previous occasions. A regular 'State of Battle' poll was prepared for each weekend, based on 2000 or so interviews nation-wide. A special version of this poll, together with a poll in marginals, had been done earlier, for the weekend of 9–10 May when Mrs Thatcher had to confirm her decision to go to the country.

The Conservatives' 'State of Battle' polls conformed closely to the findings of the published surveys: the Conservative lead over Labour varied between 8% and 12% and Alliance support fell from 21% to 19%. The measurements of likelihood to vote and propensity to vote tactically contained no surprises. Conservatives were strong on 'best leaders and best policies', but weak on health and employment. Conservatives were seen as uncaring but Labour as untrustworthy. These familiar themes were found week after week without any shift on a scale to suggest any change of tactics. The depressing news was that Labour, behind in the first week, was thereafter adjudged to be putting on the best campaign: on the final weekend it had a 15% advantage on this and a 17% advantage on being best on television.

There were also four midweek 'quickie' polls, with a 1000 sample and a short questionnaire, which offered no special additional insights – but which might have proved invaluable in a more volatile campaign.

The Conservatives sponsored a third set of weekly polls in seats marginal between Conservative and Labour and in seats marginal between Conservative and Alliance. Once again these confirmed what the public polls were saying, though they, too, were favourable to Labour, which was seen as advancing in both types of seats; however, opinions on issues and the state of the campaign did not differ from the nationwide surveys.

After the election Conservative strategists could not claim that their private polls had had any significant effect. 'They told us we were on course and, if things had been going wrong, they could have given us invaluable early guidance on specific weaknesses', someone observed. But the main polling contribution to the Conservative party's day-to-day assessment was a six-foot long 'poll of polls' chart which was brought to the meetings and which, like Figure 6.1 (on p. 127), offered three straight and well-separated parallel lines, almost horizontal throughout the campaign. It confirmed, over and over again, that the Alliance threat was not materialising and that Labour was about 10% behind.

The Alliance had less resources for polling. The Liberals did none. The SDP, with Sarah Horack as adviser, conducted a few surveys. They sponsored a qualitative report in mid-1986, and some polling on voting intentions in target seats as well as on attitudes in certain policy areas. During the election they commissioned Marplan to conduct 12 surveys in key target seats and, on 1 June, 10 of these were leaked to *Today*, their most sympathetic newspaper, which spread them on the front page, without giving any technical details. They put the Alliance ahead in two seats and within striking distance in most of the others.

There is no reason to suppose that private polling had any influence on Alliance strategy. 'I can't think of any change of tack' said one member of the planning group. But the public polls, with their obstinately depressing message, undoubtedly affected both rank and file and leaders.

Public opinion polls may have made private opinion polls less important, but they did not make polls less important. There has never been an election where the strategy of all parties was more directly linked to the evidence of surveys about the preferences of the voters. None of the parties cringed abjectly before these sometimes ephemeral indications of sometimes ephemeral opinion: each out of conviction, or party necessity, espoused policies that they knew could not win votes. But each shaped their presentation to highlight what the polls showed to be most acceptable, and each used qualitative research to mould its approach and its vocabulary. Polls shaped the election agenda both for the parties and the media. The public had to face more polls about its voting intentions than ever before – but it was also the recipient of more survey-devised presentation than ever before.

NOTES

1. This total should perhaps be 54. The 72 includes in addition to those listed in Table 6.1, a further 18 daily reports of TV-am's rolling polls, although each time these were updates involving the addition and subtraction of only one quarter of a survey (see p. 130). However, the figures were given almost equal publicity with complete nationwise polls.
2. For an excellent discussion of polling in the 1983 election see I. Crewe 'Saturation Polling, the media and the 1983 election', in I. Crewe and M. Harrop (eds), *Political Communications: the 1983 Election Campaign* (Cambridge, 1986). See also R. Rose, 'Opinion Polls as a Feedback Mechanism', University of Strathclyde, Occasional Paper, 1983. For a counterview see P. Whiteley 'The Accuracy and Influence of the Polls' in the Crewe and Harrop volume. See also R. Worcester (ed.), *Political Opinion Polling; An International Review* (London, 1983).
3. Audience Selection conducted a number of telephone polls in 1987. There were also three established regional companies, System Three in Scotland, and Beaufort Research and Market Research Wales in Wales, which published surveys in their own territory.
4. On 19 October 1987 the BBC released an independent report by Professor Martin Collins on the performance of the polls which it had sponsored. It found that the *Newsnight* surveys, while a particularly speculative venture, suffered from ill-luck, and that the separate election eve poll had been unreliable and its error had been compounded by the translation of votes into seats. This report provoked substantial controversy. For a more exhaustive discussion of the marginal and constituency polls see the chapters by Pippa Norris and Robert Waller in I. Crewe and M. Harrop (eds), *Political Communications: the General Election Campaign of 1987* (Cambridge, forthcoming).
5. This is not to suggest there were no tensions. In particular, MORI's disastrous public overprediction of Labour's chances in the Brecon by-election excited unease in some senior Labour quarters.
6. It consisted of Lord McIntosh, Peter Kellner, Robert Worcester, Brian Gosschalk, Harold Frayman, Donald Ross, Adam Sharples, Jane Bigham, Deborah Mattinson and Philip Gould, with Rex Osborne as secretary.

7 Broadcasting
Martin Harrison

As with every campaign since 1959 this was, of course, a 'television election' – only more so. Never before had the parties tailored their efforts so single-mindedly to capturing the cameras' attention. This was the year of the designer campaigns, with their blue flags, red roses and yellow umbrellas, their theatrically spectacular rallies for a generation which had never known Nuremburg, their theme tunes lifted from Brahms, Purcell and Holst and reprocessed for easy listening and, above all, their endless photo opportunities. Every party, from the largest to the Greens and the nationalists made television their first priority, and the broadcasters responded to scale. Between the election announcement and 11 June television alone carried upwards of 200 hours of programmes entirely or substantially about the election. With breakfast television joining the fray and television news on an hour during the day, the election was rarely more than 60 minutes away from the moment the sun rose on *Good Morning Britain* at 6.15 a.m. until the credits rolled for *On The Hustings*, which might be well after midnight. In the Midlands insomniac *aficionados* could even watch the news on Central at three in the morning.

It was perhaps small wonder that the campaign had scarcely begun before Gallup reported 69% of its sample expecting 'too much' coverage on television, another poll found 27% contending there should be none at all, and newspapers reported a 20% jump in video rentals. Yet the campaign never claimed all four channels, and, even in the final week, there were only 10 minutes between 6 p.m. and midnight when it took three, and about six hours when it took two. This was not too difficult an election for the apathetic or antipathetic to avoid. Nevertheless, the scale of coverage caused considerable private and public grumbling.

One reason why the election seemed so insistently invasive was that it dominated the news. This was the main battleground, both because it reached such a high proportion of the electorate, and because whatever achieved prominence there reverberated through every current affairs programme too. The news was also the point at which competition between the networks was most directly joined.

The BBC was determined to reverse what one senior editor terms 'the debacle of 1983', when the Corporation's coverage was under-resourced and ill-coordinated. It added five minutes to weekday bulletins at mid-day and teatime and expanded the *Nine o'Clock News* from a nominal 25 minutes to 50. *Newsnight* became a nightly election magazine, while *On The Hustings* carried extracts from speeches at greater length than the hurried and snippety pace of the main bulletins allowed.

By contrast, ITN's early bulletins remained at their usual length, and *News At Ten* gained only five minutes because the ITV companies were anxious to start their programmes before too much of their potential audience had departed for bed. *Channel Four News* added Saturday and Sunday to its normal Monday–Friday schedule. Even so, BBC1 carried more news time than ITV and Channel 4 combined. The BBC also made inroads on the technical superiority ITN enjoyed in 1983, hiring an additional fleet of vehicles as field editing units. It also tackled its older, more serious problems of welding its news and current affairs divisions into a coherent election team. After a slightly shaky start, the outcome was its most successful coverage for years.

Although Radio 4 had an election team of 40, its approach to the campaign was less expansive than television's. None of its bulletins was extended, though *Election Platform* was added at 11 p.m. to carry long extracts from the evening's speeches. While the election was much the biggest story, it was reported more briefly, and more often gave way to other events than on television. Radio 4's four main bulletins gave 36.9% of their time to the election, and the 'flagship' programme at 6 p.m. led on it on 11 of the last 28 days. In contrast, *Channel Four News* gave the election 72.5% of its time (3.6% up on 1983), and led with it 21 evenings out of 26. BBC1 not only had more time available than in 1983, but also gave the campaign more of it (58.9% compared with 52.9%), leading the main news with it on 18 nights out of 28. ITN had an election lead on 19 evenings but the need not to neglect other stories caused the proportion of time given to the campaign to fall below the 1983 level – from 55.0% to 51.8%.[1] Even so, *News at Ten* viewers could reckon on 'Campaign 87' running some 15 minutes most weekday evenings. All television channels moved into high intensity coverage from the very beginning. ITN broke with the usual pattern by giving less time in the second fortnight than the first, but even so the story stayed top of the bulletin or very close.[2] The broadcasters had committed such resources to it that it had a built-in momentum, and only Iran and Irangate emerged fitfully to challenge it.

While the volume of coverage varied between channels, there was little difference in the news values or formats of their hard news reporting. Even *Channel Four News* diverged sharply only once, when it led with an unpublished report about NHS funding which none of the other channels covered. As always, reporting was mainly passive and reactive, with enterprise at a premium. BBC1 and ITV news made 'leaders' day' packages a central feature, assigning a reporting team to each leader for the campaign. With reporters working cheek-by-jowl with the parties and each other for three weeks, it was scarcely surprising that much material was bland and interchangeable, the same shots and quotes turning up on both channels. Obvious pressures to 'go native', were not always resisted, though some sharper notes were struck. John Simpson noted Mrs Thatcher's tendency to visit 'islands of success in otherwise depressed areas'. Coverage of a Conservative rally jumped from a tasteless 'Paki' joke by Ted Rogers to the frozen face of a Pakistani in the audience. A report on the Kinnock campaign spoke of 'a frenetic day spent promoting the leader's image rather than the party's policies'.

However, both BBC1 and ITN showed remarkable tolerance of photo-opportunities. These were to the 1987 coverage what the walkabout had been to its predecessors. They were not, of course, an innovation: who could forget Mrs Thatcher cuddling a calf in an

Table 7.1 Relative prominence of issues in news coverage

	BBC1	ITV	C4	R4	All 1987	All 1983
Defence	2	1	1	1	1	2
Employment	1	4	2	5	2	1
Education	3	3	4	2	3=	*
NHS	4	2	3	6=	3=	6
Economy generally	5	5	6	4	5=	4
Attacks, self-praise and exhortation	6	6=	8=	3	5=	5
Taxation	7=	6=	10	6=	7	*
Hung parliament	7=	8=	8=	10	8	*
Law and order	11	9	5	12	9	*
Ireland, constitutional	9=	13	7	8=	10	8=
Industrial relations	9=	10	12	8=	11	8=

* Insufficient to rank.

East Anglian field in 1979? However, the BBC's Assistant Director-General, Alan Protheroe, had ruled that in 1983 there had been too many walkabouts. That, and the dictates of security, consigned the walkabout to unregretted near-oblivion, leaving the photo-opportunity as the most favoured device for manipulating the media. It can imply volumes while promising nothing, attracting maximum exposure for minimum political risk. Every bulletin brought its crop of visits to schools, old people's homes, bakeries or hi-tech factories. Leaders poured tea, tried their hand at wallpapering, brandished a cricket bat or even layed a brick – the same brick several times, to make sure all the cameramen had the shot. Events involving the wearing of funny hats apparently scored double. Somewhere, mused a commentator, there must be a secret youth training centre, set up for the express purpose of receiving visits from politicians. There was nothing to match that classic 1979 performance with a calf, but shots of the Prime Minister being licked by a guide dog came as close as anyone could have wished. Neil Kinnock was shown contemplating a herd of cows (but not actually handling them), apparently to demonstrate Labour concern for the environment, though some reports left the shots unexplained. Some sequences remained impenetrable. When Mrs Thatcher was pictured in a blackcurrant field, gazing through field glasses at her attendant swarm of photographers, what conceivable point were the image-makers trying to convey?

Weekends were the worst. On the first Saturday both channels showed Norman Tebbit patting a bulldog and commenting with cheerfully apt cynicism that the cameras' presence proved that an election was indeed under way. Later bulletins showed Margaret Thatcher visiting the ducks in St James's Park and Neil Kinnock wiping a stray child's nose. Labour's news conference that morning received little coverage as photo-opportunity was matched against photo-opportunity in the name of 'balance'.

Reaction set in quickly. *Channel Four News* carried a report on the way parties manipulate their images, which drew piquantly on an exceptionally supine set of cameos of the leaders' 'home lives' run on ITN only a few days earlier. Subsequently coverage of these events diminished slightly, and they tended to be shown for what they were with their attendant cameramen, an uneasy amalgam of dutiful reporting of 'what the parties were doing' and patronising comment on what was being shown. Later still, reporters tended to talk over shots of photo-opportunities – a sure recipe for non-

communication. Despite Alan Protheroe's dictum and the demise of
the walkabout, coverage of leaders' tours containing no explicit
references to policy took as much of the coverage as in 1983, and far
more than any of the campaign issues – 14.5% of ITN election news,
11.7% of BBC1's, but only 7.9% of *Channel Four News* and 3.6%
on Radio 4. While radio was by its very nature exempt from
the temptations of visual clutter, *Channel Four News* repeatedly
demonstrated that competent reporting did not require photo-opportunities. Some broadcasters were impenitent about favouring pictures
over words, others blamed the parties. But if they were rightly
hesitant about seeming to dictate the agenda of election issues, they
surely need have had no inhibitions about treating the television
equivalent of junk mail strictly on its merits (see Table 7.2).

Table 7.2   *Party shares of news coverage*[1]

	Con. (%)	Lab. (%)	Alln (%)	Others (%)	Total (%)
BBC1	31.8	32.4	31.4	4.5	100.1
ITV	31.3	33.6	32.4	2.6	99.9
C4	32.4	32.5	32.3	2.8	100.0
R4	31.6	32.1	30.7	5.5	99.9
All	31.7	32.6	31.7	4.0	100.0

1. All national bulletins on BBC1, ITV and Channel 4, Radio 4 at 8 a.m., 1 p.m.,
   6 p.m. and 10.30 p.m., 14 May–10 June 1987.

In fairness, what might have been the greatest photo-opportunity
of all – the Venice Summit – was reported with considerable spirit.
As it happened, security and the weather robbed the triumphal entry
along the Grand Canal of much of its hoped for visual impact, and
TV-am lost its link to Venice just before the Prime Minister's
breakfast meeting with President Reagan. All channels, while fully
covering the Summit outside their election packages, saw that the
Prime Minister's enthusiasm was bracketed with comments by her
opponents, such as Neil Kinnock's dismissive 'a sandwich, a sermon
and a photo-session'. All channels carried sober commentaries from
their economics correspondents; John Simpson's report for BBC1
was also notably downbeat. The Prime Minister was quite properly
displayed on the world stage, but to less advantage than her party's
managers had hoped.
    Photo-opportunities were just one facet of the parties' determin-
ation to promote their leaders. This was most obvious with Labour.

Having tried to compensate for Michael Foot's failings in 1983 by emphasis on the team, Labour's 1987 campaign focused as never before on the personal qualities of its leader. Neil Kinnock was cited more often and at greater length than anyone else. He featured in almost nine bulletins in ten; he took 56.7% of the newstime taken by statements by Labour politicians, seven times as much as his campaign manager, Bryan Gould – dominating the party's coverage even more than Harold Wilson in his heyday. By contrast, though politically Mrs Thatcher seemed as pre-eminent as ever, her 46.5% of Conservative time was a little less than in 1983, because of the decision to lighten her campaign load and give the party chairman a bigger role. The two Davids took the lion's share of Alliance coverage (63.8%), each outstripping everyone but the two party leaders. This hardly benefited them, or the Alliance; it came across as a two-man band, while television's tendency to cover each David in a sub-package had the effect of diminishing both. Even so, David Owen's proficiency at producing the bite-sized comments broadcast newsmen love made him look the dominant partner – closer to the *Spitting Image* lampoon than to Tweedledum and Tweedledee.

Yet although the four leading figures took a record 57% of all time spent quoting politicians, the editors cast their nets further than in 1983, including a record 182 different party representatives. While many were glimpsed only once and fleetingly, Gordon Wilson of the Scottish Nationalist Party (SNP) received more attention than any previous spokesman for a minor party, reflecting the nationalists' greater skill at courting the London-based media and London's greater sensitivity to the singularities of the Scottish dimension[3] (see Table 7.3).

Despite the prominence of personality politics, all networks were at pains to 'cover the issues'. On the day the Conservative and Labour manifestos were launched, *Channel Four News* gave them 23 minutes 30 seconds and the *Nine o'Clock News* 28 minutes 45 seconds – remarkable lengths in television news terms. Even *News at Ten*, with far less space, gave them 11 minutes. All channels also offered briefings on the major issues, comparing the parties' records and promises, frequently with assessments from independent experts. They also explored many of the issues further in a variety of ways, ranging from the briefest of interviews on the shorter bulletins, to lengthy discussions on the more spacious programmes and nightly extended interviews by David Dimbleby in the *Nine o'Clock News*.

This was not always as easy as it sounded. What 'the issue' was at

Table 7.3 Politicians quoted in radio and television news (number of times)

Conservative	BBC1	ITV	C4	R4	Total	Labour	BBC1	ITV	C4	R4	Total
Thatcher	140	116	47	118	421	Kinnock	147	144	59	131	481
Tebbit	46	38	16	39	139	Hattersley	26	30	10	29	95
Lawson	26	23	7	22	78	Gould	27	19	9	17	72
Younger	12	8	7	8	35	Healey	12	9	6	13	40
Baker	10	12	7	6	35	Smith	9	4	5	8	26
Young	14	7	2	5	28	Meacher	11	5	2	7	25
Hurd	7	9	3	5	24	Kaufman	9	7	3	3	22
Heseltine	8	4	3	4	19	Prescott	7	6	2	3	18
Fowler	8	1	2	9	20	Radice	3	3	2	4	12
Howe	5	2	4	3	14	47 others	38	20	22	18	98
Clarke	6	3	3	1	13						
Rifkind	7	–	–	3	10	*Alliance*					
McGregor	3	2	2	3	10	Owen	127	115	49	93	384
Parkinson	6	1	–	3	10	Steel	102	82	37	66	287
35 others	30	22	22	20	94	Williams	9	10	5	10	34
						Jenkins	9	8	5	6	28
Other parties						Pardoe	8	3	5	4	20
Wilson (SNP)	16	7	2	6	31	Bruce	10	6	1	2	19
Wigley (Plaid)	7	6	–	2	15	Ashdown	5	5	2	4	16
Powell (DUP)	2	1	1	3	7	Hughes	3	5	3	2	13
Robins (Green)	–	4	1	–	5	Meadowcroft	2	6	1	1	10
30 others	28	5	5	11	49	34 others	34	9	20	13	76

any one moment might be contentious, since every party was jockeying to promote its particular agenda and timetable. Occasionally there was agreement on 'the issue of the day'. Then, for 24 hours, law and order, say, was aired in every programme from breakfast to *Newsnight*, with Douglas Hurd, Gerald Kaufman and Shirley Williams careering from one studio to another reciting their pieces until another day and another issue took over. However, all the agreed major issues reappeared several times during the campaign.

The losers were the Alliance. They had gained equal news time as the somewhat illogical consequence of being given equality in party election broadcasts; but their distinctive policies, like proportional representation and devolution, were never generally accepted as issues, could not be imposed as 'issue of the day', and were relatively neglected. One day David Steel was even reduced to displaying a prompt card of questions he hoped journalists would raise at the other parties' news conferences. Even the larger parties could not always impose their priorities. Labour statements on women, science and technology and the arts attracted little or no coverage – sometimes because they were upstaged by the party's own photo-opportunities. However, Labour also scored the greatest triumph of the campaign. On the day it was to feature the health service it primed television that it would be raising the case of Mark Burgess, a ten-year-old boy whose hole in the heart operation had been postponed several times. Few could have been unaffected by the reports that followed on every bulletin. Caught completely unprepared, the Conservatives saw their hopes of making pensions the issue that day swept aside. They recited their statistics about hospital waiting lists and the Prime Minister suggested that the parents might write to their MP, but this was feeble stuff. 'Exploiting the sick', muttered some, but Labour knew they had scored a media coup – one they never managed to repeat.

Over the campaign all the issues on which the two larger parties agreed to join battle received substantial coverage. As Table 7.1 shows, their preoccupations had changed considerably since 1983. Foreign affairs had all but vanished apart from disarmament (classed here with defence). Britain's relations with Europe had at last disappeared from the agenda; so had inflation. In their place were education, taxation (with Nigel Lawson's assault on Labour in the final week), speculation about a hung parliament (which faded as Alliance prospects flagged), and law and order, once a Conservative preserve, but now an issue on which Labour believed it could gain ground. Some other issues reached the news surprisingly rarely. Despite attempts by Labour and the Alliance to raise housing and local government finance little was heard of them in the news, although both were the subject of controversial proposals touching the lives of millions.

It was a post-election cliché that Labour won the campaign even if it lost the election. Yet the foremost issue in the news was defence, very much a Conservative plus. While employment, education and the NHS were generally seen as Labour strengths, they were not inherent winners. This emerges most clearly from the election lead stories set out in Table 7.4. A measure of caution is essential. For whatever reason, possibly to disarm factious critics, not a few bulletins led on one story in the opening headlines and another in their election package. *Channel Four News* had a particular weakness for defensively convoluted 'intros'. So judgements about the 'real' lead are to some extent subjective. Nevertheless, it seems clear enough that, for all the meticulous counting of seconds in the newsrooms, the news more often opened with Conservative initiatives or Labour rebuttals than the converse. The Alliance tended to be marginalised.

There was no evidence of a Labour victory in the battles over either issues or personalities. Labour's television campaign was admirably calculated to dispel the tabloids' image of a party red in

Table 7.4   Election leads in main evening news bulletins

Date	Rank	BBC1	Rank	ITN
May				
14	6	Thatcher: no complacency!	3	Polls disappoint Alliance
15	1	Thatcher attacks 'iceberg manifesto' and Alliance	1	Thatcher attacks Lab. defence policy
16	3	Healey: scrap Trident, Polaris	3	Polls: Con. lead cut
17	1	Steel attacks 'smears'	1	Steel attacks 'smears'
18	1	Alliance manifesto	1	Alliance manifesto: Kinnock, Tebbit react
19	1	Con., Lab. manifestos	1	Kinnock rally, Lab. manifesto
20	1	Thatcher addresses candidates	1	Hattersley: Con. employment record
21	1	Clash over Tebbit statement	1	Clash over Tebbit statement
22	1	Thatcher, Con. education plan	1	Tebbit: unemployment under 3m
23	2	Lawson costs Lab. programme	2	Lawson: Lab. means economic disaster
24	1	Alliance tactics unchanged	1	Alliance tactics unchanged
25	1	Owen, Thatcher attack Lab. defence policy	1	Younger, Owen attack Lab. defence policy
26	1	Con., Alliance attack Lab. on defence and extremism	1	Con., Alliance attack Lab. on defence and extremism
27	1	Kinnock reply on defence, Reagan backs Thatcher	1	Reagan on Lab. defence policy, Healey reaction
28	1	Thatcher rally: attacks Lab. on defence	1	Thatcher, Owen attack Lab. on defence
29	2	Healey: Thatcher sabotages arms agreement	2	Thatcher campaigning
30	2	Con. attack switches to Lab. economic policy	3	Polls: gap narrows
31	2	Kinnock: Thatcher *is* an issue	2	Kinnock: Thatcher *is* an issue
June				
1	2	Young: Lab. means unemployment	3	Tebbit: Lab. controlled by TUC
2	1	Thatcher on union laws	1	Kinnock on North–South divide
3	3	Con. support slipping?	1	Alliance divisions over hung parliament bargaining
4	3	Kinnock, Owen attack Thatcher on private health care	3	Kinnock, Owen attack Thatcher on private health care
5	1	Thatcher answers critics of her style	1	Kinnock appeal to undecided
6	2	Lawson attacks Lab. on tax	2	Lawson attacks Lab. on tax
7	1	Party rallies	1	Party rallies
8	1	Thatcher in Venice: opposition scepticism	1	Thatcher in Venice: opposition scepticism
9	1	Venice/Thatcher's final rally: 'reach for greatness'	1	Thatcher: Venice endorsed her policies/final rally
10	1	Kinnock: last day of Thatcher	1	Kinnock: last day of Thatcher

tooth and claw. Neil Kinnock was presented as a decent, reassuring figure. Here was a man with none of Margaret Thatcher's less attractive features – but neither did he display any of her undoubted strengths – strengths which many might have come to look for in a Prime Minister since 1979.

The news of course covered more than personalities and policies.[4] About 10% was concerned with either polls or assertions about party prospects. Hardly an evening went by without mention of the next morning's newspaper polls. Presentation was as alarmingly variable as ever. At one end of the scale were bewildering comparisons between new polls and old polls, and national, regional and marginal polls, sometimes presented helter-skelter with alarming unsophistication. At the other, Peter Snow commented at considerable length in the *Nine o'Clock News*, combining a torrent of computer graphics with his mildly manic enthusiasm. Channel 4 also made a serious attempt to trace the underlying message of the polls with its own commentators and academic experts. It also polled three marginal seats, Dudley West, Cheltenham and Calder Valley on issues as well as party preference. Here as elsewhere there was a marked reticence about tactical voting, discussion of which was barred on television, due mainly to editorial anxiety about running foul of electoral law.

Both *Channel Four News* and the *Nine o'Clock News* also tried hard to guide viewers through the counter-claims and crosscurrents of the campaign. John Cole, Elinor Goodman and David Walter showed that the inhibitions of election broadcasting did not entirely preclude pointed, enlightening commentary. Many of the feature items also tried to make sense of a kaleidoscopic scene through regional and constituency surveys, reports on parties' attempts to woo the young or the ethnic vote, and pieces on the changing techniques of manipulation. Channel 4 also commissioned commentaries from American and Russian correspondents. The man from Novosti observed austerely that we had a 'bizarre' way of choosing leaders. These were serious matters, 'not to be done in the atmosphere of a Punch and Judy show'.

Yet there was much more to the coverage than that. *Election Platform* on Radio 4 and *On The Hustings* on BBC2 carried nightly extracts from speeches running anything up to 12 minutes. These showed that the traditional election speech was not entirely dead, even if only the question and answer sessions by the two Davids contained any true whiff of the hustings. They provided a glimpse of Denis Healey at his most exuberant on disarmament, proof that Nigel

Lawson really was as pedestrian as report had it, Roy Jenkins's eloquent assault on the parochialism of the campaign, and minor party leaders at greater length than anywhere else. Whether viewers who could sit through more than 60 seconds of political speech should have had to wait until midnight was another matter. Three radio news analysis programmes backed up hard news coverage. *Today*, *The World at One* and *PM* carried a similar mix of reports, briefings and discussions to television – though, like radio generally, in markedly lower key; the most 'upmarket' of the daily programmes, *The World Tonight* dealt almost entirely with foreign stories. Television's principal heavyweight offering was *Newsnight*, more systematic and thoughtful than in 1983, when it had tended to rush, underprepared, into the issue of the day. Half-hour interview/debates, with expert comment and analysis on issues like taxation, industrial policy, or the future of the welfare state were the centre-pieces, and *Newsnight* provided almost the only detailed explanation and discussion of the community charge at national level. A challenging report on the NHS also showed that, here at least, recent bruising encounters between the Corporation and the Conservatives had not induced a loss of nerve. Peter Snow regularly analysed the polls and David Sells's sketch of the campaign showed that even election reporting can be witty and pointed. His description of the Alliance leaders 'locked in this marriage of convenience, ruthlessly together' was one of many such lines.

This was breakfast television's first full-scale campaign. News at that time of day was mainly a dreary rehash of the previous evening's (or even morning's) clips, and speculation about the day ahead. TV-am's rolling poll deserved the presentation booby prize, especially for its assertion on 21 May that 'TV-am's poll predicts the Tories will lose their overall majority'. It offered a mix of interviews with showbiz personalities, politicians' wives and party spokesmen discussing the issue of the day. Inexperience was most probably at the root of the sharpest clash between a politician and a broadcaster in the entire campaign. Invited to discuss the Venice Summit, Denis Healey found himself being interrogated by Anne Diamond on a splash in that morning's *Sun* about Mrs Healey's private hip operation two years earlier. He answered several questions calmly and clearly. When she persisted at such length as to displace *Popeye* from the schedule he stalked off the set amid pungent imprecations and some pushing and shoving. Such tenacious questioning merited less shop-soiled a cause.

BBC1's *Breakfast Time* also ruffled feathers, but Jeremy Paxman's sharp questioning was directed to more central political concerns. The programme shed an interesting light on the campaign when it called on John Lloyd, at 7.10 one morning, to report 'the feeling' at Labour headquarters. Back came the reply, 'There's no one here to express the feeling' – the building was deserted. Moments later Conservative Central Office was seen to be similarly empty. *Breakfast Time* staged outside broadcasts on unemployment, the health service and education, with, for example, doctors, nurses and patients at Yarm Hospital discussing the state of the health service and questioning party spokesmen.

This was one among many examples of how, with leaders hemmed in by security and, apart from the two Davids, speaking mainly to stage-managed rallies of the faithful, only broadcasting gave ordinary voters a voice or linked them in dialogue with the politicians. Channel 4's *Election Comment* featured people discussing the election in a remarkable range of settings – from a Glasgow snooker club to a Carlisle hairdressing salon, a hill farm and a vicarage garden. Brief though it was, these were real people expressing a wider range of popular speech than television usually catches, like the lady under the hairdryer saying of Margaret Thatcher, 'She's done everything in her power to get this country where it is – rock bottom'. Authentic voices were also a feature of *Election Call*, on BBC1 and Radio 4. Only a handful of the 140 000 callers got through to the politicians, many exchanges were predictable, but danger was never too far away. Sometimes callers were better briefed than the politicians; John Wakeham revealed his ignorance of moves in Brussels that might broaden the basis of VAT. He was also unfortunate enough to meet a lady from the North-East who countered his comfortable generalisations about living stardards with the problems of a low-wage household that had not had an evening out for four years or a holiday for eight. This minor fiasco gave the Conservatives a jolt at the beginning of the campaign. John Smith fared little better at the hands of an old soldier who was invincibly sceptical about Labour defence policy.

Other opportunities for voters to challenge politicians included BBC1's *On The Spot*, with viewers in provincial studios questioning party leaders down the line, three sessions in *Channel Four News* in which a panel from three marginal seats questioned party leaders, and ITV programmes like Granada's *Election 500*, *Central Choice* and Yorkshire's *Calendar Election 87*.[5] *Question Time*, with Robin

Day and a panel of politicians again offered another form of democratic dialogue, with both vigour and courtesy.

Of the heavyweight national programmes, *World in Action* was committed to a twentieth anniversary celebration of the Beatles and Sergeant Pepper and joined the election for only the final *Granada 500*. *This Week* and *Panorama* opted for the 'traditional' straight interviews with party leaders. These very necessary occasions – the opposition challenge to a 'great debate' having been ritually issued and as ritually rejected – added little to knowledge of either leaders or policies on this occasion. The Prime Minister, below her best, seemed determined to tax her questioners with personally holding any viewpoint she disliked before slipping into her standard responses. Neil Kinnock repeatedly slipped into a fuzzy verbosity which made well-meaning attempts to answer appear evasive. And the two Davids showed that two-headed leadership had one advantage; when the questioning was tricky, one could think while the other sparred. *The Week in Politics*, *Weekend World* and *This Week, Next Week* offered what can by now be termed 'the usual mix' of attempts to lay bare the forces swaying the voters and long pieces on major issues with expert help. *This Week, Next Week* billed itself as 'an election programme with a difference', the difference being its concentration on analysing the campaign with the aid of political journalists and practitioners. Critics deplored this diversion from the issues. Yet there was a case for television providing viewers with greater insight into the ways in which the parties were attempting to influence them. If the programme had a fault it was that, for all its flavour of cynical, clinical insider talk, and outspokenness about soft targets like the Alliance's first election broadcast, it pulled more punches than it landed.

In all this there was one great contrast with 1983. Then every programme felt it must interview the party leaders. Senior figures in both the BBC and ITV felt a more balanced and varied diet was called for in 1987. As it happened, the Conservatives wanted to ease the pressure on the Prime Minister; they were ahead in the polls and had not forgotten her bruising television encounter with a lady who challenged her account of the sinking of the *Belgrano*. The result was a sharp fall in interviews with the party leaders, and Norman Tebbit represented the Conservatives on several 'leader-level' occasions, such as *On The Spot*. Uncertainty over Conservative participation almost caused the cancellation of the final *Granada 500*, which finally went ahead with Norman Tebbit. The Conservatives also wanted him to take their last *Election Call*, but reluctantly put up Mrs Thatcher when the BBC made it clear that otherwise the final programme would go to Neil Kinnock by virtue of seniority. The party's jitters on 4 June produced some last minute changes of heart. The Prime Minister suddenly became available for interview by David Frost on TV-am. He had already interviewed Norman Tebbit at the start of the campaign, and a three-party discussion had been arranged for the final Sunday. However, few producers will turn down a Prime Minister. The discussion was cancelled; Mrs Thatcher had a cosy chat with Frost – one of the few interviewers, however, with the temerity to interrupt her – and TV-am ended the campaign with a bad case of imbalance. Labour made little attempt to capitalise on the Conservatives' reluctance to expose Mrs Thatcher, despite earlier taunts over Neil Kinnock's reluctance to face the London press. The Conservatives may have made the wise decision. Although the Prime Minister was as formidable as ever when on form, several of her slips in taking the morning news conferences attracted wide coverage, and she came within an ace of disaster in her interview with David Dimbleby on the eve of poll, with an ill-phrased stab at people who 'just drool and drivel they care', for which she apologised three times over.

Much has been said about broadcasting's tendency to presidentialise campaigns. The unremitting concentration of top-of-the-bulletin reporting on the four leaders has already been demonstrated. But the other side of the coin passed unnoticed – that vast output of feature material further down the bulletins and in news analysis programmes in which the leaders were featured little, if at all. *Newsnight*, for one, was almost entirely populated by ministers and their shadows. It was as if one was watching a different election, where issues took precedence over personalities, and cabinet government looked plausible after all. Presidentialism and personality politics are not the inherent forms of television campaigning. If they come to seem so, that lies at the door of politicians and broadcasters, not of the medium itself.

In television's early days party election broadcasts (PEBs) were its sole contribution to the campaign. Since then their role has dwindled to vestigial proportions. Yet in 1987 a party broadcast, a Labour one at that, furnished the most discussed incident in the campaign.

It opened with a warplane streaking across the sky, switching to a seagull soaring effortlessly, backed by the muted strains of the party's

Independent, 22 May 1987

theme from Brahms's first symphony. Distant figures, soon revealed as Neil and Glenys Kinnock walked hand in hand across a sunny headland, with Neil Kinnock voicing over his belief that the strong should help the weak. There followed an illustrated account of the Labour leader's modest origins, school days, and early career, his commentary alternating with soft-focus soliloquy, admiring comments from Aunt Sadie and Uncle Bill, and endorsements from Jim Callaghan, Barbara Castle, Denis Healey and John Smith, before returning to Neil and Glenys gazing out over the ocean, that seagull again, and a shot of Westminster with the Labour rose and a single word – KINNOCK.

Fascinating for connoisseurs of iconography and Labour history, the programme was written by Colin Welland, directed by Hugh (*Chariots of Fire*) Hudson, scored by Michael (*Mona Lisa*) Kamer with some help from Brahms and Beethoven; it was produced by John Gau Productions, which had overall responsibility for the Labour series, with additional input from Labour's 'shadow agency' of advertising and marketing experts. It presented a decent man, rooted in family and communal values profoundly at variance with Mrs Thatcher's. The consecration by party elders was clearly aimed at deflecting criticism of his inexperience and demonstrating his courage and resolution – though Denis Healey's remark that, like Mr Gorbachev, he had 'steel teeth' was not entirely happy. A declaration of his love for his country equally obviously had an eye to inevitable attacks on his unilateralism, while a clip of his conference onslaught on Militant demonstrated his toughness and parried attacks on the strength of the 'loony left'.

Steeped in the idiom and imagery of television commercials, making at least a nod to the 'Nancy-'n'-Ron' weepie of the last Republican campaign, the film nevertheless transcended its borrowings. If some on the left were furious, most of the party were delighted. It won the rare bonus of being quoted in mainstream news coverage, and the unique accolade of Conservative complaints about Labour's 'glossy packaging'. Neil Kinnock's popularity was said to have jumped 16 points in the polls overnight. It gave Labour morale a tremendous boost, and demonstrated that this was a new style of Labour campaign that would deploy every trick in the media game with unswerving professionalism. Essentially it was a stunning invocation of the Labourism of the 1940s by the media techniques of the 1980s. For all its technical brilliance, though, its implicit defensiveness was revealing of the party's underlying weakness. To focus so deliberately on an internal dispute smacked of desperation as well as audacity. And its single-minded promotion of the leader at such cost to Labour tradition spoke volumes about the failure – in the face of a mainly hostile press – to establish him securely over the three preceding years, and about the party's vulnerability on policy. Nevertheless, it was surely this broadcast more than any that led to 36% of those polled by Mass Observation saying that Labour had 'the best PEBs', compared with 25% nominating the Conservatives and only 6% the Alliance.

Labour's next two programmes were more orthodox. Both presented a succession of consumers and practitioners to drive home Labour's 'strong' policies in health and education. The health programme scored particularly by presenting sufferers with whom viewers could readily identify, particularly the young couple describing the night when no respirator could be found for their desperately sick baby, and the man who had waited five years under the NHS for the operation on his hand Mrs Thatcher had had done privately. The fourth programme was to have been on unemployment, but was scrapped in favour of an unprecedented rerun 'by popular demand' of the opening broadcast. Repetition is of course the very stuff of advertising campaigns, but it was curious to jettison a programme on what was ostensibly the party's prime issue and give Conservatives the chance to jibe that it had run out of ideas. It was not in fact a straight repeat; a brief clip of Neil Kinnock with the shadow cabinet had been hastily stitched in, and in place of that audacious closing 'KINNOCK' was a more orthodox 'LABOUR'.

The final broadcast was curiously broken-backed. The first part tilted satirically at Margaret Thatcher. A montage of stills and Scarfe cartoons chronicled the disasters of the Thatcher years (parodying a triumphalist sequence in a Conservative broadcast), with Willie Rushton and others singing 'A Regular Royal Queen' from *The Gondoliers*. On the night of the Venice Summit this harmlessly topical piece of political fun was aimed at the many people Labour's research had suggested were wavering because of Mrs Thatcher. Whatever the effect on them, reaction within the party was mixed, and there was a jarring change of pace and mood as the programme moved to a more traditional sequence of speakers dealing rapidly with unemployment, welfare and defence, in clips interspersed with soothing 'muzak', reminders of the opening broadcast, and increasingly confident snatches of Brahms. Neil Kinnock's final call for 'one nation' ran under 30 seconds. A series which had so exalted the leader, ended without him once speaking direct to camera.

What the Labour broadcasts had, and the Conservative broadcasts lacked, was unity of style and strategy with the party's main campaign. Presenting their manifesto, the Conservatives claimed to be a radical party brimming with ideas for their third term. However, their broadcasts, produced by Jeremy Sinclair of Saatchis, said nothing about the future, concentrating on the Conservatives' achievements and Labour's failures. The first broadcasts drew on well-tried devices from earlier series with a measure of verbal and visual audacity that was remarkable even by the standards of election broadcasting. Their first broadcast epitomised the technique. A couple with their children in a sunny meadow backed by the party's theme music – Jupiter from the Planets – known also as 'I Vow to Thee My Country', by Gustav Holst (an early socialist). If 'we' have a fault, ran the narration, it was that respect for freedom led to a tolerance allowing 'imported ideologies like Marxism and its step-brother Socialism to creep into our thinking. These ideas are foreign to our nature'. So much for 150 or so years of British Socialist thought. 'We are a proud nation of individuals. We flourish under freedom', it continued over magnificent film of the climbing of Everest – so eye-catching that memory seemed churlish in recalling that Tensing was Nepalese and Hillary was a New Zealander. The remainder of the programme drove home the ways in which the Conservatives had extended freedom and the 'facts' of economic success – a barrage of international comparisons selected with such care and precision as to convey the impression that Britain was out-performing the world. A punchy presentation, but incapable of resisting overkill.

The second programme began with pictures of Neil Kinnock and a snatch of Brahms, making the unwary wonder whose broadcast they were watching. John Moore soon made it clear. Behind Labour's glossy packaging, he warned, the party was more extreme than ever. Quotations from a familiar rogue's gallery headed by Bernie Grant and Ken Livingstone were followed by clips of the excesses of 'loony left' councils, some of the more sinister-sounding parts of the Labour manifesto, and even the Alliance's list of 101 hard-left Labour candidates. A caricature, of course, but well-pitched political pamphleteering calculated to give pause to anyone reassured by Neil Kinnock.

The third programme again assailed Labour, this time devising a stagey magician, personifying Labour's approach to the economy, and producing a succession of new 'tricks' from his hat to solve the nation's problems – none of which worked. Its crudity was a reminder of why party broadcasts have a bad name. The second half celebrated the Prime Minister as world leader. It made the legitimate point that she had immense experience while Neil Kinnock had none by means of the longest non-verbal sequence in the history of party broadcasting, with 29 clips running almost $2^1/_2$ minutes, and a freshly-minted Andrew Lloyd Webber composition that could have served as a coronation anthem. Neil Kinnock had had his apotheosis; now Margaret Thatcher had hers.

The third programme, on defence, argued that the deterrent had kept the peace for 40 years, and that the Conservatives' resolute policies had finally brought the Russians to the negotiating table. With its single theme and relatively restrained presentation, it was the more telling. The final broadcast was entirely the Prime Minister's. It began with clips from her speeches to the Conservative conference, incorporating brief reminders of the Falklands spirit and the Brighton bomb, culminating in a vibrant peroration which was all but drowned by 'I Vow To Thee My Country'. A closing five-minute talk to camera, in a drawing-room set, reworked the party's principal themes: freedom, peace and the economy, in her softest and most persuasive tones. It was not one of her best performances, shot among the bustle before her departure for Venice, but it was competent enough. She was less well served technically. In her black dress she merged with the pools of darkness in a murky set, while the lighting changed her hair a curious reddish hue.

The Conservatives had hit hard and often; the Alliance seemed uncertain quite what their target was. Scripted by David Abbot of Abbot, Mead, Vickers and produced by Justin Cartwright Associates, their first programme featured Rosie Barnes, the recent victor at Greenwich. Opening with her two-year-old daughter feeding her rabbit, and shot in short takes with ultra-soft focus, like a Timotei shampoo advertisement, it had Mrs Barnes talking to an unseen, unheard interviewer about why she went into politics and the attractions of the Alliance. Although the broadcast was not as technically poor as some critics would have it, its real weakness was that Mrs Barnes meandered with well-meaning diffuseness but to no clear purpose, and the freshness and political innocence she evoked were at variance with the kind of campaign the Alliance seemed to be fighting on the nightly news.

In earlier times the Liberals had scored through the simplicity and directness of their broadcasts. Now they forgot these virtues. Pieces to camera by the two Davids and Shirley Williams were shot against a muddy-grey background; David Steel's closing appeal was so under-lit that few would have bought a used car from him. David Owen was twice shown talking to yet another unseen, unheard interviewer, his eyes never once meeting the viewer's. All four remaining broadcasts emphasised the failings of the 'old' parties and the electoral credibility of an Alliance vote. Given the message of the polls these may have been the most sensible priorities, but it was surprising that a party which was aware how little the voters knew about its policies made so little attempt to explain them – an omission tantamount to conceding defeat. In 1987 the third party had at last won equal broadcasting time with the larger parties – only to fail to profit from its opportunity.[6]

If all party broadcasts are in a sense commercials, this must be particularly true of those by minor parties which have no realistic hope of returning candidates but are building for the future. Given the political stance of the Greens their single five-minute broadcast might have consisted of unadorned pieces to camera. It was in fact a fully professional production which opened on a striking visual sequence of children's crayoned drawings of war, devastation, poverty and pollution before a series of simpler clips of party spokespersons setting out its main policies.

For all the reverberations of the Kinnock broadcast, and the efforts every party put into these television productions, broadcasting's main contribution remained that vast output the parties did not directly control but sought so energetically to influence with every stratagem at their command. Inevitably there were accusations of bias and newspapers prepared to give space to critics like Lord Chalfont, who, lacking firmer grounds, unerringly discerned dangerous leftism in the flicker of an eyebrow or a hint of a smile. In party headquarters more reasonable counsels reigned. Despite their tireless monitoring of the output there were no really serious clashes between them and the broadcasters during the campaign, just minor brushes and the unremitting tug of interests. The Conservatives had been anxious that the three-way division of airtime would put them in a constant two-against-one minority. However, although this did happen sometimes in audience participation programmes like *Granada 500*, it was much less marked elsewhere. Labour and the Alliance certainly joined against the Conservatives over the NHS or education, but

Labour suffered comparably over defence and taxation, while both
the other parties patronised the Alliance.

The public's reaction to the coverage was somewhat mixed – though
less antipathetic than early press reports suggested. Viewing was 1%
below the corresponding four weeks in 1986 and 4% less than in the
four weeks preceding the campaign. The audience for the main
evening news on BBC1 and ITV dropped more substantially, by
some 3 millions. A fortnight before polling, a BBC–IBA survey
found 65% of those who had seen some coverage saying the election
was getting 'too much' or 'far too much' time. By the end of the
campaign this had risen to 72%. However, far fewer thought
there had been too much discussion of policies than of politicians'
personalities or the polls. Only 16% still wanted to learn more about
the issues compared with 77% saying that they knew enough. 60%
of those who had seen television said that 'a great deal' or 'a fair
amount' could be learned from it, against 46% naming newspapers,
28% radio – and 50% the much-maligned party broadcasts. How
much they actually learned was less certain. The survey asked people
to match 11 policy statements to the appropriate party. Even after
so intense an electioneering barrage 9 were wrongly attributed by a
third or more of the respondents.

Most people – around 70% – felt the BBC, ITV and Channel Four
had treated all the parties fairly. Channel Four was the most widely
perceived as fair. The discontented minority was drawn from all
parties, but seemed somewhat more likely to be Conservative and to
suspect bias in the BBC rather than in the other networks. Around
half the complainants felt that BBC and ITV television coverage had
favoured the Conservatives. Somewhat fewer – between a quarter
and a third – felt that Labour had been favoured.[7]

Nevertheless, when asked to compare the election coverage of the
various media outlets (see Table 7.5) far more people mentioned
television as informative, interesting, providing good coverage of
local issues (especially ITV) – and as unbiased and useful in helping
a voting decision – than any other source.

Radio and television's vast and varied contribution to the 1987
election cannot sensibly be drawn together in one summary verdict.
That some of the output was superficial, pusillanimous and even, on
occasion, an insult to the intelligence of all concerned, can scarcely
be denied. There were issues that might have been raised, questions
that might have been pressed, and complex problems that were left
unresolved. As always the networks' specialist correspondents, who

Table 7.5 National party election broadcasts

Conservative

19 May Contrasting alien socialism and winter of discontent with Conservative freeing of individual and economic achievement. Lawson, Howe, Young.

27 May Moore contrasts glossy Lab. image with extremism of left and manifesto promises on law and order, nationalisation and defence.

2 June Attack on Lab. record on economy, NHS, education, industrial relations, nationalisation. Young, Thatcher: Con. have returned power to people. Celebratory montage of Thatcher's world role.

5 June NATO and the deterrent have kept the peace. Younger: Cruise brought Russians to negotiating table. Lab. leaves Britain vulnerable to nuclear blackmail, defenceless. Hopes of negotiated arms reduction.

9 June Thatcher conference clips: Decline not inevitable; attack on Lab. defence policy; terrorism will fail; vision of future. To camera: Setting spirit of Britain free. Prosperity allows more health, social security spending. Partnership with people in economy, law and order. Peace in industry, peace of mind, peace from independence, peace of proper defence. Heart and soul of Britain at stake.

Labour

21 May 4 June Impressionistic portrait of Kinnock through interviews, speech clips, informal shots and endorsements by Castle, Smith, Healey, Callaghan and relatives.

28 May Patients, nurse, ambulance driver, doctor illustrate NHS cuts. Kinnock attacks cuts. Lab. promises on NHS.

1 June Attack on Con. education record with clips of parents, teachers. Lab. plans. Kinnock clip on choice between past and future in education.

8 June Still sequence on Thatcher failures and scandals. Kinnock: waste of economic, human resources; we have commitment and energy. Smith: will cut unemployment. Hattersley: ask top 5% to help pensioners, families, unemployed. Kinnock on fear of crime, unemployment, speaking out; won't let anyone touch my country. Healey: need for disarmament. Kinnock: remove nuclear weapons, make welfare of each responsibility of all; one nation again.

Alliance

22 May Clips of Rosie Barnes in garden: why she came into politics, what the Alliance stands for.

26 May Williams, Jenkins and others challenge substance of Con. prosperity, waste of oil revenues; Lab. no better. Steel: originality of Alliance. Owen: Alliance speaks for all. Policies for young, old. Lab. is finished. Williams: Alliance *can* break through. Break with past now.

29 May	Steel: old values threatened; politics of envy, division. Politicians have failed. Alliance for *all* people, will heal divisions.
3 June	Owen: Consequences of Con. or Lab. victory, opportunity for something better. Trust us, you'll be amazed at what we can do.
7 June	Owen: Time for new spirit. Steel: Alliance is indivisible. Vox pops and celebrities on need for change, new policies, Alliance prospects. Owen: fight for weak. Steel attacks old parties. Alliance best vote you have.

Green

| 5 June | Children's images of destruction of environment. Lambert: Greens have answer. Kortvelyessy: Abolish nuclear weapons. Robins on weekly minimum for all. Lawson on alternative energy. Spaven advocates environment-friendly economy. Lambert: only Greens offer positive policies |

might have contributed so much to briefings or informed questioning were grievously underused. Yet there were also so many programmes that honourably illuminated, questioned, explained, and which did as much as one could reasonably hope within the limitations of a popular medium. The broadcasters could take pride in having given viewers the means of assessing Mrs Thatcher's views on private medicine and the NHS, in laying bare the tensions within the Alliance about how to respond to a hung parliament, in exploring the tenability of Labour's approach to disarmament, and much more. Nor should their role be underrated in joining voters and politicians. There are not all that many countries in which citizens can question a Prime Minister, however briefly, on air, and where her remark, 'If I could just make one more point . . .' can be greeted with a chorus of 'No!' – even if she did continue regardless! This was just one reminder of how much that is taken for granted in election broadcasting has been so hard won – and it raised the question of how such encounters will fare in the brave new world of deregulated broadcasting ahead.

NOTES

1. Detailed figures: BBC1 Lunchtime 58.4% (54.3 in 1983), early evening 51.3 (54.0), main evening 63.0 (51.6); ITN Lunchtime 49.0 (58.9), early

evening 49.0% (43.6), main evening 57.0% (57.9); Channel Four 72.5% (71.9); Radio (no comparisons available) 8.00 a.m. 30.0%; 1.00 p.m. 35.8%; 6.00 p.m. 38.1%; 10.30 p.m. 36.4%.

2. Percentages for the four weeks were: BBC1 55.0, 57.0, 59.7, 63.4; ITN 55.9, 56.7, 48.0, 47.3; Channel 4 73.9, 77.9, 64.8, 74.5; Radio 40.6, 35.2, 34.3, 37.6.

3. As in earlier studies, statistics relate either to the number of times a person was quoted or the time absorbed by these quotations. Relatively small amounts of material attributed generally to a party are not reckoned, nor are sequences, such as many photo-opportunities, containing no references to policy. The figures therefore understate the degree of 'presidentialisation'.

   There were substantial variations between channels. The four leaders took 50.0% of time given to quoting politicians on BBC1, 57.8% on Channel 4, 62.3% on Radio 4 and 66.4% on ITN. The more cramped the coverage the greater the concentration on leaders. Similarly with range; BBC1 quoted 116 different politicians, Channel 4 88, Radio 4 78 and ITN 67.

4. Radio was the most policy-oriented, with 69.2% of its output dealing with policies, compared with 54.4% on Channel 4, 55.1% on BBC1 and 60.6% on ITV. Radio bulletins normally left 'softer' items to their attendant news analysis programmes, concentrating on hard news of campaign exchanges.

5. ITV regional output was exceptionally large and varied. Most companies ran a series of late-evening specials. The Alliance was extremely hard pressed to keep these supplied with representatives of acknowledged standing. Both ITV and BBC1 covered the campaign intensively in their early evening news magazines, which the parties courted particularly assiduously, seeing them as soft targets with large audiences. One gem from Central featured that most urban and urbane of politicians, Gerald Kaufman, in green wellies, inaugurating a pig parlour. Even his ready wit failed to find words to capitalise on this incongruous occasion.

6. Labour and the Conservatives accepted without formal protest the broadcasters' decision to grant the Alliance equal time, but the SNP unsuccessfully sought a declaration from the Court of Session in Edinburgh that the two broadcasts it was allocated in Scotland did not comply with the IBA's statutory obligation to fairness and impartiality.

7. *The 1987 General Election*, BBC Broadcasting Research Special Projects, and IBA Research Department, September 1987.

8 Press
Martin Harrop

In the press, this was Mrs Thatcher's election. Not just because 7 out of 11 national daily newspapers supported her re-election; that was predictable and the endorsements were less fulsome than in 1983. The Prime Minister's triumph lay in the way her government's Industrial Relations Act had been exploited by newspaper proprietors since the last election to bring about a revolution in the production and distribution of their titles. In a perfect cameo of the enterprise culture, aggressive entrepreneurs had introduced new(ish) technology over the heads of reluctant trade unions. One immediate consequence was that by the time of the election most national papers had firm plans to move out of Fleet Street if indeed they had not already done so. It was the end of the Street.[1]

The key figures in this revolution were Eddie Shah and Rupert Murdoch. Eddie Shah made the breakthrough when his free-sheet publishing group won a hard-fought victory over the National Graphical Association at Warrington in July 1983. Inspired by this success, Shah launched a new national daily paper, *Today*, in March 1986. Using direct input of copy by journalists, colour presses, dispersed printing centres and non-print union labour, *Today* should have been an economical and flexible product. But it was also an editorial, and hence a commercial, flop. In August 1986 it was bought by Tiny Rowland's Lonrho group, publisher of the *Observer*, only to be sold again after the election to Rupert Murdoch.[2]

Eddie Shah did pave the way for fundamental changes taking place in Mr Murdoch's News International group. In January 1986, even before *Today's* launch, Rupert Murdoch had switched production of *The Times*, *Sun*, *Sunday Times* and *News of the World* to a new plant with a new work force in Wapping, East London. This blew apart the restrictive practices of Fleet Street. 'Wapping is a watershed, a great historic date in Fleet Street', said Lord Rothermere. 'There's Before Wapping and there's After Wapping. Nothing is the same'. Other proprietors were more incremental in their contacts with the print unions, but without Wapping these negotiations would have foundered and possibly never have started.

Efficient production reduces the entry costs of new papers. This was one factor in the launch of the *Independent* in October 1986, Britain's first new quality daily paper this century. The *Independent* was conceived with a professionalism wholly lacking in the case of *Today*. It quickly established a reputation for accuracy among its male, middle-class readership. But the road to commercial viability remains hard. Selling around 300 000 copies, the *Independent* was still not profitable by the time of the election.

Three new Sunday papers had been introduced since 1983. *Sunday Today* proved even less successful than its daily brother, and with a circulation of only 200 000 it ceased publication in the middle of the election campaign. *News on Sunday* had an equally difficult birth. Funded by trade unions and left-wing local authorities, this paper sought to provide a radical alternative to the rest of Fleet Street. Its launch in April 1987 was a disaster, marked by political infighting, inadequate marketing and pedestrian content. Beset by crises of finance, ownership and confidence, it surprised many by continuing to publish throughout the campaign. *Sunday Sport* was the only commercial success of the trio. Its diet of colour pin-ups and lively sports coverage soon attracted a circulation of around 500 000. It contained no news worth speaking about.

Developments in the London newspaper market confirmed that it is now easier to launch newspapers than to sell them. In February 1987 Robert Maxwell launched the *London Daily News*, an ambitious 24-hour paper. Five months later it ceased publication, killed by distribution difficulties, a revived *Evening Standard*, and the inspired, if temporary, relaunch of the *Evening News* by Lord Rothermere.

Against these dramas the three changes in the ownership of existing titles since the last election seem almost routine. First Robert Maxwell finally achieved his ambition of owning a national paper by purchasing Mirror Group Newspapers from Reed International in July 1984. Mr Maxwell said his papers would represent the sensible left, supporting a modern Britain. Secondly, United Newspapers, an expanding provincial newspaper group, bought the *Daily Express*, *Sunday Express* and *Daily Star* from Lord Matthews's Fleet Holdings in October 1985. Thirdly, Conrad Black, a Canadian businessman, acquired control of the *Daily Telegraph* and *Sunday Telegraph* in December 1985, after 60 years of ownership by the Berry family. Under Lord Hartwell, the Telegraph group had attempted a move into new technology which proved to be too expensive and too late. These three developments meant that a majority of the national dailies had changed hands in the 1980s; only the *Guardian*, the *Daily*

Mail and the *Financial Times* had the same owners in 1987 as 20 years earlier.

The main sales trend since 1983 was the continued gain of the qualities at the expense of the popular dailies (Table 8.1). Despite

Table 8.1   National daily newspapers

Name of paper Ownership group (Chairman) Editor Preferred result	Circulation[1] (1983 in brackets) ('000)	Readership[2] (1983 in brackets) ('000)	% of its readers in social class[3] (1983 in brackets)			
			AB	C1	C2	DE
Daily Mirror Pergamon Press (R. Maxwell) Ed. R. Stott Lab. victory	3 123 (3 267)	9 012 (10 400)	6 (7)	19 (18)	37 (40)	38 (36)
Daily Express United Newspapers (D. Stevens) Ed. N. Lloyd Con. victory	1 697 (1 936)	4 405 (5 608)	20 (21)	30 (27)	28 (30)	22 (22)
Sun News International (R. Murdoch) Ed. K. McKenzie Con. victory	3 993 (4 155)	11 316 (12 883)	6 (6)	18 (17)	35 (40)	41 (37)
Daily Mail Associated Newspapers Group (Viscount Rothermere) Ed. Sir D. English Con. victory	1 759 (1 834)	4,525 (5 271)	26 (26)	31 (30)	25 (26)	18 (18)
Daily Star United Newspapers (D. Stevens) Ed. L. Turner Con. victory	1 289 (1 313)	4 027 (4 588)	4 (5)	15 (13)	37 (42)	44 (40)
Today[4] Lonrho International (R. Rowland) Ed. D. Hackett Coalition	307	1 008	16	28	31	25
Daily Telegraph The Daily Telegraph plc (Lord Hartwell) Ed. M. Hastings Con. victory	1 147 (1 284)	2 775 (3 313)	53 (53)	28 (27)	12 (13)	7 (7)
Guardian The Guardian and Manchester Evening News (Scott Trust) (P. Gibbings) Ed. P. Preston Lab. victory	494 (417)	1 458 (1 453)	51 (48)	29 (28)	10 (15)	10 (9)

Name of paper Ownership group (Chairman) Editor Preferred result	Circulation[1] (1983 in brackets) ('000)	Readership[2] (1983 in brackets) ('000)	% of its readers in social class[3] (1983 in brackets)			
			AB	C1	C2	DE
The Times News International (R. Murdoch) Ed. C. Wilson Con. victory	442 (321)	1 216 (924)	55 (60)	28 (22)	8 (10)	8 (8)
Independent Newspaper Publishing (Lord Sieff) Ed. A. Whittam Smith No endorsement	293	816	48	32	12	8
Financial Times Pearson (Viscount Blakenham) Ed. G. Owen Con. victory	280 (161)	743 (711)	53 (53)	30 (30)	11 (11)	6 (6)

Notes
1. Average of ABC figures for Jan.–June 1987. *Morning Star* (circulation about 30 000) excluded.
2. Joint Industry Committee for National Readership Surveys (JICNAR), July 1986–June 1987 average.
3. JICNAR's definition classifies the population aged 15 and over as follows: AB (professional, administrative, managerial) – 17%; C1 (other non-manual) – 23%; C2 (skilled manual) – 28%; and DE (semi-skilled or unskilled, residual) – 32%.
4. *Today* was acquired by Rupert Murdoch's News International in July 1987.

the *Independent*, all the qualities except the *Daily Telegraph* increased their circulation. By 1987 the five qualities were selling half a million more copies than the four qualities had done in 1983. In the middle of the market the *Daily Mail* achieved its long-term goal of overtaking the *Daily Express*, though just by virtue of a slower decline. At the bottom end the *Sun* finally ceased to soar away, but this did not help either the *Daily Star* or the *Daily Mirror*, both of which also lost sales.

Table 8.2 presents the statistical bones of election coverage in the national dailies. This shows that the new papers fitted neatly into their niches, *Today* giving just a shade less coverage to the election than the *Daily Mail* and the *Daily Express* while the *Independent's* coverage was comparable in scope to the other qualities.

Compared to 1983, this was not a high-profile election in the press. All the papers except the *Sun* led less frequently on the campaign in 1987; indeed the *Daily Star* did not have a front-page election headline until three days before polling. The messages were still strident but they were shouted less loudly than in 1983.

In the press the central focus of this election was the Labour Party and its flaws. All the popular papers except the *Daily Mirror* gave

Table 8.2 Profile of press content, 18 May–11 June 1987

Press content	Daily Mirror	Daily Express	Sun	Daily Mail	Daily Star	Today	Daily Telegraph	Guardian	The Times	Independent
Mean number of pages (June 1983 in brackets)	33 (32)	41 (36)	32 (31)	41 (36)	30 (29)	44 (–)	37 (32)	33 (27)	43 (28)	30 (–)
Lead stories on election Number (22 days) (June 1983, 23 days)	9 (14)	18 (20)	11 (5)	15 (19)	3 (7)	13 (–)	16 (23)	18 (22)	16 (23)	19 (–)
Leading articles on election										
Number	14/22	27/31	27/54	29/39	14/42	21/29	24/43	31/55	22/55	25/40
Per cent	64	87	50	74	33	72	56	56	40	62
(June 1983 %)	(96)	(63)	(58)	(58)	(54)	(–)	(61)	(55)	(39)	(–)
Election coverage Column inches	5 859	7 985	4 973	7 400	4 743	6 515	9 431	14 762	14 366	12 900
Coverage of parties (%) (1983 in brackets)										
Conservative	48 (59)	40 (37)	22 (44)	35 (43)	34 (35)	32	31 (44)	36 (37)	34 (35)	35
Labour	44 (30)	44 (41)	73 (41)	54 (35)	46 (40)	36	39 (37)	32 (34)	34 (40)	35
Alliance	6 (9)	15 (16)	5 (13)	10 (18)	17 (16)	25	26 (15)	27 (19)	28 (16)	24
Other	1 (3)	1 (6)	– (2)	1 (4)	4 (9)	6	4 (4)	5 (10)	4 (9)	5
Opinion polls Agency	IFF Research	Marplan	Audience Selection	–	Programmes Opinion Research	Marplan	Gallup	Marplan	MORI	NOP
Poll coverage as a percentage of all election coverage (June 1983)	2.6 (0.6)	2.5 (3.7)	1.7 (6.6)	4.0 (3.5)	4.1 (6.9)	4.7 (–)	5.9 (3.2)	4.6 (4.7)	5.7 (3.1)	5.7 (–)

more of their coverage to Labour than to the Conservatives – and all gave more of their space to Labour this time than last. The *Sun* devoted three column inches of vitriol against Labour for every inch in defence of the Conservatives. Despite the Alliance's relatively healthy position in the polls at the start of the campaign, none of the tabloids significantly increased their coverage of the Alliance over 1983 levels. Overall the ratio of coverage for Conservative, Labour and Alliance in the popular press was 5:6:3.

The qualities were more balanced. Except for the *Daily Telegraph*, which also concentrated on Labour's defects, the quality dailies gave no more coverage to Labour than to the Conservatives. They also gave more attention to the Alliance this time than in 1983, another contrast with the tabloids. In the qualities the ratio of coverage for Conservatives, Labour and Alliance was 5:5:4. This distribution was agreed for television in the last election but was less favourable to the Alliance than the 5:5:5 split on television in the 1987 campaign. The ratios in the quality press strongly suggest that the Alliance received more coverage on television than was justified by news values alone.

In terms of photographs of politicians, the two main parties received rough equality of treatment, with the Alliance lagging behind (Table 8.3). The patterns here reveal some evidence of a more presidential campaign. Mr Owen and Mr Steel provided a far higher proportion of Alliance photographs than Mr Jenkins and Mr Steel had done in 1983. For Labour, the presidential theme is captured not by more emphasis on the leader (though photographs of Mr Kinnock certainly projected a more purposeful image than Mr Foot achieved last time) but by Mrs Kinnock's success in the photographic charts. She came second only to her husband in the list of most frequently photographed Labour figures. The numerous photographs of Mrs Thatcher at the Venice Summit also conveyed a statesmanlike, presidential flavour, even if the Grand Canal was not available as background.

To ascertain how the Conservative press views an election, consult the big, bold headlines on the best-selling *Sun*. The *Sun's* coverage was basic, bigoted and brilliant. Basic because its main theme was the incompetence of the Labour Party – its Marxist ideology, its loony lefties, its fantasy defence policy, its windbag leader, and its indebtedness to robber baron union bosses. Bigoted because the *Sun* not only made hay with any scandal it could find about Labour politicians, but also linked the party as a whole with sexual minorities:

Table 8.3   *Photographs of leading party politicians in national dailies*

Politician	14 May–9 June, 1983	18 May–11 June, 1987
Conservative	335 (36% of total)	509 (39% of total)
Margaret Thatcher	125 (37% of Conservative)	196 (39% of Conservative)
Tebbit		38
Baker		20
Denis Thatcher		20
Lawson		19
Heseltine		18
Currie		15
Other		184
Labour	324 (35% of total)	525 (40% of total)
Neil Kinnock	17 (5% of Labour)	175 (33% of Labour)
Glenys Kinnock		38
Healey		37
Hattersley		31
Livingstone		18
Grant		17
Gould		15
Other		194
Foot	104 (32% of Labour)	
Alliance	225 (24% of total)	245 (19% of total)
Owen	22 (10% of Alliance)	79 (32% of Alliance)
Steel	48 (21% of Alliance)	78 (32% of Alliance)
Williams		14
Jenkins	40 (18% of Alliance)	6
Other		68

'LABOUR USES GAY JIMI TO WIN OVER YOUNG VOTERS' and 'LABOUR PICKS RENT BOY AS SCHOOL BOSS'. Brilliant because this was all presented with a verve which no other paper could match. Only the *Sun* could launch a 'SPECIAL NIGHTMARE ISSUE – LIFE UNDER THE SOCIALISTS. SEE P.5, 6, 8, 9 AND 13'. Only the *Sun* could announce that p. 3 would be banned under Labour: 'THE LOVELIEST GIRLS ARE IN THE SUN – BUT ONLY UNDER THE CONSERVATIVES'. Only the *Sun* could dream up 'WHY I'M BACKING KINNOCK, BY STALIN'. How-ever, much of the *Sun's* coverage was audacious to the point of caricature, thus possibly reducing whatever impact it had on its readers.

The *Daily Mirror* lacked the *Sun's* extravagance, but still fought its weightiest campaign for many a year. It covered individual issues in a neat three-part format: what the Tories promised, what has happened, what Labour will do. The selection of issues highlighted the *Daily Mirror's* theme of divided Britain and, of course, Labour's own agenda. Whereas the *Sun* invited readers to say how much profit they had made from buying their council house, the *Daily Mirror* invited people to ring in with examples of Tory heartlessness.

Occasionally the *Daily Mirror's* coverage became routine, as with photographs of decaying cities which could have been taken at any time since the invention of the camera. At other times its headlines were excessive: 'THOUSANDS OF DISABLED PEOPLE FACE DEATH BECAUSE OF BENEFIT CUTS'. But its front page editorial on 10 June was powerful:

> The Conservative Party exists to preserve its privileges. That is what it was created for. That is its historic role. The Labour Party was created to fight privilege, the degradation of poverty, the humiliation of unemployment, the misery of the slums. That is its historic duty.

Echoing the 'VOTE FOR HIM' campaign of 1945 ('he' being the exhausted serviceman), *Daily Mirror* readers were invited to 'VOTE FOR THEM – the old, the young, the sick'. Throughout the campaign, the *Daily Mirror's* election coverage drew strength from its own traditions but, in so doing, failed to establish a new style for the future.

Compared with the *Sun* and the *Daily Mirror*, the *Daily Star* was less politicised and less partisan. True, there was a clear Conservative tone to its limited campaign coverage, culminating in a signed leader from the editor on election day:

> If Kinnock's bandwagon rolls to success, it will mean more borrowing, higher taxes, the return of undemocratic trade union power and a halt to the property-owning, share-owning democracy. You can't overcome social problems if you are bankrupt. Mrs Thatcher is the only leader who can take us forward.

But there was at least an attempt at balance: Labour MP Joe Ashton continued his column and Ken Livingstone was given a chance to air his views. Inside the *Daily Star's* Manchester offices a good popular newspaper was still struggling to emerge.

In the middle of the market, the *Daily Mail* and the *Daily Express* continued their traditional role as defenders of the Conservative faith. Both papers made some play with the contrasting styles of the party leaders. In the *Daily Express*, the formidable Jean Rook portrayed Mrs Thatcher as 'Mega Maggie – the kind of neighbour who, if the roof fell in, would hold up the ceiling with one hand while she dialled emergency with the other'. The 'bawling boyo', on the other hand, was a prisoner of the unions:

watch mangy caged lions like Scargill crouching again to roar, claw
back and slit a recovering nation's throat. And where would rose-
cheeked, sweet-smelling Nice Guy Neil end up if he got in on June
11? Firmly clamped between their teeth.

Ms Rook notwithstanding, political leadership was less important in
the *Daily Mail* and the *Daily Express* in 1987 than 1983. These papers
correctly judged that Mrs Thatcher's position was not as strong as
last time while Mr Kinnock's image was infinitely better than Mr
Foot's.

If in doubt, run a red scare. This traditional maxim of the Tory
press was followed by the *Daily Mail* and the *Daily Express*. Labour's
extremism was the insistent theme of both papers. They made a large
contribution to photographs of Ken Livingstone and Bernie Grant
appearing in the press more often than any other Labour politicians
except Kinnock, Hattersley and Healey (Table 8.3 on p. 169). The
Daily Express in particular took extremism to extremes. 'OUR
CONSPIRACY, BY RED KEN' was its front-page headline on 22
May, followed the next day by 'NEIL DENIES TRUTH ABOUT
LEFT PLOT'. Militants, gays, educational lunatics, unilateral
disarmers – all were presented as alien, dominant elements in the
Labour Party. 'Labour is today more extremist than it has ever been',
pronounced the *Daily Express* on 9 June. 'Fighting this election is
the largest collection of left-wing nasties West of the Berlin Wall.
Kinnock will be their prisoner in the Commons'. On election day the
Daily Express finally turned its attention to the positive virtues of
the government: the Conservatives, it said, had produced prosperity,
home-ownership, share-ownership, low inflation and falling unemployment. But even this editorial devoted more space to the threat
from Labour.

Judged against these indifferent standards, *Today's* election coverage was refreshing. *Today* made clear from the start that it thought
the Alliance should hold the balance of power in Parliament. The
Alliance manifesto was described as a 'radical, attractive document'.
The Conservatives, despite Mrs Thatcher's drive, offered little to the
have-nots while Labour's vision was impractical even if superficially
more attractive. *Today's* main object was to end Mrs Thatcher's
unhindered grip on power; it published a list of 100 seats where
tactical voting was recommended to defeat the Conservative MP.
Few people could object to the Alliance receiving this degree of
support from a national paper, but it was unfortunate that *Today*

should resort to the traditional practice of over-praising its friends
and condemning its enemies. For example, its opinion poll coverage
found glimmers of hope for the Alliance where most commentators
could detect no light at all. This bias was mild compared to the *Daily
Mail* and *Daily Express*, but it was unfortunate that it should exist at
all in a new paper.

The quality dailies provided a depth and range of election coverage
sufficient to satisfy the most demanding enthusiast. The contrast with
the populars could never have been sharper. Under the editorship
of Max Hastings, even the *Daily Telegraph's* coverage read less like
the house-journal of the Conservative Party than in previous years.
The *Daily Telegraph's* traditional loyalties did reassert themselves to
an extent as the campaign proceeded. The Alliance's manifesto was
dismissed as the philosophy of the 1970s while Labour's policies
on taxation and defence were attacked fiercely. But even the
Conservatives were chided on occasion. Mrs Thatcher was invited
to show more sympathy for the underprivileged, Mr Tebbit was
encouraged to be bolder in his assertions that only the Conservatives
were fit to rule, and Mr Hurd was advised to be a shade more liberal
on immigration. The *Daily Telegraph* remained a solidly Conservative
paper, puzzling over how the 'fiscal flagellants' of the middle-classes
could be other than right-wing, but its commitment now was to
conservatism as well as the Conservative Party. In the *Daily Telegraph's* news coverage, too, there were slight signs of a more modern
approach. Endless constituency profiles gave way to a broader range
of coverage, including more detailed reporting of the Alliance.

Under Rupert Murdoch, *The Times* entered the campaign with
increased circulation but reduced authority. However, it would be
difficult to spot any 'decline of *The Times*' in its election coverage.
The paper caught up with the *Guardian* in quantity of coverage and
offered well-packaged background material. For the first time *The
Times* commissioned its own polls, the final one accurately predicting
a Conservative majority of just over 100 (George Gale made a similar
prediction in the *Spectator* without troubling the pollsters). In
its leader columns, *The Times* showed more enthusiasm for the
Conservative manifesto than in 1983: 'this Tory manifesto is a
revealing snapshot of a government in power, still thinking, still
taking risks, not always getting the means right but ready to fight for
clear and critically important ends'. Labour's manifesto was dismissed
as obscuring the party's socialist if not Marxist essence: 'in drafting
the modern Labour manifesto, the art of the leaders is lavished on

obscuring the wishes of the led'. The Alliance received less criticism but also less attention. *The Times* argued that it lacked a philosophical base, offering only the out-dated theory that Britain's problems could be solved by changing the system of government.

The *Guardian's* strength lay in the variety of viewpoints expressed in its columns. These included Terry Coleman's individual commentaries, Agenda pages on such issues as the health service, and a double-page spread on the political preferences of well-known writers. The *Guardian's* own views can only be described as obscure. *The Times* rightly described the *Guardian's* key editorial as 'couched in an embarrassed (and embarrassing) jokey and vulgar prose, which was a disgrace to a quality newspaper'. This leader praised Mrs Thatcher for her capacity to achieve, but argued that her government had no solution to the problem of declining social cohesion. The Alliance was no alternative because, although its policies were radical and attractive, 'the spark hasn't come'. Labour, on the other hand, had blossomed as an alternative government. Its policies on defence, inflation and the unions were still unconvincing, but Mr Kinnock would probably behave sensibly in office. With help from an Alliance challenge in Conservative seats, Labour deserved victory.

The *Independent* had a radical and long-overdue solution to the tortured ramblings of *Guardian* leader-writers. It declined to endorse any party at all. None the less, it did offer a review of the campaign which was sympathetic to a social market philosophy and David Owen in particular. The errors of the Alliance were tactical, in failing to overcome internal divisions on defence and unemployment, whereas the defects of the other parties were strategic. The Conservatives espoused the market but did little to attack its distortions – business monopolies, the housing market and low pay for teachers. Labour, on the other hand, offered only a return to the discredited corporatism of the 1970s; the party's leaders had failed to develop the more positive concept of market socialism. The tone of the *Independent's* editorials reflected its news coverage: accurate, thoughtful, detailed. Peter Kellner provided expert poll commentaries, the Viewpoint series offered the perspective of commentators ranging from anarchists to law professors, and the paper provided detailed facts on the North/South divide, the interpretation of economic statistics and Mrs Thatcher's health. Its photographs, quite the best of any paper, added much-needed flair to this worthy diet.

Readers of the *Financial Times* (as numerous as those of the *Independent*) were offered election coverage which was both broad and varied. The breadth came from interpretive front-page reports on the current state of play; the variety emerged in detailed, inside-page reports on the by-ways of the campaign – the contest in the Western Isles, the voting intentions of expatriates in Belgium, the parties' proposals on agriculture. The *Financial Times* was also the only party to print the manifestos in full. Politically the paper remained an unenthusiastic member of the Conservative camp. Its support for Mrs Thatcher rested on the government's capacity to operate a market economy effectively; its doubts concerned the Conservative's lack of concern for the bottom 15% of the population. The *Financial Times* regretted the Alliance's failure to break through; had it done so, the paper's support might well have switched.

Labour fared slightly better in the Sundays. It was supported by three papers, the *Sunday Mirror*, the *People* and the new *News on Sunday*. These provide 36% of all Sunday newspaper readers, compared with 27% of daily paper readers who took a Labour title – that is, the *Daily Mirror* or the *Guardian*. The *Sunday Mirror* and the *News on Sunday* were the most partisan of the Sundays. The *Sunday Mirror* devoted five pages of its pre-election issue to pro-Labour material while the *News on Sunday*, in its equivalent issue, included a 16-page glossy photo portrait of the 'strife and bitterness' of the Thatcher years. The *People* was less politicised and less partisan. Although it declared for Labour on 17 May, subsequent leaders were more critical of the Conservatives than enthusiastic about Labour. However, its limited news coverage of the campaign did retain a pro-Labour bias.

The Conservatives were supported by the *News of the World* (whose sole contribution to the campaign was to smear Labour politicians and officials), the *Sunday Express*, the *Sunday Times*, the *Sunday Telegraph* and the *Mail on Sunday*. Perhaps the only surprise here was the *Mail on Sunday*. After a phase of sympathy for the Alliance, the paper declared in a full-page editorial on 7 June that the Conservatives had snatched from the Alliance the title of the modern party for the modern world. Several other Sundays also presented the Conservatives as the party in tune with the times. But there were doubts, not least in the *Sunday Telegraph*. In a signed leader Peregrine Worsthorne argued that Mrs Thatcher's 'utopia was riddled with worms', finance capital bringing economic benefits at the cost of civilised governance. The *Observer* decried even the economic achievements of Thatcherism, which it suggested owed

more to artful presentation than solid achievement. The *Observer*
concluded that

> what many of our readers would find attractive is the result that
> the Alliance set out to get, which was a substantial influence on a
> minority government . . . If there were to be a hung Parliament,
> the best outcome would probably be a Thatcherless Conservative
> Party supported by the Alliance.

Sunday Today, in its last issue, also advocated a coalition, following
a hung parliament produced by tactical anti-Conservative voting.

Regional, evening, and especially local, newspapers were generally
less intense in their partisanship. There was certainly more sympathy
for Labour than in 1983, particularly among Northern papers, but
doubts about Labour's defence policy remained. The *Yorkshire Post*,
firmly Conservative, said Mr Kinnock's views were frightening while
Newcastle's *Evening Chronicle* argued that for Mr Gould to say
that Trident would be 'virtually useless' was as unconvincing as a
shopkeeper saying he was 'virtually certain' he could supply a turkey
for Christmas.

In Scotland, too, the tone was generally less strident than in some
of the London-based newspapers. The *Scotsman*, the *Glasgow Herald*,
and the *Press and Journal* (Aberdeen), all gave extensive coverage
to the campaign, proportionately not far short of that provided by
the English 'heavies'. Their reporting was non-partisan, though
feature articles repeatedly drew attention to the decline in Scottish
industry since 1979 and the severity of unemployment. Both the
Scotsman and the *Glasgow Herald*, while paying tribute to the last
two Conservative Secretaries of State, looked towards tactical voting
to put a brake on Thatcherism, and both also called for the creation
of a Scottish Assembly. The *Glasgow Herald* was seen by the
Conservatives as being hostile, mainly because it published a series
of System 3 polls showing – correctly, as it turned out – that the party
was likely to lose half its seats in Scotland. The most strident
contributions came from the Maxwell-owned *Daily Record*, which
has, relatively, the highest sales of any daily newspaper in the UK
(current daily average about 775 000 copies in a circulation area of
5.5 million people). The *Daily Record* took little interest in the
campaign until near the end, but then fired front-page salvoes on 6
of the last 12 days. Its final comment began 'Margaret Thatcher has
a blind spot . . . It's called Scotland'.[3]

Political periodicals had little impact on the campaign. Despite its assessment of Labour's campaign as 'triumphal', the *New Statesman* advocated proportional representation and tactical anti-Conservative voting for the Alliance. However, this latter advice, in contrast to 1983, attracted little attention elsewhere in the media. The *Economist*'s position was also unchanged: it advocated a Conservative victory and reckoned that Labour deserved to be replaced by the Alliance as the principal opposition. The *Spectator* was less Thatcherite than the *Economist*, but equally Conservative; it claimed that a vote for Labour was a moral posturing, not a moral act. *New Society* set out the arguments against each party, concluding that its case against the Alliance was least convincing. The Alliance was not going to win while the others did not deserve to. The only trend of note among the periodicals was that both the *Spectator* and *Punch* commissioned opinion polls.

Press advertising has now become a standard feature of election campaigns. Its effect on voting behaviour is undoubtedly slight – for example, the Alliance's campaign, which included some press advertisements, was less successful than its 1983 campaign, which did not. But as long as parties have the money, they are reluctant to concede any possible advantage to their opponents, and advertising can at least boost the morale of the party's own supporters and leaders.

In the 1987 campaign the parties took 336 pages of advertisements in the national press at a rate-card cost of £5.6 million (Table 8.4). In addition some parties advertised in regional, especially Scottish, papers. This was a three-fold increase on the record spending in 1983. As last time the Conservatives outspent Labour by more than two to one. Both parties would have spent more had their material not been rejected by some papers. The *Daily Mirror* refused to accept the rush of Conservative advertisements in the final week, Robert Maxwell arguing that 'blanket advertising puts the principle of freedom to advertise – which in this case is the power of money to influence an election – above any other'. In similar vein the *Daily Express* and the *Sun* rejected Labour's election day advertisement, claiming that a section on education was misleading.

Conservative advertising began slowly. Saatchi's early advertisements attempted a more positive tone than in earlier campaigns but were widely considered unsuccessful. However, even before the

Table 8.4   Political advertising in national daily and Sunday newspapers

Parties/Pressure groups	16 May–9 June 1983		17 May–11 June 1987	
	Pages	*Cost (£'000)*	*Pages*	*Cost (£'000)*
Parties				
Conservative	67	1 282	217	3 620
Labour	27	399	102	1 581
Alliance	–	–	17	352
Green/Ecology	0.4	–	0.1	–
Pressure groups				
Committee for a Free Britain	–		6.0	
Aims of Industry	4.3		3.5	
ISIS Association for Independent Schools	0.3		3.4	
CND	1.6		3.0	
Friends of the Earth	–		1.3	
Alliance businessmen	–		1.0	
Other	49.5		1.2	
Total	150.1		355.5	

Note: Costs calculated by (MEAL) at rate-card prices.

involvement of other agencies knocking copy took over. The best example, repeated on several occasions, showed 'LABOUR'S POLICY ON ARMS' – a young soldier with his arms up (see p. 104). This was undoubtedly the most memorable image produced in the press advertising war. Other advertisements attacked Labour's extremism and its policy on secondary picketing. In the final week, in a change of direction, the Conservative campaign reverted to the traditional Saatchi formula of splashing selective statistics across several pages: 'FACT 1 – OVER 1,000,000 NEW JOBS CREATED SINCE 1983. FACT 2 – UNEMPLOYMENT FALLING FASTER IN BRITAIN THAN IN ANY OTHER COUNTRY IN EUROPE'. This last minute, £2 million blitz was dramatic in scale but hardly innovative in content.

Labour's material was less extravagant but more consistent. It used full-page advertisements, an improvement over the small insertions of 1983, but their impact was reduced by appearing later in the paper than the Conservative advertisements. The hopeful slogan was 'THE COUNTRY'S CRYING OUT FOR CHANGE – VOTE LABOUR', though in the final week this was shortened to the even more optimistic 'THE COUNTRY'S CRYING OUT FOR LABOUR'. One advertisement caused controversy by quoting Mr Tebbit as saying in 1983 that 'if unemployment is not below three million in five years, then I'm not worth re-electing'. In fact Mr Tebbit had said, when asked if unemployment would be below three million within four or five years, 'If I did not think we could do that, I don't think we would be in a position to win the next election'. But, in the main, Labour's advertisements were visual rather than textual. They portrayed a dark, Dickensian land of poverty and suffering, but readers may simply have associated this gloomy image with the source (Labour) rather than the target (the Conservatives).

The Alliance's complex message was squeezed between the aggressive simplicities of the major parties. One Alliance advertisement listed its policies on the back of an own-label pack and said, 'THE BEST PRODUCTS RARELY COME IN THE FLASHIEST PACKS'. The other used the same policies to claim 'ONLY THE ALLIANCE CAN SATISFY YOUR HEAD *AND* YOUR HEART'. It was the best that could be done on a small budget.

Advertising by interest groups was less prevalent than in 1983. Most of it was pro-Conservative, a return to the situation existing before the exceptional campaign of 1983. Advertisers included the old stalwart Aims of Industry, an organisation which shared offices with the 'Committee for a Free Britain'. This latter, self-effacing body placed several full-page anti-Labour advertisements in the *Sun*. The Labour Party sought, and initially obtained, an injunction banning these advertisements on the grounds that they featured people from specific constituencies and should be charged against the expenses of Conservative candidates from those seats. However, this injunction was overturned later in the same day.

All this advertising had limited effects. Qualitative research by Horner, Collis and Kirvan suggested that knocking copy increased voter cynicism, sharpening distinctions between the parties but not contributing to voter preferences. Quantitative research by Mass Observation on 13 June showed that 41% of electors thought the Conservatives had the best press or poster advertisements, compared to 24% mentioning Labour and 9% the Alliance (the figures for worst advertisements were reversed: Alliance 30%, Labour 14%, Conservatives 10%). So the Conservatives got something from their expenditure of £3 million plus – even if it was not extra votes.

The opening leader columns of the campaign established one of Fleet Street's main themes: progressive Conservatism versus a backward-looking Labour Party. 'Neil Kinnock will captain the reactionaries', said the *Daily Mail*, and 'Margaret Thatcher will lead for the radicals'.

**UNDER THE
TORIES
YOUR CHILD'S
EDUCATION
COULD DEPEND
ON JUST
ONE BOOK.**

**YOUR CHEQUE
BOOK.**

The Tories plan to let State schools charge fees if they want to.
If you don't want to pay, don't vote Tory.

THE COUNTRY'S CRYING OUT FOR CHANGE. VOTE LABOUR.

**IN BRITAIN
THE POOR HAVE
GOT POORER
AND THE RICH
HAVE GOT...
WELL, THEY'VE
GOT THE
CONSERVATIVES.**

For 60 years there has been a trend towards more equal distribution of wealth in Great Britain.

In the last eight years this has been reversed.

The top 5% of the population now own 20% of the nation's wealth. (By contrast, the bottom 50% own just 4%).

Last week Margaret Thatcher's comment on the effect of Tory policies was 'Life gets better for some. It gets worse for others.'

We're afraid we can't argue there.

What we can say is that it's about time life started getting better for the 'others.'

THE COUNTRY'S CRYING OUT FOR CHANGE. VOTE LABOUR.

**THE
CONSERVATIVE MANIFESTO
DOESN'T SAY
ANYTHING ABOUT REDUCING
UNEMPLOYMENT.**

**IT DOESN'T SAY
ANYTHING ABOUT IMPROVING
THE HEALTH SERVICE.**

**IT DOESN'T SAY
ANYTHING ABOUT INVESTING
IN EDUCATION.**

**IT DOESN'T SAY
ANYTHING ABOUT BUILDING
MORE HOUSES.**

**IT SAYS A LOT
ABOUT THE CONSERVATIVES.**

THE COUNTRY'S CRYING OUT FOR CHANGE. VOTE LABOUR.

**"IF
UNEMPLOYMENT
IS NOT BELOW
THREE MILLION IN
FIVE YEARS,
THEN
I'M NOT WORTH
RE-ELECTING."**

Norman Tebbit 1983

NO WONDER THEY'VE CALLED THE ELECTION A YEAR EARLY.

THE COUNTRY'S CRYING OUT FOR CHANGE. VOTE LABOUR.

The *Daily Express* wrote that 'a vote for Labour is a vote for yesterday, a vote for the Tories is a vote for tomorrow'. The *Guardian* noted that 'the momentum of change remains with the Conservatives', and the *Independent* said 'Labour is identified more with resistance to necessary change than with efficiency and modernity'. The outdated nature of Labour's policies, coupled with the party's left-wing extremism, were the basis of Labour's image as portrayed in the press.

Well-prepared smears against individual politicians were the most distinctive feature of press coverage of the campaign. Again the pattern was quickly established. On 16 May the *Daily Star* reported allegations circulating about the personal life of Mr Steel. Subsequent apologies did not prevent a lawsuit (for this was the election in which the politicians bit back, going straight to the courts and by-passing the Press Council). The next day 'revelations' about a Labour official appeared in the *News of the World*. A week later the same paper investigated Mr Hattersley in a story which subsequently made the front pages of the *Daily Mail* and the *Sun*. Some of these 'smears' were trivial in the extreme. Did the nation need to know that Ken Livingstone had been seen visiting a council house purchased by his sister (*Sun*), that Mrs Thatcher was having hormone treatment (*Daily Mirror*), that Mrs Castle (the *Sunday Telegraph*) and Mrs Healey (the *Sun* again) had used private health care? Most of the media sensibly ignored these reports, in fact several papers ran 'keep it clean' leaders. But when, two days before the election, Mr Healey reacted angrily to a television interviewer's questions about his wife's operation, an excuse was provided for the *Daily Mail* and the *Daily Express* to headline the story the next day.

This neatly illustrates the role of the press in election campaigns. Newspapers raise issues which television reports but would not have initiated. The press 'legitimises' issues for television; and the subsequent coverage on TV then generates additional reporting in the press. Hence the capacity of the press to influence the election agenda should not be understated even in such a television-dominated campaign as 1987.

Newspaper coverage of the manifestos provides a useful indicator of the press's attitudes to the parties. Despite publishing first, the Alliance must have been disappointed with the limited coverage it achieved. No paper led on the manifesto; none of the populars even mentioned it on their front page. The editorial reaction was equally lukewarm. *The Times* said the Alliance lacked a philosophical base, the *Independent* wrote that it had hundreds of policies but no theme, and the *Daily Express* commented that no one should vote for such a flimsy prospectus. *The Financial Times* was more sympathetic ('it is serious, comprehensive and costed') but only *Today* enthused. Comment on the major parties' manifestos was largely predictable. The *Daily Express* said Labour's proposals were wall-to-wall white-wash, while the *Daily Mirror* consistently criticised the Conservatives for appealing to selfish instincts. But common themes were visible beneath these knee-jerk reactions. The main criticism of the government was its lack of concern for the have-nots; of Labour, that its policies were out-of-date and a camouflage for extremism.

As the campaign progressed, even the most pro-Conservative papers acknowledged Labour's progress. 'Yes but' was the usual reaction. The *Daily Mail* commented on 21 May:

> Never before has a Labour campaign been so glossed with genteel schmalz. Very professional. Very transatlantic. But what's really on offer? Neither the bland phrases nor the evasive brevity of Labour's manifesto can mask the musty smell of the failed policies of yesteryear.

In the *Guardian* David McKie compared Labour's revival to Wolves almost winning promotion from Division Three – progress perhaps, but hardly a great achievement by past standards. Still there were signs of edginess in the Conservative camp. On 22 May the *Daily Express* asked 'Are the Tory supporters still asleep at nine in the morning? Or are they as complacent as the Frime Minister was afraid they might be?' On 25 May the *Daily Mail* referred to the Conservative's lacklustre campaign and called for bolder measures.

As perceived in the press, Labour's recovery was based on the packaging of Neil Kinnock. It was indeed in the treatment of the party leaders that press coverage of this campaign differed most from 1983. Last time Mrs Thatcher was glorified and Mr Foot treated with contempt. By 1987 the Falklands factor afforded the Prime Minister less protection. Her drive, determination and achievements were still praised but in a respectful rather than adulatory way. Several papers commented on her uncaring image and her stumblings over education. But the real transformation lay in the treatment of Labour's leader. Mr Kinnock received widespread praise for his campaigning ability. After the first seven days the *Independent* commented, 'one way and another, it was Neil Kinnock's week. Labour does have a theme and that theme is Mr Kinnock himself'. The *Daily Mail* noted that

'Kinnock speaks with passionate sincerity rarely conveyed by other leaders' while in the *Daily Express* even Jean Rook wrote twice of the Labour leader's 'pleasing personality'. The only criticism early on was of Mr Kinnock's decision not hold daily London press conferences. This policy may have helped to avoid distraction from Labour's planned themes, but the criticism of his absence might suggest that the press was still a significant campaigning forum in elections.

And then came defence. Mr Kinnock's unfortunate words on weekend television inspired three papers to lead on the issue on Monday, 25 May (the *Daily Express*, *Today* and the *Daily Telegraph*). The *Daily Mail* and *The Times* followed the next day. Indeed the *Daily Express* led on the issue three times in the week: 'IF THE ENEMY COMES – BY NEIL' (Monday, 25 May), '"WHITE FLAG" KINNOCK ACCUSED' (Wednesday) and 'MAGGIE NUKES KINNOCK' (Saturday). *The Times* was also concerned: 'THATCHER GOES ON ATTACK OVER DEFENCE' (Tuesday) and 'TORIES ATTACK KINNOCK POLICY OF NO SURRENDER' (Wednesday). There were more front-page headlines on defence in 1987 than in 1983, more than on any other election topic except opinion polls (Tables 8.5 and 8.6). Just as the Anne Diamond interview with Mr Healey on breakfast TV shows how a press story can be picked up by television, so Mr Kinnock's comments to David Frost show the reverse influence. A short comment on television became the dominant issue in the press for the next week. The sheer scale of the press's reaction surely helped to project the defence issue to the centre of the campaign stage.

Press comment on Labour's defence policy was, with the possible exception of the *Guardian*, firmly critical. The *Sun* ran a cartoon of Kinnock fleeing into the Fens like Hereward the Wake. The next day, perhaps realising the obscurity of this allusion, it published a full-page front-page cartoon showing Kinnock being trampled by a Soviet soldier. The leader writers, and not just in the populars, were equally unsympathetic. The *Independent* described Labour's defence policy as 'frail' while even the *Guardian* said Mr Kinnock was 'half way round Spaghetti Junction in a thick fog' about how he would achieve the laudable aim of nuclear disarmament. Several papers saw in Kinnock's comments on defence a shallow, glib quality which called into question his credibility as a potential Prime Minister. Thus Labour's difficulties over defence prised open broader, more damaging issues of competence and leadership.

Table 8.5   Lead stories on the election in daily newspapers

Lead story	10 May–9 June, 1983	18 May–11 June, 1987
Opinion polls	14	24
Defence	16	19
'Scandal' stories	–	12
Party strategy and prospects	19	11
Taxation	–	9
Health	–	7
Education	–	6
Manifestos	9	6
Editorials	6	5
Divided Britain	–	5
Unemployment	7	3
Trade unions	–	3
Hard left	–	3
Falklands	9	–
Other	–	10

Defence apart, the issues which received most attention from the press were education, taxation and health. There were 22 front-page headlines about these areas in 1987 compared to none at all in 1983. However, the education issue was well-contained by the Conservative press. All the lead stories on education bar one were in the quality papers, the exception being the *Sun's* 'LABOUR PICKS RENT BOY AS SCHOOL BOSS'. In the Conservative populars the education issue was left-wing domination of schools not the controversial Conservative proposals on opting out.

The health issue also received more attention from non-Conservative papers. The *Daily Mirror* made full play with the Mark Burgess case. 'DEAR MRS. THATCHER', said a front-page headline on 5 June, 'WHEN WILL THEY MAKE ME BETTER?' On the same day *Today* discovered its own victim: 'FOUR TIMES THEY GOT HIM READY FOR SURGERY, FOUR TIMES THEY SENT HIM HOME'. The Conservative papers soon counter-attacked with a rehashed story in the *Sun* about Mrs Healey's private operation two years earlier and a front-page lead in the *Daily Star* on Mr Kinnock's admission that he would pay for private treatment in an emergency.

The more effective response was to shift the agenda. This the Conservative press did in the last 10 days of the campaign with the *Daily Express*, *Daily Mail*, *Daily Telegraph* and *The Times* each leading twice on Labour's tax policies. The Conservative press gave much more prominence to taxation than did the more neutral medium of television. The *Daily Mail* announced that anyone earning over £9000 a year would be worse off under Labour and that the standard

Table 8.6   Lead stories during the election, 18 May–11 June 1987

Date	Guardian	Daily Telegraph	The Times	Independent	Daily Express	Daily Mail	Today	Daily Star	Daily Mirror	Sun
MAY 18	Parties condemn 'Dirty tricks'	(Judges outlaw Fiji coup)	Steel attacks 'Smears, lies and slanders'	Privatisation to fund Alliance	IRA killer stalks Maggie	Steel smear fury	Lies, Smears and Dirty Tricks	(Britons in mid-air horror)	(What a Cock Up)	(Mansell in track punch-up)
19	(Attack in Gulf)	(U.S. Gulf Policy)	(Reagan to keep Gulf open)	Kinnock predicts Labour Landslide	(Child Rapist Jailed)	(Telecom Tory in Court)	Big Chance for Davids (Poll)	(Gone Fishing)	(My Hell by Elton John)	(Wogan bans Pam)
20	Thatcherism sets battleground	Thatcher & Kinnock draw battle lines	Tories offer Radicalism & tax cuts	Battle plans for the nation	Wall-to-Wall Whitewash	(The Distress of Prince Charles)	(Gay Plot)	(Hospital woman shot Dead)	(Gunned down under cop's nose)	(Girl shot dead in ward)
21	Alliance attack Thatcher	Alliance poll disaster	Teachers will strike	Labour gains panic City	Alliance poll disaster	Hospital shooting	Proctor Ruined	His obedient servant	Tea at Commons for Proctor schoolboy	(Let him die!)
22	Thatcher attacks Alliance	Defence made top issue by Thatcher	(Ferry disaster clues)	Unemployment figures	Our conspiracy by Red Ken	Labour's secret tax plan	Tories in turmoil	(Track star jailed)	(Get lost Beasties)	(Exam panic victim)
23	Thatcher schools speech	Thatcher schools speech	Schools split Tories	Muddled Tory campaign	Kinnock on Left	(Disney war)	(Child drug ring)	(I want your sex)	(Bottoms up ma'am)	(BBC ban on sexy George)
25	Thatcher schools speech	Kinnock on defence	Education	Young's unemployment plans	Kinnock on defence	(Broadmoor drug shock)	Fight them in the street	(Peril of the water judges)	(Coach fired)	Hattersley's girl fights cancer
26	Tory attacks on Labour	Jobless tide turned	Thatcher on defence	Tories and Alliance attack Labour	(Tycoon dies)	Kinnock on defence	Crisis for Hattersley	(Holiday horror)	(Hamburger blinds baby)	IRA hunt Maggie
27	Reagan attacks Labour's defence	Thatcher attacks Kinnock	Tories attack Kinnock	Kinnock under fire	Kinnock on defence	Kinnock on defence	(Police expose phone tap mob)	(Bruce jailed)	(Test stars beat up fans)	Labour picks rent boy as school boss
28	Tories attack Kinnock	Reagan attacks Labour's defence	Tories attack Kinnock	Owen revitalizes Alliance	(Girl murders)	Kinnock runs from press	Reagan interferes	(The Life of Riley)	Attack on Mrs Thatcher	(What a lovely Di for tennis)
29	Thatcher attacks Left	Defence fury	Kinnock on defence	Kinnock on defence	Maggie nukes Kinnock	The iceberg manifesto	Let's have more jobs	(Murder rape)	(Wallop!)	Labour on defence
30	(Iran releases envoy)	(Plane beats Soviet defence)	(Iran releases envoy)	Tories and NHS figures	(Girl in spy outrage)	(Diplomacy of terror)	(Envoy freed)	(Plane crazy)	Thatcher's butler sacked	(Mass Aids scare)

JUNE									
1	Thatcher under attack	(Envoy faces death charge)	Labour flagging	Kinnock on schools	Labour tax threats	(Don't throw it all away)	Alliance poll success	(Royal marriage)	Divided Britain	(Cripple's con)
2	Kinnock on inflation	Tories attack Labour	Thatcher attacks	Tebbit forces BBC to interview Tory	Labour's jobs cost	(Mother attacks judges)	8m say we'll wait and see	(Free our man)	Crisis in Jim's hospital	(Soap star in dinner brawl)
3	Opinion polls	Thatcher warning on unions	Polls cause City panic	Election is Alliance's last chance	Owen's desperate last throw	The tyrants are waiting	(Girl raped)	(Rape trap girl)	Cabinet puddings	(Ferry skipper's wife threatens suicide)
4	Opinion polls	Tory lead cut	Opinion polls	Alliance divided	What kind of people are we?	Labour gives 'em the money	Yard foil plot to murder Maggie	(First lady)	(Army louts gas a pub)	Opinion polls
5	Thatcher on NHS	(Iranian diplomats expelled)	(Envoy in Iran shreds papers)	(Iranians expelled)	Union mob rule threat	Labour on taxation	Ordeal by NHS	(Sex in church)	Heart-boy plea	Union power
6	(U.S. threat on Iran missiles)	Tories on taxation	Poll spending climax	Thatcher seeks Christian votes	Labour's tax fiasco	Labour's attack on pensions	Maggie takes a tumble	(Bingo fraud)	(Bingo fraud)	(Bingo fraud)
8	(Autumn summit)	Labour tax disarray	Opinion polls	(U.S. threatens Tehran)	Labour tax divides	Labour and tax	If you care about Britain	(Bingo fraud)	That's rich	Labour nightmare victory
9	Thatcher willing to lead 'minority'	Venice Summit boost	Lawson attacks Labour tax plans	(U.S. threaten Iran)	Summit success	Militant menace	(Glue sniffer dies)	Don't throw it all away	Dirty Liars!	Mrs Healey's private op
10	'Switch loyalty' call for by Thatcher & Kinnock	Venice boosts Thatcher	Thatcher attack on Labour	Tory job proposals	Healey the hypocrite	Healey's gaffe	Power cut for Maggie	Kinnock's private agony	Privilege and poverty	Half way there
11	Thatcher sure of victory	Thatcher set for victory	Polls favour Thatcher	Tories set for victory	Vote for Maggie	Thatcher set for victory	Tory lead	Anti-Tory warning	Chuck her out!	Three times a lady

rate of income tax would go up to 32p. The *Daily Express* and the *Daily Telegraph* highlighted divisions within the Labour Party over taxation, seizing on that most heinous of campaign sins – muddle. So the modest headway which Labour had made in the press on education and health was more than lost at the end on the old issue of living standards.

Press coverage of the election will be remembered for smears against Labour and Alliance politicians. These were undoubtedly a new trend but it would be wrong to conclude that they indicated a greater bias against Labour than in previous contests. As in the election generally, Labour did better in the press in 1987 than in 1983; its problem was that it did not do well enough. The Conservative press acknowledged the skill of Labour's presentation, the attractiveness of Mr Kinnock, and the momentum which the party achieved in the first week of the campaign. For the first time in several elections the Conservative press was forced on to the defensive over health, education and the 'caring' issues. But there was still plenty to criticise about Labour: its extremism, its union links, its defence policy, its questionable competence, and above all its backward-looking philosophy. Still, for better or worse, the Labour Party was the central focus of press coverage in this campaign.

How much difference the press made to the outcome of the election is a difficult question to answer. It seems clear that any impact of newspapers on voters was largely indirect, mediated through television and the response of politicians themselves to press coverage. The television interview with Mr Healey about the story in the *Sun* concerning his wife's private operation illustrated the continuing capacity of the press to influence the campaign agenda on television. The heavy emphasis of the Conservative press on defence and taxation may also have accentuated coverage of these issues on the broadcast media. The importance of how politicians respond to the press was illustrated by the Labour Party's plan to keep Mr Kinnock away from half the London press conferences. Not surprisingly, this policy attracted substantial criticism from newspapers themselves – initially from the Conservative populars ('NO QUESTIONS PLEASE I'M KINNOCK' said the *Daily Mail*) but then from the qualities. More seriously, these comments then began to be picked up by television, conveying to a mass audience an image of a leader attempting to hide from critical scrutiny. In the event, of course, Mr Kinnock performed well when he did meet the London press.

The direct effect of newspapers on voting behaviour is still limited

largely to the reinforcement of existing loyalties.[4] It is true that there
is some correlation between the partisanship of newspapers and the
voting patterns of readers (Table 8.7) but this is probably due more
to self-selection of newspapers than their impact on readers. The
press may be able to increase the salience of abstract concepts such
as 'the loony left' or 'the robber baron trade unions', notions which
are remote from the voter's own experience, but even here there
must be a pre-existing chord in public opinion for the press to strike.
Research on the impact of the press on elections held between 1964
and 1979 suggests that even when the readership of Conservative
papers is two-and-a-half times as great as that of Labour papers
(approximately the situation in 1987), this is unlikely to produce a
swing of more than 1% to the Conservatives between a pair of
elections.[5] Apart from the inherent limits of the press in a television

*Table 8.7   Party supported by daily newspaper readers and perceptions of
newspaper partisanship by readers, 1987*

Daily newspaper	Party supported by readers			Readers' perceptions of paper's partisanship			
	Con. %	Lab. %	Alliance %	Con. %	Lab. %	Alliance %	Don't know %
Daily Mirror	20	55	21	2	84	8	6
Daily Express	70	9	18	87	0	4	9
Sun	41	31	19	63	12	7	18
Daily Mail	60	13	19	78	2	5	15
Daily Star	28	46	18	23	16	7	54
Today	43	17	40	11	4	18	67
Daily Telegraph	80	5	10	85	0	3	12
Guardian	22	54	19	13	30	43	14
The Times	56	12	27	61	0	33	6
Independent	34	34	27	12	6	20	62

Source: MORI/*Sunday Times*, 27–28 May (N = 1188).

era, reasons for this modest impact include the fact that some Labour
voters do not take a paper at all, and that Labour readers are still
concentrated on the *Daily Mirror*. For what it is worth, voters
themselves reported after the 1987 campaign that newspaper coverage
of the campaign had more effect on their attitudes to parties than
leaflets and posters, about the same effect as party election broadcasts,
but less effect than television.[6]

188 *The Election Nationally*

NOTES

1. L. Melvern, *The End of the Street* (London, 1986). Other useful works on the press published since 1983 include: M. Hollingsworth, *The Press and Political Dissent* (London, 1986); M. Cockerell, P. Hennessy and D. Walker, *Sources Close to the Prime Minister* (London, 1985); A. Hetherington, *News, Newspapers and Television* (Basingstoke, 1985); S. Jenkins, *Market for Glory: Fleet Street Ownership in the Twentieth Century* (London, 1986) and H. Porter, *Lies, Damned Lies and Some Exclusives* (London, 1984).
2. D. Goodhart and P. Wintour, *Eddie Shah and the Newspaper Revolution* (London, 1986).
3. The *Press and Journal*, in keeping with its custom, remained neutral in comment.
4. M. Harrop, 'The Press and Post-war Elections', in *Political Communications: the 1983 Election Campaign*, I. Crewe and M. Harrop (eds) (Cambridge, 1986, pp. 137–49. For additional data on newspaper readership and voting, see B. MacArthur, 'The Press and Its Politics', *Sunday Times*, 23 August 1987, p. 41.
5. Harrop, 'The Press and Post-war Elections', p. 148.
6. R. Worcester, 'Trying the Food on the Dog', *New Statesman*, 24 July 1987, pp. 12–13.

The author is grateful to Deborah Lund for her help in preparing the tables in this chapter.

III

The Election Locally

9 Candidates
Byron Criddle

Candidates, despite a necessary belief in their own importance, contribute little to the outcome of British general elections. They are the mere bearers of party labels, the anonymous footsoldiers in a battle waged far away in television studios. Yet they have always had a symbolic value, their social, occupational and ideological characteristics saying much about the parties they represent. Moreover, candidates not only voice the issues in a campaign, they can become one of the issues themselves, as in 1987 when the Conservative and Alliance parties pointed to what they claimed would the the most left-wing Parliamentary Labour Party ever.

The 650 MPs elected in 1987 were drawn from a field of 2325 candidates (fewer than the 2577 in 1983), 82% of whom represented the four main parties. The Conservative and Labour parties and the Alliance parties between them each fought all 633 British seats. In Scotland the Scottish National Party fought 71 of the 72 seats and in Wales Plaid Cymru contested all 38 seats.[1]

Of the 650 successful candidates, 144 were new to the House in the sense of not having been elected at the previous general election, though 14 of them had been returned at by-elections since that election and 10, including one of the by-election victors, had sat in earlier parliaments.[2] Eighty-eight MPs – a post-war record – had retired at the dissolution (and two more who had already announced their retirement had died shortly before it). The vast majority of retiring members went voluntarily on grounds of age, health or disillusionment but, as in 1983, a number of Labour MPs were pushed unwillingly into retirement.

For only the second time since its introduction in 1980, Labour's mandatory reselection process was applied to all 177 Labour MPs seeking to retain their seats. Because the process had on its first use before 1983 seen the deselection of eight MPs and the harrying into retirement or defection of a number of others, it was understandable that the first major initiative taken by Neil Kinnock after his election as leader in 1983, was to try to draw the teeth of mandatory reselection by seeking to introduce 'one member one vote' in selections involving sitting MPs.

191

The proposal was that each General Management Committee (GMC) should have the option of polling the entire membership in the reselection process, and it met with predictable hostility from the hard left who had worked hard to secure, and had benefited from, mandatory reselection under the aegis of activist-controlled GMCs. They saw the involvement of the probably less radical wider membership as a device for saving the skins of a number of beleagured MPs, not least the front benchers Peter Shore, Gerald Kaufman, John Silkin and Michael Cocks. On the other hand, moderate critics were unhappy with a proposal which left hardline GMCs with the power to determine whether the wider membership should be involved or not. The proposal was narrowly defeated at the 1984 Conference, for lack of support from the unions, notably the TGWU, who feared that a greater role for the wider membership would dilute the power of trade union delegates in the selection process.

Reselection thus went ahead unamended, and by 1986 had claimed the scalps of six MPs, four from the right of the party and two from the left.[3] Two of the six were ostensibly casualties of the 1984–5 miners' strike. Michael McGuire, the 59-year old NUM-sponsored MP for Makerfield, was a moderate in the tradition of the Lancashire coalfield. An unobtrusive MP since 1964, he had defied his union's national leadership by supporting working Lancashire miners and lost his NUM sponsorship. He was beaten by 59 votes to 15 by Ian McCartney, son of a retiring MP and Labour agent in Wigan, who duly joined the soft left *Tribune* group on getting to Westminster.

Alec Woodall, another little-heard and little-known NUM-sponsored member, who had represented Hemsworth since 1974, was ousted for similar reasons. He too paid for his non-Scargillite views; he had praised the local police in clashes with striking miners in July 1984. He also had his age (67) against him, though he was at pains to point out that 'in all its long history, the Yorkshire NUM has allowed its MPs to die in office, or retire with honour: I am the first to be sacked for no reason'. His replacement, after a 60-28 vote defeat, was another local miner, 50-year-old George Buckley.

A third casualty from among the ranks of obscure, ageing, right-wing back-benchers, was the 61-year old John Forrester, who had represented Stoke-on-Trent North since 1966, during much of which time, though not at the time he faced reselection, he had also doubled up as his own constituency secretary and used the position to screen membership applications. Blaming his demise on Militant infiltration, he went under to the locally-born, but London-based, Joan Walley, a surcharged, suspended Lambeth councillor, whose London left politics were in stark contrast to Mr Forrester's. On reaching Westminster, Ms Walley joined both *Tribune* and *Campaign* groups.

Of far greater celebrity was the deselection at Bristol South of Michael Cocks, Chief Whip from 1976–85. The trouble at Bristol South dated from 1983 when Mr Cocks had defeated Tony Benn for the nomination in the enlarged seat on which both men had a claim. Although Mr Benn's defeat effectively eliminated him from parliament until his return at the Chesterfield by-election in 1984, his erstwhile Bristol supporters built up strength in the new Bristol South CLP, which they saw as 'a rotten borough serving little purpose than to secure the reselection of Michael Cocks', and in March 1984 they took control of the GMC.[4] Claiming irregularities in the conduct of that meeting, Cocks petitioned Labour's NEC, under threat of legal action if they refused, to investigate the local party. They did so, but despite it, at a re-run AGM the left triumphed even more convincingly. In advance of the reselection vote, the MP sought more NEC intervention when the left challenged the credentials of some of his delegates, but in January 1986, all delays exhausted, he lost by 56 to 71 to Dawn Primarolo, 31, a Bristol University researcher in urban affairs and, more significantly, Tony Benn's former CLP secretary. Michael Cocks, who had sued the *Mail on Sunday* in 1985 for claiming he was intending to join the SDP, was given a peerage in 1987.[5]

The deselections of both Norman Atkinson (Tottenham) and Ernie Roberts (Hackney North & Stoke Newington) were different; both men were ardent left-wingers, but they fell victim to a new phenomenon in the Labour Party which emerged after 1983, the Black Sections campaign. This aimed at specific representation for blacks and Asians on GMCs, Labour groups and the NEC, and for the nomination of blacks/Asians as candidates in winnable seats. A number of seats were targeted for this purpose and it was the misfortune of Mr Atkinson and Mr Roberts to occupy the sort of seats – those with a high percentage of black and Asian voters – on which the black campaigners had set their sights. Norman Atkinson, the 63-year-old Amalgamated Engineering Union sponsored member for Tottenham since 1964 and a former Labour Party treasurer, was deselected in favour of the 41-year old Guyanan-born local government officer and leader of Haringey council, Bernie Grant. Ideologically this involved a Marxist Tribunite making way for a former member of the Trotskyist Socialist Labour League, but it was more a question of race than dogma, even though Mr Grant joined the *Campaign* rather than the *Tribune* group in 1987.

Ernie Roberts, like Mr Atkinson an AEU-sponsored member (and a former Assistant General Secretary of the union), was additionally vulnerable on grounds of his advanced age; he was 74, though he argued that his health and fitness and his very late entry to parliament at the age of 67 in 1979 rendered this irrelevant. He was also an MP of impeccably hard left credentials. He was ousted nevertheless, in a 42-35 vote by 31-year old Diane Abbott, a local government officer (formerly a civil servant and trade union official), Cambridge educated and of Jamaican parentage. With many more nominations than Ms Abbott, Mr Roberts claimed he should have won, but 'they wanted a woman, a black woman'. Race and gender politics were tough on the old white left, but there was little they could do about it. Ms Abbott duly replaced Mr Roberts in the hard left *Campaign* group.

To these six deselections must be added the demise of Reg Freeson at Brent East. Saved in 1983 only by NEC-intervention, he sought to delay the inevitable by getting the Party's national officers to continue investigating alleged irregularities in the local party, where supporters of GLC leader Ken Livingstone, and other left-wingers, were in commanding control. Because Walworth Road did not meet Mr Freeson's demands, he withdrew from the selection procedure, thus acknowledging the inevitability of his defeat. He did, however, threaten legal action against the NEC if they endorsed Mr Livingstone's selection. Mr Livingstone was selected and, after denouncing him as an 'overwhelmingly ambitious man who has campaigned and caucused against me for three to four years', Freeson fell silent. Ken Livingstone duly won Brent East on a much-reduced majority and joined both *Tribune* and *Campaign* groups.

Other 'retirements' were forced, most notably John Silkin's. Mr Silkin had not been forgiven by left-wingers in his Deptford seat for standing against Tony Benn in the deputy leadership election in 1981, and since then he had taken legal action to wrest control of *Tribune* from the Bennites; in addition his legal firm had acted on behalf of Michael Cocks in his battle to stay afloat in Bristol. Eventually, under NEC instructions, local CLP officers agreed to give Silkin a list of the local membership, which they had long denied him, but instead of using it to try to replace a hostile GMC, Silkin opted to retire, and died shortly before the dissolution. His replacement in Deptford was the former CND chairperson, Joan Ruddock.[6]

It was the view of Labour's national officials that mandatory reselection had become a more routine matter, with the party taking it in its stride, and that most of the vulnerable MPs had in any case been shaken out before 1983. Proportionately fewer MPs (one in four) faced contested reselection votes in 1985–6 than had done so in 1981–2 (one in three).[7] The short-list of one, decried by the left before 1983 and formally discouraged by the NEC thereafter, was very much the norm and drew few complaints to Walworth Road. Nevertheless, many MPs had to employ a variety of skills and devices to ensure survival, whether it was the time-consuming cultivation of wards and union branches to secure their GMCs,[8] or, as in the case of Frank Field in Birkenhead, threatening to resign and fight a by-election if deselected.[9] It was hardly surprising that the leadership put 'one member one vote' back on the agenda after the election.

Conservative selection procedures were unchanged, and characteristically few problems arose. In the wake of revelations in a Young Conservative publication, repeated on a BBC *Panorama* programme in January 1984, alleging the involvement of named Conservative MPs with extreme right-wing racist groups, some of the MPs concerned sued for damages and won. But a consequence of these embarrassing accusations was that Central Office tightened up on its scrutiny of would-be candidates and encouraged local associations to be vigilant in interviewing candidates. (In 1983 the Conservative candidate in Stockton South was revealed as having been a National Front candidate in 1974.) In mid-parliament there was some talk of marginal seat MPs, elected unexpectedly in 1983 and envisaging certain defeat at the coming election, wanting to migrate to safe seats being vacated by retiring members. Central Office rejected such an idea, which would involve very unseemly problems in the event of retiring members dying and provoking by-elections, and which could not be expected anyway to appeal to the Vice-Chairman responsible for candidates, Tom Arnold, who had himself for 10 years managed to retain a marginal seat.

Without the disruptive force of a boundary revision, as in 1983, few opportunities arose to unseat unpopular MPs. Some young MPs made an early exit. Lord Cranborne, 40, left South Dorset after only eight years, citing his opposition to the Anglo-Irish Agreement. John Watson, 43, quit Skipton and Ripon, disillusioned with parliament's low standards of behaviour and quality of debate, and critical of the poor financial rewards and interrupted career patterns of ministers.

He returned to industry. Christopher Murphy, 40, left Welwyn & Hatfield amid allegations that he was an absentee MP. Some older MPs, with a history of trouble in their constituency associations, had a bumpy ride: Sir Anthony Meyer, after a finger-nail survival in 1983, scraped through at Clwyd North-West by a 66-51 vote. He had criticised the government for allowing the use of UK bases for the American raid on Libya. At Windsor & Maidenhead, Dr Alan Glyn evaded attempts to remove him on grounds of age (68).

Much is made by Central Office of the autonomy of local associations and its inability to determine their choice. There was some evidence of local resistance to parachuted-in metropolitan barristers or bankers. After the loss of Ryedale to the Liberals in the 1986 by-election, the defeated candidate, Neil Balfour (Ampleforth & Oxford and a banker) was rejected in favour of a grammar school-educated former policeman. In Norfolk South-West an Oxford-based barrister approved by the local executive was rejected in favour of a well-known local woman, Mrs Gillian Shephard.

Three Conservative MPs were obliged to retire for personal reasons.[10] Keith Best (Ynys Mon) and Eric Cockeram (Ludlow) quit after disclosure that they had made more than one application for British Telecom shares. Mr Best had made multiple applications for both Telecom and Jaguar shares and became the subject of fraud squad investigation. More awkward was the case of Harvey Proctor (Billericay), who was dogged in 1986 by newspaper allegations about his private life, over which he refused to sue. He won a 220-62 vote of confidence in March 1987 from his local association, but when finally charged in April, within four weeks of the election, with gross indecency, he resigned. In Winchester a large minority in the local association was unsympathetic to the MP, John Browne, who was suing his former wife for money as part of a divorce settlement, with the possibility of her being sent to jail for non-payment. But in March 1987 Mr Browne survived by a vote of 325-182.

For the Liberal–SDP Alliance the main preoccupation was how to share out the candidacies between the two parties. The 50-50 split in 1983 had rankled with the Liberals, given the fact that they claimed three times as many members in the constituencies and that they were after 1983, three times as strong in the House. There was therefore an immediate Liberal demand for 'joint open selection', whereby members of both parties would vote in candidate selections without prior allocation of seats to either party. The SDP leadership saw this as threatening the swamping of the party by the Liberals, and initially resisted, but pressure from parts of the SDP's own grass roots where the parties were working amicably together, led to some 80 seats being allocated through joint open selection and many more by joint closed selection (where seats were allocated in advance, but where members of both parties were able to participate fully in the selection process). Joint open selection led to a new switch of some 20 seats between the parties, with a slight advantage to the Liberals, who ended up with five more seats (327) than in 1983. The whole process was highly complex and subject to much local variation, but national officials of the parties had to monitor the situation carefully so as to ensure parity in seat allocations and to resolve deadlocks.[11] After the election the extremely tortuous and elongated process of candidate selection was cited by those in the SDP who favoured merger with the Liberals as a reason for so doing. Candidate selection, whilst generating conflict, had served to bring the parties closer together and to standardise procedures; by 1986, for example, the Liberals had adopted the SDP's practice of mandatorily short-listing women. It was also remarkable how in the outcome, Liberal and SDP candidates were virtually indistinguishable in terms of age, education and occupation (see Tables 9.1, 9.3, 9.4). The Alliance fielded a large crop of former MPs, all but three of them, one-time Labour MPs.[12] Of the 23 SDP MPs defeated in the 1983 election, 13 had by 1987 left the political scene, 4 (including Mrs Shirley Williams) had migrated to 'more winnable' seats, with only 6 remaining to fight their old constituencies.

The 1987 election was most noteworthy for the advances made in the representation of gender and race. A record number of 243 women candidates were selected by the main parties: 46 Conservative, 92 Labour and 105 Alliance (of whom 60 SDP and 45 Liberal), and a record number of 41 women were elected: 21 Labour, 17 Conservative, 1 Liberal, 1 SDP and one SNP. (Only Plaid Cymru, of the six parties representing British constituencies, failed to elect a woman MP).[13] Individually, the parties themselves were breaking records: the Conservatives had never returned as many women MPs, and Labour elected, in defeat, as many women as it had done in its landslide victory of 1945. In the past, in elections where Labour did badly overall, the number of Labour women MPs fell (viz., 10 in 1970 and 11 in 1979), but in 1987 Labour had selected more women in safe seats than ever before. (In the 44 seats where Labour MPs retired, 3 retiring women were replaced by 11 women candidates). Traditionally women have failed to reach Westminster because constituencies are less keen to select them than party headquarters are to enlist them, and when chosen it has rarely been for safe seats.[14] By 1987 Labour was doing much to remedy this; the idea of greater representation of women was to be found everywhere in the party, from demands for including a woman on every short-list (a demand finally conceded at the 1986 Conference, though not implemented before the election), to organisations such as Target Labour Government, set up by London activists to press for greater representation for all 'minorities', including women, in the allocation of candidacies. In two London Conservative-held marginal seats, the executive committee decided on all-women short-lists to ensure a woman's selection (Westminster North and Hornsey & Wood Green).

The Conservative Party made slighter gains in this area, although that was not without the efforts and energies of Emma Nicholson, who was appointed Vice-Chairman with special responsibility for the advancement of women. She increased the number of women on the Central Office candidates list to 80 (out of about 650), but resistance to selecting women at local level remained strong. In the event, Miss Nicholson was herself selected to fight the safe seat of Torridge & West Devon, and three other women inherited safe seats at Maidstone, Norfolk South-West and Billericay.

Although the Alliance selected more women than the other parties, it had no safe seats into which they might be placed. Nevertheless, Mrs Ray Michie, by winning Argyll & Bute, became the first woman to win a seat for the Liberals at a general election since Lady Megan Lloyd George last held Anglesey in 1950.

As with gender, so with race: 1987 saw the election of the first Asian MP since 1929,[15] and the first Afro-Caribbean MPs ever. The number of black/Asian candidates fielded by the main parties did not rise dramatically: 28 were selected (compared with 18 in 1983) – 14 Labour, 6 Conservative and 8 Alliance (of whom 6 SDP and 2 Liberal). But what was different in 1987 was the selection of 6 of Labour's 14 candidates for safe or winnable seats, and 4 duly triumphed: Keith Vaz, a Cambridge-educated solicitor of Goan parentage who won Leicester East; Paul Boateng, a solicitor of Anglo-Ghanaian parentage and former GLC councillor, who inherited Brent South on an all-black short list; Diane Abbott (Hackney North & Stoke Newington) and Bernie Grant (Tottenham).[16] All four had won seats with a high proportion of black and Asian voters and which had been targeted by black activists for that reason. The Black Activists Campaign (BLAC), an outgrowth of the black sections movement, called on white MPs to 'stand aside' in 'black seats', a proposal rejected by one of the target-seat MPs, Jeff Rooker, who dismissed the idea as 'apartheid in reverse'. One MP who resisted such pressure successfully was the veteran 69-year old Syd Bidwell at Southall. He was able to do so after successful appeals to the NEC over alleged irregularities surrounding the rapid inflation of membership in a heavily Asian ward of the constituency, largely because his Asian opponents, some Sikh, some Hindu, were divided among themselves. As Mr Bidwell put it: 'The opinion is that if the candidate wears a turban there will be quite a defection in the Labour vote. I'm the bridge-man and I'll stay the bridge-man in these circumstances'.[17] Thus 'Bidwell singh' survived for at least one more parliament. Elsewhere, the involvement of unconstitutional 'black section' delegates in candidate selection in five seats (the NEC had not acceded to the black sections demand) led to NEC-invalidation. In three of these cases (at Newham North-West, Norwood and Vauxhall) sitting MPs were involved, but rerun selections excluding black section delegates were impossible because of local insistence on their inclusion.

If Labour made great strides in the election of black and Asian MPs, its once dominant role in Jewish representation continued to decline. Twenty-three Jewish MPs were elected, five fewer than in 1983, and for the fifth election in succession the number had declined from the record high of 45 in 1974. But more significant, for the second successive election, Conservative MPs (16) outnumbered Labour (7), in stark contrast to the 1950s and 1960s when between 25 and 30 Labour MPs were regularly returned, as against a mere 2 Conservative. The trend would appear to reflect changes in political loyalties within the Jewish community where social mobility and foreign policy considerations have drawn voters away from the Labour Party and towards the Conservatives.[18]

The number of old (70+) MPs, as shown in Table 9.1, continued to decline. Only five were elected, one Labour and four Conservative. The oldest of all was Labour's Michael Foot (b.1913). The oldest Conservative was Sir Bernard Braine (b.1914), whose slightly younger septuagenarian colleagues were Sir Julian Ridsdale (b.1915), Sir Raymond Gower (b.1916), and Edward Heath (b.1916). On the last occasion, before 1987, when Labour suffered its third defeat in succession – in 1959 – as many as 21 Labour MPs were over 70. Since that time the job of an MP has become more arduous, and since 1979, when 10 Labour septuagenarians were returned, it had become

Table 9.1   Age of candidates, 1 January 1987

Age on 1 Jan. 1987	Conservative elected	Conservative defeated	Labour elected	Labour defeated	Liberal elected	Liberal defeated	SDP elected	SDP defeated
20–9	4	52	—	37	1	29	1	24
30–9	70	114	44	196	4	128	–	111
40–9	146	65	94	126	7	88	2	106
50–9	111	22	63	40	4	56	2	50
60–9	43	4	27	5	1	9	–	10
70–9	4	–	1	–	–	–	–	–
Total	376	257	229	404	17	310	5	301
Median age								
1987	48	37	47	38	45	40	47	41
1983	47	36	51	38	43	39	45	39

more insecure, with mandatory reselection making it more likely that older MPs would either retire, or be retired. Conservative MPs, on the other hand, had rarely sought to linger into their 70s.[19]

A few of the new MPs in 1987 did however come late to the fray. Two of Labour's new intake were in their 60s: Mildred Gordon of Bow & Poplar (b.1923), and John Hughes of Coventry North-East (b.1925). The oldest Conservative newcomer was Irvine Patnick from Sheffield Hallam (b.1929).

Four MPs were under 30: two were Conservatives – Patrick McLoughlin from Derbyshire West (b.1957), and Tim Devlin from Stockton South (b.1959); one was SDP – Charles Kennedy re-elected for Ross, Cromarty & Skye (b.1959); and one Liberal, Matthew Taylor (b.1963), who had become the baby of the House on winning the Truro by-election in March 1987, and who was still the only MP born in the 1960s to be returned at the election in June. The youngest Labour MP was Keith Vaz of Leicester East (b.1956).

As well as being the oldest MP, Michael Foot was the sole remnant of the 1945 election (Table 9.2). He was not, however, the MP with the longest continuous service. That distinction was held by Sir Bernard Braine (Castle Point) who had served uninterruptedly alongside his colleague Edward Heath since 1950, but, because he had taken the oath in 1950 ahead of Mr Heath, it was Sir Bernard who became the new Father of the House in 1987.

Only 5 of Labour's MPs remained from the elections of the 1950s (Tony Benn, Denis Healey, Denis Howell, Bruce Millan and John Morris). Twenty-two Conservatives survived from the same period, 12 of them, including Mrs Thatcher, from the large 1959 intake.[20] Of Labour's post-war record 1964 intake of 90 MPs a mere 12 remained

Table 9.2   Parliamentary experience of MPs

First entered parliament	Conservative	Labour	Liberal	SDP
1945–9	–	1	–	–
1950–9	22	5	–	–
1960–9	44	31	2	2
1970–4	99	53	3	1
1975–9	68	34	1	–
1980–3	85	39	6	1
1984–7	58	66	5	1
Total	376	229	17	5

in 1987, and of the large 1966 influx of 69, only 15 (two of whom had joined the SDP). Conservative and Labour front benches were now dominated by MPs first elected in the 1970s; only 107 of the 650 MPs predated the election of 1970 (66 Conservatives, 37 Labour, 2 Liberal and 2 SDP). A majority of Labour (132) and Conservative (199) MPs now had no parliamentary experience of any Prime Minister but Margaret Thatcher.

The proportion of Conservative MPs educated at public schools was barely different from 1983 (Table 9.3), although the percentage (68%) had been falling by about two points over a series of elections. In 1987 the trend was reflected in the new 53-strong intake, at least 40 of whom were inheriting safe seats and replacing members with traditional public school backgrounds. It was noteworthy that only 61% of the new intake had been to public schools, and few of them to the famous boarding schools.[21] For a third election in a row, and following a longer trend than that, the number of Conservative Etonians declined, to 43.[22] The figures reflect both a drift of the party away from the upper middle class: and a drift of the upper middle class away from political careers now seen as less rewarding both in pay and status.[23] The educational characteristics of Alliance candidates were essentially unchanged, with a large graduate component and one-third of both Liberal and SDP representatives being public school educated. Only Labour relied almost exclusively on the products of state education.

The occupational profiles of the parties showed more continuity than change. In the Conservative case what had altered was not so much the candidates' occupations, as the social background – reflected in education – from which they had come. The Alliance drew rather fewer of its candidates from professional occupations and more from

Table 9.3 Education of candidates, 1987

Type of education	Conservative		Labour		Liberal		SDP	
	elected	defeated	elected	defeated	elected	defeated	elected	defeated
Elementary only	–	–	4	1	–	–	–	1
Elementary +	–	1	11	1	–	1	–	1
Secondary only	25	25	32	63	3	30	1	25
Secondary +	26	41	50	91	2	45	–	51
Secondary & University	69	84	100	194	4	121	2	133
Public School only	41	12	1	4	–	7	–	4
Public School +	21	13	1	5	–	10	–	4
Public School & University	194	81	30	45	8	96	2	82
Total	376	257	229	404	17	310	5	301
Oxford	90	32	22	35	2	33	1	51
Cambridge	76	25	12	14	2	31	1	26
Other university	97	108	95	190	8	154	2	139
All universities	263 (70%)	165 (64%)	129 (56%)	239 (59%)	12 (71%)	218 (70%)	4 (80%)	216 (72%)
Eton	43	9	2	–	–	7	–	6
Harrow	8	5	–	–	–	2	–	2
Winchester	4	3	1	–	–	2	–	3
Other	201	89	29	54	8	102	2	79
All public schools	256 (68%)	106 (41%)	32 (14%)	54 (13%)	8 (47%)	113 (36%)	2 (40%)	90 (30%)

business than in 1983, but what was most remarkable about the Alliance was how alike the profiles of the two parties were. Labour's enduring characteristic, that of a large minority of MPs drawn from manual occupations, remained, but in 1987 the proportion of manual workers (29%) was the lowest since 1974. The percentage normally declines when Labour *wins* elections, as in October 1974 when of 319 Labour MPs only 28% were manual workers. But in a PLP reduced to 229 MPs representing mostly safe seats, a higher proportion could be expected. As well as the large number of teachers and lecturers, more Labour MPs and candidates were being drawn from the ranks of local government officers, full-time politicians and trade union officials, mostly 'middle-class' graduates. Of Labour's 69 entrants in 1987, comprising a third of the PLP, only 12 were formerly manual workers.

The number of trade union sponsored Labour MPs (see Table 9.5) rose to 129, restoring the figure to where it had been in the 1970s, though in a much-reduced PLP the proportion of union-sponsored MPs was higher (56%). The TGWU's dominance was even more marked, with a record number of 33 sponsored by the union. The AEU fell from second place in the list only because it was no longer organically linked with the white-collar union TASS. Some unions increased representation, notably USDAW, and NUPE, which made a special effort to sponsor women candidates. Of Labour's 21 women MPs, 13 were union-sponsored (6 by TGWU, 2 by NUPE, 2 by GMBATU, and one each by ASTMS, NUR and USDAW). The NUM's representation continued a gradual decline, mirroring the contraction of the mining industry. Five of the union's nominees were new to the House, reflecting the troubles caused by the miners' strike; opposition to what Arthur Scargill did cost three NUM-sponsored MPs their sponsorship (and in two cases their seats) and probably contributed to the decision of the pro-UDM MP Don Concannon to retire. With Mr Concannon's retirement and the loss of sponsorship by Frank Haynes (Ashfield), there were, after the election, no longer any NUM-sponsored MPs from seats on the Nottinghamshire coalfield.[24] The new NUM-sponsored MP for Barnsley Central, Eric Illsley, represented a sign of the times: he was the first NUM-sponsored MP to have come from a desk job in the union's offices and never to have worked in the mining industry. But he was not alone in the wider context; two-thirds of the 130 union-sponsored MPs elected in 1987 had no experience of manual work.

Co-operative party representation revived slightly from its 1983

Table 9.4   *Occupation of candidates, 1987*

	Conservative		Labour		Liberal		SDP	
Occupation	*elected*	*defeated*	*elected*	*defeated*	*elected*	*defeated*	*elected*	*defeated*
Professions								
Barrister	43	33	9	4	4	11	1	15
Solicitor	21	19	9	13	1	19	–	17
Doctor/dentist	3	4	2	4	–	5	1	11
Architect/surveyor	7	2	–	–	–	3	–	1
Civil/chartered engineer	6	7	–	4	–	5	–	6
Chartered sec./accountant	17	12	2	6	–	9	–	4
Civil Servant/local govt.	13	3	8	28	–	15	1	9
Armed services	15	7	–	–	1	1	–	2
Teachers:								
University	6	3	11	15	2	13	–	15
Adult	2	8	15	47	–	24	–	20
School	17	18	29	82	2	34	–	39
Other consultants	3	3	2	5	–	11	–	10
Scientific research	3	1	6	2	–	3	–	4
Total	156 (42%)	120 (50%)	93 (40%)	210 (52%)	10 (59%)	153 (50%)	3 (60%)	153 (51%)

Business								
Company director	39	21	2	1	–	14	–	12
Company executive	75	39	12	6	–	39	–	41
Commerce/insurance	18	13	9	9	–	10	–	12
Management/clerical	4	7	16	18	2	12	–	7
General business	3	8	2	2	–	8	–	3
Total	139 (37%)	88 (34%)	41 (10%)	36 (9%)	2 (12%)	83 (27%)	0 (0%)	75 (25%)
Miscellaneous								
Miscellaneous white collar	8	5	18	54	1	21	1	17
Politician/pol. organiser	21	14	12	21	1	17	–	8
Publisher/journalist	26	12	14	9	2	13	1	16
Farmer	16	6	2	1	1	2	–	7
Housewife	7	–	–	4	–	6	–	5
Student	–	2	–	1	–	2	–	3
Local administration	–	2	4	7	–	9	–	2
Total	78 (20%)	41 (14%)	50 (21%)	97 (24%)	5 (30%)	70 (22%)	2 (40%)	58 (19%)
Manual workers								
Miner	1	1	16	1	–	–	–	2
Skilled worker	2	7	44	41	–	4	–	13
Semi/unskilled worker	–	–	6	14	–	–	–	–
Total	3 (1%)	8 (3%)	66 (29%)	56 (14%)	0 (0%)	4 (1%)	0 (0%)	15 (5%)
Grand Total	376	257	229	404	17	310	5	301

Table 9.5   *Sponsored candidates, 1987*

	Total	Elected
Transport and General Workers Union (TGWU)	44	33
National Union of Mineworkers (NUM)	13	13
Amalgamated Engineering Union* (AEU)	15	12
General Municipal Boilermakers' and Allied Trades Union (GMBATU)	12	11
National Union of Public Employees (NUPE)	16	9
Association of Scientific Technical and Managerial Staffs (ASTMS)	9	8
National Union of Railwaymen (NUR)	9	8
Union of Shop Distributive and Allied Workers (USDAW)	9	8
Technical and Supervisory Staffs* (TASS)	7	5
Confederation of Health Service Employees (COHSE)	8	4
Association of Professional Executive Clerical and Computer Staffs (APEX)	3	3
Electrical Electronic Telecommunications and Plumbing Union (EETPU)	3	2
National Communications Union (NCU)	2	2
National Graphical Association (NGA)	2	2
Society of Graphical and Allied Trades (SOGAT)	2	2
Transport Salaried Staffs Association (TSSA)	2	2
Fire Brigades' Union (FBU)	1	1
Iron and Steel Trades Confederation (ISTC)	3	1
National Association of Colliery Overmen Deputies and Shotfirers (NACODS)	2	1
National Union of Seamen (NUS)	1	1
Union of Communication Workers (UCW)	1	1
Union of Construction Allied Trades and Technicians (UCATT)	1	1
Trade union sponsored	164	129
Co-operative Party	20	10
All sponsored candidates	184	139

* In previous Nuffield studies AEU and TASS candidates were aggregated. In 1985
the unions became quite separate organisations.

trough, but was still, at 10, lower than the average figure of 16 during
the 1970s. The picture reflected the decline of the co-operative
movement. All but three Co-operative-sponsored MPs were new to
the House; the party is the only sponsoring organisation not to 'back-
sponsor' existing MPs.

The Conservative and Alliance election campaigns had predicted
a Parliamentary Labour Party dominated by extremists. The Alliance

published a list of dubious validity headed '101 Damnations', listing candidates with allegedly known hard left associations. In the event the new PLP did have a majority for the left as measured by the aggregation of *Tribune* and *Campaign* group membership. By the time the House rose for the summer recess in July 1987, 100 members had joined *Tribune* and 42 *Campaign*, with 14 of these taking dual membership. Thus, in total, 'the Left' numbered 128, or 56% of the PLP. It was also clear that a larger proportion (70%) of the 69-strong new intake had aligned with *Tribune* and *Campaign*, with five of these taking joint membership.[25] But it was a moot point how 'left' many of the *Tribune* group were; it already included Neil Kinnock, Bryan Gould and Tony Blair and many others who were not identified with extremist zeal. *Tribune* had become a very broad church whose membership was inflated by MPs taking out insurance against troublesome GMCs, in some cases doubling their insurance by embracing *Campaign* as well.

The Conservative benches also retained their political heterogeneity. Although the new intake contained some obvious right-wingers, it also contained some noted moderates. The new House was notable less for ideological polarisation than for its reflection of broader social trends, especially the mounting political aspirations of the black and female graduate class, the slow erosion of social exclusivity and the gradual demise of the traditional working class.

NOTES

1. Only one other party fielded sufficient candidates to earn air time: the Green Party, with 133 candidates.
2. Forty former MPs sought to return to the House in 1987: 18 for Labour, 18 for the Alliance, 3 for the SNP and 1 for the OUP. Only 9 were successful: 7 Labour and 2 SNP.
3. *Labour MPs failing to gain reselection 1985–6*

Name	Age in 1986	First elected	Left-group membership	Left-group membership of new MP
N. Atkinson	63	1964	*Tribune*	*Campaign*
M. Cocks	57	1970	–	*Campaign*
J. Forrester	62	1966	–	*Campaign*

Name	Age in 1986	First elected	Left-group membership	Left-group membership of new MP
M. McGuire	60	1964	–	*Tribune*
E. Roberts	74	1979	*Campaign*	*Campaign*
A. Woodall	68	1974	–	–

4. See, 'Anatomy of a Takeover: How the Left is ousting Labour's Chief Whip', *Sunday Times*, 15 July 1984.

5. By being deselected, Mr Cocks became the third Labour chief whip in succession to fall foul of his local party. Bob Mellish had been driven out of Bermondsey in the previous parliament, and John Silkin was heading for deselection in Deptford before he announced his retirement in 1985.

6. Other MPs judiciously opted for retirement where the omens looked poor. Mrs Renee Short was in a weak position in Wolverhampton North-East, and other MPs, such as Tom Torney (Bradford South) and Gordon Bagier (Sunderland South) had expressed their hostility to facing the reselection process.

7. Forty-two MPs faced contested reselections; apart from the six who were defeated, three others later retired and one died. Not all the contests involved right-wing MPs; 18 were *Tribune* or *Campaign* group members.

8. Controversy arose at Dudley East where left-wingers objected to new delegates allegedly recruited to sustain the MP, John Gilbert, one of whom (representing a local GMBATU quarry-workers branch) was the MP's wife, a London-based designer. The secretary of the union branch involved happened to be Neville Hough, a senior right-wing figure on Labour's NEC, and recent party chairman; Dr Gilbert survived. At Swansea West Alan Williams's survival on a short-list of one came after the exclusion from the short-list of an active Militant-backed nominee.

9. Frank Field, who eventually survived by 52-21 votes, was one of a group of Merseyside MPs targeted by Militant or an assortment of 'hard left' activists. John Evans (St Helens North), NEC spokesman for the 'one member one vote' proposal in 1984, and Gerry Bermingham (St Helens South) were both under threat, but on account of long-running investigations into irregularities in their CLPs, they were exempted from the reselection process. Robert Kilroy-Silk (Knowsley North), resigned from parliament in 1986, making allegations about Militant infiltration. Mr Kilroy-Silk's successor, George Howarth, was imposed on the suspended local party. Elsewhere, in the North-East, two MPs, John Ryman (Blyth Valley) and Jim Tinn (Redcar), faced with local opposition and *claiming* Militant infiltration, survived contested votes, but later retired. John Ryman, a fox-hunting barrister, objected to his left-wing successor, Ronnie Campbell, an unemployed miner, and called for an NEC investigation into the local party, threatening to fight Mr Campbell in a by-election.

10. Two Labour MPs also attracted unfavourable personal publicity. Dr

Roger Thomas (Carmarthen) was obliged to announce his retirement following a conviction for indecency, and Gerry Bermingham (St Helens South) suffered publicity concerning extra-marital affairs. He, however, survived, with his CLP suspended by the NEC.

11. Local options varied. In Bristol, the 'Ferguson formula', named after a local Liberal, was devised to break the deadlock between the parties. It was agreed to pair Bristol North-West and Bristol West, to allow for joint open selection in both, but that to ensure that whichever party got one candidacy, its supporters would vote only for a member of the other party for the candidacy in the other seat. The formula was applied elsewhere.

12. Two of the SDP candidates with past parliamentary experience were, if anything, over-experienced. Humphrey Berkeley (Southend East) was donning his third party rosette, having previously been a Conservative MP and a Labour candidate. Similarly, Dr Edmund Marshall (Bridlington) was adding SDP colours to the ones he wore as a Liberal candidate prior to becoming a Labour MP from 1971–83.

13. The percentage of women candidates in each of the parties was: Conservative 7%, Labour 15%, Liberal 14%, SDP 20%, the Scottish National Party 9% and Plaid Cymru 24%.

14. See E. Vallance, 'Women Candidates in the 1983 General Election', *Parliamentary Affairs*, vol. 37, No. 3 (1984) pp. 301–9.

15. There had been three Asian MPs previously: Dadabhai Naoroji, Liberal, Finsbury Central, 1892–5; Sir Mancherjee Bhownagri, Conservative, Bethnal Green North-East, 1895–1906; and Shapurji Saklatvala, a Labour-supported Communist, Battersea North, 1922–3 and 1924–9.

16. Labour would probably have taken a fifth seat with a black/Asian candidate had not Sharon Atkin (Nottingham East) been sacked for insulting Neil Kinnock at a black sections rally shortly before the campaign opened. The NEC imposed an Asian candidate in her place, but the Conservatives narrowly retained the seat.

17. See Patrick Bishop, 'Labour MP seeks action over reselection tactics', *The Sunday Times*, 13 January 1985.

18. See G. Alderman, 'London Jews and the 1987 General Election', *Jewish Quarterly*, vol. 34, No. 3, pp. 13–16, September 1987.

19. Notwithstanding the arduous nature of the MP's job, 1987 saw with the election of David Blunkett, Labour leader of Sheffield City Council, the first blind MP since 1958.

20. The 22 Conservative MPs first elected in the 1950s (with date of first election in brackets) were:

Julian Amery (1950)*	Julian Critchley (1959)*
Sir Bernard Braine (1950)	Sir Peter Emery (1959)*
Edward Heath (1950)	Sir John Farr (1959)
Sir Raymond Gower (1951)	Dr Alan Glyn (1959)*
Sir Julian Ridsdale (1954)	Sir Geoffrey Johnson-Smith (1959)*
Sir John Biggs-Davison (1955)	Sir Fergus Montgomery (1959)*
Sir Richard Body (1955)*	Nicholas Ridley (1959)
Sir David Price (1955)	Sir Trevor Skeet (1959)*
Sir Philip Goodhart (1957)	Sir Dudley Smith (1959)*

Paul Channon (1959)   Sir Peter Tapsell (1959)*
Sir William Clark (1959)*   Mrs Margaret Thatcher (1959)

    * denotes interrupted service

21. In South Dorset Lord Cranborne (Eton and Oxford) was replaced by Ian Bruce (technical school and Bradford). At Harrow West, 'Harrow and Cambridge' was replaced by 'grammar school and technical college'; at Leeds North-East, 'Harrow and Oxford' by 'direct grant grammar school and law college'.

22. The slow decline of the Etonians implied a decline in political families, since as many as 16 of the 45 (43 Conservative and 2 Labour) Etonians were the sons of former MPs. 1987 saw the election of 30 MPs who were the offspring of MPs, one (Andrew Mitchell) of a current MP. The Mitchells were the first father and son pair since the 1960s. Two husband and wife pairs, the Bottomleys and the Wintertons were returned. Two sets of brothers, the Morrisons and the McNair-Wilsons, all Etonians, retained their seats. Of the 30 MPs whose fathers had been MPs, seven were Labour: Hilary Armstrong, Tony Benn, Mark Fisher, Michael Foot, Llin Golding, Greville Janner and Ian McCartney. Hilary Armstrong in 1987, like Greville Janner in 1970 and Paul Channon (Con.) in 1959, succeeded her father as MP for the same constituency.

23. See M. Burch and M. Moran 'Who are the new Tories?', *New Society*, 11 October 1984, and for some impressionistic whimsy, Hugh Montgomery-Massingberd, 'Top and bottom of the Tory class', *The Spectator*, 3 May 1986.

24. Uncharacteristically, the election saw the return to the Conservative benches of a former miner, Patrick McLoughlin, who had won the Derbyshire West by-election in 1986.

25. Despite the expulsion of Militant Tendency leaders from the Labour Party, the new intake included one MP with Militant links (Pat Wall, Bradford North), to add to the two returning Militant-linked MPs Terry Fields (Liverpool, Broadgreen) and Dave Nellist (Coventry South-East).

10 Constituencies[1]

The rise of a mass electorate over the last century, with no counter-vailing rise in the parties' resources to deal with it, has resulted in ever less emphasis on personal contact with the individual voter, and ever greater reliance on the mass media, above all on television. Increasingly, technology has concentrated power over election campaigns in the hands of national party managers.

The constituency campaign, meanwhile, has come to be regarded by most observers as little more than a ritual. The anachronistic local rites of canvassing and public meetings are performed at each election, but they are not thought to have any real bearing on results.[2] Yet hundreds of thousands of people spend what amounts to millions of hours, devotedly trying to influence the votes of their fellow citizens. What did they do? Was there anything new at the grass roots in the electioneering of 1987?

In the hot-house world of national campaigning and campaign-watching, it is easy to lose perspective. The party *apparatchiks* in Smith Square, Walworth Road and Cowley Street, tended to assess the progress of the campaign by the performances of a few party spokesmen, and focused on the daily cut and thrust, the point-scoring, and the stumbles. The public often came to be perceived as mere statistics in a succession of opinion polls rather than as flesh-and-blood voters. But across the nation, in 650 constituencies, a very different sort of election campaign was being fought. With 40 million electors, over half a million campaigners, and over 2000 candidates, the election in the constituencies defies easy description. The patterns of activity are too varied to be recorded or assessed in any detail; generalisations must suffice. What follows is largely influenced by the answers given by 200 or more candidates to our post-election enquiries.

In the constituencies in June 1987 candidates and canvassers were, as usual, busy with the routine of campaigning, dealing with printers, paperwork and postal votes. For most of the time they had little opportunity to follow the national campaign on television or in the press. On the doorsteps they met electors who were often even less involved with the matters absorbing the strategists and observers in London than they were, and whose patience was severely tried by what most of them saw as excessive media coverage of the campaign.

The scandal-mongering in the tabloid press found little echo in the constituencies. Canvassers were faced with concern over a number of national issues, notably health, schools, defence and taxation. Some evidence that the Conservative and Alliance campaigns had penetrated the voters' consciousness could be found in the extent to which fears of the so called 'loony left' were expressed. Labour's first election broadcast clearly struck a chord too, at least with Labour sympathisers. Less frequently there were references to specific press conferences and national campaign incidents. These were, however, restricted to those perceived as detrimental to the party concerned; notably Mrs Thatcher's remarks on health and education, and Mr Kinnock's on taxation, and on making an occupation of Britain 'untenable'. However, voters were often too courteous to allow party workers a clear sense of what was going on in their minds. Agents would candidly admit that they were in no position to tell London how the campaign was being received. Candidates across all parties, isolated among their party zealots, usually became increasingly optimistic – but they could not all be right.

From 1984 onwards, candidates were duly selected and adopted by their local parties and, under the guidance of a professional agent, or more usually an amateur one, a local strategy of fund-raising, canvassing, literature distribution and meetings was devised. Candidates and workers soldiered on and convinced themselves that they were making a difference. The varying outcomes in contiguous and comparable seats indicate that in some cases, to some degree, they did.

Often campaigning was a nominal activity, with a handful of people performing a shadow of the traditional routines in a hopeless seat. But sometimes there was an elaborate and well-executed plan, involving hundreds of enthusiasts. Indeed, in some instances, 1987 marked a rehabilitation for the constituency campaign. Certainly there was a divergence of trends between different sorts of seat. Whereas there was less and less activity in seats that were safe for one or other of the parties, in some marginal constituencies there was more campaigning, more canvassing, and more money being spent than in 1983. New campaign techniques were also being tried.

The impetus for these stirrings came largely from the centre. The organisation departments at the parties' London headquarters encouraged constituency agents and activists to take a fresh, more business-like, approach to campaigning in their key seats. The strategy of targeting was important. Parties have always had target seats, but this often meant little in practical terms. In 1987, however, it involved direct, daily contact and advice from members of the parties' national or regional staff, special training and guidance before the election, and, in some cases, substantial financial grants.

Targeting can work at two levels; effort and resources can be aimed at particular seats, and also they can be aimed at individual voters within seats. In 1987 the parties put a new and special focus on the latter: they knew that not every seat in an election was of importance to them, but neither was every voter. The trick, they believed, was to avoid spreading their resources too thinly, which meant, in practice, spreading them unevenly, to give that extra bit of attention to their marginal supporters. The efficient exploitation of this strategy was, they claimed, made possible by the new availability of cheap and powerful personal computers. Some press accounts during the election exaggerated the role of computers, giving the impression that they had become the norm. In fact, most constituencies did not have computers at all, and most of those which had them failed to exploit their full potential. But they did emerge as the new 'ideal' of efficient campaigning, and their use is bound to grow in the future.

Canvassing provides campaigners with the data they need for targeting. Apart from the distribution of literature, it is canvassing that makes most demands on manpower in a constituency campaign. In a perfect campaign every house would be visited and the likely voting behaviour of every elector recorded. The advent of three-party politics had caused the parties in some constituencies to become more sophisticated, asking for other information besides the canvasser's traditional 'For', 'Against' and 'Doubtful'. In some seats party workers were told to record electors' sex, age, and type of housing, in addition to seeking more specific answers about their voting intention. As well as for campaigning purposes during the election, canvass data is traditionally used on polling day to ensure the maximum turnout of a party's supporters: as electors reach the polling booths their names are ticked off the parties' lists, so that any laggards can be knocked up in the final hours of voting.

When canvassing is done well – in reasonable quantity and in a well-resourced campaign – there is reason to believe that it is not as inaccurate as some commentators claim. In research into the efficacy of canvassing, based on the Greenwich by-election, Kevin Swaddle[3] found that the canvass was generally quite efficient in identifying a party's opponents, that about two-thirds of the people a party identified as one of its supporters did really support it, and did vote, and that people who were not visited by the parties were less likely to vote than those that were. However, even if people were on the whole correctly identified, the number of additional votes to be garnered by good organisation remains few. And since the resources available to a party in the ideal circumstances of a by-election are many times greater than even the best organised constituencies can manage in a general election, the message from Greenwich is not an unequivocal endorsement of canvassing.

In 1987 the number of constituencies where there was a comprehensive canvass, and an efficient polling-day organisation, was small. In some safe and many hopeless seats, there was no attempt at systematic canvassing. Candidates and their workers confined themselves to mingling in shopping areas and other places, and on polling day to making appeals by loudspeaker in their strongest areas for people to go out and mark their ballot. Gallup found that only 16% of people remembered anyone approaching them on polling day; 6% were Conservative supporters, 7% were Labour, and 3% Alliance.

In some constituencies – mostly marginals – the canvass was aided by computers. The spread of computers was greatly encouraged by the new availability of electoral registers on computer tape (sold by the local council for about £100).[4] They were used in a few areas for the preparation of canvass cards. When canvass data was also inputted, they could be used for the printing of polling day knock-up sheets, and when linked to a good printer, could be used for sending out direct mail letters – often specifically targeted. Unlike the parties' national direct mail programmes, constituency letters were mainly used for political persuasion and not for fundraising. In theory there is little that a computer can do in a campaign that could not be done manually. But it is significant in practice because of the speed and power of data manipulation it gives to the campaigner.

When the electoral register was stored by local parties, much time could be saved by automatic preparation of addressed envelopes rather than laborious handwriting by party workers.[5] For the most part, however, computers were used in 1987 to facilitate internal party communications. Since regional and area offices also had their micro-computers, it was possible to keep in constant touch via a telephone modem. In their efforts to co-ordinate the election nationally, both Conservative and Labour headquarters sent out daily messages to marginal seats by Telecom Gold – and hoped to receive them back, thus maintaining a continuous two-way contact.

Before the election a number of Conservative Associations in target seats had made use of telephone canvassing to find out about local concerns and to identify potential switchers; telephone canvassing was also tried in the Fulham by-election. The SDP also experimented with the technique. Though the parties claimed that it had a lot of advantages, telephone canvassing has a major disadvantage when conducted during an election campaign, namely, the cost of the phone calls.[6] Even if calls were made by party members on

Table 10.1   Campaign activity

Since the start of the election campaign have you . . .

	Total	Con.	Lab.	All.
	%	%	%	%
Had any leaflets through door?	92	94	94	93
Had Con.	85	88	85	89
Had Lab.	84	86	89	84
Had Alln.	81	84	82	88
Seen any PEBs on TV?	75	74	80	77
Seen Con.	69	70	72	68
Seen Lab.	71	69	76	72
Seen Alln.	66	64	69	70
Been called on?	49	41	41	41
By Con.	19	25	18	18
By Lab.	20	16	30	17
By Alln.	14	13	12	23
Seen any political ads on hoardings?	46	48	51	42
Seen Con.	38	42	40	34
Seen Lab.	32	31	38	29
Seen Alln.	23	24	21	25
Received any leader's letter?	17	20	18	19
Received Con.	11	17	6	9
Received Lab.	9	8	14	9
Received Alln.	6	6	4	13
Listened to any phone-ins?	16	18	15	22
Listened to Con.	13	16	11	17
Listened to Lab.	13	15	12	16
Listened to Alln.	10	11	8	15
Heard any PEBs on radio?	15	18	15	15
Heard Con.	14	16	13	14
Heard Lab.	14	16	13	14
Heard Alln.	12	14	11	12
Attended any meeting?	3	3	5	3
Attended Con.	1	3	1	*
Attended Lab.	2	*	5	1
Attended Alln.	1	*	1	2

Source: MORI/NOP.

their own telephones, counsel advised that the cost of the calls should be entered on the agent's budget. The Conservatives had also sought counsel's advice about conducting national telephone canvassing and been told that, unless the cost of such activity was included in the official expense limits of the constituencies affected, it would be illegal.

Post-election polls demonstrate how far the parties' constituency campaigning permeated through to the mass of people – and the figures are very close to similar findings from 1983. According to Gallup, 49% read an election address, 12% put up a party poster in the window, 2% actually canvassed for their side, 3% attended an indoor meeting, and 2% an outdoor meeting. As Table 10.1 shows, MORI found that there was little difference in the extent to which supporters of different parties were touched by the election campaign. However, the Labour campaign seems to have had a more favourable impact than that of the other political parties (see Table 10.2).

Most candidates spoke at joint meetings organised by churches or local associations because they offered an audience which, in cities at least, they could not attract to their own meetings. In most instances a prominent front-bencher was required for an audience to rise above 100. But most of the 3% of voters who claimed to have attended meetings must have been the party faithful. Except when they drew coverage from the local press or broadcasters, the candidates' spoken utterances reached few wavering voters. Local radio offered a larger outlet – but not one that they rated very highly. The main way in which ordinary candidates could get any message to their constituents was thus through their election addresses and other literature – 94% told MORI they had received such documents.

Gallup's figures also suggest that the part of a constituency campaign that greatest numbers of electors are exposed to, is the parties' election addresses. Consequently, this long-standing element of electioneering still gives candidates and local parties the opportunity to express their concerns to their electorate. Published early on in most campaigns, the addresses inevitably reflect the manifestos of their respective parties. However, an analysis of their content does serve to indicate which issues the candidates, freed from the requirements of comprehensiveness, really thought worth stressing, in addition to providing interesting evidence of divergent regional concerns.[7]

The addresses of all three parties dealt largely with the record of eight years of Conservative government. The most frequently

Table 10.2   Campaign impact

Q: *Which, if any, have made you more/less favourable towards the . . . Party?*

		More %	Less %	Net +/− %
Party political leaflets through	Con.	5	8	−3
the letterbox	Lab.	8	7	+1
	Alln.	6	7	−1
PEBs on TV	Con.	15	21	−6
	Lab.	24	16	+8
	Alln.	16	12	+4
Been called on by a representative	Con.	6	7	−1
	Lab.	7	6	+1
	Alln.	4	3	+1
Political advertisements on	Con.	4	9	−5
billboards or hoardings	Lab.	7	6	+1
	Alln.	3	6	−3
PEBs on radio	Con.	7	13	−6
	Lab.	13	7	+6
	Alln.	6	9	−3
Interviews on TV with	Con.	11	19	−8
party representatives	Lab.	18	14	+4
	Alln.	15	11	+4
General coverage of the	Con.	12	15	−3
election on TV	Lab.	15	11	+4
	Alln.	13	11	+2
General coverage of the	Con.	10	12	−2
election in newspapers	Lab.	10	10	0
	Alln.	6	9	−3

Source: MORI.

mentioned issue in Conservative addresses was defence (80%). Unilateralism was, predictably, savaged, and some claims were made that Alliance policy would leave Britain similarly vulnerable. A 'Soviet threat' was seldom mentioned explicitly, and 34% stressed the more positive side of arms control talks, with several referring to the new 'special relationship' of Mrs Thatcher and Mikhail Gorbachev. But central to the Conservative candidates' messages was the government's economic record. As in 1983, the continued low level of inflation was given a lot of attention (64%), but in 1987 the government's record on economic growth (42%) and unemployment (78%) were paraded as successes, rather than pointed to as costs of painful but unavoidable adjustment, as in 1983.

The growth of productivity levels (21%), of Gross Domestic Product, and of employment since the previous general election were all contrasted favourably with those of Britain's European partners. Whilst some candidates recognised that more needed to be done to help those out of work, there were some addresses where self-congratulation gave way to a certain statistical extravagance. David Shaw, for example, standing for Dover, listed 'reducing unemployment' among 'Conservative achievements of the last eight years'.

The vision of a wealth-owning, low tax, high enterprise economy also loomed large with 71% of Conservatives mentioning the growth of home-ownership, and, specifically, the sale of council houses. David Gilmartin, the vociferous and defeated candidate in Leyton, even went so far as to say, 'I am totally opposed to the notion of council estates and the concept of public sector housing for families'. 39% celebrated the growth of share-ownership, and 43% praised income tax cuts, which it was claimed had contributed, along with reform of the trade unions (33%) to the growth of enterprise and initiative (24%). The whole experience was summed up by 38% as marking the 'reversal of Britain's economic decline' and the restoration of British pride (39%), or, as the MP for Havant, Ian Lloyd, poetically put it, 'Under Mrs Thatcher winters of discontent have been succeeded by summers of high performance'.

It is interesting that eight years on, half as many Conservative addresses sought to remind readers of the 'winter of discontent' as had mentioned it in 1979. Fear of Labour, not just its 'extreme left' (28%), was the vital corollary of the eulogy of Thatcherism: the 'high inflation, high borrowing years of the IMF and the Lib–Lab pact' is a typical reference. In promoting this image of the opposition, several of Conservatism's less conciliatory advocates came into their own. Frank Rogers (candidate for Gateshead) claimed that 'Many Socialists have sympathy with rioters, Scargill-style pickets, terrorists'. The never reticent Peter Bruinvels warned that Britain's new found

> self respect, pride and strength would be undermined by a state-controlled Labour/Trade Union backed government, destroying enterprise, competition and initiative at the hands of the Militant left . . . Family life would be undermined and discipline removed from our schools. Our children would suffer political and sexual indoctrination.

Iain Picton, defeated in Sunderland North, devoted space to a costing of how income tax at 53 pence, the alleged consequence of Labour's spending plans, would hit a variety of different income groups. For voters in Sutton and Cheam there was 'no alternative' for voters but to help Neil Macfarlane 'Keep Britain flourishing and . . . defeat the sinister presence of Socialism'. 14% of Conservatives sought specifically to stress that wealth creation enabled real caring. 78% discussed the National Health Service and education, and the Conservative proposals for reform of the latter were mentioned by 59%.

The opposition parties devoted even more attention to the social issues such as the NHS (Lab. 94%, SDP 91%, Liberals 86%) and education (Lab. 71%, SDP 93%, Liberals 84%). Voters were asked to compare their own experiences of these services with the Conservatives' claims of increased expenditure, and several addresses illustrated their point with local instances of inadequate provision. 27% of Labour and 44% of Alliance addresses made appeals for a more caring society, and about a quarter of opposition candidates castigated the government as 'uncaring'.

Other social issues also featured prominently. 71% Labour, 84% SDP, 59% Liberal, but only 47% of Conservative addresses discussed pensions, an issue perceived as a weak one for the government. For the Alliance, 64% also discussed other aspects of help for the elderly; among Conservatives this was almost exclusively mentioned only in the context of the benefits of low inflation for savers. One strident analysis of the uncaring nature of both Thatcherism and capitalism in general came from Dave Nellist, MP for Coventry South-East, who claimed that the Conservatives thought, 'Pensioners are "disposable"', because they no longer work and therefore do not contribute to profits'.

Opposition addresses also discussed social security benefits (38%), poverty (21%) and homelessness (28%), areas almost entirely neglected by Conservatives. Labour was strongest on women's rights (35%), with 15% mentioning the proposed Ministry for Women, and 36% mentioning nursery education.

On the economy, Labour naturally stressed unemployment (91%), although the figure was down from the 100% of 1983, perhaps reflecting a belief among some sections of the public that the government had made progress on the issue. Labour's programme of public sector spending and investment (56%) was clearly an important element in the party's economic strategy, as was training (54%) and reviving manufacturing industry (35%). Perhaps the most glaring omission was any recognition of the need for any counter-inflation policy. Whereas in 1983 36% of addresses had dealt with inflation (in most cases by the advocacy of price controls), in 1987 only 1% gave it any attention. It was a somewhat disturbing feature of the local campaigns, and to some extent the national campaign too, that on the whole range of issues, such as inflation, council house sales, women's rights, poverty and social security, there was scarcely a hint of consensus between the two major parties even on defining the problems.

The theme of divided Britain wrought some of Labour's toughest rhetoric, even from Southern candidates. Fred Inglis in Winchester wrote that,

> Since 1979 Mrs Thatcher has made naked greed acceptable. She has split the country against itself. She promised harmony and has brought riot. She has brought toadies to office. She has laid waste huge tracts of the country's greatest cities.

Only 38% of Labour candidates tackled the question of defence, with 28% also stressing Labour's plans for increased spending on conventional arms. There were no references to withdrawal from NATO, but some hard-hitting remarks were made from the left. Ken Livingstone referred to Europe as 'Reagan's preferred battleground', and Dave Chapple (Woodspring) stated that, 'David Steel, David Owen and Thatcher have all said they would perform the opening ceremony to a nuclear war in Europe'.

Alliance election addresses had a quite distinctive flavour and set of priorities. They offered a clear strategy for the economy: a 'carefully costed' programme of public investment (SDP 55%, Liberal 65%) to reduce unemployment (SDP 91%, Liberal 92%), combined with an incomes policy (SDP 28%, Liberal 30%) to prevent inflation (SDP 47%, Liberal 57%). In line with the other parties, training (SDP 58%, Liberal 51%) was a high priority. On defence also the clear outline of joint policy, a minimum nuclear deterrent without Trident, was mentioned by virtually all the 75% of addresses mentioning defence. Arms control was mentioned by 66%, and strengthening the European voice in NATO was another frequently-expressed aspiration. There were no dissenting voices; Liberal unilateralists kept a very disciplined silence.

A distinctive feature of the Alliance addresses lay in their stress on concepts – 'consensus and cooperation' (SDP 63%, Liberal 68%), 'adversary/see-saw politics' (SDP 47%, Liberal 32%), 'divided Britain' (SDP 58%, Liberal 51%) – and in their emphasis on political reform as an important means to solving problems. Electoral reform received attention from 58% of Alliance candidates, freedom of information from 36%, devolution and recional assemblies from 34%. 42% of Alliance addresses also advocated 'tactical' voting.

One interesting feature of 1987 was the extent to which 'law and order' ceased to be an exclusively Conservative issue (Con. 74%, Lab. 65%, Alln. 70%). This was in marked contrast to the 1979 and 1983 general elections when only 34% and 21% of Labour addresses respectively touched upon the issue. Moreover, the emphasis has switched from the almost exclusive concentration on the 'social origins of crime' that used to be found in Labour discussions of the subject. But on the advocacy of tougher sentences (30%) and capital punishment (19%), Conservatives still have a monopoly. It is interesting that on these issues, as well as on immigration, race relations, rates, and Labour's 'hard left', the most virulent pronouncements came from defeated Conservatives. It seems that in a particular type of seat, notably Northern, urban, Labour strongholds, the Conservative message consists in large measure of a more specific attack upon the Labour candidate or high-spending Labour council, and contains a more authoritarian populist message than would normally be found in a more winnable seat.

As usual, the election addresses of all parties demonstrate the insular nature of the election (see Table 10.3). Little was said on the Third World, South Africa or the EEC, the latter having been a major issue in 1983 addresses. The danger posed by AIDS was also a non-issue, drawing only this comment from one rather irresponsible Conservative: 'We will protect society from AIDS by public health measures, and stop the promotion of homosexuality which is encouraged by the other parties'.

The style of addresses was generally traditional, although some unusual individualistic touches were displayed. Many candidates featured messages from prominent party or public figures, as well as photographs of themselves accompanying them. Neil Thorne, Conservative MP for Ilford South, chose to be photographed with President Zia of Pakistan, not obviously an overwhelming electoral asset. Pictures of candidates and their families in domestic settings remain prevalent in many addresses from all parties, and the accident-prone 'wife's message' is still not dead. Edna Healey was ambiguous, 'The children who, 35 years ago shouted "Healey for Labour" have grown up', when trying to stress the longevity of local respect for her husband. Just under half the addresses analysed used glossy paper, but Labour were far ahead in the use of colour photography (34%).

Table 10.3 Themes in election addresses (%)

Issues/Themes	Conservative			Labour			Alliance	
	All	Elected	Defeated	All	Elected	Defeated	SDP	Liberals
1. IMAGE/IDEAS								
Use of party slogan	21	23	13	47	65	52	65	51
Britain's place in the world	39	40	36	1	–	2	–	–
Divided country	3	3	4	21	22	21	58	51
Consensus/co-operation	1	1	–	5	4	5	63	68
Oppose adversarial politics	–	–	–	–	–	–	47	32
Own party moderate	3	1	8	1	–	2	21	16
Labour left extreme	28	18	41	–	–	–	12	24
Con. right extreme	–	–	–	–	–	–	12	11
Own party caring	14	15	9	27	34	24	51	35
Conservatives 'uncaring'	–	–	–	25	26	24	23	24
Mention 'socialism'	11	12	9	8	17	5	–	–
Freedom/choice	21	18	28	9	13	8	2	5
2. STRATEGIC VOTING								
Lab./Con. wasted: vote tactically	–	–	–	1	–	2	42	43
Dismiss tactical voting	–	–	–	5	–	6	–	–
Alln. lets in Lab./Con.	13	12	18	12	4	15	–	–
Alliance vote wasted	–	–	–	8	4	10	–	–
Hung Parliament.	9	10	5	–	–	–	7	3
3. POLITICAL REFORM								
Electoral reform	2	3	–	–	–	–	60	54
Devolution/regionalism	1	1	–	4	13	–	37	30
Other constitutional	1	1	–	–	–	–	23	43
Freedom of information	–	–	–	5	9	3	40	32
Civil liberties	–	–	–	5	9	3	7	16

4. STYLE OF ADDRESS

Background of candidate	71	72	68	72	57	77	81	81
Candidate's constituency record	56	63	32	24	43	16	14	5
Stress on 'local' candidate	7	5	14	29	35	27	28	30
Local issues	39	36	50	54	57	53	51	46
Wife's message	7	8	4	6	13	2	–	–
'Glossy' address	46	44	54	46	53	42	37	39
Colour photographs	2	1	4	34	35	34	2	3
Thatcher (mention)	17	19	10	10	13	8	7	5
Thatcher photo	4	4	4	–	–	–	–	–
Kinnock (mention)	1	–	4	25	22	26	–	3
Kinnock photo	–	–	–	22	22	22	–	–
Owen (mention)	1	–	4	1	–	2	51	26
Owen photo	–	–	–	–	–	–	55	30
Steel (mention)	–	–	–	1	–	2	44	32
Steel photo	–	–	–	–	–	–	49	38

5. ECONOMIC ISSUES

Reversal of economic decline	38	44	18	–	–	–	5	5
Enterprise/initiative	24	27	14	4	4	3	16	22
Unemployment	78	80	73	89	91	89	91	92
Inflation	64	64	64	1	–	2	47	57
Growth	42	45	32	–	–	–	5	8
Income tax	43	42	45	18	9	21	5	8
Indirect tax	1	–	4	6	–	8	2	3
Tax burden	20	23	9	6	–	8	5	3
Productivity	21	24	9	–	–	–	–	–
Public borrowing	15	15	14	–	–	–	2	–
Public spending/investment	14	13	18	56	57	56	55	65
Private investment	5	6	–	4	–	5	7	8
National investment bank	–	–	–	10	–	10	–	–
Incomes policy	1	1	–	6	9	–	28	30
Balance of payments	16	17	14	6	9	5	5	3

Issues/Themes	Conservative			Labour			Alliance	
	All	Elected	Defeated	All	Elected	Defeated	SDP	Liberals
Manufacturing industry	3	3	4	35	39	34	14	19
Interest rates	6	5	8	4	4	3	7	8
Poverty/redistribution	–	–	–	21	39	15	16	11
Minimum wage/low pay	–	–	–	25	30	23	2	–
Public/private sector co-operation	4	5	–	3	4	3	28	27
Nationalisation/social ownership	14	15	9	8	4	2	–	–
Privatisation	39	42	27	8	–	11	5	8
Share-owning democracy	11	12	9	–	–	–	–	–
Small businesses	3	4	–	6	4	6	14	5
New technology	–	–	–	8	4	10	5	14
City regulation	–	–	–	3	4	2	2	–
Trade union reform	33	34	32	8	13	6	37	30
Strikes	29	29	27	–	–	–	–	–
Trade union 'barons'/winter of discontent	15	18	5	1	4	–	35	38
Industrial democracy	–	–	–	11	17	8	2	8
North Sea oil	–	–	–	12	13	11	7	19
Energy	2	3	–	9	13	8	7	14
Nuclear power	–	–	–	20	22	19	23	35
Environment	21	24	8	4	–	5	9	3
Green belt	19	22	9	7	–	10	5	19
Agriculture	9	12	–	13	13	13	28	43
Local government	7	3	23	–	–	–	14	19
Rates	18	15	27	4	4	3	9	41
Poll tax	20	21	18	12	13	11	12	19
Local income tax	–	–	–	12	13	11	5	8
Transport	3	4	17	–	–	–	–	–
Lab./Alliance pact and the 1970s	17	17	17	8	–	11	–	–
Programme 'costed'	–	–	–	–	–	–	21	16

6. *SOCIAL ISSUES*

Housing (general)	20	24	9	38	30	40	65	62
Homeless	–	–	–	28	35	26	35	32
Council house sales/Home ownership	70	73	60	5	9	3	21	38
NHS	78	78	77	94	87	97	91	86
Private health care	3	3	4	6	–	8	–	–
Disabled	10	13	–	8	22	3	12	11
Drug abuse	6	–	–	–	–	–	5	–
AIDS	1	8	4	–	–	–	2	–
Education	59	59	59	71	74	67	93	84
Education reform	59	62	50	5	–	6	40	32
Nursery education	1	1	–	36	30	39	23	11
Higher education/'brain drain'	13	15	5	19	13	21	49	51
Training	39	38	41	54	64	50	58	51
Law and order	74	72	82	65	57	68	74	65
Tougher sentences	30	26	45	–	–	–	–	–
Capital punishment	19	14	36	–	–	–	–	3
Labour 'anti-police'	14	14	14	–	–	–	–	–
Pensions	47	53	27	71	80	66	84	59
Whole 'deal' for elderly	14	17	5	27	35	24	77	49
Social security benefits	7	9	–	38	35	39	23	11
Reform of tax/benefit system	2	3	–	–	–	–	21	14
Services (general)	13	17	–	21	26	19	21	–
Inner cities	11	9	18	–	–	–	5	11
Women's rights	–	–	–	35	35	35	14	16
Abortion	2	1	4	–	–	–	–	–
Family/moral issues	6	5	8	3	9	–	–	–
Immigration	6	4	14	1	4	–	–	3
Race relations	3	1	9	5	13	2	2	5
Northern Ireland	–	–	–	1	4	–	–	–
Animal welfare	3	4	–	2	4	2	–	–

7. DEFENCE/FOREIGN AFFAIRS

Issues/Themes	Conservative			Labour			Alliance	
	All	Elected	Defeated	All	Elected	Defeated	SDP	Liberals
Defence nuclear/unilateral	80	78	86	38	46	34	74	76
Defence conventional	11	10	14	28	30	27	35	24
Arms control	34	38	18	11	4	13	67	65
NATO	14	14	14	15	30	10	56	57
EEC	3	4	–	5	9	3	9	30
South Africa	–	–	–	6	9	5	–	3
Soviet Union	3	3	4	2	9	–	2	–
Foreign affairs (general)	2	3	–	7	9	6	–	3
Third World	4	5	–	11	22	6	5	14
Terrorism	8	5	16	–	–	–	–	–

About three-quarters of candidates stress their personal backgrounds, and claims of a record of service to the constituency could be found from local councillors and even pressure group activists, as well as sitting MPs.

In contrast to the somewhat 'presidential' campaign fought on the mass media, relatively few candidates carried photos, messages or even mention of their party's leader. The high figure for the Alliance is largely due to the centrally circulated photos and messages that came from the two leaders. It is ironic that the parties which stressed their national leadership most in their local addresses, were perceived as the campaign unfolded, to have had the weakest national image and the least effective leaders. Most surprising, perhaps, was the lack of personal criticism and attacks upon other parties' leaders; this was an attractive feature of addresses, for elsewhere they were often far from moderate in tone.

Labour, and to a lesser extent the Conservatives, wanted the issues raised in the morning press conferences, and throughout the day by the principal party spokesmen, to be echoed at the same time in the constituencies' campaigns. Labour hoped that its 'people's agenda' – concentrating on jobs, health, schools, housing and pensions – would be driven home locally. The activities of candidates were to be linked with the press conferences, leader's photo-opportunities and advertising.

Labour strategists tried to monitor opinion in their 144 target seats. Initially they planned to contact each seat on a three-day cycle, but in fact were able to contact the agents or candidates every other day. In previous elections regional officers had the job of reminding the constituency agent to take action on the postal vote or follow up the issue of the day. In 1987 Labour's Organisation Department did this directly with the constituencies, taking the view that officers in the regions should be freed for direct activity on the ground.

As part of their monitoring exercise all parties received nightly reports from their regional or area offices which were then collated and formed the basis of a summary for the early morning meeting of campaign strategists. Conservatives were getting positive feedback from London and the West Midlands, but less encouraging news from Scotland. Labour received good reports from Scotland and Wales.

Daytime visits by party notables imposed great strains upon local and regional organisations. Mr Tebbit and Mr Heseltine for the Conservatives, and Mr Hattersley and Mr Healey for Labour, demonstrated an ability to garner crowds when they visited shopping centres. On the Alliance side only Dr Owen and Mr Steel possessed a similar drawing power.

There appeared to be less activity by pressure groups in this election than its predecessors. Whilst CND seemed to be much less visible than in 1983, candidates reported more activity by Life and SPUC, the anti-abortion groups. SPUC in particular was criticised by several Labour and Alliance candidates for producing aggressive and misleading literature, and there were protests at the literature sent to local clergy about the voting records of particular MPs.

For Labour, the trade unions lent officers, cars and equipment. The TGWU and the GMB tried to concentrate on the party's target seats. There were cases of unions failing to co-operate with the Trade Unions For Labour (TUFL) because they wanted to focus their efforts on their own sponsored candidates. A post-election report for Labour by Bill Keys, the former printers' leader, complained that too often trade unions were not able to provide effective help because so little preparatory work had been done.[8]

Labour's agency service, long in decline, had recovered a little since 1983. The number of full-time agents had increased from 60 to 68, covering nearly 100 seats. The party had also appointed assistant regional organisers for North Wales, Liverpool, Lothian and North Nottinghamshire. In Nottinghamshire the miners' strike had divided a number of constituency parties, and the entrenchment of the Union of Democratic Miners posed a threat in some Labour-held seats. (In marginal Mansfield, the retiring Labour MP, Don Concannon, urged voters not to support the Labour candidate.) Organisers tried to keep out of constituency disputes to concentrate on electioneering. Labour regional officers, particularly in the North-West, London and the East Midlands, often encountered hostility from some constituency parties because of the many troubles since 1983. The Conservatives had about 300 full-time agents, and by the time of the election had full-time agents in all but two of their 72 target seats (see p. 26). An indication of the comparative strength of the two parties is that in the 58 constituencies in the West Midlands, Labour had two full-time agents while the Conservatives had 33.

There was the usual crop of alleged malpractices in the constituencies. Labour's headquarters said that there was 'more consorting with lawyers' than in any previous election. Libel writs were issued by at least 15 candidates, but almost all were dropped after the election. John Horam, a Labour, and then an SDP MP for Gateshead West up to 1983, wrote to SDP supporters appealing for them to back the Conservative candidate, so as not to split the anti-Labour vote; his letter gave no indication that he had recently joined the Conservative party or that it was sent out by the local Conservative party. There were also objections to the activities of TV87 and other groups seeking to inform electors as to how best to cast an effective tactical vote against the Conservatives (see p. 58). A number of Conservatives complained privately of Labour opponents infringing the expenses limit, due to the cost of the high quality leaflets and envelopes which they were using; Conservatives also expressed worries about the volume and lavishness of some local trade union literature. Similar suspicions were voiced from the other side about the Conservative campaign. Generally, disregard for the official limits on constituency spending seems to have been more widespread and systematic than in other recent general elections.

In Scotland and Wales the Nationalist parties imparted a different flavour to the campaign, the contrast being heightened because these two regions were so clearly part of Labour's heartland. The Labour and the Alliance parties were pledged to introduce devolution and an elected Scottish Assembly. The Nationalists called for an independent Scottish parliament, as a prelude to national independence. All the non-Conservative parties emphasised the industrial decline in Scotland and related this to the North/South divide in Britain. Thus, although Mrs Thatcher chose to open her campaign at Perth, the Conservatives were clearly on the defensive because they had so few MPs (only 21 out of 72) to start with, unemployment was high, the rating revaluation had caused unpopularity, and there was continuing gloom over the future of Ravenscraig, Scotland's only steelworks. In Wales there were complaints when the Conservatives selected another non-Welsh speaker to defend Ynys Mon from Plaid Cymru – but in general the Plaid challenge was constrained by the fact that only five of the 38 Welsh constituencies are, to a substantial extent, Welsh speaking. It is a strength of Scottish nationalism that it has a base that is primarily economic and not linguistic.

The issues for the candidates in Northern Ireland differed from those on the mainland, although surveys suggested that voters in the province, like other United Kingdom voters, were primarily concerned with unemployment, defence, law and order and education. While the domestic politics of Northern Ireland hardly figured in the election in Great Britain, the threat of IRA terrorism necessitated strictest security for the Prime Minister wherever she went.

The constitutional question has long been dominant in the province. It received a fresh twist from the 1985 Anglo-Irish Agreement, which, by giving the Irish Republic a consultative voice in Ulster affairs, deeply affronted the Unionists. Both Official Unionist (OUP) and Democratic Unionist (DUP) politicians regarded the election as a second referendum on the Agreement (the first having arisen when Unionist MPs resigned their seats to cause by-elections in 1986 – see p. 15). In contrast to 1983 when they had competed with each other in 13 of the 17 seats, in 1987 they formed an electoral pact, neither party putting up candidates against the other. The Unionist leaders had some difficulty in making their pact stick. In Antrim East the 1983 DUP candidate, Jim Allister, who had lost to the OUP by only 367 votes, wanted to try again. The opening drama of the campaign was whether Mr Allister, who had been the DUP's Chief Whip at Stormont, would defy his party and stand as an Independent. On 21 May he announced that he would not, but at the same time resigned from the DUP denouncing the 'self-serving charade' of the Unionist pact. In North Down James Kilfedder, who had sat under various Unionist labels since 1970, was challenged by Robert McCartney, who stood as a Real Unionist, and was expelled from the Official Unionist Party. This inter-Unionist fight was one of the three highlights of the election in Northern Ireland – and although the established Mr Kilfedder won by 45% to 35%, it was his lowest majority in seven elections. The other Unionist battle which attracted attention was in South Down, where in an increasingly Catholic area Enoch Powell had to defend his seat against an opposition that was less divided than before.

Catholic division, however, was most acute in West Belfast, where Sinn Fein's sole representative faced an SDLP challenge which, in contrast to 1983, did not have to split the vote with Gerry Fitt. Sinn Fein fought 14 seats in all, competing with the SDLP, the party of constitutional nationalism, for the Catholic vote. The Unionist parties' hopes rested on a deadlocked parliament which would enable them to exploit their votes and insist that the Agreement be revoked. It was also suggested that Orange indignation at the Hillsborough agreement explained some of the Conservative slump in the Protestant Irish areas of Liverpool and Strathclyde.

In their replies to our post-election questionnaires, many Conservatives were remarkably outspoken about their party's campaign. They commented that voters had decided views on Mrs Thatcher and that supporters and opponents were equally matched. Some 'wet' MPs, who had not been favoured with promotion under Mrs Thatcher, were highly negative about her impact on voters. One commented: 'The victory was dampened by the 15% of our previous Conservative voters who cannot abide that awful woman. In effect Conservatives won on an unfair electoral system and *despite* Mrs Thatcher'. Another MP in the Midlands commented, 'on balance she was a liability, having been an asset in 1979 and 1983'.

There was also much criticism of the quality of presentation and the absence of an overall theme in the Tory campaign. One prominent junior minister remarked that this was 'the worst campaign I have seen in a long time'. A Thatcherite MP in a Northern marginal commented: 'No clear themes were established and the message was essentially negative . . . I wonder whether Central Office added a single vote to my total'. Another Conservative MP, noted for his independence, reflected: 'A party that goes into an election, making up policies [on education and housing] as it goes along, deserves to lose. Fortunately there is no justice in this world'.

Candidates from the Alliance were even more critical of their parties' national campaigns and leadership. One outspoken Liberal MP forcefully summed up the general feeling: 'Abysmal! No passion, no theme, no content and no idea of what to do when the polls kept on dropping'. Some candidates saw the campaign as 'purer' than those of their adversaries, seeking to present the issues in a more serious, deliberative manner, but too often it was precisely this which was seen as lacking in feeling: 'too A-level' as one Liberal put it. The goal of a hung parliament was also viewed as 'lacking sex appeal'. However, many of the campaign's deficiencies arose from a genuine dilemma rather than specific blunders. Different regions tended to benefit or suffer from differing aspects of the national campaign. One candidate bemoaned that he 'could feel us losing the tactical vote each time Dr Owen attacked Labour'. By contrast, candidates for whom Labour was the chief adversary, or those seeking to present the Alliance as 'safe' to Conservative waverers, were critical of the early decision not to attack Labour.

There was also general dismay about the first election broadcast which featured Rosie Barnes and a rabbit. Alliance candidates reported a growing lack of credibility as their opinion poll ratings remained poor, and candidates from all parties claimed to have noticed a tendency for some voters to move tactically from the Alliance to the Conservatives for fear of Labour, as the two Davids languished in the polls.

One area of almost universal agreement was that the 'dual leadership' was a disaster, with some Liberals drawing early lessons on the need for a merger. Frequent comments were made about 'Tweedledum and Tweedledee'. David Steel's leadership was considered a weakness by a few respondents who felt that the *Spitting Image* television caricature of him had made a mark on the voters' minds. However, the most specific criticism was reserved for David Owen. A perceptible rift emerged on this, more than on any other question, between Liberals and Social Democrats. Several Liberals went so far as to say that he was 'universally disliked' and 'a vote loser', and one senior Liberal stated that 'Tories like Owen, Labour like Steel'. Indeed, it did sometimes seem that Neil Kinnock was more in tune than David Owen with the aspirations of Liberal candidates in less prosperous constituencies. In particular, Liberals were critical of David Owen's 'obsession' with defence, and his failure to be even-handed between the Labour and Conservative parties when discussing coalition possibilities.

Alliance respondents in general seemed contented, but not delighted with, the quality of service which the constituencies received from national headquarters, although longstanding Liberals commented that it was an improvement upon former times.

Labour candidates were virtually unanimous in their praise, and often their surprise, at the quality of help from Walworth Road. Superlatives such as 'magnificent', 'outstanding', and 'fantastic' were common. The generally favourable media reaction to the Labour campaign, was, not surprisingly, reflected in the remarks of Labour respondents to our questionnaire. Frequent contrasts were made with the 1983 campaign, and the performance of Michael Foot was adversely compared with that of Neil Kinnock. As one *Tribune* MP wrote: 'We took pride in the sheer professionalism of our national TV campaigning. In 1983 we strongly believed that every national Labour effort was another nail in our coffin locally'.

There was also considerable agreement that the Party Election Broadcast featuring Neil Kinnock was the highlight of the media campaign, contrasting well with Rosie Barnes's broadcast for the Alliance. With Kinnock's passionate rhetoric, its effect in generating activist enthusiasm was clearly immense, and it did much to restore party pride amongst Labour voters.

However, respondents had to face up to the scale of Labour's defeat and seek reasons. The party's wings differed. From the right came, 'Sanity broke out four years too late'. And from the left: 'After three years in which the leadership had attacked the left, melted down the policies, and reaffirmed its commitment to the status quo, just three weeks to attack the cabinet was not enough'.

Reaction to the campaign itself was not uncritical. The performances of Roy Hattersley and Denis Healey were contrasted unfavourably with those of Bryan Gould and Neil Kinnock. More generally some complained that, despite good presentation, much of the policy analysis they received was somewhat superficial. One of the more individualistic Labour MPs wrote:

> In the excitement of the election the Kinnock approach was successful but in the aftermath questions remain about the presentation of the substance of policy . . . the repetition of the glory of Kinnock should have been replaced by a more detailed presentation of policies.

However, a majority blamed specific issues: defence, taxation, and, in the South particularly, the right to buy council houses. A typical comment was, 'the taxation issue hurt – C1, C2 voters are greedy for the tax cuts and it was difficult to deal with this by telling them to think about the pensioners'. And again: 'I believe people quite deliberately chose not to run the risk of being less well off. Compassion did not extend to personal sacrifice'.

The increasing public antipathy towards the saturation coverage of the election by the media, wrought a sympathetic response from candidates of all the major parties. One candidate stated, 'I saw little of the national media campaign, and this was agreed by one and all to be an advantage'. Conservatives in particular stressed this, and some expressed regret at what they saw as the belittled role of the individual candidate and the local campaign. A Conservative respondent attributed the whole outcome of the election to 'the opinion polls and the media interviewers'. 'I wonder if the result of the election would have been any different if all the candidates had spent the month abroad', commented another. One respondent suggested that there should be three media-free days a week, to encourage voters to return to public meetings. In spite of all the reporting of the election on the TV and in the press, many candidates reported political interest to have increased during the election.

The weather on polling day was good over most of the country, although there were some thunderstorms and heavy showers in the South-East (London had 0.41 inches of rain). In 1979 and 1983 there had been a similar pattern in the time of voting on election day. In 1987, however, as Table 10.4 shows, more voters cast their ballots earlier in the day, continuing a long-term trend. By 3 p.m. 51% had voted; 30 years earlier over half the votes were cast after 6 p.m., even though the polls then closed at 9 p.m. The Conservative advantage that used to come from their supporters polling first seems to have evaporated.

Table 10.4   Time of voting

Time	All voters 1983 (%)	1987 (%)	Con (%)	1987 Lab (%)	Alln.(%)
7.00 a.m.–11.59 a.m.	34	38	36	38	38
12 noon–4.59 p.m.	21	25	25	26	25
5.00 p.m.–7.59 p.m.	32	27	29	27	26
8.00 p.m.–10.00 p.m.	11	9	9	7	9
Postal vote	1	1	–	–	–

The Representation of the People Act 1985 had greatly expanded the facilities for absent voting. It provided that Britons living overseas could stay on the register in their old constituencies for up to five years. In the event, only about 13 000 people availed themselves of this contentious arrangement. More important, it allowed people away on holiday to claim a proxy or postal vote, which, in a summer election, offered great opportunities for efficient party organisation. In fact, the numbers were not as great as expected, and most of the applications came from individual enterprise. A rather confusing Home Office advertisement on television and in all the national papers on Thursday 21 May and Sunday 24 May prompted many claims (many of which had to be disallowed because husband and wife had used the same witness). People holidaying abroad had to appoint proxies, as postal votes could not be sent overseas. No exact statistics on the use of proxies were collected but local reports suggested that almost twice as many voted by proxy as in 1983, and that proxy votes amounted to about half of all the absent votes cast. The more generous regulations on postal voting did not bring the expected increase in numbers.

The total number of postal electors was 950 000 compared to 624 000 in 1983, and the number of valid postal votes was 780 000, compared to 624 000 in 1983 and 875 000, the highest on record, in October 1974. The 150 000 increase was less than might have been expected in view of the new facilities for holiday makers and the Home Office advertising. The largest number recorded in mainland Britain was 2687 in Taunton and there were 41 other seats with a postal vote of over 2000. At the other extreme there were six seats with less than 300 postal votes, the lowest being 231 in Newham North-West. If the postal vote divided 75-15-10 in favour of the Conservatives (with the 15% going to the largest opposition party) they would owe 10 seats to it. If it divided 50-25-25 the figure would be five seats. But the old assumption that the Conservatives gain an overwhelming advantage from the postal vote may be misconceived. An Independent Television News (ITN) study in ten marginal seats showed Labour closer to the Conservatives among postal electors than among those who voted in person (Con. 43%, Lab. 40%, Alln. 16%).

As always, the highest postal votes came in Northern Ireland: Fermanagh and South Tyrone (6715) was once again easily top and, with three other seats, exceeded any in mainland Britain – Mid-Ulster (4343), Newry & Armagh (4325) and South Down (4296). But another change in the law cut turnout in those constituencies: the 1985 Act required voters in Northern Ireland to provide proofs of identity and, accordingly, the local custom of personating absent and dead voters fell sharply. Turnout over the whole of the province was reduced from 72.8% to 67.4%, and in Fermanagh from 88.6% (the highest in the UK in 1983) to 77.4%.

Centrally the parties spent £15m compared to £7.6m in 1983 – a real increase of 65% allowing for inflation. Table 10.5 gives estimates for the expenditure of the parties:

Table 10.5   Party expenditure, 1983 and 1987

	Central expenditure*		Constituency expenditure	
	1983	1987	1983	1987
Conservative	£3.6m	£9.0m	£2.1m	£2.8m
Labour	£2.2m	£4.2m	£1.8m	£2.5m
Alliance	£1.9m	£1.7m–£2.0m	£1.6m	£2.2m

* Central expenditure in some cases includes direct grants towards constituency expenses.

In the localities, the maximum permitted expenses rose from £4200 in an average borough in 1983 to £5400, and in the average county constituency, from £4700 to £5800. Some agents complained that this limit forced them to engage in creative accountancy, but most kept well within the limit. The average expenditures were appreciably higher than in 1983, as Table 10.6 shows.

Rough estimates available for the central expenses of the parties are as follows:

Table 10.6   Total amount spent by candidates

Party	Average expenditure	% of maximum all candidates	victors	% 1983 all candidates
Conservative	4400	78	88	72
Labour	3900	69	81	63
Alliance	3400	61	93	56
SNP	2000	43	90	45
Plaid Cymru	1900	40	91	30
Green Party	800	14	–	24
Communists	1100	20	–	19
Ulster Unionists	3200	55	62	56
SDLP	3100	54	98	33
Sinn Fein	2300	42	96	44

The election cost the government £2m for returning officers' expenses, quite apart from the annual cost of preparing the electoral register – £28.9m in the financial year 1986–7. In recompense, the Treasury gained £145 000 from lost deposits, £500 each from the 290 candidates who failed to get more than one-twentieth of the vote. The Green Party, paying £66 500, was hardest hit. The 1987 general election was the first in which the new deposit regulations applied. Formerly a £150 deposit was lost if a candidate failed to achieve one-eighth of the vote in his constituency. If deposits had been forfeited for less than 12.5% not 5%, a further 222 candidates would have lost their deposits, raising the total amount forfeited to £256 000 (or £76 300 on the old £150 tariff).

The fact that the total central expenses now exceed local expenses by a factor of 2:1 does suggest the need for a review of the law which so constrains constituency campaigning, while allowing the centre a free hand. However it is worth pointing out that press advertising accounted for two-thirds of central expenditure. If press advertising (which no one has shown to have any effect on votes) were banned, as television advertising has always been, elections would be much

cheaper and no one, except newspaper owners, would suffer any
loss.

NOTES

1. This chapter owes a great deal to the work of Kevin Swaddle and Peter
   Wells.
2. The Labour MP Austen Mitchell wrote, 'It is arcane irrelevance, a
   background noise which distracts from the decisive national campaign
   coming over on the box'; 'Taking it Personally', *New Society*, 7 June
   1987.
3. Kevin Swaddle, 'Doorstep Electioneering in Britain: An Exploration of
   the constituency Canvass', *Electoral Studies*, April 1988. The research
   involved a comparison of the three parties' canvasses and the official
   record showing which electors voted.
4. About 100 Conservative seats had the constituency register on the
   computer and about 270 seats in all had computers. In recent years firms
   have been developing election packages which allow for databases on the
   attitudes, interests and voting intentions of voters. See Jon Haber, 'The
   Party Machines', the *Guardian*, 4 June 1987. But the use of computers is
   still in its infancy and regional and party officials reported many cases of
   computers either not being used or being used in an unsophisticated way.
5. In any case, the task of leaflet delivery – particularly in less well
   organised constituencies – was considerably eased by the Post Office's new
   regulations for the free delivery of election literature, operative for the
   first time in 1987. Whereas previously the free post facility had involved
   constituency parties in hundreds of hours of writing election address
   envelopes, they could now choose to have their literature delivered
   unaddressed.
6. It is legal for private individuals to spend up to £5 each in support of their
   chosen candidate without effecting his agent's budget, so long as that
   expenditure is spontaneous and in no sense co-ordinated.
7. The tables and discussion in this section are based upon quantitative
   analysis of the themes found in a random sample of election addresses.
   About one-sixth of all addresses from the Conservatives, Labour and
   Alliance were used. A slight overrepresentation of elected Conservative
   and defeated Labour candidates affects the sample, largely due to the
   small number of Scottish addresses available.
8. See the interesting article by Phillip Basset, 'Many Unions Caught Napping
   at the Last Election', *Financial Times*, 21 August 1987.
9. For more detail on party expenditure see M. Pinto-Duschinsky, 'Last
   minute charge by the Head Office Big Spenders', *Financial Times*, 23
   October 1987; see also M. Pinto-Duschinsky, article in *Parliamentary
   Affairs*, 1985 and his chapter in I. Crewe and M. Harrop (eds), *Political
   Communications: the 1983 Election Campaign* (Cambridge, 1986).

IV

The Assessment

11 Retrospect

Parties devote immense effort and resources – manpower, money and planning – to general election campaigns. However, in terms of the voting decisions of some three-quarters of the electorate, and the election outcome of some four-fifths of seats, the results are largely decided before the dissolution of parliament. Party strategists have to remind themselves of the limits which can be achieved by even the best-run campaign. For many voters electoral choice is a product of a life-time of influences, rather than a response to the stimuli associated with the four hectic weeks of an election campaign.[1]

Yet party leaders constantly review their campaigns during and after the election. There may not be much they can do about the cards they were dealt at the outset of the campaign, but they can ask if they played them to the best of their ability. How might things have gone better? What were the missed opportunities? What mistakes in policy or presentation were uncovered by the campaign? What can be learnt from the efforts of their rivals? Election campaigns also present opportunities for individual politicians to emerge or increase their reputations – like Neil Kinnock, Bryan Gould and Lord Young in 1987 – or conversely to lose some standing – like John Wakeham and even Denis Healey.

The 1983 Labour campaign was generally judged to be the most inept fought by any major party in the post-war period; Labour actually lost a quarter of its support in the four weeks of the campaign.[2] The 1987 election has been widely regarded as one in which Labour, although it failed to win the election and, indeed, finished a poor second, was thought to have fought the best campaign. 1987 may confirm the old adage that elections are won over the long haul. Voters had experienced eight years of Mrs Thatcher's rule and three and a half years of an invigorated Labour party under Mr Kinnock; perhaps they had sufficient time to have arrived at settled views. Many Labour campaigners, in their post-election evaluations, spoke of their vain efforts to combat memories of past disasters – the winter of discontent, the divisions of 1981, the exit of leading right-wingers to the SDP, and the activities of left-wing councils.

Only three among the many voting surveys conducted during the campaign held out the possibility of a hung parliament, and even those saw the Conservatives as comfortably the largest party. At the end of the first week, according to the average of the opinion polls, Labour had picked up three points when the Conservatives stood at an average of 42%, Labour 33% and the Alliance 23%, and by election day those figures had hardly changed. With three-party politics, each party not only fights on two fronts, but there are also two battles, one for first place and one for second place. According to MORI's eve of election poll the Conservatives started with an 11% lead over Labour (43% to 32%) and ended on polling day with a 10.5% lead (42% to 31.5%). The campaign may have had more effect on the battle for second place; Labour's narrow pre-election lead over the Alliance was increased to nine points on election day. Yet commentators made much of volatility and claimed that many voters 'were up for grabs'. Some of these claims may have been an attempt to whip up interest in an election which the Conservatives seemed assured of winning decisively.

The 1987 election campaign gained a bad press. Tory supporting tabloids criticised their party's lack of vigour (which could not be said of their own efforts) and seemed to fear that the professionalism of Labour's public relations might 'con' voters. The quality papers complained about the issues being inadequately discussed, the parochialism of the debate, and the evasions and economies with truth. Dr Owen's interest in the social market was hardly mentioned; Labour spokesmen's habit of cross-referencing between the manifesto and various party policy documents was convoluted and, ultimately, on taxation, self-confusing; the Conservatives backed off their radical proposals for social policy after the first week. Hugo Young, in the *Guardian* on 10 June, complained of the parties' deceptions and evasions, for example, over Conservative plans for schooling and over Labour plans on taxation and trade unions. The recently born *Independent* was so dissatisfied that it withheld endorsement from any party on the grounds that each had shown itself too fallible. On 9 June its main editorial was headlined: 'AN ELECTION CAMPAIGN WHICH HAS FAILED TO SATISFY'.

For Peter Jenkins, in the *Independent*, what passed as debate 'has been no better than crude propaganda'. Such issues as higher education, the world debt crisis, Northern Ireland and South Africa, were hardly mentioned. The *Spectator* (13 June), writing before the election result was known, deplored the Conservative's timidity on health and education and the parties' boasting on how much they had spent and how much more they would spend: 'the Tories boasted of their profligacy: Labour accused them of meanness'. Yet, as Martin

Harrop shows in Chapter 8, elements of the press contributed to such trivialisation by their sensationalism, over-simplification and smears about the private lives of prominent politicians. Television also erred by its passive transmissions of the photo-opportunities staged by the parties – the equivalent of 'junk mail', as Martin Harrison describes them (p. 193).

But although an election campaign is not a course in civic education, many television programmes and quality newspapers covered issues and themes thoroughly. On such programmes as *Granada 500*, *On the Spot*, and *Election Call*, front-bench politicians faced direct questions from members of the public. Some of the main themes of the election were well brought out, notably the Conservative belief in the superiority of market forces for allocating resources and achieving economic growth, versus Labour's advocacy of economic redistribution, state intervention in the economy and collective provision of social services. The government's claim that Britain was enjoying an economic renaissance (accompanied by selected statistics to show that Britain was top of various international league tables) was rejected by Labour spokesmen who pointed to an industrial wasteland, poor quality public services, sharpening economic in-equalities, social divisions and low investment. Again such claims could be backed by selected statistics. By the end of the campaign the Conservative appeal of 'Don't trust Labour' was opposed to Labour's claim that it was the only party that could oust Mrs Thatcher and produce a change of direction. On defence, education and industrial relations too, the differences between Labour and Conser-vative were clearly brought out.

Mrs Thatcher's speeches emphasised the themes of freedom, personal choice, private property and individual opportunity, and the threat Labour posed to these values. Mr Kinnock's speeches concentrated on Labour's plans for the future, the contribution good public services made to the quality of life, and criticised the Conservative version of freedom as one that was primarily for the well-off, not the have-nots.

This was a media-oriented campaign, with television being domi-nant in getting the parties' messages and images across. Parties were ruthless in planning policy statements, schedules, photo-opportunities and initiatives to meet television deadlines, particularly news bulletins at breakfast, lunchtime, early evening and late evening. The leaders' activities were designed to provide good 'photo-opportunities' for the press or for television. All-ticket party rallies for Mrs Thatcher and Mr Kinnock ensured that they addressed party loyalists. The enthusiastic responses of adulatory audiences (hecklers were an extinct breed at the Labour and Tory rallies) were designed to persuade television viewers at home. The Labour campaign was about the selling of Mr Kinnock and the Conservative one, to a lesser extent, focused on Mrs Thatcher. In spite of the efforts of the party strategists to control the campaign agenda, the media still picked up unintended gaffes. On the Conservative side there was Mrs Thatcher's early talk of seeking a fourth term, of 'going on and on'; her unscripted remarks about the Conservative plans for education which had to be corrected later by Mr Baker, her dismissal (immediately withdrawn) in a television interview of those who 'drivel and drool' about caring; and also Mr Wakeham's floundering performance on *Election Call*. On the Labour side there was John Smith's discomfiture in handling questions on defence on the same programme, Mr Healey's angry confrontation with Anne Diamond on television, and Mr Kinnock's interview with David Frost when he spoke of British resistance in the event of a Soviet occupation. On the Alliance side there was the muddle between the two Davids as to whether they would serve under Mrs Thatcher.

A number of important election issues were pursued more in the press than on television – particularly the pro-Conservative tabloid's interest in taxation, left-wing extremism, defence (in the wake of Neil Kinnock's interview with David Frost), and charges that the Labour leader was avoiding questions on policy. Journalists certainly used the daily press conferences to put tough questions to party spokesmen, and at times the encounters rivalled Question Time in the House of Commons.

There was a good deal of published and private survey research about the issues that mattered to voters during the election campaign. The three major policy areas appear to have been health and social security, unemployment and jobs, and education (which rose strikingly in importance during the election). Labour outscored the Conservatives as the party judged best for handling these issues, and managed to get its so-called 'people's agenda' across. Yet the campaign did not have much effect on changing the parties' relative standing on these social issues. The Conservatives enjoyed a success of sorts in holding off further Labour advances as Table 11.1 shows:

But on the second order issues the parties' standings were reversed. All surveys showed that on defence, law and order and taxation, the Conservatives enjoyed a big lead. A third of the final Harris survey

Independent, 4 June 1987

Table 11.1   Campaign trends on issues, 1987

Which party do you think has the best policies to deal with:	May 19/20 (%)	June 8/9 (%)	Change (%)
(a) Inflation and prices?			
Conservative	51	54	+3
Labour	21	23	+2
Liberal/SDP	12	11	−1
Dont's know/other	16	12	−4
(b) Unemployment?			
Conservative	30	30	–
Labour	38	41	+3
Liberal/SDP	16	16	–
Don't Know/other	16	13	−3
(c) Britain's defence?			
Conservative	49	54	+5
Labour	22	21	−1
Liberal/SDP	14	15	+1
Don't know/other	15	11	−4
(d) Common Market?			
Conservative	40	41	+1
Labour	20	20	–
Liberal/SDP	10	10	–
Don't know/other	30	30	–
(e) Strikes and industrial disputes?			
Conservative	48	51	+3
Labour	28	25	−3
Liberal/SDP	10	12	+2
Don't know/other			
(f) The National Health Service?			
Conservative	24	25	+1
Labour	41	44	+3
Liberal/SDP	17	19	+2
Don't know/other	17	12	−5
(g) Education and schools?			
Conservative	33	31	−2
Labour	35	38	+3
Liberal/SDP	17	20	+3
Don't know/other	16	12	−4
(h) Law and order?			
Conservative	43	42	−1
Labour	23	27	+4
Liberal/SDP	13	14	+1
Don't know/other	20	17	−3

Source: Gallup.

respondents mentioned 'defence' or 'nuclear weapons' as influences on their votes, and Labour's private polls indicated that the party's defence policy was costing it some 5–6% of the votes. Peter Kellner in the *Independent* (13 June 1986) thought that the actual figure might have been higher than 6% because one had to take account of the pre-1983 defectors from Labour who were confirmed in their defection and the alienation of potential converts. Defence cost Labour dear. By the end of the campaign Labour's private polls also made clear that the general issue of managing the economy was another major barrier to its advance (see p. 134).

Surveys give some idea of the public's rank order of importance of issues and approval of the parties' stands on them. However, few voters actually decide how to vote on the basis of one issue alone. A voter might think a party's policy is superior on a particular issue area but doubt its competence to delivery, or fear the negative consequences of that policy on, for example, unemployment or inflation. It is also worth noting that the surveys seldom explored such broader topics as the parties' ability to deliver economic prosperity or their competence to govern, both issues on which the Conservatives outscored Labour heavily.

The polling evidence shows how limited is the impact of specific issues on voting. All surveys found that unemployment was the one issue which a majority of voters considered most important. And, by a clear majority, voters regarded Labour as the best party to handle the issue (though private polls showed the Conservatives were seen as the best party for creating jobs). Other concerns, however, prevented many voters from translating this preference into a vote for Labour. For example, Gallup in the second week of the campaign found that inflation (a strong Conservative issue), rather than unemployment, was seen as a bigger threat to voters and their families (Table 11.2). A calculation about the effects of a policy on oneself and family is likely to shape one's vote more than a view about issues in general.

Table 11.2   Inflation versus unemployment as an influence on vote

Which do you think threatens your family most?	%
The threat of rising prices	49
The threat of unemployment	43
Don't know	7

Source: Gallup, 21–26 May 1987.

The dominance of television helped to presidentialise the message of the parties. As noted in Chapters 7 and 8, press and broadcasting coverage concentrated overwhelmingly on the party leaders. Party messages were carried through and by the party leaders, and secondary figures gained little coverage. Mr Kinnock dominated the broadcasting coverage of his party more than any previous Labour leader had ever done (see p. 144). He substantially improved his image during the election and was judged to have had the best campaign of any leader. It is worth noting, however, that he always trailed behind Mrs Thatcher when voters were asked who would make the best Prime Minister (Table 11.3). When the Harris exit poll asked voters for the ONE most important reason 'which decided their vote' only 6% mentioned a party leader, of whom 8% were Conservative, 6% Labour and 4% Alliance.

The Conservatives did not have a happy campaign. It is worth remembering that the party and Mrs Thatcher had a lot to lose – including office itself – and little to gain. The party entered the election with a huge parliamentary majority and a year of office remaining. The choice of election date was ultimately her own personal decision and she would bear a heavy responsibility if the outcome was disappointing. The government had enjoyed a remarkably fortunate approach to the election, with a popular budget, a triumphant trip to Moscow, and the fragile state of the Labour party, as demonstrated by the Greenwich by-election. Yet the Conservative campaign, planned long in advance, stumbled at the start with Mrs Thatcher's answers on education at the party's press conference. 'We fell at the first hurdle', said one adviser, and another resignedly said, 'that was supposed to be the jewel in our crown'. Although the education gaffes seemed to create little impact in the constituencies, the Conservative campaign never caught fire and even a normally friendly *Daily Telegraph* called it 'lacklustre'. A good part of the dissatisfaction was because Labour's campaign was going so smoothly; the Kinnock election broadcast had been well received, and the issue-a-day format was paying off. Although the central thrust of the Labour campaign, with its emphasis on Neil Kinnock and social issues in an attempt to distract attention from Labour's weak points, had been largely anticipated by Central Office and by Saatchi, few expected it to be carried out in such a disciplined and professional fashion.

The reports of Mrs Thatcher's dissatisfaction with the campaign, particularly with Mr Tebbit, the Saatchi and Saatchi advertisements and the television performances of some of the party spokesmen, sapped morale at the centre. Staff at Central Office were made uneasy by the frequent and increasingly public reports of tensions between Lord Young and Norman Tebbit in the building. The self-promoting (and anti-Saatchi and, by extension, anti-Central Office) leaks about the activities of Tim Bell and Young and Rubicam were also distracting.

Some of the problems could be foreseen. Much of Central Office thinking and planning was to cope with an Alliance upsurge – which never occurred. Mrs Thatcher's doubts about the ability of Norman Tebbit to manage the Central Office and her campaign were known beforehand. That is why she posted Lord Young to Central Office in March; he also had lines of communication to other advertisers, who became known as 'the exiles'. Poor co-ordination between 10 Downing Street and Central Office was in part a consequence of there being almost two separate campaign centres. If Downing Street felt that Norman Tebbit was running his own campaign, Central Office were also impatient with the No. 10 staff. In retrospect, Mr Tebbit would have liked to have had more control on the Prime Minister's schedule, and to have chaired the press conferences. In a situation where the clients (Mrs Thatcher and Mr Tebbit) disagreed over advertising and strategy, Saatchi had an impossible task.

It was Mrs Thatcher's idea to ask John Wakeham to marshall spokesmen for broadcasts, selected by Mr Tebbit – unfortunately Mr Wakeham thought his brief included selection as well. One campaign adviser complained that: 'Tory spokesmen on television in the first week looked like cost accountants, saying how much they had spent on services. They cut very poor figures beside the visionaries of the other two parties'.

There was a lack of clear lines of responsibility in Central Office for communications, and Michael Dobbs reluctantly found himself in an ill-defined role co-ordinating with Saatchi and Saatchi over the advertising. Although Conservative leaders mourned the absence of a Peter Mandelson type figure, somebody experienced in television and able to act authoritatively in communications, they had consciously failed to make such an appointment before the election.

It was also Mrs Thatcher, egged on by freelance advertising advisers, who wanted to change the party strategy on the Wednesday and Thursday of the penultimate week. Amongst some disparaging comments made were the following: 'She panicked', 'She was in a bloody funk', 'She was aware that for the first time she might actually lose a general election'. Her confidence was eroded on 3 June by what turned out to be two 'rogue' polls, first the subsequently discredited *Newsnight* marginal seats poll, and then the Gallup survey arriving on Wednesday night. As noted on p. 112, it was only when the party chairman presented a more reassuring poll by Marplan 24 hours later that Mrs Thatcher relaxed. The so-called 'Wobbly Thursday' (4 June) has attracted much publicity, as rival advertising agencies and their supporters have leaked selective versions to the media. Indeed a book, *Campaign: The Selling of the Prime Minister*, graphically reports the state of panic in 10 Downing Street, particularly on the part of Mrs Thatcher, and purports to describe how Tim Bell, a former Saatchi director, almost single-handedly turned the campaign round.[4] In fact, apart from a more positive thrust to the advertisements, there was little change in the planned strategy (see above, p. 109), and claims that the Conservatives were faced with defeat (or at least from being denied a majority) rested on two rogue polls.

A hectic election campaign, conducted by increasingly exhausted and nervous people, will not always run smoothly; fluctuations in morale and scares are part of the game. But one rogue poll should not raise the question of changing strategy, advertising, or even the advertising agency. The Conservatives campaign structure was faulty from the start, and there was a lack of complete agreement and understanding between Mr Tebbit and Mrs Thatcher. One 'secret' campaign, apart from the official one of Central Office, is remarkable, but two is extraordinary. There were three different agencies linked to different senior Cabinet ministers: Saatchi to Mr Tebbit, Tim Bell to Lord Young, and Young and Rubicam to Lord Whitelaw and Mr Wakeham. Each was vying for Mrs Thatcher's attention. It was no surprise that, with the overlaps of authority, some second-guessing, and some personal rivalries (all reminiscent of the pre-Kinnock Labour party), the Tory campaign nearly came unstuck in face of the Labour advance. Mr Tebbit complained publicly after the election 'too many cooks spoil the broth, especially when the chef does not know who is putting in what behind his back'. The diverse recommendations from so many directors resulted in a 'cacophony of discordant and ill-considered advice'.

In defence of Mrs Thatcher it may be suggested that by seeking alternative advice to that from Central Office she was able to make more informed decisions. It could also be said that her nervousness (understandable enough) illustrated her lack of complacency and her determination to improve the campaign. 'An election is like a war', said one of her staff. 'Even if you win easily, it may not have appeared that you would do so at the time. You always try and do better because, in the end, it may make the difference'. Mrs Thatcher was under another self-imposed pressure. A majority of 40 or even 80 seats would not satisfy her, a 100-seat majority was a minimum target. She was now a major figure on the international political stage. She did not want to be regarded as a leader who had lost support at home.

Mrs Thatcher was understandably frustrated at the party's inability to make more of what she regarded as her government's excellent spending record on the national health service. She wanted to be positive about this and to confront Labour on its chosen ground. But Central Office advisers and Saatchi were adamant that this was the wrong strategy. It was necessary, they maintained, to convince the electorate of the contrasts between the parties before they could be positive. 'The problem was that we forgot to ensure that the electorate saw that it had a clear choice before we could sell a positive line', said one. It was Mrs Thatcher who changed the issue of the day at some press conferences and it was her well-known propensity for talking at length on all subjects at press conferences which led to her remarks on education and private health. She was frequently mentioned by voters as a positive reason for voting Conservative, but equally often as a negative reason for not doing so. (Labour's private polls found the same reaction to Mr Kinnock.)

There is, however, a positive case to be made for the Tory campaign. In terms of pacing it proved better than Labour (see p. 256). Compared to the substantial erosion of its leads in the opinion polls in 1979 and 1983 the Conservative party ended the campaign where it began – 42%–43% – and actually improved its standing on most of the issues. There was no dip in the final days. As seen in Table 11.3, it held its commanding lead as the party having the best policies and best leaders, as did Mrs Thatcher as the best Prime Minister. Labour's big improvement (perhaps its only single achievement) was that Mr Kinnock easily outscored other party leaders as the best campaigner. The Conservatives' 'knocking' campaign in the middle of the election – on defence and the loony left – halted Labour's progress at the end of the first week. Some Labour strategists felt that the party had little more to say after the final weekend, when it was clearly on the defensive over taxation, and how it would pay for its programme. Yet in the final week the Conservatives outspent Labour by four-to-one (both Labour and the

Conservatives spent an average of half a million pounds per week on press advertising in the first three weeks of the campaign; in the final week the Conservatives spent some £3 million). The Conservatives launched what was probably the heaviest advertising blitz ever seen in Britain, covering 154 press pages. Having started the campaign with the slogan 'Don't undo 8 years work in 3 seconds', Saatchi (and Tim Bell) finished with 'Britain is great again. Don't let Labour wreck it'. The campaign also ended with a much higher mass media profile for Mrs Thatcher (see p. 109).

Table 11.3   Changes in campaign impact

		May 19/20 (%)	June 8/9 (%)	Change (%)
1.	*Taking everything into account, which party has the best policies?*			
	Conservative	36	37	+1
	Labour	25	27	+2
	Liberal/SDP	16	18	+2
	Don't know/other	23	19	−4
2.	*And which party has the best leaders?*			
	Conservative	49	46	−3
	Labour	21	27	+6
	Liberal/SDP	16	14	−2
	Don't know/other	14	12	−2
3.	*Who would make the best Prime Minister: Mrs Thatcher, Mr Kinnock, Mr Steel or Dr Owen?*			
	Thatcher	46	42	−4
	Kinnock	22	28	+6
	Steel	11	8	−3
	Owen	12	15	+3
	Don't know	9	7	−2
4.	*Setting aside your own preferences, which leader do you think has campaigned most impressively so far?*			
	Thatcher	19	20	+1
	Kinnock	18	43	+25
	Steel	15	8	−5
	Owen	14	11	−3
	Don't know	34	19	−15

Source: Gallup.

To win, the Conservatives had to hold on to the 40% or more of the vote they started with. They did this comfortably; the 'brick wall' strategy was vindicated (see p. 43). Campaign analyses may be too easily influenced or rationalised by the result; the victorious parties' decisions are vindicated by winning, the losers' are judged as almost inevitable contributions to defeat. An alternative perspective is to judge a campaign in organisational (did the operation run smoothly?) and media terms (was it 'good' television?), and discount the result. Labour did well on the first two tests in 1987. Yet a campaign is also a means to an end – winning votes, and winning more than any other party. The ballot result offers a crude but effective judgement of the totality of the parties' campaigns. One person close to Mrs Thatcher reflected that during the election he had thought that the Conservatives had no strategy. He added,

> In fact we probably did have one, but only realised it at the end. We stood for something which the voters wanted, whereas the opposition stood for something they did not want. That is why we won.

In a television interview, Norman Tebbit said that he would rather have a lacklustre campaign and a good victory than a brilliant campaign and a poor result. He may have had the former and Labour the latter. After the election John Sharkey of Saatchi was critical both of many commentators and the Labour campaign. He argued that it was not much use for Neil Kinnock to improve his own ratings if this did not carry over to voting figures; he felt that too many commentators had been beguiled by the television ratings which, at the end of the day, did not matter: 'In what other market could you be twelve points behind and still say that you won the campaign?' He also took the view that Saatchi could not have got away with using the Labour style of presentation on behalf of the Conservative party. Labour's broadcasts had ignored issues, whereas 'people are interested in issues and any advertising has to be linked to that. The British public is not ready for the presidential style of campaigning'. He added that Mrs Thatcher came across better, for 'the Prime Minister is a real person, even if this means she has dislikeable attributes. People know where they are with her'.

Labour's euphoria about its campaign lasted for some time after the result. The BBC Gallup election survey found that 47% of voters thought that Labour had run the best television campaign, compared to 21% for the Tories and 17% for the Alliance. Marplan found that two-thirds of Labour said that Labour had fought the best campaign, compared with 53% of Alliance voters who claimed the distinction for their party, but only 44% of Conservatives who felt the same about their campaign. Labour clearly managed to appeal to its own side more successfully than did the other parties to their supporters. Virtually all surveys reported that Neil Kinnock came over best among the party leaders and, as noted, Labour did well on the important issues. Private polls by MORI also found that Labour's communications (advertising, election broadcasts, leaflets and presentation) decisively outscored those of other parties (see p. 215). A number of Conservatives paid tribute to the sharpness of the Labour advertisements, and thought that Saatchi's efforts generally lacked the impact they had had in 1979 or 1983.

Labour strategists took pride in their single-mindedness and how they stuck to the chosen issue of the day. Bryan Gould conducted his Transport House press conferences without cameras (because pictures might rival Neil Kinnock's regional press conferences; Peter Mandelson's golden rule was 'do not compete with your own news pictures'). The activities of Neil Kinnock were also cleverly keyed in to the chosen press conference of the day, for example, on an education day the Kinnocks visited schools and addressed teachers. In the constituencies candidates were urged to do the same. Mr Kinnock's passion, warmth and sheer eloquence at the evening rallies also came over effectively on television. Some Conservatives admired Labour's resolute refusals to answer challenges from the other parties and wished that Mr Tebbit had done likewise over the unemployment charge (see p. 114). Labour's campaign reaped the rewards of discipline, advance planning, and the concentration of communications in the hands of the professional volunteers in the well-disciplined Shadow Communications Agency. It offered a marked contrast to the fragmentation of decision-making in the Conservative camp and, indeed, to some previous Labour election campaigns.

In spite of effectively having two campaigns – the travelling press conference with Mr Kinnock in the regions, and the London campaign conducted by Bryan Gould and Peter Mandelson – there were few problems over co-ordination. Quite soon these two figures marginalised the rest of the Campaign Committee in Walworth Road, and in effect ran the Labour show; the fact that the campaign was seen to be successful stilled criticism from others in the Labour party headquarters. Preparations for the campaign had been ruthelssly centralised in the hands of Bryan Gould and Peter Mandelson, together with Pat Hewitt and Charles Clarke. Although leading members of the Shadow Cabinet were consulted, they did not have a significant input and this remained the case during the election. The plan of the campaign, outlined on pp. 65–6, was largely adhered to.

Yet there were flaws in the Labour arrangements. The party may have suffered from its rigidity in sticking to the pre-chosen issues of the day. Keeping control of the campaign at one time looked like a strategy for avoiding the London journalists' tough questions on defence. Mr Kinnock, however, geared his provincial press conferences to specific themes, and succeeded in talking about what he wanted to. 'The questions that bother Paul Johnson [the *Daily Mail* columnist] do not necessarily interest the British voter', said Charles Clarke. Some strategists felt that Mr Kinnock should have called an immediate press conference when the Conservatives were floundering on education. The party was also slow to deal with concern over defence following Mr Kinnock's appearance on the Frost television programme. One Labour campaign planner, challenged on this, commented, 'We could not call a press conference because we had nothing to say'. In talking about their social issues Labour leaders felt that they were controlling the campaign and were reassured by private polls which showed voters wanted politicians to spend more time talking about jobs, health, education (and law and order) and less on defence. But the MORI panel survey in the *Sunday Times* showed an increase from 10% to 20% in those thinking defence important. It was only after polling day that some were prepared to acknowledge that in the campaign they were failing to resolve public doubts about their weak issues, notably defence, taxation and the economy.

In spite of the largely negative findings from the private polls there was very positive feedback from the constituencies. This was sustained by the odd published poll, and above all by the *Newsnight* marginal seats survey. Ron Todd, the general secretary of the Transport and General Workers Union, was so carried away at the Campaign Committee on 4 June that he said, 'We are on the verge of a great victory of 1945 proportions'. Above all, morale was high because of the widespread sense that the campaign was going well. Labour party strategists (in contrast to Tory counterparts) did not talk much about 'timing'; 'we are going flat out from the start', was one view. They had plans for a strong finish which were predicated on some sort of breakthrough in the opinion polls to create a bandwagon effect over the final weekend. In particular they hoped to attract support from the Alliance. But there was no breakthrough. By the final weekend, when the party was on the defensive over its economic and taxation package, various strategists spoke of themselves being 'shattered', 'becalmed' and unable to fight back. 'We ran out of steam' said one senior spokesman.

Labour did little to counteract its pre-election weaknesses on defence, trade unions, extremism and the question, 'Where's the money coming from?' to pay for its programme. Day after day the party's quantitative and qualitative research showed how weak its position was on defence and how vulnerable it was on the economy – paying for its programme, tackling inflation and dealing with strikes in the public services. On these two major issues it had not got its message over to voters before the election began and its image on both deteriorated in the campaign. It was dogged by long-standing doubts among voters about its ability to govern.

Labour's manifesto may not have been as 'suicidal' as in 1983 but it still inflicted damage. One person close to Neil Kinnock condemned it as 'inadequate in thought, design and presentation' and blamed the leader's determination to keep a close rein over the process, which resulted in only a handful of people discussing it. At the manifesto launch Mr Kinnock had said: 'What you see is what you get'. The implication was that if an item was mentioned in the manifesto then it was official party policy; if it was not included then it was not party policy. The trouble was not that the manifesto was brief, but that it omitted detail on a number of crucial policy areas. During the course of the campaign various party spokesmen referred questioners seeking clarification about policy to other documents which the party had released in the months prior to the election. Labour spokesmen revealed a number of 'official' policies which had not been mentioned in the manifesto including: the abolition of the upper limits of £15 000 per annum on national insurance contributions and of the married man's tax allowance; extending the right to buy to private tenants, relegalisation of secondary picketing and support for compulsory pre-strike ballots. Most damaging of all, the manifesto provided no authoritative guidance about the party's tax and benefit plans which were in confusion at the end of the campaign.[5]

Neil Kinnock's image improved during the campaign especially among Alliance supporters, among whom he turned a 12% deficit *vis-à-vis* Mrs Thatcher into a 6% lead. However, the BBC Gallup survey found that while 31% of all voters stated that he would make 'the best Prime Minister', 44% said he would make the 'worst' (by far the most negative figure for any party leader) giving a net score of −13%. For Mrs Thatcher the respective figures were 34% and 41% – a net score of −7%. Mr Kinnock may have had the best campaign, but he still ran well behind Mrs Thatcher on ratings for 'the best Prime Minister'. After the first week there was no improvement in Labour's share of the projected vote. In spite of the appreciation for Labour's election broadcasts, it is worth noting that the party's recovery to 33% in the opinion polls occurred before the first election broadcast and, according to the BBC Gallup Survey, fewer switchers to Labour mentioned the broadcasts as a positive influence on their votes compared with the number of switchers to other parties mentioning their parties' broadcasts.

Once again the private polls showed that Labour was most frequently blamed by voters for 'slanging' (Labour 30%, Conservatives 23%, Alliance 6%), though its score was well down on 1983. This may have been a consequence of the anti-government and anti-Thatcherite thrust of the party's messages. But the party's credibility gap on its economic policy was more worrying. Nearly half the voters (including a fifth of Labour voters) thought it was making promises the country could not afford (Table 11.4) and 63% thought Labour

Table 11.4   Unaffordable promises

Are the parties making promises which the country cannot afford?	%
Labour	46
Conservative	18
Alliance	16

Source: MORI private polls 29 May 1987.

would handle inflation badly (28% thought it would do well). In answer to a question about 'raising your standard of living', 49% thought Labour would do badly versus 43% who thought it would do well. People feared that a Labour government would put up taxes, boost inflation rapidly and could not afford its programme.

Labour strategists had little success with Alliance voters who had voted Labour in the past. One central figure said, 'there was little we could do about this because these voters now had an investment in Thatcherism – they were home-owners and had bought shares'. The private polls also showed that voters' perceptions of the party

on defence and extremism also deterred potential converts from the
Alliance. Attempts in the last week to attract weak Alliance supporters into the Labour fold, on the grounds that Labour was the main
anti-Thatcher force, reaped little reward. Labour was more successful
in recovering support among first-time voters, women and skilled
workers. But it made little impression on the Conservative vote. The
advertising efforts improved morale among Labour workers and
candidates and, for a good part of the campaign, appeared to keep
the Conservatives off balance. 'We wanted to lob a hand grenade
over Central Office's front door every day' claimed Philip Gould, on
behalf of the Shadow Communications agency. He took consolation
at least in the fact that they had forced the Tories to increase their
spending from half a million pounds a week to £3 million in the last
week.

After the election some Labour strategists were more sober in
their calculations about the effects of the campaign. Winning the
television or advertising battles is not the same as winning votes. 'We
could change their minds, but not their votes; that takes four years,
not four weeks', said Philip Gould. Criticism of the professional
public relations approach did not come only from the party's left
wing – 'the glitter was counter-productive; in a way it showed up the
emptiness of what we were saying', said one senior Shadow Cabinet
member. Another member of the Communications Agency said that,
'The presentation was nearly as good as it could be. It was the
product that was poor'. Serious policy weaknesses were demonstrated
in the contradictory statements on taxation from senior party figures
in the last days of the election. According to Peter Mandelson, 'what
decides elections is economic prosperity and the climate of good
economic times. The Conservative government created these and,
unless something extraordinary happened, there was no reason why
they should lose'. He also thought that if Labour had won on the social
issues the Conservatives had won on the economy and effectively
exploited Labour's weaknesses.

After the election Labour leaders argued that the campaign should
be seen as the first in a two-stage road to Labour recovery. Some
had considered the party's prospects to be so poor at the outset that
it would be battling the Alliance for second place. After 11 June they
claimed that Labour had now re-established itself as the main
alternative to the Conservatives. 'We have shaken the great dam
against voting Labour. Labour is now a serious contender and Neil
Kinnock a credible leader of the nation' said Philip Gould. 'Historians

will see this as the campaign that saved the Labour Party', said another. Claims that the party's aim was to consolidate its second place (and hope that it might deny the Tories a clear majority) are consistent with Labour's failure to bid for the solid Tory vote, which it had to loosen, if it wanted to win a majority of seats. A well-crafted campaign failed totally to dent Conservative support.

Post-mortems were being written on the Alliance campaign well before polling day. The campaign came to look even more disastrous in the wake of the acrimony which broke out over merger proposals within a few days of the election result. Talk of 'partnership' and a new style of politics looked hollow indeed.

A number of difficulties with the Alliance campaign were outside their control. As the Labour party recovered and Neil Kinnock gained much admiration for his campaign, so the Alliance was caught in the old two-party squeeze. There was no repeat of 1983, when the poor Labour campaign did so much for Alliance fortunes. Without the momentum of a rise in the opinion polls (which had been a feature of three of the previous four Liberal or Alliance general election campaigns) criticisms grew. The charge that the Alliance lacked a cutting edge was in part a consequence of its being a centrist party. Many of its policies were indeed 'in between' the other parties, as was clearly seen in the many three-cornered debates on television and radio. The Alliance advocacy of coalition and constitutional reform was hardly newsworthy; a hung parliament was unpopular with the public, and surveys showed that the idea of coalition was disliked because people thought it would produce divided and weak government.

Throughout its short life the Alliance has depended on by-election upsets or surges in the opinion polls to make headlines and give it momentum. 1987 was not 1983. Spokesmen had to cope instead with media queries about 'what is going wrong?', why the Alliance was not doing better in the polls, and campaigning problems like David Steel's complaint that the joint TV appearances made himself and Dr Owen look like Tweedledum and Tweedledee. Alliance policies were largely ignored. The 'Ask the Alliance?' question sessions, although well-attended and spontaneous, did not make for good television. Neither David Steel nor David Owen ('there's no actor in him' said John Pardoe) spoke with the passion of Mr Kinnock or Mrs Thatcher. But David Gow, in his reports of David Owen's tour in the *Guardian*, while admitting that Dr Owen was not a striking television campaigner, added 'he has been verbal, rational, intellect-

ual, where others plugged a brand image straight into the viewers' sitting rooms' (*Guardian*, 11 June).

The dual leadership was a popular target for criticism by commentators both during and after the campaign, although survey research did not indicate that this in itself was significant in turning voters away from the Alliance. The format was in part a reaction to the 1983 campaign, when Roy Jenkins and David Steel were rarely in touch. It was also designed to show the theme of inter-party co-operation in action. But there was indeed a Tweedledum and Tweedledee problem. When the two Davids were asked by the planning group not to look bored on television when the other was speaking, one of them said 'But we are bored'. There were times when the pair did try to outscore one another, and the media inevitably inflated differences of emphasis into serious disagreements.

Alliance activists looking back on the campaign were critical of the leaders' strategy. Many in the SDP felt that they should have started with an assault on Labour, as in 1983, rather than concentrate their fire on the Tories. But that, of course, might have alienated some voters for whom Mrs Thatcher was the prime enemy.

It was predictable that some Liberal candidates, and many Liberal activists, would complain to their headquarters about Dr Owen's 'obsession' with defence, his hostility to the Labour party, and his reputation as a stalking horse for Mrs Thatcher. Many well-placed Liberals were trying to squeeze the Labour vote in seats where that party ran a poor third in 1983 and reported a negative reaction to the SDP leader among target Labour voters.

It was also predictable that the *apparatchiks* at the Alliance headquarters would feel frustrated with the two Davids.[6] The campaign managers simply lacked the authority to instruct the leaders. David Owen was a loner, and David Steel had never been trusted by his party bureaucrats. What galled the headquarters strategists was that the two leaders talked so freely to journalists on the battlebus and jet. Colourful stories based on these conversations were written up the next day and often received more coverage than did issues for the day set by the Alliance. 'It was as though we had three bloody separate campaign centres', said one disillusioned strategist. The classic case of this was on the first Sunday of the campaign when, during prime television time, David Owen was seen promising an attack on Labour, followed by David Steel promising an attack on the Tories, and concluding with John Pardoe stating that the Alliance would not be attacking anybody. For Mr Pardoe, the campaign was 'the greatest disappointment of my life'.

Some Alliance leaders indulged in post-election 'if onlys'. What if the Alliance had gone for Labour, in the first week, as Dr Owen wanted? What if there had been a merger of the two parties and perhaps David Owen had been leader? But David Owen wanted to lead his own party; he despised many Liberals, and they suspected him. It is doubtful that a merger was possible, even if he had not fought it so fiercely. But if Dr Owen had become leader he would still have fallen out with many Liberals – if not over defence then over something else. It is also doubtful that an Alliance campaign under David Steel would have made much difference. Mr Steel would probably have made the same remarks over Mrs Thatcher and there would have been no co-leader to draw him back. Dr Owen was a commanding political figure, but it is doubtful that he could have prevailed in any popularity competition with Mrs Thatcher and Mr Kinnock. Indeed, the issue of a merger is probably irrelevant. A merger would have involved time-consuming negotiations and compromises and would not necessarily have given the Alliance a sharper cutting edge or a clearer sense of direction. As Labour support rose in the opinion polls, so fear of a Labour government drove some wavering Alliance supporters into the Tory camp. The Alliance balance of power strategy had little appeal. The Alliance was squeezed between the other two parties, and probably there is no alternative scenario which would have placed it in a much better position, say, with more than 25% of the vote.

This chapter began by warning how easy it is to overstate the importance of the campaign from the point of view of the voters (undeniably, it matters for the politicians). For all the backstage drama (particularly in the Conservative party) which accompanied the parties' election broadcasts and advertising, the evidence is that these had little impact on the voters.[7] The BBC Gallup survey found that less than 2% of voters admitted to having been influenced by a press advertisement or posters. Labour's campaign won much praise (not least from other party strategists) and was a great improvement on 1983. Yet the party added only 3% to its 1983 share of the vote. The Conservative campaign was widely judged to have been poorer than that of 1983, yet the party held its share of the vote. Campaign strategists should not accord themselves too much praise or blame. Compared to the influence of the social structure, prosperity and the mood created by the events of the previous years, their efforts did not count for very much.

NOTES

1. See I. Crewe, 'The Campaign Confusion', *New Society*, 8 May 1987.
2. *The British General Election of 1983* (London, 1984) pp. 274–83.
3. For the argument that television should ignore the photo-opportunities staged by politicians, see David Cox, 'Does election broadcasting meet the needs of the voters?', *Listener*, 18 June 1987, p. 16.
4. R. Tyler, *Campaign: The Selling of the Prime Minister* (London, 1987).
5. On this see R. Oakley, 'Tangle of Labour Tax and Benefits Policy Fuels Doubts', *The Times*, 9 June 1987.
6. For one insider's account, see D. Wilson, *Battle for Power* (London, 1987).
7. See R. Eliahoo 'What the voters thought of the election circus', *Campaign* 26 June 1987, for a very negative verdict on the quality and impact of the party advertising. It showed how few people had noticed the press and poster advertisements. Among those who had, the Conservative presentation was seen as more effective than Labour's. 'Although [Labour] scored top marks for its [broadcasts], their radical new style was extreme enough to turn more people off than the Conservatives' more pedestrian broadcasts'.

12 Conclusion

Mrs Thatcher's victory, giving her a third term in 10 Downing Street will stand out in history. Although the Conservatives lost a net 20 seats compared to 1983, their final majority of 102 over all other parties was the second largest since 1945. Mrs Thatcher became the first leader since Lord Liverpool in the 1820s to win three elections in a row. Harold Wilson scored more victories, but two of his four successes (1966 and October 1974) were essentially the second stages of an earlier narrow outcome.

In some respects the 1987 result was more remarkable than those of 1979 and 1983. In 1979 the Labour government's position had been destroyed by the trade unions in the 'winter of discontent', and in 1983 the Conservative task was made easy by the successful Falklands campaign, the split opposition, and the election of Mr Foot as leader of the Labour party. But in 1987 the Conservatives faced a relatively united Labour party fighting a far more professional election campaign under an attractive and youthful leadership, and still they won overwhelmingly, at least in seats; as in 1983 they profited greatly from being the largest party in a three-party race under the British electoral system; 43% of the vote secured them 57% of the seats.

The election results are fully analysed by John Curtice and Michael Steed in the Appendix. Here we summarise some of their main findings:

1. The country did not cast a national verdict. Labour's vote increased more sharply in the North of England, Wales and Scotland than in the South of England and the Midlands. In general the opposite was true for the Conservatives. There was actually a swing from Labour to Conservative in London and the surrounding metropolitan area, but the extra Conservative support appears to have come more from the Alliance than Labour.

2. There was, unusually, a social and geographical pattern in Alliance performance. The Alliance vote fell back particularly heavily in working class seats in the North of England, Wales and Scotland. It suffered a serious setback in its attempt to erode the Labour vote in traditional Labour 'heartlands'.

3. In contrast to previous elections, the Conservative vote did not fall particularly heavily in big city constituencies. In some cities such as London and Bristol they fared notably well. In contrast

to 1983 there was no evidence of the Conservatives doing especially badly in constituencies with high unemployment. The results do not fit a simple pattern of prosperous constituencies endorsing the Conservatives and less prosperous ones rejecting them.

4. There was considerable evidence that MPs could win personal votes for themselves. The Alliance and the SNP lost in each of the three constituencies where the incumbent MP retired. In constituencies gained by new Conservative MPs for the first time in 1983, new personal votes were on average worth 2% of the vote. Such support helped the Conservatives to retain as many as half a dozen North of England seats which they would otherwise have lost.

5. The campaign to promote tactical voting had some limited success. There was further new tactical voting by Labour voters in constituencies where the Alliance was second to the Conservatives. Alliance voters also appear to have drifted tactically to Labour in some Conservative/Labour marginals where there was not a strong personal vote for the incumbent Conservative MP. Such switching was more common in the North of England, Scotland and Wales than elsewhere. But tactical voting was strongest between Alliance and Nationalist voters. Without tactical voting, the Conservative majority would have been at least 16 seats larger.

6. Turnout rose by 2.6% to 75.3%. Only in Northern Ireland, where the unionist pact appears to have dissuaded some loyalists from turning out, did it fall. There was some tendency in the South and Midlands for an above average increase in turnout to occur where there was an above average Alliance performance.

7. There was little real difference in the performance of Liberal and SDP candidates. Liberals did better on average by 1%, but this was largely due to their fighting more of the seats in which the Alliance could be expected to do well.

8. The electoral system again hurt third parties whose vote was geographically evenly spread. The Alliance won 3.5% of the seats for 23.1% of the vote. Plaid Cymru, in contrast, won 0.5% of the seats on 0.4% of the total vote. The long-term decline in the number of Conservative/Labour marginals was slightly reversed, but the ability of the electoral system to ensure that the largest party has an overall majority remains seriously eroded. On a uniform shift of votes from 1987, both Conservative and Labour need a 4% lead in votes to be sure of an overall majority. Labour's vote has become more concentrated in constituencies with smaller

electorates and lower turnouts, but this bias is counteracted because it also wastes votes by winning more seats than the Conservatives by large majorities. The 28 safest seats are now all Labour held.

Press reactions were varied. The *Sun* epitomised the ecstatic reactions of the Tory tabloids:

> Okay, maybe the Tory campaign was lacklustre.
> ### Control
> The Conservatives had Mrs Thatcher – thank
> goodness – and precious little else in the way
> of personality.
> Against here was Neil Kinnock, with his oratory,
> his razzmatazz and his Chariots of Fire.
> *But when push came to shove, YOU – the voters –*
> *plumped as ever for policy and not personality.*
> YOU wanted more money in your pay packet to spend
> as you choose.
> *And you voted for Maggie.*
> YOU wanted firm control of the union bullies and
> the right to choose when and where you can go to work.
> *And you voted for Maggie.*
> YOU wanted strong defence based on the nuclear
> deterrent, not the white flag of surrender.
> *And you voted for Maggie.*
> ### Tolerant
> YOU wanted freedom to choose the best education,
> the best health care and the best home for your family.
> *And you voted for Maggie.*

The *People*, for Labour, had a very different emphasis:

> The anti-Thatcher vote in Thursday's election exceeded that of her supporters. The haves triumphed over the have-nots and the Prime Minister is now on course to take the creed of Thatcherism into the 1990s.
> Labour fought a brilliant campaign. They put the message across, but it did not reach out sufficiently to the uncommitted.
> It is now up to Mr Kinnock to look again at his vote-losing non-nuclear defence policy, and the selection process which allows the unpopular hard-left to hijack constituency parties.

The *Independent* gave a measured verdict.

> THE CONSERVATIVES have won this election in spite of themselves. They fought a disorganised and strangely hesitant campaign. They boasted about radicalism of their manifesto, but appeared to be vague about what was in it . . .
>
> The reason why Mrs Thatcher has secured a third term is that the current of the times still flows with the Conservative Party.
>
> What Labour did achieve, however, was an undeniably respectable result when set against the very low expectations with which it started out a month ago.
>
> The Alliance has failed in both of its key objectives to hold the balance in a hung Parliament and to overtake Labour in the total number of votes cast.

The Times made no such attempt at balance:

> The election result is a triumph for two great, indomitable predictable forces. One is Mrs Margaret Thatcher. The other is the good sense of the majority of voters.

The *Economist* warned:

> The challenge for the third term can be summed up in two facts: more people are still voting against her than for her, and most of those opponents are still voting Labour. Even in the dawn of this third Thatcher triumph, it is possible to imagine Labour winning next time.

The *Guardian* described the election as 'barely a semi-colon in the stretching sentence of the Thatcher years'.

Both the *Economist* and the *Guardian* found warnings in Mrs Thatcher's landslide victory. They pointed to the rejection of the Conservative party in Scotland and the North of England as evidence that the imbalance in economic prosperity and opportunity was producing a more divided Britain. In Scotland the Conservatives held only 10 of the 72 seats and in Wales only 8 of the 38. Although the Conservatives retained such northern marginals as Bolton North-East and Bury South, and Labour made four gains in the Midlands,

The Times, 13 May 1987

there was a political line between the affluent parts of South-East Britain and the economically deprived parts of North-West Britain.

Mrs Thatcher clearly took on board the uneven pattern of the Conservative strength in the country and the North-South political divide. Acknowledging victory in the early hours of 12 June at Central Office she also said:

> We have a big job to do in some of those inner cities . . . to help the people get more choice and politically we must get right back in there.

The Alliance parties' sense of disappointment was in part a product of their high expectations at the start of the campaign. In the May local elections they had won 27% of the vote. They were undoubtedly beguiled by their record by-elections and recent general elections, when a significant improvement in their position had almost always developed in the course of the campaign. Their final vote of 23% was a fall of 3% from the 1983 figure and not much advance on the Liberal post-war high point – 19% in February 1974. The Alliance failed to advance in most of their target seats and did badly in three-way marginals. The 1983 result had turned out to be a peak rather than a springboard.

The problems that dogged the Alliance were hardly new. They suffered, predictably, from the relatively even geographical spread of their vote and from the first-past-the-post electoral system. Under pure proportional representation the Alliance would have gained an extra 127 seats (149 instead of 22), the Conservatives would have had 96 fewer (279 instead of 375) and Labour 27 fewer (202 instead of 229). But the Alliance remained the main rival from the point of view of most Conservative MPs, since they came second in two-thirds of the Conservative-held seats.

As usual the Alliance vote was the 'softest' of the three main parties and proved vulnerable to Conservative claims that a vote for them could open the door for Labour, and to Labour charges that only Mr Kinnock could unseat Mrs Thatcher. After the election many SDP and Liberal activists, and even David Steel himself, were critical of the dual leadership approach. The concept was not understood by the public and differences of emphasis between Mr Owen and Mr Steel became public during the campaign. However, Ivor Crewe quotes survey evidence that the old 'wasted' vote argument was more damaging.[1] Nearly a quarter of the electorate, according to the BBC Gallup poll, claimed either to have voted Alliance in the past or to have seriously considered voting Alliance in 1987 and then, in the event, failed to deliver their support. Of these, 68% feared that the Alliance could not win, or that voting for it would let in either Labour or Conservative. It is significant that among defectors from the Alliance, twice as many feared helping the Conservatives as letting Labour in, the reverse of the pattern at the 1983 election. The Alliance, like the Liberals, remained a protest party without a solid social or geographical base and, for much of the electorate, it failed to present a clear alternative to the other parties.

Labour optimists could discover some consolation in the result. The party started in poor heart – the Greenwich by-election had seriously raised the spectre of the Alliance taking second place in popular votes. Labour clearly won that battle, with a lead of 9% over the Alliance. It confirmed itself as the main rival to the Conservatives and Mr Kinnock enhanced his position in the party and the country. The optimists could also look back to 1959. Labour had then lost its third successive election, and many commentators, and even some Labour MPs, were sceptical about the party's electoral future. Yet it went on to win four of the following five elections. Moreover, in Australia, New Zealand, and Sweden, parties with Labour or Socialist labels have gone on showing they could win elections among affluent electorates.

There is, however, another side to the outcome. The party gained an additional net 20 seats for a 3% increase in votes, but it still stood 11% behind the Conservatives (in 1959 it was only 5% behind). The 1987 election produced the party's second lowest return of MPs (229) and its second worst performance in votes since 1945. To have a majority at the next election it needs a swing of over 8% and an extra 97 seats – an electoral Everest. In spite of Mr Kinnock's brave campaigning, based on his determination to bury the memories of the 1983 disaster, Labour's support in the voting booths was actually lower than it was when he took over the leadership three and a half years earlier. The party had recovered from the 28% of 1983 but was far from the 1979 level when it gained 37% of the vote. In the 1983 parliament Labour's support in the opinion polls scarcely touched the 40% barrier. Not since 1970, five general elections earlier, has the party gained more than 39% of the vote.

The Gallup election day survey found that 36% of voters expressed an identification with Labour even if they did not vote for it. It is close to the 35%–38% of the vote the party gained in the local elections and in the opinion polls for most of 1986. This may be Labour's 'normal' vote, the basic level of support it can rely on. On this reckoning Labour 'under-polled' by some 4%. Indeed, in all general elections since 1966, Labour has failed to gain its full 'natural' vote in terms of its share of party identifiers in the electorate – and in 1987 it fought what was widely regarded as a good campaign, had an attractive leader, and enjoyed a useful lead on the social issues.

What was different to the 1960s and 1970s, however, was that the existence of the Alliance meant that Labour was no longer the exclusive home for anti-Tory voters. The longer-term social and politico-geographical trends hold out little encouragement for the party. Liverpool and Glasgow swung sharply to Labour, although

London edged away. Scotland, Wales and Northern England swung to Labour, while the rest of the country hardly changed. This had the effect of producing an even sharper geographical division between a Labour North and a Conservative South. Labour now has only three seats in the south, outside of London. It relies more than ever on its regional strongholds; three-quarters of its 229 MPs are from North Britain and Wales. There is little more for Labour to gain in these areas. To reach 40% of the votes, to gain an extra three million votes and 100 seats, it has to make inroads in the South and the Midlands, in constituencies dominated by skilled workers and the middle class. On the other side the Conservatives are left with no MPs in the major cities of Manchester, Leicester, Bradford, Liverpool, Newcastle-upon-Tyne and Glasgow.

The Labour party still has an image problem. John Lloyd's editorial in the *New Statesman* (19 June 1987) called on Labour to change its habit of mind:

> Labour has got into the bad habit of talking to itself: of using debates and resolutions and the composition of committees as proxies for the real world even as the party – sociologically, numerically, rhetorically – was removing itself further and further from most people's experience. Some of that habit has been lost: but not enough.

The steady expansion of home-ownership, the growth of the middle class and a share-owning society, combined with the decline of trade unions, the manual working class and council tenancy, also undermined the traditional institutional supports for Labour voting. Robert Worcester, in *The Times* on 13 June, traced the socioeconomic changes in voting behaviour since October 1974, when Labour last won a general election and had a lead over the Conservatives of 3%. He showed that Labour support had fallen over the 13-year period among every group, according to age, class and geography. Each group, except the middle class, was more Conservative, and in every group, except for 18 to 24-year-olds, the Alliance was scoring higher than did the Liberals in that year.[2]

There were other interesting developments. The Scottish and Welsh nationalists each made one gain, ending with three seats apiece. Four black MPs were elected (all for Labour) with swings comparable to those in adjoining seats. A record number of women

MPs (41) were elected and Diane Abbott (Hackney North) became the first black woman MP.

What did the election result suggest about the future of the political parties, particularly the opposition parties, the political agenda in the 1990s, and the changing values of the British electorate? The survey evidence hardly suggests that the electorate wholeheartedly approved of the Thatcherite revolution on social questions. Labour was preferred over the Conservatives on handling jobs, health and education (see p. 247). A MORI poll for *The Times* on election day found little support for many of the more radical proposals in the Conservative programme. Only a third of voters favoured selling water authorities and electricity to private shareholders, replacing Polaris by Trident, and allowing state schools to opt out of local authority control. Replacing domestic rates with a poll tax was supported by 43% (with 38% against). Surveys also showed a clear majority of voters preferring more state spending on public services even at the cost of higher taxes, rather than tax cuts accompanied by a reduction in such expenditure. On the basis of such opinion polls the Conservative mandate was a brittle one.

But survey evidence can be read in a number of ways. Voting behaviour is more often influenced by the individual's calculation about what is best for his or her family – and on the issue of 'prosperity' the Conservatives were clearly regarded (by 55% to 27%) as more likely to deliver increased living standards than Labour. As Ivor Crewe noted in the *Guardian* on 16 June: 'Here, quite simply and obviously, lies the key to the Conservative victory'.

A majority of voters thought that the economy in general and their own family finances were improving. Perceptions of whether the economy was getting better were clearly correlated with changes in voting behaviour since 1983. Those who thought their family fortunes had improved were highly likely to defect to the Conservatives. A reverse pattern was found among switchers to and from the Labour party. Pocket-book politics – the voters' perceptions of the economy and their family finances – were potent electoral forces, and the Conservatives were seen by enough voters to have delivered the goods.

Labour's private polls showed that the party's ability to manage the economy was widely distrusted – particularly among key voters living in the South and leaning to the Alliance. 49% thought the party would do a bad job of 'raising your standard of living' compared to 43% who thought it would do well. Voters' major concerns about

Table 12.1   *The flow of the vote from 1983 to 1987*

Vote in 1987	Con. (%)	Lab. (%)	Vote in 1983 L/SDP (%)	Did not vote (%)	Too young (%)
Con.	77	4	10	21	28
Lab.	5	75	12	19	24
L/SDP	12	11	70	14	14
Other	–	1	1	1	1
Did not vote	6	8	8	45	32
Total	100	100	100	100	100

Note: Columns do not always add up to 100% because of rounding.
Source: Ivor Crewe, *Guardian*, 15 June 1987.

Labour's economic policy were over higher taxes, rapidly rising inflation, and the making of promises the country could not afford.

Although the opinion polls did not uncover much movement in the parties' fortunes in the campaign, underneath the apparent stability there were many moves by individual voters. Table 12.1 examines the flow of the vote between 1983 and 1987. Although the movements it records are dependent upon the voters' uncertain recall of their 1983 vote, it is significant that Conservative 1983 voters appear to have been marginally more loyal to their party than were those who voted Labour or Alliance in 1983. The 23% of the 1983 Conservatives who defected – to the Alliance, Labour and abstention – were almost matched by the Conservatives' capture of deserters from the other two parties. Labour's modest recovery from 1983 was gained in part from the 1983 abstainers and a net advantage from two-way movements of voters between the Conservatives and Labour parties.

The BBC Gallup survey provides further sociological detail about the changing behaviour of the British electorate. The Conservative vote was at its lowest in the 23–44 age group, perhaps due to concern over the social issues among this category. Among first-time voters (aged 18–22) the Alliance was the major loser compared to 1983. The correlation between social class and voting behaviour has diminished in recent years, with the emergence of three-party politics. But divisions between the manual and middle-classes remain important. The Conservatives gained just over a half (54%) of the middle-class employed vote.[3] But among the middle class in the public sector only 44% voted Conservative compared to 65% in the private sector and Tory support also fell among the well educated.

The government's handling of schools and higher education obviously cost it support.

Perhaps the most significant feature of the Conservative party under Mrs Thatcher is its strength in the working class (C2 and DE) as Table 12.2 shows. It gained 36% of the vote (compared to Labour's

Table 12.2   *How Britain voted in 1987*

	Class			Trade union member	Sex		Age				
	ABC1	C2	DE		Men	Women	18–24	25–34	35–54	55+	All
All	43	27	30	23	48	52	14	19	33	34	100
Con.	54	40	30	30	43	43	37	39	45	46	43
Lab.	18	36	48	42	32	32	40	33	29	31	32
Alln.	26	22	22	26	23	23	21	25	24	21	23
Other	2	2	2	2	2	2	2	3	2	2	2

Source: MORI.

48%), its largest post-war share. As in 1979 and 1983 Conservative victories were built on the support of what Crewe has called the 'new working class', manual workers who live in the south, who are home-owners, who are employed in the private sector, and who are not members of unions (see Table 12.3). The MORI post-election poll showed how housing tenure divided the working-class. The Conservatives had a 12% lead over Labour among working-class home-owners, but ran 32% behind among working-class council tenants. Labour recovered some ground among the unskilled, less among the skilled workers. Between 1979 and 1987, support for Labour among the last group has fallen from 45% to 36%.

Elections may be as significant for what they fail to produce as for what they lead to. With less than 75% of the vote between them, the 1987 election was not a full-hearted endorsement of the old Labour/Conservative duopoly. The third force vote was still strong. For all the disappointment of the Alliance, its vote stood at nearly three-quarters that of Labour.

Inevitably, perhaps, there was much post-election speculation about how the non-Conservative parties might co-operate to end the Conservative hegemony. Yet Alliance supporters were divided from Labour on many issues and in social background they had more in common with Conservative voters. For all the talk of harnessing the so-called anti-Conservative majority, represented by the combined vote for the Alliance and Labour parties, it could equally be observed that there were even larger anti-Labour and anti-Alliance majorities. So long as Labour finds a ceiling below 40% of the vote and remains

Table 12.3 How the working class voted (%)

	The new working class				The traditional working class			
	Lives in south (40%)[1]	Owner-occupier (57%)[1]	Non-union (66%)[1]	Works in private sector	Lives in Scotland/North	Council tenant	Union member	Works in public sector
Con.	46	44	40	38	29	25	30	32
Lab.	28	32	38	39	57	57	48	49
Lib./SDP	26	24	22	23	15	18	22	19
Con./Lab.	Con.	Con.	Con.	Lab.	Lab.	Lab.	Lab.	Lab.
maj. 1987	+18	+12	+2	+1	+32	+17	+28	+18
Con./Lab.	Con.	Con.	Con.	Lab.	Lab.	Lab.	Lab.	Lab.
maj. 1983	+16	+22	+6	+1	+38	+17	+10	+21
Change from 1983	+4	+3	+7	+2	-1	-4	(-7)	(-2)

Source: I. Crewe, Guardian, 15 June 1987.
[1] % of all manual workers.

virtually unrepresented not only in the South but in most of the other economically dynamic parts of Britain, and so long as a third party can score at least 20% of the vote, the Conservative position remains strong. In a three-party system the Conservatives' 43% of the vote compared favourably with the 45% it won on average during the old two-party domination of the 1950–70 period. Since 1979 the Conservatives have located a large constituency of 'winners', people who have an interest in the return of a Conservative government. It includes much of the affluent South, home-owners, share-owners, and most of those in work, whose standard of living, measured in post-tax incomes, has improved appreciably since 1979. The rub is that continued economic prosperity may be the necessary lubricant to maintain the coalition.

The conduct of the 1987 election will leave its mark. Professionalism and media management took a significant step forward. Parties learnt new lessons in how to package themselves and their leaders. Careful handling meant that gaffes, though still perpetrated, were fewer and less serious than in previous contests. These trends are likely to continue and elections to become duller as party headquarters get more and more skilled at putting on a safe and smooth campaign. Perhaps it is as well that the nation's destiny should not be decided by the accidents of electioneering and that the four weeks of a campaign should merely be used to test and confirm the judgements that voters have formed over the previous four years. But by reducing its vitality and excitement the packagers may have diminished the educational potential of an election.

Some commentators dismissed the 1987 election as a minor event, a small landmark along the Thatcherite continuum, as the Conservatives were again confirmed in office with a handsome majority. But it was more than that; the Conservative victory had not seemed at all inevitable during the disastrous by-elections of 1983–7 or at the time of the Westland affair. The failure of the Alliance or the Labour party to make any significant breakthrough left the Conservatives without serious opposition as both the other groupings looked inwards to see what was wrong with themselves or with society that they could not win more support against a leader and against policies that were to them so transparently objectionable. The electorate, or 43% of them, had endorsed a capitalist, free-enterprise approach to the country's problems, a set of solutions that reversed the Socialist ratchet with a vengeance. In many of the election post-mortems of the opposition there was a rueful recognition of the need to move towards policy positions that they used to oppose and that Mrs Thatcher had shown were plainly acceptable to a large chunk of solid middle Britain.

Our story ends with Mrs Thatcher's return to Downing Street on 12 June. But a number of immediate post-election events were decisively shaped by the conduct of the campaign and the outcome of the election. Conservatives could claim that their radical plans for schooling, housing and local government, all trailed in the manifesto, were legitimised by victory. Mr Kinnock's authority in the party and his bid to remake the Labour challenge were helped by both the professionalism of his campaign and the comprehensive nature of the election defeat. For the third election in succession Labour faced a 'what went wrong?' inquest. After 1987 it appeared inevitable that the party would have to mount a fundamental review of its policies and its approach to the electorate. The leaders of the two Alliance parties drew different lessons from the disappointing election result for the future of the Alliance and for policies: the rows over party merger were coloured by the traumas of the Tweedledum-Tweedledee strategy and balance-of-power strategies. If the mould of politics has been broken in the 1980s, 1987 was not a happy follow-up to the creation of the SDP in 1981. The politics of the 1990s will certainly have been shaped by the 1987 election.

Mrs Thatcher will have a secure position in the history books. Apart from the psephological records from winning three successive elections and becoming the longest continuous serving Prime Minister in the twentieth century, she may also be said to have effectively changed the direction of British politics. On 12 June 1987 she was granted a prospect given to no previous British Prime Minister for over a century – a third full term of office, a clear parliamentary majority and a renewed opportunity to shape the agenda of British politics.

NOTES

1 See the *Guardian*, 16 June 1987.
2. There was evidence that the race of voters, like the race of candidates, plays a diminishing part in electoral choice. None the less a poll conducted by Harris in late May for the *Asian Times*, and the *Caribbean African*

Times, found that electors of West Indian origin divided 86% Labour, 6% Conservative and 7% Alliance; Electors from the Indian sub-continent divided 67%, 33%, 10%. Blacks are, of course, concentrated in areas of urban deprivation where a high Labour vote could be expected. For a discussion of electoral trends associated with race see M. Anwar, *Race and Politics* (London, 1986). See also Z. Layton-Henry and P. B. Rich (eds), *Race Government and Politics in Britain* (London, 1986).

3. Middle-class meaning professional, administrative and managerial groups, as well as the lower-middle class and clerical and office workers.
4. The extent to which class voting has declined has been the source of much controversy. See A. Heath et al, *How Britain Votes* (London, 1985); I. Crewe's critique in *Political Studies*, vol. 38 (Dec., 1986), pp. 620–38; and A. Heath's rejoinder in *Political Studies*, vol. 35 (Jun., 1987), pp. 256–77.

V

Appendices

Appendix 1   Statistics

Table A1.1   Votes and seats, 1945–87 (seats in italics)

	Electorate and turnout	Total votes cast	Conservative	Labour	Liberal (1983–87 Alliance)	Welsh & Scottish Nationalist	Communist	Others (mainly N. Ireland)
1945[1]	73.3%	100% – 640	39.8% – 213	48.3% – 393	9.1% – 12	0.2%	0.4% – 2	2.1% – 20
	32 836 419	24 082 612	9 577 667	11 632 191	2 197 191	46 612	102 760	525 491
1950	84.0%	100% – 625	43.5% – 299	46.1% – 315	9.1% – 9	0.1%	0.3%	0.9% – 2
	34 269 770	28 772 671	12 502 567	13 266 592	2 621 548	27 288	91 746	262 930
1951	82.5%	100% – 625	48.0% – 321	48.8% – 295	2.5% – 6	0.1%	0.1%	0.5% – 3
	34 645 573	28 595 668	13 717 538	13 948 605	730 556	18 219	21 640	159 110
1955	76.8%	100% – 630	49.7% – 345	46.4% – 277	2.7% – 6	0.2%	0.1%	0.8% – 2
	34 858 263	26 760 493	13 311 936	12 404 970	722 405	57 231	33 144	230 807
1959	78.7%	100% – 630	49.4% – 365	43.8% – 258	5.9% – 6	0.4%	0.1%	0.5% – 1
	35 397 080	27 859 241	13 749 830	12 215 538	1 638 571	99 309	30 897	145 090
1964	77.1%	100% – 630	43.4% – 304	44.1% – 317	11.2% – 9	0.5%	0.2%	0.6%
	35 892 572	27 655 374	12 001 396	12 205 814	3 092 878	133 551	45 932	169 431
1966	75.8%	100% – 630	41.9% – 253	47.9% – 363	8.5% – 12	0.7%	0.2%	0.7% – 2
	35 964 684	27 263 606	11 418 433	13 064 951	2 327 533	189 545	62 112	201 032
1970	72.0%	100% – 630	46.4% – 330	43.0% – 288	7.5% – 6	1.3% – 1	0.1%	1.7% – 5
	39 342 013	28 344 798	13 145 123	12 178 295	2 117 033	381 818	37 970	486 557
Feb. 1974	78.1%	100% – 635	37.8% – 297	37.1% – 301	19.3% – 14	2.6% – 9	0.1%	3.1% – 14
	39 770 724	31 340 162	11 872 180	11 646 391	6 058 744	804 554	32 743	958 293
Oct. 1974	72.8%	100% – 635	35.8% – 277	39.2% – 319	18.3% – 13	3.5% – 14	0.1%	3.1% – 12
	40 072 971	29 189 178	10 464 817	11 457 079	6 346 754	1 005 938	17 426	897 164
1979	76.0%	100% – 635	43.9% – 339	37.0% – 269	13.8% – 11	2.0% – 4	0.1%	3.2% – 12
	41 093 264	31 221 361	13 697 923	11 532 218	4 313 804	636 890	16 858	1 043 755
1983	72.7%	100% – 650	42.4% – 397	27.6% – 209	25.4% – 23	1.5% – 4	0.04%	3.1% – 17
	42 197 344	30 671 136	13 012 315	8 456 934	7 780 949	457 676	11 606	951 656
1987[2]	75.3%	100% – 650	42.3% – 376	30.8% – 229	22.6% – 22	1.7% – 6	0.02%	2.6% – 17
	43 181 321	32 536 137	13 763 066	10 029 778	7 341 290	543 559	6 078	852 368

Note:
1. The 1945 figures exclude University seats and are adjusted for double voting in the 15 two-member seats.
2. See p. 310 for Northern Ireland percentages for 1987 and p. 344 for votes for others.

Table A1.2 Regional results, 1987

THE UNITED KINGDOM

	Seats won in 1987 (Change since 1983 in brackets)				Share of votes cast 1987 and change since 1983						
Region	Cons.	Labour	Alliance	Nat. & Other	Turnout 1987	Change since 1983	Conservative	Labour	Alliance	Nationalist	Other
England	358 (+0)	155 (+1)	10 (−3)	–	75.4	+2.9	46.2 +0.2	29.5 +2.6	23.8 −2.6	–	0.4
South	209 (+3)	25 (−3)	6	–	74.9	+2.7	51.8 +1.2	20.9 +1.1	26.8 −1.9	–	0.5
Midlands	86 (−2)	34 (+3)	0 (−1)	–	76.3	+2.7	47.8 +1.0	30.0 +1.9	21.8 −2.7	–	0.4
North	63 (−5)	96 (+7)	4 (−2)	–	75.4	+3.4	36.6 −1.8	42.1 +5.4	21.0 −3.5	–	0.3
Wales	8 (−6)	24 (+4)	3 (+1)	3 (+1)	78.9	+2.8	29.5 −1.5	45.1 +7.3	17.9 −5.3	7.3 −0.5	0.2
Scotland	10 (−11)	50 (+9)	9 (+1)	3 (+1)	75.1	+2.4	24.0 −4.3	42.4 +7.3	19.2 −5.3	14.0 +2.3	0.3
Great Britain	376 (−21)	229 (+20)	22 (−1)	6 (+2)	75.7	+3.0	43.3 −0.2	31.5 +3.2	23.7 −2.9	1.7 +0.2	0.4
Northern Ireland	–	–	–	17	67.0	−5.8	–	–	–	–	100.0
United Kingdom	376 (−21)	229 (+20)	22 (−1)	23 (+2)	75.3	+2.6	42.3 −0.1	30.8 +3.2	22.6 −2.8	1.7 +0.2	2.6

REGIONS

	Seats won in 1987 (Change since 1983 in brackets)				Share of votes cast 1987 and change since 1983						
Region	Cons.	Labour	Alliance	Nat. & Other	Turnout 1987	Change since 1983	Conservative	Labour	Alliance	Nationalist	Other
South-East	165 (+3)	24 (−3)	3	–	74.1	+2.7	52.2 +1.7	22.3 +1.1	25.0 −2.4	–	0.6
Inner London	13 (+1)	17 (−1)	1	–	66.1	+3.4	37.2 +2.2	42.4 +2.1	19.2 −3.0	–	1.2
Outer London	45 (+1)	6 (−2)	2 (+1)	–	73.4	+2.4	51.3 +2.9	25.8 +1.4	22.4 −3.8	–	0.5
Outer Met. Area	57 (+1)	0 (−1)	0	–	76.3	+2.2	55.8 +2.0	17.8 +1.0	25.9 −2.8	–	0.5
Rest of S.E.	50	1 (+1)	0 (−1)	–	76.1	+2.8	55.3 +0.0	15.7 +1.2	28.5 −0.8	–	0.4
South-West	44	1	3	–	78.3	+2.8	50.6 −0.8	15.9 +1.2	33.0 −0.2	–	0.5
Devon & Cornwall	14	0	3	–	78.8	+2.2	48.8 −2.9	12.9 +2.5	37.7 +0.6	–	0.7
Rest of S.W.	30	1	0	–	78.0	+3.1	51.5 +0.2	17.3 +0.6	30.8 −0.5	–	0.4
East Anglia	19 (+1)	1	0	–	77.1	+2.3	52.1 +1.1	21.7 +1.2	25.7 −2.5	–	0.5
East Midlands	31 (−3)	11 (+3)	0 (−1)	–	77.5	+3.2	48.6 +1.4	30.0 +2.1	21.0 −3.1	–	0.4
West Midlands	36	22	0	–	75.0	+2.4	45.5 +0.5	33.3 +2.1	20.8 −2.6	–	0.4
W. Mids Met. Co.	14 (+1)	17	0	–	72.6	+2.2	42.6 +0.9	39.8 +2.4	17.3 −3.2	–	0.3
Rest of W. Mids	22 (−1)	5 (+1)	0	–	77.4	+2.5	48.3 +0.1	27.1 +2.0	24.2 −2.1	–	0.4
Yorks & Humber	21 (−3)	33 (+3)	0 (−2)	–	74.5	+3.5	37.4 −1.2	40.6 +5.3	21.7 −3.9	–	0.3
S. Yorks Met. Co.	1	14	0	–	72.5	+3.0	24.9 −3.1	56.0 +7.3	18.9 −4.1	–	0.2
W. Yorks Met. Co.	9 (−2)	14 (+4)	0 (−2)	–	75.6	+3.8	37.9 +0.5	41.0 +5.3	20.8 −5.2	–	0.4
Rest of Yorks & H.	11 (−1)	5 (+1)	0	–	74.9	+3.6	47.0 −2.3	27.6 +4.2	25.1 −1.9	–	0.3
North-West	34 (−2)	36 (+1)	3 (+1)	–	75.3	+3.2	38.0 −2.0	41.2 +5.2	20.6 −3.0	–	0.2
Gtr Man. Met. Co.	10 (−1)	19 (+1)	3	–	74.9	+3.1	35.9 −0.2	44.0 +4.4	19.9 −3.8	–	0.1
Merseyside Met. Co.	4	11	2 (+1)	–	72.5	+3.0	30.6 −2.3	48.3 +5.3	20.8 −3.3	–	0.3
Rest of N.W.	20	6	1	–	77.8	+3.0	45.7 −1.5	34.4 +4.8	19.6 −3.3	–	0.3
Northern	8 (−1)	27 (+1)	1 (−1)	–	75.3	+3.5	32.3 −2.3	46.4 +6.2	21.0 −4.0	–	0.3
Tyne & Wear Met. Co.	1	12 (+1)	0	–	72.5	+3.1	27.6 −3.7	53.6 +8.2	18.6 −4.7	–	0.3
Rest of Northern	7	15	1 (−1)	–	76.9	+3.7	35.0 −1.6	42.3 +5.1	22.4 −3.6	–	0.2
Wales	8 (−6)	24 (+4)	3 (+1)	3 (+1)	78.9	+2.8	29.5 −1.5	45.1 +7.5	17.9 −5.3	7.3 −0.5	0.2
Industrial Wales	4 (−3)	20 (+3)	0	0	78.2	+3.3	26.3 −0.9	54.3 +9.1	15.4 −7.0	3.7 −1.0	0.2
Rural Wales	4	4	3 (+1)	3 (+1)	80.1	+2.0	35.0 −2.6	29.2 +4.9	22.2 −5.3	13.5 +0.3	0.2
Scotland	10 (−11)	50 (+9)	9 (+1)	3 (+1)	75.1	+2.4	24.0 −4.3	42.4 +7.3	19.2 −5.3	14.0 +2.3	0.3
Central Clydeside	1	23 (+3)	0	0	74.9	+2.4	16.6 −5.7	56.1 +9.6	15.6 −6.4	11.4 +2.6	0.3
Rest of indust. belt	1 (−2)	22 (+2)	0	0	76.5	+3.0	24.7 −3.3	47.0 +7.8	16.6 −6.8	11.5 +3.0	0.3
Highlands	0 (−1)	1 (+1)	5 (+1)	0	72.2	+0.8	22.3 −6.8	20.9 +6.4	40.8 +2.7	13.6 −4.6	2.5
Rest of Scotland	5 (−5)	4 (−2)	4	3 (+2)	74.1	+2.1	33.6 −3.8	21.5 +4.0	22.8 −?	?	2.5

Table A1.3   Constituency results – Great Britain 1987

This table lists the votes in each constituency in percentage terms.

The constituencies are listed alphabetically within counties.

The figure in the 'Other' column is the total percentage received by all 'Other' candidates. (When there was more than one candidate the number is indicated in brackets.)

In Scotland and Wales Greens are listed with Others but indicated by a °.

† denotes seats held by a different party in 1983 and 1987.

‡ denotes seats that changed hands in by-elections during the 1983–7 parliament.

Swing is given in the total-role (or Butler) form – the average of the Conservative % gain and of the Labour % loss – but only in those seats where those parties occupied the top two places both in 1983 and in 1987. This is the practise followed in all Nuffield Studies since 1955.

Distribution of Census Characteristics by Constituency

On the left of these tables there are listed for the 633 constituencies in Great Britain (but not for the 17 in Northern Ireland) some basic social data, mainly drawn from the 1981 census:

% car owners: % of households with access to at least one car (1981 Census).

% working class: % of economically active and retired males in the Registrar-General's socioeconomic groups, 7, 9, 10, 11, 15 (1981 Census). This definition differs from that conventionally used in excluding socioeconomic groups 8 (foremen and supervisors), 12 (own-account workers) and 14 (own-account farmers). It provides the best possible approximation to the definition of the working class authored by Goldthorpe and used in A. Heath, R. Jowell and J. Curtice, *How Britain Votes* (Oxford: Pergamon, 1985).

% with degree: % of population aged 18+ with a degree, professional or vocational qualifications (1981 Census).

% unemployed 1987: Registered unemployed, 12 March 1987, (*Source: Employment Gazette*, May 1987) as a percentage of the June 1987 electorate less the % of the population aged over 60 (1981 Census).

Outer Metropolitan Area includes those seats wholly (mostly) in the Outer Metropolitan Area as defined by the Office of Population Censuses and Surveys (OPCS). It includes the whole of Surrey and Hertfordshire, those constituencies in Kent north-west of Faversham and Ashford, the Crawley and mid-Sussex divisions in West Sussex, the whole of Berkshire less Newbury, constituencies in Buckinghamshire to the south-east of Aylesbury, those constituencies in Bedfordshire from Luton southwards, constituencies in Essex from Chelmsford south-westwards, together with the Aldershot division of Hampshire.

The Central Clydeside Conurbation includes those constituencies wholly or mostly in the Clydeside conurbation as defined by the Registrar-General (Scotland). It includes the city of Glasgow and those surrounding seats in the Strathclyde region which lie to the north of East Kilbride and the east of Renfrew West & Inverclyde.

The *English Regions* and the eight *Standard Regions* are defined by the Office of Population, Census and Surveys.

Appendix 1

Electorate change: change in size of electorate, June 1983–June 1987, as a percentage of the June 1983 electorate.

The following information was published in *The British General Election of 1983*: % owner-occupied, % council tenants and % employers and managers.

The following table is designed to show the approximate rank ordering of all constituencies in terms of these characteristics as well as the range between the highest and lowest figures for each characteristic.

Ranking order of decile (%)	Rank order in number	Car-owners (%)	Working class (%)	Degree holders (%)	Unemployed (%)	Change in electorate (%)
0	1	18.1	23.5	1.0	2.6	−15.3
10	63	42.9	36.1	2.8	4.7	−2.0
20	126	49.2	41.5	3.6	5.9	−0.5
30	190	53.5	44.5	4.1	7.2	0.6
40	253	58.1	47.7	4.6	8.2	1.3
50	316	61.2	50.7	5.2	9.4	2.2
60	380	65.5	53.3	5.7	10.8	2.9
70	443	69.4	59.1	6.3	11.9	3.8
80	506	72.1	62.9	7.1	13.3	5.0
90	570	75.6	67.1	8.6	16.1	6.5
100	633	84.7	80.8	16.5	27.7	22.5

The correlation between the social composition of a constituency and the percentage level of support for each party can be seen in the following table:

	Conservative	Labour	Alliance
% unemployed 1987	−0.73	0.75	−0.42
% working class	−0.77	0.82	−0.48
% with degree	0.41	−0.50	0.31
% car-owners	0.74	−0.78	0.45
% council tenants	−0.72	0.68	−0.38
% owner-occupiers	0.68	−0.60	0.31
% employers & managers	0.78	−0.83	0.48

Constituency results, Great Britain, 1987

Swing	% Other	% Green	Alln. change 1983-87	% Alln. (*SDP)	Lab. change 1983-87	% Lab.	Con. change 1983-87	% Con.	% change in voting	% voting	ENGLAND	Electorate change %	% Unemployed	% with degrees	% Working class	% Car-owners
–	–	1.3	6.6	42.7*	–4.5	10.6	–1.7	45.4	5.0	79.4	Avon, Bath	1.4	7.8	7.6	42.2	58.8
2.3	0.6	–	–0.8	20.4	–1.5	35.4	3.1	43.6	4.8	78.7	Bristol, East	–3.7	10.6	3.2	57.2	59.4
0.4	–	–	–4.7	18.8*	2.0	34.6	2.7	46.6	2.5	79.4	North-West	–0.2	8.7	5.0	54.0	64.0
3.1	0.3	1.2	0.0	19.5*	–3.1	40.9	3.0	38.1	5.2	74.0	South	–4.6	13.4	1.9	63.0	56.3
–	0.3	2.0	1.9	31.3	1.4	20.9	–3.6	45.5	4.3	75.0	West	–1.1	11.8	15.9	32.5	60.0
2.1	–	–	–4.8	17.7	0.3	37.4	4.5	44.9	2.6	80.2	Kingswood	1.3	7.0	3.0	56.4	66.5
–	–	–	0.6	31.7	–0.5	13.9	0.7	54.4	2.2	80.2	Northavon	6.7	5.1	6.5	42.2	82.7
–	–	–	–2.2	25.2	1.6	23.3	1.0	51.5	2.3	81.3	Wansdyke	5.8	6.3	6.3	43.1	77.8
–	–	3.6	0.2	35.6	0.3	11.4	–4.1	49.4	2.6	75.6	Weston-super-Mare	6.9	8.4	5.5	41.0	67.9
–	–	2.0	–3.3	27.0	2.7	14.4	–1.0	56.6	1.3	79.1	Woodspring	7.0	4.7	7.6	35.2	79.9
–	–	–	–4.0	22.9	1.9	18.1	2.1	59.0	1.7	78.6	*Bedfordshire*, Mid	6.8	4.4	5.9	45.5	75.6
–	–	–	–2.8	23.5	2.1	23.1	0.6	52.6	2.0	77.2	North	2.9	7.5	7.1	47.2	66.1
–	–	–	–5.5	22.3*	1.1	18.3	3.1	58.1	3.1	78.7	South-West	3.5	5.8	6.3	45.2	75.2
2.4	0.8	1.3	–6.1	19.4*	0.6	26.8	5.5	53.8	0.2	77.6	Luton, North	6.3	7.2	4.8	53.1	73.0
0.5	–	–	–7.8	17.1	3.4	36.7	4.4	46.2	–0.6	75.2	South	0.3	12.0	4.3	60.5	58.7
–	–	–	–4.5	25.4*	1.0	14.3	3.5	60.3	0.5	73.8	*Berkshire*, East	6.8	4.3	7.7	36.2	78.0
–	–	–	–3.3	31.7	2.5	8.1	0.8	60.2	2.8	78.0	Newbury	5.4	3.6	6.7	42.2	76.8
0.6	–	1.3	–4.2	23.2*	2.1	21.5	2.2	53.8	2.9	73.3	Reading, East	7.1	6.4	8.4	43.6	65.1
–	0.2	1.1	–5.9	22.3	2.0	21.3	3.2	55.3	–0.2	72.2	West	6.5	5.6	6.6	44.9	67.7
–	–	–	–5.1	13.4*	2.7	39.6	4.0	47.0	4.4	75.9	Slough	2.1	7.7	4.0	57.0	65.6
–	3.8(2)	1.2	1.7	27.0	–0.4	11.2	–1.4	56.8	5.0	75.4	Windsor & Maidenhead	0.9	3.8	8.3	36.0	76.2
–	–	–	–1.7	29.9	0.7	8.7	1.0	61.4	–0.1	75.9	Wokingham	19.2	2.6	9.7	27.0	84.7
–	–	–	–0.8	28.6*	1.6	13.9	–0.5	57.5	3.0	74.5	*Buckinghamshire*, Aylesbury	5.7	3.9	7.1	42.4	75.3
–	–	–	–1.8	23.7	–0.4	10.3	2.2	66.0	2.2	74.6	Beaconsfield	2.3	3.0	8.0	31.0	81.4
–	–	–	–3.2	24.9	1.5	16.5	1.7	58.6	1.2	78.3	Buckingham	11.6	4.4	7.6	42.2	75.0
–	–	1.4	–4.0	27.1	1.5	9.3	1.1	62.2	1.4	77.3	Chesham & Amersham	2.5	2.6	8.9	28.0	81.9

ENGLAND	% voting	% change in voting	% Con.	Con. change 1983–87	% Lab.	Lab. change 1983–87	% Alln. (*SDP)	Alln. change 1983–87	% Green	% Other	Swing	Electorate change %	% Unemployed	% with degrees	% Working class	% Car-owners
Milton Keynes	76.3	2.2	47.8	−0.2	21.8	−0.5	29.3*	0.9	1.1	–	–	22.5	8.0	5.2	50.4	68.9
Wycombe	72.8	1.2	53.9	−0.4	18.6	1.5	27.5*	−0.5	–	–	–	2.6	4.7	6.0	44.4	74.7
Cambridgeshire, Cambridge	78.0	2.8	40.0	−1.5	28.3	0.1	30.6*	0.9	1.1	–	–	3.5	6.4	11.3	46.8	57.6
Cambridgeshire, North-East†	77.4	1.1	47.0	6.2	8.5	−0.2	44.5	−6.0	–	–	–	6.2	8.0	3.6	54.9	70.6
South-East	76.5	2.3	58.8	1.2	13.7	1.1	27.5*	−2.3	–	–	–	9.5	3.2	7.3	42.8	76.6
South-West	77.7	1.7	57.7	1.5	13.3	1.7	29.0	−3.3	–	–	–	7.1	3.8	9.2	39.2	76.9
Huntingdon	74.0	2.4	63.6	1.2	13.9	2.4	21.1*	−4.2	1.4	–	–	12.4	5.1	5.8	44.0	77.7
Peterborough	73.5	0.2	49.4	2.3	33.7	4.6	16.1	−6.6	0.8	–	−1.1	6.7	11.9	3.6	59.9	61.0
Cheshire, City of Chester	79.8	5.3	44.9	−2.3	35.6	7.4	19.5	−5.2	–	–	−4.8	2.1	11.4	7.4	48.9	60.1
Congleton	80.5	3.6	48.3	−0.3	17.9	−2.0	33.8	2.4	–	–	−4.8	6.7	5.4	7.1	44.8	75.6
Crewe & Nantwich	79.3	4.6	42.1	1.6	44.0	2.9	13.9*	−4.5	–	–	−0.7	1.6	8.1	5.3	58.8	62.5
Eddisbury	78.0	3.7	51.1	−2.3	23.5	2.5	23.7	−1.9	1.7	–	–	3.3	8.0	7.2	45.1	75.7
Ellesmere Port & Neston	81.0	5.2	44.4	−1.5	41.2	8.6	14.1*	−7.4	–	–	−5.1	1.9	10.8	5.7	58.7	70.6
Halton	78.3	5.0	30.2	−3.4	55.5	9.0	14.3*	−5.7	–	0.3	−6.2	1.5	13.2	3.2	66.3	57.0
Macclesfield	77.4	2.4	56.4	0.0	19.6	1.5	24.0	2.3	–	–	–	4.1	5.2	9.2	38.4	71.5
Tatton	76.7	2.4	54.6	3.4	21.3	3.1	23.6*	−3.6	–	0.5	–	4.6	6.7	7.4	41.2	72.0
Warrington, North	75.2	2.6	34.1	0.0	48.2	7.0	17.7*	−9.9	–	–	−1.8	8.3	11.0	4.0	61.5	59.9
South	77.6	3.1	42.0	−5.2	35.8	5.9	22.2	−5.2	–	–	−2.9	4.7	10.1	5.8	51.2	69.8
Cleveland, Hartlepool	73.0	3.2	33.9	−2.6	48.5	2.9	14.0	−1.3	–	–	−4.1	−1.0	17.0	3.2	68.9	47.7
Langbaurgh	78.8	3.8	41.7	−2.4	38.4	7.0	19.9	−7.0	–	3.6	−3.5	2.3	11.8	5.7	56.6	65.3
Middlesbrough	71.0	4.5	25.0	−0.8	59.7	9.0	15.3	−5.9	–	–	−5.8	−3.4	21.7	3.1	73.2	40.1
Redcar	76.1	4.8	31.3	−1.5	47.3	6.8	21.4*	−4.3	–	–	−4.6	−0.1	16.9	2.8	68.7	51.9
Stockton, North	75.4	5.0	32.5		49.2	12.0	18.3*	−11.3	–	–	−6.8	0.1	15.0	3.3	67.1	51.8
South†	79.0	6.9	35.0		31.3	5.0	33.7*	−3.0	–	–	–	2.0	11.9	5.9	52.6	65.7
Cornwall, North	79.8	−0.6	51.7	−0.7	6.4	2.5	41.9	−1.1	–	–	–	8.3	11.8	4.0	42.3	74.0
South-East	79.5	0.9	51.6	−3.7	8.7	3.8	39.7	0.8	–	–	–	7.8	8.0	4.7	44.5	72.3

Constituency																
Falmouth & Camborne	67.4	4.6	12.7	4.2	50.2	78.8	3.8	43.9	-6.1	20.8	-0.4	34.6*	7.0	—	0.7	—
St. Ives	65.4	5.4	13.1	4.9	43.7	77.2	3.3	48.4	-3.0	17.8	6.6	33.8*	-0.9	—	—	—
Truro	73.2	5.7	10.0	5.7	44.6	79.9	0.3	40.8	2.7	10.2	5.6	49.0	-8.3	—	—	-0.9
Cumbria, Barrow & Furness	57.2	2.1	8.4	4.0	60.2	79.0	3.8	46.5	2.8	39.3	4.6	14.2*	-7.4	0.7	—	-1.0
Carlisle	53.1	1.0	10.0	3.7	60.2	78.8	2.4	40.1	2.8	42.2	4.7	17.7*	-7.5	—	—	0.0
Copeland	60.1	0.9	8.9	4.8	64.0	81.3	3.1	43.0	3.1	47.2	3.0	9.1*	-6.7	0.7	—	—
Penrith & Border	74.8	4.2	6.3	5.4	44.8	77.5	4.4	60.3	1.4	11.0	-2.2	28.7	0.8	—	—	0.3
Westmorland & Lonsdale	71.6	4.6	5.1	7.5	42.3	74.8	2.5	57.6	-3.7	13.2	3.4	29.2	2.0	—	—	5.3
Workington	59.6	1.4	10.0	4.4	60.6	80.6	1.0	37.0	1.0	52.4	0.3	10.6	-1.3	—	—	0.8
Derbyshire, Amber Valley	60.9	2.6	8.2	3.8	61.5	81.2	4.0	51.4	9.7	34.4	-0.9	14.2	-7.1	—	—	—
Bolsover	54.5	1.1	11.2	2.4	70.2	77.3	4.7	28.3	1.4	56.2	-0.1	15.5*	-1.3	—	—	2.4
Chesterfield	53.8	2.7	11.4	4.1	61.7	76.7	4.1	25.0	-7.5	45.4	-2.6	29.6	10.0	0.5	—	-1.1
Derby, North	57.5	1.9	9.8	5.2	57.3	75.8	3.3	48.9	5.2	37.2	0.4	13.4	-6.1	—	—	-1.4
South	49.6	0.4	15.5	3.8	62.8	69.9	2.5	40.5	2.1	43.7	4.3	15.8*	-5.8	—	—	0.6
Derbyshire, North-East	64.6	3.0	9.9	5.7	55.6	79.3	3.6	37.7	0.8	44.4	3.6	17.9*	-4.3	—	—	—
South	70.7	6.2	7.1	5.7	55.8	81.3	2.8	49.1	5.3	33.2	4.0	17.7*	-9.3	—	—	-2.0
West	70.1	3.1	5.5	7.2	46.5	83.1	5.7	53.1	-2.8	11.7	-5.4	35.2	8.2	—	—	—
Erewash	60.5	4.3	8.6	4.1	59.1	77.4	1.7	48.6	3.2	32.1	7.2	19.3*	-2.9	—	—	—
High Peak	63.2	3.8	7.3	5.7	50.0	80.5	2.0	45.7	-0.7	28.8	2.8	25.5*	-2.0	—	0.3	—
Devon, North	71.1	6.0	8.9	4.6	43.4	81.7	1.6	50.9	-4.2	6.3	0.6	42.8	4.9	2.0	1.3	—
Devon West & Torridge	74.0	5.5	7.9	5.0	44.1	78.7	2.6	50.3	-7.7	8.5	1.9	39.2	4.2	1.0	—	—
Exeter	62.8	2.4	8.6	6.5	46.0	80.6	2.6	44.4	-2.1	22.5	-0.3	31.8*	2.5	—	—	—
Honiton	69.5	7.0	6.8	6.6	36.7	76.4	1.9	59.2	-1.4	8.4	2.2	31.1*	-2.0	—	—	—
Plymouth, Devonport	55.6	4.7	10.0	2.6	63.4	76.9	0.8	29.3	-4.6	28.4	7.5	42.3*	-2.1	1.3	—	—
Drake	50.0	-2.3	16.8	5.1	52.6	76.6	2.3	41.3	-9.3	24.1	3.8	33.3*	4.7	—	—	—
Sutton	70.0	7.1	7.7	4.7	46.8	79.0	2.7	45.8	-9.4	16.4	2.1	37.8	8.3	1.9	—	—
South Hams	70.8	5.8	8.3	6.1	38.0	78.6	3.7	55.4	-1.9	8.2	1.3	34.1	-0.9	—	0.4	—
Teignbridge	68.5	6.5	8.8	5.7	41.9	80.3	2.8	53.2	-0.8	11.1	3.9	35.1	-3.2	—	0.6	—
Tiverton	75.8	6.9	6.0	6.2	41.5	79.7	2.2	54.9	0.2	6.3	-0.1	38.0	-0.8	—	0.8	—
Torbay	61.2	4.6	14.4	4.5	39.7	76.3	3.7	54.0	1.4	8.4	1.2	37.6	-1.6	—	—	—
Dorset, Bournemouth, East	58.9	6.3	11.2	4.3	41.3	70.5	4.0	58.3	4.8	11.1	2.5	30.6	1.4	—	—	—
West	64.4	3.0	8.5	3.5	47.6	73.3	4.2	55.2	-1.7	12.8	0.4	32.0*	1.7	—	—	—
Christchurch	77.9	8.4	5.2	6.2	31.4	76.3	4.0	65.9	-1.2	9.6	2.0	24.5*	-0.8	—	—	—

ENGLAND	Car-owners %	Working class %	% with degrees	% Unemployed	Electorate change %	% voting	% change in voting	% Con.	Con. change 1983–87	% Lab.	Lab. change 1983–87	% Alln. (*SDP)	Alln. change 1983–87	% Green	% Other	Swing
Dorset, North	78.6	41.5	6.7	4.5	7.9	79.1	2.5	57.0	−1.1	6.6	1.4	36.4	0.3	—	—	—
South	66.3	44.9	5.1	8.2	5.6	75.5	2.9	54.8	−2.3	17.3	1.6	27.5	0.5	—	0.4	—
West	73.0	42.3	7.5	5.0	5.5	78.3	4.0	56.2	−3.5	12.2	0.7	31.6	2.8	—	—	—
Poole	70.4	43.2	5.5	7.6	8.4	77.5	3.9	57.5	−0.8	9.9	−0.8	32.6*	2.0	—	—	−2.3
Durham, Bishop Auckland	54.7	63.3	3.9	11.2	1.4	74.1	1.9	34.8	−1.1	48.0	3.5	17.2	−2.4	—	—	−0.9
Darlington	52.1	59.3	4.8	11.5	1.1	80.8	3.7	46.6	2.0	41.6	3.8	11.8	−5.6	—	—	—
Durham, City of	57.3	53.2	8.0	8.1	−0.5	78.2	3.8	21.9	−9.1	44.9	8.4	33.2*	0.6	—	—	—
Durham, North	52.7	61.6	4.3	11.3	1.2	75.9	3.3	21.2	2.8	56.2	5.3	22.6	−2.5	—	—	—
North-West	52.4	66.4	4.3	12.5	0.9	73.5	2.9	28.4	−1.4	50.9	6.3	20.7	−4.9	—	—	−3.9
Easington	43.2	74.2	2.4	11.9	−1.3	73.4	5.9	16.3	−0.2	68.1	9.7	15.6	−9.4	—	—	—
Sedgefield	54.2	62.7	4.3	10.6	−1.4	76.1	3.2	27.9	−1.3	56.0	8.5	16.1*	−6.5	—	—	−4.9
East Sussex, Bexhill & Battle	67.6	32.3	6.8	5.7	5.7	77.4	4.5	66.5	−0.9	7.7	−0.2	25.8*	2.3	1.6	—	—
Brighton, Kemptown	48.2	48.1	4.5	11.6	−1.0	74.5	2.9	53.5	2.4	32.9	3.3	13.6	−5.1	—	—	−0.5
Pavilion	51.0	37.1	8.0	12.0	−1.4	73.7	4.5	50.8	−0.7	29.7	5.9	19.5*	−5.1	—	—	—
Eastbourne	54.4	38.6	5.5	3.7	1.6	75.6	2.5	59.9	0.8	8.8	1.7	29.7	−4.1	—	—	—
Hastings & Rye	54.7	41.7	4.6	10.4	4.3	71.8	2.9	50.1	−3.2	13.1	−2.1	36.0	5.6	—	—	—
Hove	49.3	36.8	5.9	9.7	1.0	67.8	2.0	58.8	−1.7	18.3	4.5	21.8*	−2.3	1.7	0.8(2)	—
Lewes	69.3	36.6	7.2	5.1	8.6	77.0	2.7	56.8	−1.6	8.8	0.4	32.7	2.0	—	1.1	—
Wealden	78.1	33.3	7.3	3.4	5.5	75.0	3.1	64.2	0.0	8.3	2.2	27.5	−2.2	—	—	—
Essex, Basildon	64.4	57.2	2.6	10.5	4.4	73.3	4.3	43.5	4.9	38.3	2.6	18.2	−7.5	—	—	1.1
Billericay	79.9	43.6	5.4	5.3	6.4	77.2	3.5	54.9	1.2	19.4	0.4	25.7*	−1.6	—	—	—
Braintree	71.6	44.5	5.3	5.2	5.3	79.0	2.9	54.2	1.6	19.3	0.5	26.5*	−2.1	—	—	—
Brentwood & Ongar	78.1	34.5	6.8	4.1	4.7	79.0	2.4	60.5	2.1	13.2	1.8	25.0	−5.2	1.3	—	—
Castle Point	74.7	42.5	3.2	6.0	2.3	75.1	3.7	59.9	1.4	19.0	2.3	21.1*	−3.7	—	—	—
Chelmsford	74.0	37.1	7.5	4.2	3.1	82.2	2.8	51.9	4.3	6.9	1.7	40.5	−6.5	0.7	—	—
Colchester, North	70.3	41.5	6.1	6.1	6.6	76.0	2.9	52.3	−0.7	17.2	−1.2	30.5*	4.2	—	—	—
South & Maldon	72.0	42.2	5.2	6.4	6.0	75.3	2.0	54.9	1.3	14.5	0.9	30.6*	−2.2	—	—	—

290

					Constituency												
73.5	37.4	5.4	5.5	2.2	Epping Forest	76.3	3.3	60.9	4.4	18.4	1.2	19.4*	-5.4	1.3	—	—
70.2	48.7	4.3	6.8	0.8	Harlow	78.4	1.9	47.2	6.1	36.6	2.4	16.2*	-8.0	—	—	1.9
58.5	43.9	3.5	10.8	6.9	Harwich	73.5	3.3	51.8	-2.4	17.5	1.1	30.4	1.0	—	0.3	—
77.6	36.7	5.3	4.4	9.6	Rochford	78.1	4.6	60.4	2.6	12.3	2.3	27.3	-4.9	—	—	—
77.3	41.2	6.8	3.9	5.5	Saffron Walden	79.0	2.1	57.7	-0.2	11.5	0.2	29.0	-0.3	1.4	0.4	—
54.8	43.0	3.6	11.0	2.4	Southend, East	69.3	1.8	58.0	2.2	17.8	1.9	24.2*	-4.2	—	—	—
61.7	33.5	4.9	7.3	1.4	West	75.3	3.6	54.4	0.1	7.6	-0.0	38.0	0.2	—	—	—
64.1	62.1	2.3	10.4	2.0	Thurrock†	71.5	3.8	42.5	7.1	41.0	1.9	16.5*	-5.2	—	—	2.6
65.5	41.2	6.7	6.8	4.2	*Gloucestershire*, Cheltenham	78.9	3.1	50.2	-0.4	7.5	-0.1	42.3	1.3	—	—	—
76.0	44.2	6.4	4.3	5.0	Cirencester & Tewkesbury	77.9	3.0	55.4	-1.8	8.2	-0.6	36.0	1.9	—	0.4	—
65.4	53.6	4.7	8.1	3.6	Gloucester	78.1	2.4	49.7	1.2	29.6	3.5	20.7	-3.3	—	—	-1.1
74.5	49.2	4.6	7.5	5.0	Gloucestershire, West	81.1	1.5	46.2	0.4	27.8	3.1	26.0*	-3.5	—	—	—
72.1	46.5	6.9	5.9	4.8	Stroud	80.6	3.0	50.2	-1.1	18.5	1.7	31.3	-0.6	—	—	0.9
49.7	65.3	1.4	9.7	-1.4	*Greater London*, Barking	66.9	1.5	34.5	4.1	44.3	2.2	21.2	-4.4	—	—	0.8
54.3	62.3	1.5	8.6	-2.0	Dagenham	67.3	3.9	38.5	6.7	44.4	5.2	17.1*	-9.9	—	—	-1.0
72.5	28.2	8.7	4.6	4.2	Barnet, Chipping Barnet	70.0	-0.7	57.9	1.8	19.1	3.1	23.0	-3.1	—	0.5(2)	—
63.3	30.9	9.5	6.7	3.8	Finchley	69.4	0.4	53.9	2.9	31.7	4.9	13.9	-6.3	—	—	—
64.9	37.4	6.0	6.7	1.1	Hendon, North	65.8	-2.1	55.6	5.8	25.5	1.7	18.9*	-6.7	—	—	—
62.7	26.1	8.9	7.1	1.2	South	63.8	-1.5	55.5	6.9	20.9	-0.2	23.6	-6.7	—	—	—
70.8	38.4	3.9	5.2	0.3	Bexley, Bexleyheath	77.8	3.4	53.7	0.7	17.8	0.6	28.5	-1.3	—	—	—
62.6	51.8	2.9	8.5	5.8	Erith & Crayford	75.4	1.9	45.2	8.1	29.5	2.2	25.3*	-9.6	—	—	—
74.0	32.0	5.6	4.5	1.1	Old Bexley & Sidcup	77.1	3.0	62.1	1.9	17.3	3.5	20.6	-5.4	—	—	—
44.9	45.8	7.8	15.3	-0.8	Brent, East	64.5	0.9	38.4	3.8	42.6	-4.4	14.5*	-2.4	1.8	2.7	4.1
68.4	31.5	7.5	6.7	0.6	North	71.0	0.6	59.9	3.6	24.8	1.7	15.3*	-5.3	—	—	0.9
48.5	60.0	4.5	13.3	0.0	South	64.9	1.2	32.4	5.5	51.9	-1.4	15.7	-3.3	—	—	3.4
63.7	30.9	8.7	6.8	2.4	Bromley, Beckenham	73.6	3.5	56.3	-1.1	17.8	2.3	25.9	-0.7	—	—	—
68.2	35.1	6.8	5.3	1.8	Chislehurst	75.5	2.8	57.6	1.9	19.4	0.9	23.0	-2.3	—	—	—
76.9	28.1	6.9	4.3	1.4	Orpington	78.5	2.6	58.2	1.0	10.7	3.0	31.1	-3.5	—	—	—
74.8	27.3	7.6	4.5	0.9	Ravensbourne	75.7	2.5	63.0	-0.1	11.3	1.9	25.3*	-1.7	—	0.4	—
45.5	27.6	15.1	12.2	-4.9	Camden, Hampstead & Highgate	71.5	4.6	42.5	1.3	37.6	3.9	19.3*	-5.5	—	0.6(2)	1.3
31.6	51.5	9.4	15.7	-1.4	Holborn & St. Pancras	64.3	4.1	31.1	0.4	50.6	3.1	17.6	-3.8	—	0.7	-1.3
64.9	38.8	6.5	7.2	-2.0	Croydon, Central	70.5	1.9	56.6	2.8	24.4	1.0	19.0*	-3.8	—	—	0.9

Swing	% Other	% Green	Alln. change 1983-87	% Alln. (SDP*)	Lab. change 1983-87	% Lab.	Con. change 1983-87	% Con.	% change in voting	% voting	ENGLAND	Electorate change %	% Unemployed	% with degrees	% Working class	% Car-owners
—	—	—	-6.6	18.5*	4.1	26.5	2.5	55.0	2.2	69.7	North-East	0.3	7.7	6.6	38.1	60.4
—	—	—	-15.9	16.0	12.7	37.0	4.7	47.0	1.6	69.2	North-West	-1.7	8.8	5.1	46.9	58.6
1.6	—	1.9	-2.8	24.3	2.0	9.8	-1.1	64.0	2.7	73.7	South	0.9	3.8	8.7	23.7	78.8
0.0	—	1.1	-4.8	18.8*	1.1	27.8	4.2	53.4	-1.1	71.0	Ealing, Acton	8.2	9.2	10.3	35.9	54.1
3.3	—	—	-6.3	15.1	-5.0	27.8	10.9	56.0	0.2	75.1	North	4.5	6.8	5.6	46.2	64.9
6.3	0.5	—	-2.5	13.3	-1.6	50.7	5.0	35.5	-1.6	69.7	Southall	4.8	9.2	5.6	55.7	58.9
1.6	—	1.3	-4.1	12.8*	-3.8	36.0	8.7	51.2	3.7	72.5	Enfield, Edmonton	2.0	8.3	3.9	47.4	59.7
—	—	1.4	-4.5	14.7*	0.6	28.5	3.8	55.5	2.1	74.5	North	2.2	6.9	4.0	26.9	64.1
-1.5	—	—	-2.5	20.9	1.0	18.9	0.8	58.8	3.0	72.6	Southgate	1.8	6.0	7.9	43.2	70.2
—	—	—	-1.6	20.5	2.7	32.0	-0.4	47.5	2.9	76.9	Greenwich, Eltham	-1.8	8.6	5.2	49.6	60.2
—	0.3(2)	0.9	15.5	40.6*	-3.4	34.9	-11.5	23.3	5.7	73.4	Greenwich‡‡	-1.5	12.2	8.2	58.3	51.0
—	—	—	1.2	41.7*	3.6	37.0	-3.9	21.3	2.7	70.7	Woolwich	3.2	13.6	3.2		49.9
											Hackney					
1.8	0.6	2.6	3.4	19.2*	-3.3	48.7	0.3	28.9	3.5	58.1	North & Stoke Newington	0.0	19.1	5.7	54.2	35.1
0.6	1.0	1.1	-5.5	22.4	4.4	47.9	5.5	28.7	1.5	55.4	South & Shoreditch	-0.6	19.7	4.9	63.0	33.7
1.4	0.6(2)	1.3	-7.9	10.4*	2.7	36.7	5.6	51.8	1.0	77.1	Hammersmith, Fulham‡	5.1	12.5	8.8	44.2	42.1
-0.5	—	1.9	-5.9	14.9	3.5	45.0	2.6	38.2	1.5	72.7	Hammersmith	4.6	18.2	8.5	50.8	36.0
-2.2	1.7(2)	1.5	-5.8	15.1*	4.9	40.0	0.5	43.0	2.1	73.3	Haringey, Hornsey	9.1	11.9	12.5	36.3	52.4
6.8	—	—	1.6	17.9	-8.4	43.6	5.1	35.3	2.6	66.1	Tottenham	12.0	16.1	4.7	58.9	44.5
—	—	—	-5.7	22.2	1.2	23.6	4.4	54.2	1.0	73.4	Harrow, East	1.5	5.7	7.0	33.6	68.9
—	—	—	-5.0	27.2*	2.8	17.5	2.2	55.3	2.1	74.5	West	1.2	4.6	8.8	27.5	71.2
—	—	—	-4.3	20.4	1.5	28.4	4.1	51.2	1.7	75.3	Havering, Hornchurch	1.1	5.5	3.0	46.7	71.1
—	—	1.0	-6.0	20.2	3.6	22.8	2.6	56.0	3.2	72.9	Romford	-0.2	6.2	3.5	43.6	70.3
—	—	—	-3.6	22.1*	1.6	22.1	3.3	55.8	3.1	75.2	Upminster	0.3	5.5	4.0	41.9	71.3
1.7	—	—	-13.7	15.3*	5.6	35.5	8.9	49.2	3.6	74.5	Hillingdon, Hayes & Harlington	1.1	6.4	3.1	52.8	68.8
—	—	—	-4.1	23.9	1.1	13.5	3.1	62.6	4.7	77.7	Ruislip-Northwood	0.0	3.8	6.8	31.3	74.8
—	—	1.1	-5.8	19.0*	1.8	23.4	2.8	56.5	4.3	76.5	Uxbridge	2.5	5.1	5.3	46.0	70.2

59.5	41.7	8.8	7.3	3.7	Hounslow, Brentford & Isleworth	76.7	1.9	47.7	0.3	33.2	4.0	17.5*	-4.6	1.6	—	-1.8
66.8	52.3	3.4	7.3	3.4	Feltham & Heston	73.7	3.8	46.5	3.1	37.4	-2.0	16.1*	0.2	—	—	2.6
36.1	54.6	9.1	20.6	-1.8	Islington, North	66.5	4.9	25.3	0.0	50.0	9.5	21.8*	-0.5	2.9	0.3(2)	-4.7
34.1	54.9	6.5	16.7	-3.2	South & Finsbury	71.2	9.2	20.6	-6.1	40.1	3.8	38.1*	2.8	0.9	—	—
44.0	28.1	14.5	9.8	-8.0	Kensington & Chelsea, Chelsea	57.7	1.5	64.6	1.3	15.4	2.6	17.9	-5.5	2.1	0.3(2)	-1.1
40.4	36.6	12.1	13.3	-3.3	Kensington	64.7	2.4	47.5	1.5	33.3	3.7	17.2*	-4.9	1.7	0.4	—
66.9	32.9	9.4	5.8	-3.4	Kingston-upon-Thames, Kingston	78.5	6.6	56.2	2.1	13.2	1.0	30.2	-2.2	—	—	—
69.0	31.4	8.3	4.3	-3.2	Surbiton	78.3	7.0	55.8	1.3	14.4	-1.1	28.5*	0.1	1.3	0.9(2)	-2.3
43.3	50.2	7.3	18.6	1.7	Lambeth, Norwood	67.0	1.4	36.0	-0.7	48.4	3.9	14.7*	-2.7	—	—	-4.7
47.6	41.2	9.4	13.7	0.8	Streatham	69.5	4.1	45.0	-1.6	39.2	7.7	15.8	-5.4	—	0.8(2)	-0.7
32.8	59.1	7.1	19.7	2.6	Vauxhall	64.0	3.5	29.0	2.3	50.2	3.7	18.2*	-6.0	1.8	—	-0.6
43.2	58.2	5.4	17.6	-0.9	Lewisham, Deptford	64.9	3.7	31.7	0.1	49.6	1.2	17.2*	-1.5	1.5	—	3.2
52.0	49.7	6.0	10.5	-2.6	East	73.9	4.4	45.1	4.8	34.2	-1.7	20.7*	-1.3	—	—	1.3
53.5	46.6	6.2	11.3	-0.7	West	72.3	1.9	46.2	2.2	37.9	-0.5	15.9	-0.9	—	—	-0.5
59.5	48.3	4.1	8.2	-1.2	Merton, Mitcham & Morden	75.7	2.6	48.2	5.5	35.2	6.4	16.6*	-10.8	—	—	—
61.4	29.4	11.3	5.6	-2.7	Wimbledon	76.1	3.7	50.9	-1.2	21.6	2.7	27.5	0.3	—	—	0.4
50.0	59.7	3.1	12.2	-4.5	Newham, North-East	64.1	2.0	30.7	3.0	51.9	2.2	17.4	-3.1	1.8	—	-2.7
43.6	61.2	3.8	15.0	-0.2	North-West	59.4	3.3	25.4	3.5	55.4	8.8	17.4*	-1.2	—	—	—
42.7	69.1	1.9	14.7	0.3	South	59.1	5.5	34.2	11.2	43.5	-6.7	22.3*	-0.9	—	—	—
66.6	37.5	4.6	6.4	0.6	Redbridge, Ilford North	72.6	1.4	54.9	3.6	27.4	2.1	17.7*	-5.7	—	—	0.7
62.0	42.2	6.4	9.0	0.4	Ilford South	71.8	1.2	48.4	2.9	37.5	3.2	14.1	-5.4	—	—	-0.1
69.7	26.3	9.2	4.9	-2.1	Wanstead & Woodford	72.4	4.1	61.3	1.0	16.6	3.1	22.1	-1.7	—	—	—
61.5	27.3	13.8	6.2	0.9	Richmond, Richmond & Barnes	83.2	3.6	47.7	1.2	7.1	0.0	43.9	-2.5	1.3	—	—
68.8	31.6	10.6	4.6	-0.4	Twickenham	81.5	3.7	51.9	1.5	8.4	0.9	38.3	2.4	1.4	—	—
50.4	44.6	8.8	10.9	0.2	Southwark, Dulwich	69.3	2.1	42.4	1.9	42.0	6.3	14.5*	-7.5	1.1	—	-2.2
33.7	64.8	3.5	19.6	-0.7	Peckham	55.6	1.1	25.7	1.5	54.5	2.9	17.9	-3.9	1.9	—	-0.7
32.5	67.6	2.4	18.7		Southwark & Bermondsey	64.9	3.2	12.6	-0.4	39.7	4.8	47.4	-2.4	—	0.3	—
66.3	39.7	5.7	5.4	0.6	Sutton, Carshalton & Wallington	75.0	3.0	54.0	2.6	18.2	0.7	26.2*	-3.4	1.6	—	—
71.8	30.9	8.3	4.5	1.2	Sutton & Cheam	76.6	2.3	60.8	3.6	10.6	3.0	28.6	-6.6	—	—	—

Swing	% Other	% Green	Alln. change 1983-87	% Alln. (*SDP)	Lab. change 1983-87	% Lab.	Con. change 1983-87	% Con.	% change in voting	% voting	ENGLAND	Electorate change %	% Unemployed	% with degrees	% Working class	% Car-owners
											Tower Hamlets					
—	0.7	—	1.3	31.8	-3.0	48.3	5.2	19.2	2.0	57.6	Bethnal Green & Stepney	0.8	19.2	3.2	68.3	29.5
—	0.8	1.5	1.4	32.7	-3.2	46.4	4.0	20.1	2.0	57.4	Bow & Poplar	2.4	17.5	3.0	68.1	35.5
—	—	—	-3.7	21.0	-2.4	15.3	7.1	62.2	3.9	76.7	Waltham Forest, Chingford	1.0	6.5	4.6	41.4	65.2
4.1	1.1	1.2	4.7	29.7	-2.3	41.2	-2.5	29.1	3.9	69.6	Leyton	-0.2	12.2	5.1	55.5	48.1
4.6	0.3	1.0	3.5	25.1*	-5.1	34.8	3.1	39.0	3.6	72.4	Walthamstow†	0.8	10.7	4.2	57.9	48.5
1.9		1.3	-5.6	11.9*	-1.4	42.4	7.9	44.2	4.1	70.7	Wandsworth, Battersea†	1.6	12.4	9.0	47.1	41.9
1.4			-3.9	12.4	0.2	36.1	4.0	50.5	2.4	75.9	Putney	-1.2	8.0	9.1	39.5	52.2
			-4.9	13.2*	1.5	44.2	4.3	41.3	3.7	71.2	Tooting	0.0	10.6	8.8	43.3	48.0
											Westminster					
—		1.1	0.8	21.8*	3.3	20.4	-1.3	57.8	6.4	58.2	C of London & W'ster S.	-15.3	11.7	11.7	33.3	39.1
2.0		—	-3.6	12.1*	0.1	39.5	4.1	47.3	6.9	71.1	Westminster North	-14.1	19.3	8.6	43.2	34.7
—			-3.8	26.0	4.5	20.5	0.9	53.5	3.7	76.7	*Greater Manchester, Altrincham*	2.5	5.7	8.7	34.5	70.0
-1.6			0.1	17.9	2.0	51.8	-1.2	30.3	2.4	74.0	Ashton-under-Lyne	-0.9	11.5	3.0	62.2	48.3
-1.8			-5.3	13.0*	4.3	42.6	1.2	44.4	1.6	78.7	Bolton, North-East	0.8	11.7	5.0	52.9	53.7
-2.7			-5.9	14.5	6.0	54.3	0.6	31.2	1.3	74.9	South-East	-2.4	12.3	2.6	66.0	48.5
-2.7			-3.8	19.6*	4.6	36.1	-0.8	44.3	1.9	80.0	West	3.7	9.1	6.5	48.7	60.0
3.5			-2.2	12.1	-2.4	37.8	4.6	50.1	2.9	82.5	Bury, North	2.9	7.9	6.3	47.6	61.7
-1.2			-6.5	13.1*	4.4	40.9	2.0	46.0	3.6	79.7	South	0.3	9.0	5.1	47.1	60.1
—			-1.5	35.9	2.1	9.1	-0.7	55.0	4.2	81.0	Cheadle	2.8	4.5	9.6	24.1	80.7
-2.7			-4.2	23.0	3.6	30.4	0.6	46.6	3.5	77.3	Davyhulme	0.9	8.9	5.8	45.9	64.9
-3.3			-5.2	16.6*	5.3	49.6	-0.1	33.8	2.7	75.5	Denton & Reddish	1.3	11.3	2.3	62.7	51.2
—			-2.0	17.9*	4.9	50.8	-1.8	31.3	4.4	74.5	Eccles	-0.4	11.2	3.0	63.3	49.0
—		0.7	0.1	42.0	-0.2	11.8	-0.6	45.5	4.4	81.6	Hazel Grove	3.3	6.7	7.4	40.5	68.6
-3.0			-6.3	15.8*	6.6	49.9	0.5	34.3	3.9	73.8	Heywood & Middleton	-0.6	12.3	3.3	61.1	49.2
-3.7			-6.2	15.1*	6.8	58.6	-0.6	26.3	2.0	74.1	Leigh	1.6	11.4	3.2	63.4	52.2
—			-0.1	30.9	0.7	26.0	0.2	43.1	2.6	77.4	Littleborough & Saddleworth	3.2	7.0	6.7	46.1	61.7

294

Constituency																
Makerfield	63.9	60.7	4.5	10.8	2.4	75.8	2.1	27.3	−0.7	56.2	7.0	16.5	−6.3	–	–	−3.8
Manchester, Blackley	40.2	63.1	2.9	16.1	−2.1	72.9	3.2	28.8	−3.8	52.4	4.4	18.8*	−0.5	–	–	−4.1
Central	24.7	77.2	2.1	23.7	−9.0	63.9	3.4	18.8	−2.4	68.2	2.9	13.0*	1.2	–	–	−2.6
Gorton	39.5	62.5	4.5	14.5	−0.6	70.4	2.6	23.3	−5.2	54.4	3.2	21.7	2.7	1.0	0.6	−4.2
Withington†	50.6	45.4	10.6	14.5	1.1	77.1	4.9	36.2	−3.0	43.0	8.8	19.8	−6.4	–	–	−5.9
Wythenshawe	43.9	64.9	2.6	15.5	−4.4	72.1	2.6	28.6	−0.8	56.8	2.2	14.1*	−1.9	–	0.5	−1.5
Oldham, Central & Royton	43.5	65.2	2.8	12.0	−2.3	69.2	2.3	34.3	0.2	48.1	6.7	17.6*	−6.9	–	–	−3.3
West	50.1	61.2	2.3	10.0	−0.5	71.9	2.0	34.8	−1.3	49.4	5.3	15.8	−3.5	–	–	−3.3
Rochdale	49.2	57.4	4.7	11.7	2.6	74.6	3.8	18.6	−3.7	38.0	7.9	43.4	−2.7	–	–	–
Salford East	32.8	69.1	2.8	19.7	−9.2	66.0	3.8	27.4	−2.4	58.8	−5.1	13.3*	−2.2	–	–	−3.7
Stalybridge & Hyde	52.3	60.3	3.3	11.1	0.1	74.2	3.7	37.1	0.7	48.4	2.8	14.5*	−2.9	–	0.5	−1.1
Stockport	57.8	47.8	7.0	10.3	2.0	78.1	3.5	41.4	−0.8	35.3	6.3	22.1*	−5.5	1.2	–	−3.5
Stretford	45.8	57.5	4.6	20.1	0.2	71.9	1.9	32.4	−1.6	55.2	10.3	12.4*	−7.9	–	–	−6.0
Wigan	51.3	64.0	4.2	12.9	−0.5	76.6	1.0	24.5	1.9	61.5	7.0	14.0	−8.9	–	–	–
Worsley	60.5	57.0	4.1	10.3	1.7	77.2	2.5	35.1	2.5	48.1	7.8	16.8	−10.2	–	–	−2.6
Hampshire, Aldershot	76.4	39.0	6.9	4.0	4.1	74.0	1.3	59.0	3.5	11.8	1.0	29.2	−4.6	–	–	–
Basingstoke	72.8	48.7	6.2	4.3	8.4	77.0	0.2	56.0	4.7	17.7	−1.5	26.3*	−2.6	–	–	–
Eastleigh	74.3	48.5	5.7	6.1	6.2	79.3	2.2	51.3	0.3	16.7	−1.8	32.0	1.5	–	–	–
Fareham	77.3	42.0	6.4	5.2	7.1	78.2	4.5	61.1	−0.7	9.0	1.9	29.9	−1.2	–	–	–
Gosport	64.1	48.7	5.0	7.3	5.0	74.8	3.2	58.5	−2.1	9.9	0.6	31.6	2.0	–	–	–
Hampshire, East	80.7	33.3	7.6	3.5	8.9	77.4	3.2	64.5	1.7	6.6	1.1	28.9	−2.8	–	–	–
North-West	76.0	46.0	5.3	3.9	6.4	77.9	3.5	57.8	0.4	9.1	−1.0	33.1	0.6	–	–	–
Havant	69.4	45.2	5.0	8.6	4.4	74.6	2.5	57.1	1.8	14.1	2.1	28.1*	−4.5	–	–	–
New Forest	76.1	37.6	7.2	5.4	7.2	76.6	3.1	64.7	−1.7	8.4	0.5	26.9	1.1	–	0.7	–
Portsmouth, North	59.5	50.8	3.7	7.9	3.3	74.8	1.8	55.3	0.0	20.0	−1.2	24.7*	1.1	–	–	–
South‡	45.5	52.5	5.1	14.5	2.4	71.3	3.9	43.3	−6.7	13.0	−9.6	42.9*	17.5	–	–	–
Romsey & Waterside	79.6	45.7	6.3	5.6	11.8	79.0	3.3	56.3	−0.2	11.5	−0.8	32.0*	0.9	–	0.8	–
Southampton, Itchen	56.4	58.4	3.9	12.4	0.6	75.8	2.6	44.3	2.8	32.1	5.0	23.6*	−7.9	–	–	–
Test	59.5	55.4	5.3	10.4	−1.0	76.4	3.3	45.6	0.4	33.2	5.2	21.2	−5.6	–	–	−2.4
Winchester	75.0	39.4	7.9	3.6	5.1	80.4	4.2	52.3	−5.2	6.6	−1.6	40.2*	6.2	0.9	–	–
Hereford & Worcester, Bromsgrove	76.6	45.1	6.5	7.5	5.1	76.4	1.3	54.7	−1.5	23.3	2.6	22.0*	0.3	–	–	–
Hereford	70.4	50.3	4.9	8.1	4.7	78.0	2.3	47.5	−0.6	7.7	0.1	44.8	1.4	–	–	–

ENGLAND	% voting	% change in voting	% Con.	Con. change 1983-87	% Lab.	Lab. change 1983-87	% Alln. (*SDP)	Alln. change 1983-87	% Green	% Other	Swing	Electorate change %	% Unemployed	% with degrees	% Working class	% Car-owners
Leominster	77.5	0.1	57.9	-0.9	8.2	4.4	31.9	-6.0	2.0	—	—	5.6	6.5	6.0	43.6	78.9
Worcester	76.7	2.6	48.2	-1.3	28.4	5.7	23.4*	-4.0	—	—	—	3.7	8.6	5.5	51.1	65.9
Worcestershire, Mid	76.6	2.1	51.6	0.7	27.4	2.2	21.0*	-2.3	1.9	—	-0.8	8.5	8.6	5.5	50.3	72.5
South	75.6	1.9	55.3	-0.5	10.9	3.2	31.9	-2.7	—	—	—	5.4	6.2	6.9	41.8	74.6
Wyre Forest	77.6	2.5	47.1	1.2	18.9	-0.3	34.0	1.6	1.4	—	—	3.6	9.3	5.5	51.7	71.9
Hertfordshire, Broxbourne	75.2	1.2	63.2	4.4	16.9	0.5	19.9	-3.9	—	—	—	4.8	5.0	4.2	41.0	77.2
Hertford & Stortford	77.7	2.1	57.5	1.6	12.8	0.8	28.3*	-2.7	—	—	—	10.0	3.3	8.3	36.3	76.8
Hertfordshire, North	81.1	1.9	49.7	0.7	18.5	-0.1	31.8	-0.6	—	—	—	4.3	5.0	7.2	44.3	71.3
South-West	77.7	1.9	55.8	2.2	15.3	1.4	28.9	-3.0	—	—	—	1.7	3.7	7.0	36.7	75.2
West	80.9	1.5	49.7	3.0	24.0	1.7	26.3*	-4.6	—	—	—	3.1	4.8	7.0	35.7	73.5
Hertsmere	75.4	1.6	56.6	3.4	19.6	0.4	23.8	-1.7	1.3	—	—	0.5	4.8	6.7	29.6	74.6
St. Albans	80.2	2.0	52.5	0.5	11.5	0.6	34.5	-2.5	—	0.2	—	3.3	3.9	11.1	45.1	75.6
Stevenage	80.5	2.6	42.1	2.6	25.4	1.4	32.5*	-3.6	—	—	—	2.7	6.6	5.8	44.6	69.4
Watford	77.9	1.8	48.7	0.8	28.2	2.2	23.1*	-3.0	—	0.7	—	2.2	5.4	6.2	40.7	68.8
Welwyn & Hatfield	80.9	1.5	45.6	-2.1	26.4	0.5	27.3*	0.9	1.7	—	—	1.3	4.7	6.7	38.2	72.8
Humberside, Beverley	76.3	3.1	52.2	-4.0	16.5	4.0	31.3	0.0	—	—	—	4.1	5.9	7.5	53.9	71.7
Boothferry	75.8	2.6	55.7	-2.0	21.9	4.4	22.4	-2.4	—	—	—	3.9	8.0	5.4	47.7	69.7
Bridlington	73.7	3.1	54.8	-3.0	18.0	4.4	25.5*	-1.6	—	—	—	4.4	9.3	4.7	55.6	64.7
Brigg & Cleethorpes	76.3	2.7	48.7	-2.0	22.7	2.7	28.6	-0.7	—	—	—	3.4	10.2	3.8	64.2	65.6
Glanford & Scunthorpe†	78.1	4.6	42.6	4.1	43.5	6.2	13.6*	-10.6	—	0.3	-1.1	1.2	11.3	3.8	63.5	61.7
Great Grimsby	75.3	1.5	28.4	-6.4	45.5	9.2	26.1*	-2.7	—	—	-7.8	0.2	13.9	2.9	68.2	51.0
Hull, East	70.6	3.0	26.0	-2.6	56.3	6.4	17.7	-3.8	—	—	-4.5	-2.0	14.4	1.9	62.8	43.3
North	69.6	2.2	27.3	-3.1	51.2	8.7	21.5*	-5.1	—	—	-5.9	-1.7	15.3	4.1	68.3	46.0
West	67.6	4.1	30.3	-1.6	52.0	10.0	17.7*	-8.4	—	—	-5.8	-3.6	19.2	2.2	61.3	37.7
Isle of Wight	79.6	-0.4	51.2	4.8	5.9	3.5	42.9	-8.0	—	—	—	4.7	11.2	4.4	41.3	63.8
Kent, Ashford	75.7	2.4	56.5	-0.3	14.7	1.8	27.3*	-0.5	1.5	—	—	7.0	6.7	5.2	48.7	69.6
Canterbury	74.0	4.0	53.8	-2.6	16.9	1.5	27.3	1.5	1.7	0.3	—	3.5	7.8	6.7	42.2	64.7

Dartford	71.9	46.1	5.5	5.7	1.4	79.0	2.6	53.5	1.9	27.5	0.7	18.2*	-2.3	–	0.8	0.6
Dover	57.8	54.0	3.7	9.4	1.6	79.8	2.3	46.0	-2.3	34.1	3.3	19.9*	-0.3	–	–	-2.8
Faversham	64.8	53.6	3.7	8.8	3.4	76.9	3.4	51.1	-2.0	20.8	1.0	28.1*	1.0	–	–	–
Folkestone & Hythe	61.2	46.1	4.7	11.1	-5.0	78.3	7.7	55.3	-1.6	7.4	-2.4	37.3	4.7	–	–	–
Gillingham	66.3	46.7	4.8	7.8	3.7	75.3	1.7	53.1	1.3	17.0	-0.8	29.9	-0.6	–	–	0.0
Gravesham	67.0	51.3	4.2	8.3	2.3	79.3	1.7	50.1	3.0	34.8	3.1	15.1	-4.5	–	–	–
Kent, Mid-	69.2	45.4	4.7	7.3	8.9	71.9	0.5	55.1	1.7	18.1	-0.7	26.8	-0.3	–	–	–
Maidstone	71.3	43.5	5.6	5.8	3.7	76.0	2.3	52.4	1.5	12.5	0.4	33.8	-3.2	1.3	–	–
Medway	65.4	55.8	4.1	9.1	1.1	73.0	0.4	51.0	2.1	29.8	-0.3	18.1*	-2.9	1.1	–	-1.2
Sevenoaks	76.7	38.0	6.9	3.9	2.6	76.4	2.7	58.9	0.5	13.2	1.0	27.9	-0.7	–	–	–
Thanet North	55.6	43.9	3.8	13.2	4.6	72.2	3.4	58.0	-0.4	16.7	2.5	23.3*	-3.4	–	–	–
South	55.8	48.6	3.9	11.5	1.2	73.7	3.7	54.3	-2.1	20.9	1.5	24.8	0.7	2.0	–	–
Tonbridge & Malling	74.1	41.4	6.3	4.3	5.9	77.8	3.0	56.9	0.8	13.1	0.3	29.4*	-1.8	–	0.6	–
Tunbridge Wells	68.7	38.1	6.9	4.0	3.5	74.3	1.6	58.4	0.2	11.8	0.3	30.0	0.0	–	–	–
Lancashire, Blackburn	47.8	62.9	3.3	13.4	-1.7	74.9	0.3	40.1	0.7	49.9	5.2	10.0*	-4.4	–	–	-2.2
Blackpool, North	49.4	49.2	3.1	15.4	2.3	73.1	3.2	48.0	-3.1	31.0	9.3	21.0	-5.0	–	–	–
South	51.7	51.7	2.5	16.4	2.4	73.5	3.6	48.0	-2.5	32.1	7.3	19.9*	-4.1	–	–	-4.9
Burnley	50.1	60.9	4.1	11.1	-0.9	78.8	2.5	33.5	-4.4	48.4	8.6	17.8*	-4.3	1.2	–	-6.5
Chorley	68.9	49.6	5.7	7.2	7.8	76.9	-2.3	48.0	-0.2	34.7	4.2	16.1	-4.2	0.6	–	-2.2
Fylde	69.0	33.7	7.5	6.8	1.6	77.0	5.8	60.7	-2.2	14.3	3.4	24.2*	-0.1	–	0.8	–
Hyndburn	53.9	59.7	4.1	8.1	2.0	80.5	3.1	44.4	2.1	39.8	-2.4	15.2*	0.6	–	–	2.3
Lancashire, West	68.1	49.8	5.2	11.5	2.8	79.7	5.3	43.7	-2.5	41.5	7.7	14.8*	-5.2	–	–	-5.1
Lancaster	61.2	50.2	7.1	8.3	2.1	79.2	4.5	46.7	-3.6	32.4	7.5	19.9	-4.5	1.0	–	–
Morecambe & Lunesdale	61.2	44.3	5.6	13.1	4.7	76.1	3.2	52.6	-3.9	22.5	4.8	24.9*	-0.3	–	–	–
Pendle	54.5	59.0	3.3	9.0	-1.4	81.8	2.1	40.4	-3.9	35.3	3.0	24.3	0.9	–	–	-3.4
Preston	40.8	67.4	2.4	14.9	-0.8	69.0	-2.8	28.5	-3.2	52.5	5.7	19.0	-2.5	–	–	-4.5
Ribble Valley	76.0	38.6	8.6	4.2	4.4	79.1	2.3	60.9	-2.6	17.7	4.2	21.4*	-1.7	–	–	–
Rossendale & Darwen	55.7	57.4	5.2	7.3	0.9	80.3	2.5	46.6	-0.5	38.3	6.5	15.1	-6.1	–	–	-3.5
South Ribble	71.8	50.0	5.0	7.2	-0.3	82.5	4.8	47.2	-1.9	33.1	6.5	19.7	-4.6	–	–	-4.2
Wyre	63.6	45.8	4.3	3.7	1.7	75.4	4.0	53.1	-3.4	21.2	2.6	24.0*	-0.9	1.7	–	–
Leicestershire, Blaby	78.2	44.0	6.3	4.3	7.2	80.9	3.5	60.5	1.8	14.5	2.2	25.0	-3.0	–	–	–
Bosworth	72.5	53.3	5.2	5.6	5.6	81.3	3.1	54.4	-1.0	17.2	-2.3	27.3	2.2	1.1	–	–
Harborough	75.7	41.6	6.0	3.9	3.5	79.3	3.4	59.4	-0.7	12.9	1.3	27.7	1.3	–	–	–

ENGLAND	% voting	% change in voting	% Con.	Con. change 1983–87	% Lab.	Lab. change 1983–87	% Alln. (*SDP)	Alln. change 1983–87	% Green	% Other	Swing	Electorate change %	% Unemployed	% with degrees	% Working class	% Car-owners
Leicester, East†	78.6	5.4	42.5	3.5	46.1	9.1	11.4*	−9.7	—	—	−2.8	−1.0	10.6	2.5	61.6	51.2
South†	77.0	4.7	40.8	0.6	44.2	3.9	13.8	—	0.7	0.5(2)	−1.7	−0.5	12.1	5.0	57.9	47.5
West	73.4	4.7	42.0	1.0	44.5	−0.3	13.5*	0.7	1.0	—	0.6	0.2	12.6	3.2	66.9	46.5
Leicestershire, North-West	82.9	1.8	47.6	3.0	34.3	1.7	17.1	−4.5	1.1	—	0.7	3.1	7.9	5.2	58.2	68.3
Loughborough	79.2	1.5	54.7	1.8	24.5	1.0	19.7*	−2.5	—	—	0.4	4.2	5.8	6.8	48.5	67.5
Rutland & Melton	76.8	3.5	62.0	1.6	14.5	2.9	23.5	−3.6	—	—	—	3.5	4.7	5.7	48.5	73.8
Lincolnshire,																
Gainsborough & Horncastle	76.9	1.9	53.3	2.4	11.5	3.8	35.2	−5.6	1.2	—	—	3.9	8.0	5.2	50.5	72.6
Grantham	75.0	1.5	57.0	−0.4	20.5	1.1	21.3	−1.9	—	—	—	5.8	7.6	5.0	52.2	70.3
Holland-with-Boston	72.3	1.2	57.9	2.6	20.5	5.1	20.7	−8.6	—	0.9	—	3.1	8.8	3.2	54.4	71.0
Lincoln	75.6	1.0	46.5	0.1	33.7	6.1	19.4*	−5.6	—	0.4	−3.0	5.7	12.0	4.3	57.5	57.5
Lindsey East	75.2	2.0	52.2	−1.1	11.1	2.9	36.7	−1.8	—	—	—	6.2	12.3	3.7	50.5	70.2
Stamford & Spalding	77.8	3.4	56.5	0.0	12.5	1.6	31.0	−1.6	—	—	—	7.0	6.5	5.1	51.7	73.1
Merseyside, Birkenhead	72.3	2.6	26.4	−2.5	58.7	9.1	14.9	−5.9	—	—	−5.8	−2.4	19.6	4.4	63.3	44.9
Bootle	72.9	4.5	20.1	−3.5	66.9	13.9	13.0*	−10.4	—	—	−8.7	−4.8	19.2	1.9	66.3	38.7
Crosby	79.6	1.8	46.2	−1.1	17.9	7.8	35.9*	−6.1	—	—	—	0.8	8.0	7.2	33.9	74.1
Knowsley, North	74.2	4.6	12.5	−7.5	69.9	5.4	16.2	1.4	—	1.4	—	−4.8	21.1	1.4	75.4	37.4
South	74.1	3.9	21.6	−7.5	64.5	10.7	13.9*	−3.2	—	—	−9.1	3.6	17.6	2.6	63.8	49.4
Liverpool, Broadgreen	75.9	3.8	15.5	17.1	48.6	7.7	35.9	9.4	—	—	—	−1.2	18.5	4.4	59.1	43.1
Garston	75.7	4.1	23.9	14.0	53.6	7.0	22.3*	6.8	—	0.2	−10.5	−4.7	16.8	3.6	60.1	45.7
Mossley Hill	75.1	1.8	17.5	14.3	38.8	12.0	43.7	2.8	—	—	−7.1	−2.9	16.9	7.0	50.7	47.2
Riverside	65.3	2.9	13.8	−5.9	73.2	8.3	11.3	−2.8	—	1.7	—	−13.5	27.7	3.9	69.3	20.7
Walton	73.6	4.0	14.4	−10.8	64.4	11.7	21.2	−0.2	—	—	−9.6	−0.6	20.6	2.1	67.2	34.7
West Derby	73.4	3.9	19.2	−8.3	65.3	10.8	15.5*	−2.4	—	—	—	−4.1	20.2	1.9	61.1	39.1
St. Helens, North	76.3	1.8	27.3	−3.1	53.6	5.8	19.1	−2.7	—	—	—	−0.3	12.1	4.4	61.4	61.1
South	71.3	0.6	26.7	−0.4	54.6	7.7	18.7*	−3.7	—	—	−4.5	0.4	14.3	4.4	63.6	54.3
Southport†	76.3	3.8	44.5	−5.9	6.4	−1.9	47.9	7.4	1.2	—	−4.1	1.9	10.0	6.3	36.7	60.8

Constituency																
Wallasey	53.3	53.0	3.9	15.6	-1.8	79.8	7.2	42.5	3.5	41.9	9.5	15.6*	-6.0	–	–	–
Wirral South	70.3	43.7	7.3	8.2	2.3	79.4	3.7	50.2	-3.5	28.0	5.4	21.8	-1.9	–	–	–
Wirral West	68.2	40.2	7.4	9.3	3.2	77.9	4.5	51.9	-3.9	31.2	4.5	20.2	-2.2	1.6	–	–
Norfolk, Great Yarmouth	59.0	51.9	3.0	16.1	4.7	74.5	3.7	51.7	1.3	17.8	5.9	17.1*	-7.2	–	–	-2.3
Norfolk, Mid.	78.3	46.1	5.5	5.9	7.2	78.2	2.9	56.7	0.8	19.9	0.5	25.5*	-0.5	1.8	–	–
North	70.9	48.7	4.6	8.3	7.2	77.5	2.9	53.3	-0.7	17.5	0.7	25.0*	-1.8	–	–	–
North-West	69.5	55.4	4.0	9.0	6.6	78.9	1.2	50.6	7.1	12.7	-1.4	31.9*	-5.7	–	–	–
South	77.5	44.5	5.9	5.3	6.6	81.0	3.8	53.4	-0.7	21.0	-0.4	33.9	1.1	–	–	–
South-West	74.4	55.2	3.6	7.3	5.5	76.0	3.0	57.6	1.9	30.2	3.3	21.4	-5.3	–	–	–
Norwich, North	65.1	52.4	3.7	8.2	-0.1	79.2	3.0	45.8	1.2	37.9	-2.2	24.0	1.4	–	–	-0.7
South†	54.3	52.2	6.6	12.7	0.5	80.6	4.2	37.2	-1.6	40.9	2.6	24.9*	0.4	–	–	-0.2
Northamptonshire, Corby	61.1	63.4	3.5	9.0	4.8	79.6	2.1	44.3	1.7	20.5	4.8	14.8	-5.4	–	–	-0.5
Daventry	77.1	44.5	6.1	4.8	7.6	78.2	1.3	57.9	4.6	19.7	0.6	21.6	-5.2	–	–	–
Kettering	65.8	51.5	4.9	6.1	5.0	78.8	2.4	51.0	2.7	30.1	-1.4	29.3*	-1.2	–	–	–
Northampton, North	60.0	53.4	3.8	8.6	1.4	74.6	2.6	48.0	1.0	24.6	3.1	20.7	-5.4	0.9	0.3	-1.1
South	63.8	50.0	5.3	6.7	10.4	75.2	2.6	55.7	2.1	27.2	1.5	18.6*	-4.8	1.1	–	–
Wellingborough	64.9	56.1	4.2	6.7	4.2	78.1	0.3	52.7	3.9		1.2	20.1	-4.6	–	–	1.3
Northumberland,																
Berwick-on-Tweed	60.7	57.8	4.2	9.7	1.5	77.3	-0.5	29.5	-3.5	17.5	3.2	52.1	-0.6	0.9	–	–
Blyth Valley	58.1	58.8	4.3	10.8	2.5	78.1	5.3	16.9	-10.8	42.5	3.0	40.6*	8.8	0.7	–	–
Hexham	69.8	40.1	7.3	5.7	3.7	80.0	3.7	49.6	-1.9	18.0	1.0	31.7	0.2	–	–	–
Wansbeck	52.2	63.0	4.2	11.2	-1.2	78.0	5.1	19.4	-3.4	57.5	10.4	23.1	-7.0	–	–	–
North Yorkshire, Harrogate	65.8	36.3	7.9	6.0	4.0	74.1	5.0	55.6	-4.7	10.1	-0.1	34.3*	5.7	–	–	–
Richmond (Yorks)	73.5	42.4	6.5	6.2	5.4	72.1	3.4	61.2	-1.4	11.8	2.1	27.0	-0.7	–	–	–
Ryedale‡	72.4	45.0	6.3	5.2	6.1	79.2	7.4	53.3	-5.8	8.1	-2.2	38.6	8.1	–	–	–
Scarborough	55.2	46.7	5.1	11.2	3.1	73.2	2.0	50.7	-3.6	23.6	5.1	25.7*	-1.5	–	–	–
Selby	71.2	46.0	7.1	6.6	9.2	77.7	5.6	51.6	-5.1	26.7	6.2	21.7	-1.1	–	–	–
Skipton & Ripon	70.3	41.2	6.0	5.1	4.0	77.8	2.9	59.0	-1.6	11.1	3.4	28.4	-3.2	1.5	–	–
York	47.9	58.6	5.8	10.7	1.3	78.4	3.2	41.7	0.3	41.4	6.3	15.9*	-7.1	1.0	–	–
Nottinghamshire, Ashfield	56.8	67.4	2.6	9.6	1.6	77.2	3.5	33.6	3.0	41.7	-0.8	24.7	-2.1	–	–	–
Bassetlaw	60.5	62.9	4.2	10.5	3.5	77.6	3.4	37.5	-0.3	48.1	2.5	14.4*	-2.2	–	–	-3.0
Broxtowe	67.0	48.0	6.2	7.0	2.9	79.2	2.7	53.6	0.1	24.3	3.0	22.1	-3.1	–	–	1.9
Gedling	66.3	48.5	5.8	7.4	2.6	79.1	3.7	54.5	0.4	23.9	3.4	21.6*	-3.4	–	–	-1.4

ENGLAND	% voting	% change in voting	% Con.	Con. change 1983-87	% Lab.	Lab. change 1983-87	% Alln. (*SDP)	Alln. change 1983-87	% Green	% Other	Swing	Electorate change %	% Unemployed	% with degrees	% Working class	% Car-owners
Mansfield	78.4	7.7	37.3	1.7	37.5	-3.0	22.2*	-1.8	–	3.0	2.4	2.3	10.6	3.7	64.5	59.0
Newark	77.6	1.2	53.5	-0.3	27.7	3.1	18.8*	-1.8	–	–	-1.7	5.5	9.0	5.8	52.4	65.6
Nottingham, East	68.8	5.2	42.9	2.5	42.0	4.9	14.7	-4.6	–	0.4	-1.2	-0.5	19.0	4.5	64.6	39.8
North†	72.6	6.5	41.6	2.2	44.9	6.2	11.7*	-7.7	–	–	-2.0	-3.0	14.3	1.5	70.6	45.2
South	73.0	2.8	45.0	-0.9	40.8	6.7	14.2*	-5.9	1.7	–	-3.8	5.4	11.6	5.5	57.2	48.7
Rushcliffe	80.0	3.1	58.8	-2.7	16.5	3.1	23.0*	-1.1	–	–	–	3.5	6.5	9.1	36.5	73.0
Sherwood	81.9	5.6	45.8	4.9	38.2	-1.6	16.0*	-3.3	–	–	3.2	3.3	8.8	4.2	59.6	65.2
Oxfordshire,																
Banbury	76.2	0.9	56.2	2.8	19.8	1.4	24.0*	-3.4	–	–	–	6.3	5.3	5.1	50.2	72.1
Henley	74.9	2.0	61.1	1.4	12.6	3.1	26.3	-3.0	–	–	-2.7	5.3	3.2	8.5	37.9	80.6
Oxford, East†	79.0	5.0	40.4	0.4	43.0	5.7	15.6	-7.1	0.9	0.1	–	-2.3	7.7	7.2	57.6	59.6
West & Abingdon	78.4	4.5	46.4	-1.3	14.9	-2.0	37.4*	4.0	1.3	–	–	2.6	4.6	12.8	40.7	67.2
Wantage	77.9	1.0	54.0	1.1	15.5	1.1	30.5*	-1.8	–	–	–	4.0	3.5	7.9	44.8	76.8
Witney	77.3	2.6	57.5	2.1	15.1	2.9	25.8	-5.1	–	–	–	8.5	3.3	6.4	45.5	78.9
Shropshire,																
Ludlow	77.1	2.5	53.9	-1.8	15.1	2.5	31.0	-0.8	–	–	–	4.6	7.2	5.5	46.1	74.3
Shrewsbury & Atcham	77.0	3.0	47.8	-1.7	19.8	1.4	31.2	-0.9	1.2	–	–	6.2	7.4	6.9	45.7	70.2
Shropshire North	75.5	2.8	52.2	-1.3	20.4	5.6	27.4	-4.1	–	–	–	5.2	7.3	5.0	48.7	72.9
Wrekin, The†	78.3	2.8	40.6	1.6	42.8	6.1	16.6*	-7.8	–	–	-2.3	6.9	13.5	3.2	64.2	63.6
Somerset,																
Bridgwater	78.2	3.4	51.5	-0.7	18.2	0.4	30.3*	0.3	–	–	–	5.1	8.5	4.6	51.9	70.9
Somerton & Frome	79.4	2.7	53.7	-0.7	10.0	0.2	36.3	0.5	–	–	–	6.3	5.4	5.7	47.8	76.8
Taunton	82.3	6.8	53.1	0.2	14.3	-3.5	32.6*	3.3	–	–	–	5.4	7.0	5.7	42.4	70.6
Wells	79.6	2.0	53.5	0.9	8.7	-0.9	37.6	-1.5	–	0.2	–	8.1	6.7	5.6	44.9	74.2
Yeovil	79.7	-0.1	41.3	-2.7	7.3	-1.8	51.4	1.0	–	–	–	6.5	6.0	4.8	49.3	72.2
South Yorkshire,																
Barnsley Central	70.0	3.8	18.1	-2.9	66.8	7.0	15.1	-4.1	–	–	-4.9	1.4	14.4	3.0	69.3	47.6
East	72.6	6.1	14.0	-2.1	74.5	8.6	11.5	-6.4	–	–	–	-0.2	13.9	2.2	73.1	46.0
West & Penistone	75.6	2.4	26.6	-0.9	57.4	6.5	16.0*	-5.6	–	–	-3.7	0.7	12.9	4.6	63.8	54.2

Constituency																
Doncaster, Central	49.4	62.0	4.0	14.5	-1.9	73.7	2.8	35.2	-1.9	51.2	9.1	13.6*	-7.3			-5.5
North	51.3	71.9	2.2	14.9	1.1	73.1	3.2	24.4	-3.2	61.7	9.0	13.9*	-5.8			-6.1
Don Valley	56.1	62.1	4.7	12.1	1.9	73.8	3.9	32.3	-0.2	53.1	8.0	14.6	-7.9			-4.1
Rotherham	48.2	65.5	3.8	14.8	0.6	69.2	2.3	22.1	-3.6	59.7	5.4	18.2	-1.8		0.3	-4.5
Rother Valley	62.0	60.9	4.1	11.2	2.0	75.6	3.6	24.9	-3.2	56.4	9.9	18.4*	-7.0			
Sheffield, Attercliffe	51.5	66.7	2.2	12.5	4.4	72.9	3.2	22.7	-2.9	57.8	6.3	19.5*	-3.3	0.8		-4.6
Brightside	38.6	75.2	1.8	17.7	-3.4	68.7	3.3	15.7	-2.2	69.9	11.9	14.4	-9.0		1.3(2)	
Central	30.0	76.1	3.6	23.0	-8.4	62.5	0.8	17.1	-2.1	67.7	7.6	13.9*	-5.4			
Hallam	65.4	29.4	14.9	8.8	1.8	74.7	1.9	46.3	-4.3	20.4	-0.7	32.5	4.1			-5.6
Heeley	45.9	61.9	3.5	14.6	-1.0	72.0	1.4	26.3	-3.6	53.4	7.6	20.3*	-4.0			
Hillsborough	58.0	56.7	4.9	10.5	2.5	78.0	2.6	17.5	-10.8	44.0	6.8	38.5	4.0			-3.2
Wentworth	52.0	69.0	3.4	13.5	2.9	72.5	2.9	21.8	-0.4	65.2	6.1	13.0*	-5.7			-2.1
Staffordshire, Burton	63.9	58.6	4.5	8.3	2.0	78.5	2.7	50.7	-0.4	33.6	3.8	15.7	-3.4			0.5
Cannock & Burntwood	70.3	57.7	3.8	9.6	2.9	79.8	2.4	44.5	3.5	39.5	2.6	16.0	-6.1		0.7	
Newcastle-under-Lyme	59.7	59.6	4.5	8.0	1.0	80.8	3.5	27.9	-8.6	40.5	-1.5	30.9	9.3			
Stafford	71.7	43.7	7.1	7.1	2.6	79.5	2.9	51.3	0.1	21.2	-2.5	27.5*	2.8		1.5	
Staffordshire, Mid	73.4	49.8	6.3	7.3	5.7	79.4	1.9	50.6	-1.4	24.7	2.3	23.2	-2.3			-2.7
Staffordshire Moorlands	72.5	52.6	5.0	5.8	2.5	80.4	3.2	52.9	-0.8	28.8	4.6	18.3*	-3.8			
South	79.1	44.4	6.4	8.0	8.5	78.2	2.4	60.9	1.7	19.0	1.8	20.1	-3.4			
South-East	73.3	54.9	4.8	10.5	4.5	80.4	3.9	47.2	-3.5	26.1	-2.1	26.7*	5.6			-1.4
Stoke-on-Trent, Central	48.1	70.5	2.6	11.0	-1.4	68.8	2.9	31.0	1.7	52.5	4.5	16.5*	-5.0			-0.2
North	55.5	69.9	2.0	9.8	-1.4	72.9	1.9	31.3	0.4	47.1	0.8	21.6*	-1.2			2.4
South	57.7	66.1	3.2	8.4	0.3	73.7	4.1	37.8	4.2	47.5	-0.5	14.7	-3.7	1.9		
Suffolk, Bury St. Edmunds	72.5	51.9	4.4	5.3	5.1	74.1	1.8	59.3	0.3	17.3	4.7	21.5*	-6.9		0.3	1.9
Ipswich	58.6	57.5	4.3	8.7	1.3	77.1	1.7	44.4	2.8	42.7	-1.0	12.6*	-1.7			
Central	73.3	51.9	4.3	5.3	4.7	76.2	1.8	53.7	0.2	19.6	0.3	26.7	-0.6	1.8		
Coastal	72.8	44.5	5.6	5.2	5.8	77.9	2.9	55.7	-2.6	12.8	0.1	29.7*	0.6			
South	73.4	49.0	5.5	5.4	7.5	77.7	1.2	53.4	2.8	18.7	0.6	27.9	-3.4			-3.0
Waveney	63.4	55.0	3.7	11.3	5.0	78.4	3.1	48.4	-3.4	30.0	2.6	21.6*	0.7			
Surrey, Chertsey & Walton	77.4	36.0	7.3	3.7	1.8	75.5	3.0	59.5	1.2	13.3	-0.2	27.2*	-0.3			
Epsom & Ewell	77.3	26.5	8.8	3.7	0.1	75.4	3.4	62.2	1.8	14.6	1.6	23.2	-3.4			
Esher	80.7	23.5	9.9	2.9	0.6	76.9	3.8	65.5	2.3	8.8	1.6	25.7	-2.4			

ENGLAND	% voting	% change in voting	% Con.	Con. change 1983-87	% Lab.	Lab. change 1983-87	% Alln. (*SDP)	Alln. change 1983-87	% Green	% Other	Swing	Electorate change %	% Unemployed	% with degrees	% Working class	% Car-owners
Guildford	75.3	2.8	55.5	0.4	10.6	-0.1	33.9*	0.6	–	–	–	3.6	3.1	8.7	35.0	73.0
Mole Valley	77.0	2.0	60.8	-0.1	9.3	0.8	29.9	-0.7	–	–	–	4.1	2.8	8.6	31.2	78.1
Reigate	72.5	0.4	59.3	0.2	14.3	2.2	24.4*	-2.4	2.0	–	–	2.3	3.6	7.6	34.6	74.5
Spelthorne	74.1	3.1	60.0	7.6	17.1	1.6	22.9*	-3.1	–	–	–	1.0	3.8	5.6	38.1	79.4
Surrey, East	77.2	3.1	63.4	0.5	10.4	0.6	23.9	-3.4	2.3	–	–	1.8	3.3	8.3	30.9	78.6
North-West	72.5	2.3	64.0	-0.2	11.2	1.3	24.8	-1.1	–	–	–	6.0	3.1	8.1	34.9	81.0
South-West	78.4	3.9	59.5	-0.3	5.6	-2.5	34.4	2.3	–	0.5	–	4.5	2.9	8.8	34.1	75.7
Woking	75.1	3.4	58.1	-0.2	10.5	-1.1	31.4	2.0	–	–	–	5.3	3.3	7.8	32.5	77.0
Tyne & Wear, Blaydon	75.7	-2.5	24.2	-5.1	50.3	6.0	25.5*	-0.8	–	–	–	1.3	10.1	5.4	57.5	52.3
Gateshead East	71.8	-2.2	23.9	-2.7	59.2	10.9	16.9*	-8.2	–	–	-6.8	-0.6	13.1	2.7	66.5	40.0
Houghton & Washington	71.2	4.4	22.7	-1.2	59.1	7.4	18.2*	-6.2	–	–	–	2.9	12.5	3.6	64.8	52.1
Jarrow	74.4	3.0	23.2	-1.5	63.5	8.2	13.3	-6.6	–	–	-4.9	-1.5	15.8	3.2	67.1	42.5
Newcastle-upon-Tyne, Central†	72.5	1.5	38.8	-2.0	44.2	8.4	15.8*	-6.5	0.9	0.3	-5.2	1.6	12.7	9.6	45.7	45.8
East	70.6	-0.3	26.6	1.1	56.5	10.9	16.0	-10.7	–	0.9	–	-0.4	18.7	4.1	64.8	32.7
North	75.9	3.1	24.6	-7.9	42.7	5.1	32.7	2.8	–	–	-6.5	-0.4	12.0	5.1	55.7	52.5
South Shields	70.7	4.5	25.7	-5.2	57.9	11.4	15.5*	-7.2	–	0.9	-6.9	-1.9	16.8	3.0	68.4	38.5
Sunderland, North	70.5	4.0	28.3	-4.2	55.8	9.5	15.9	-5.3	–	–	-6.3	-3.6	18.8	2.5	70.7	38.4
South	71.1	4.5	30.4	-4.2	54.0	8.4	14.6*	-5.1	1.0	–	-5.6	-0.2	14.4	4.3	64.4	46.4
Tyne Bridge	63.1	1.6	20.6	-4.6	63.0	6.6	16.4*	-1.9	–	–	-6.4	-4.4	21.5	2.5	73.4	27.2
Tynemouth	78.1	3.5	43.2	-5.4	38.8	7.5	18.0	-2.1	–	–	-5.3	-0.2	12.1	5.8	48.3	50.7
Wallsend	75.0	3.9	23.2	-2.8	56.8	7.8	20.0*	-4.9	–	–	–	0.6	13.9	3.2	84.0	43.7
Warwickshire, Nuneaton	80.4	3.1	44.9	4.4	34.6	4.0	19.2*	-8.7	1.3	–	0.2	3.4	9.2	4.2	58.8	65.1
Rugby & Kenilworth	79.6	1.5	51.6	0.7	24.9	2.3	23.5	-2.9	–	–	–	2.9	7.0	7.4	46.0	70.5
Stratford-on-Avon	76.5	3.5	61.9	1.0	10.2	-0.1	27.9	-1.0	–	–	–	6.0	5.1	6.1	42.5	77.2
Warwick & Leamington	76.0	2.4	49.8	-1.1	23.5	1.6	24.5*	-1.4	2.2	–	–	2.7	7.5	7.8	49.1	68.4
Warwickshire, North	79.9	1.9	45.1	3.1	40.1	3.0	14.8*	-6.1	–	–	0.1	3.0	9.1	4.1	61.5	67.7

71.2	49.0	5.1	8.2	2.2	*West Midlands,* Aldridge-Brownhills	79.8	1.5	53.4	2.6	28.3	3.4	18.3*	-6.0			-0.4
55.5	44.8	9.7	13.5	-1.2	Birmingham, Edgbaston	68.6	2.3	49.8	-3.9	26.9	5.9	21.0*	-1.4	1.5	0.8	
47.1	65.5	3.5	20.0	-3.3	Erdington	68.5	1.5	39.2	0.1	45.9	6.1	14.9*	-6.2			-3.0
57.5	54.2	4.0	13.3	0.2	Hall Green	74.7	4.1	44.8	-4.2	28.2	0.8	27.0*	3.4			-2.5
44.2	72.0	1.6	17.6	-3.2	Hodge Hill	68.8	1.3	36.9	1.7	48.7	1.1	14.4	-1.5	1.7		0.3
41.0	66.2	3.7	20.5	-2.8	Ladywood	64.8	2.3	31.3	4.3	57.7	6.7	9.3*	-11.2			-1.2
51.9	64.4	3.9	14.9	-1.4	Northfield	72.6	1.4	45.1	2.4	50.4	1.7	15.6*	-3.4			0.3
48.9	67.5	2.3	14.8	-0.8	Perry Barr	69.6	0.4	36.9	-1.3	39.3	-2.1	12.7	3.4			0.4
54.2	53.1	8.0	11.5	0.8	Selly Oak	73.1	1.6	44.2	-0.7	66.3	4.9	15.4	-5.3	1.1		-2.8
30.8	79.2	1.3	22.9	-4.5	Small Heath	60.6	0.2	21.1	0.9	60.8	2.5	10.5	-5.5	1.6		-0.8
39.0	71.0	3.0	21.8	-1.0	Sparkbrook	63.5	2.0	25.7	-2.3	36.6	0.9	11.3*	0.9	1.5	0.5	-1.6
52.9	64.4	2.3	12.6	-1.3	Yardley	73.9	1.7	42.6	0.6	54.3	0.3	20.8	1.3		0.7	-0.4
52.2	69.6	2.7	15.3	0.7	Coventry, North-East	70.6	1.4	29.3	0.4	49.0	6.4	15.8	-6.3			-3.0
58.4	63.0	3.9	12.6	2.0	North-West	74.8	0.0	34.7	-1.8	47.4	4.7	16.3*	-3.0	1.3	0.6	-3.2
51.8	64.8	3.8	16.3	-1.3	South-East	73.0	2.1	29.9	-4.0	37.0	6.4	21.4*	-3.6			-5.2
66.6	50.5	6.4	8.7	0.8	South-West	78.7	2.8	43.3	-1.7	45.9	5.1	19.7	-2.9			-3.4
54.6	66.2	2.5	14.0	0.6	Dudley, East	72.3	1.0	39.5	4.6	34.0	0.0	14.6*	-4.6			2.3
69.1	50.8	4.7	9.7	5.1	West	79.1	3.2	49.8	3.7	27.8	2.6	16.2	-6.3			0.5
68.6	48.4	5.6	8.3	2.1	Halesowen & Stourbridge	79.4	3.0	50.1	1.7	26.1	2.8	22.1*	-3.5			—
68.2	51.1	4.4	11.0	5.9	Meriden	73.9	2.3	55.1	1.5	15.0	0.7	18.8*	-1.3			0.4
78.1	35.2	6.9	5.6	6.0	Solihull	75.1	3.8	61.1	0.3	11.3	3.4	23.9	-3.7			—
78.2	30.0	8.9	6.4	6.8	Sutton Coldfield	74.5	2.7	64.0	-1.4	42.6	3.0	24.7	-1.6			—
53.1	69.3	1.9	14.1	-0.8	Walsall, North	73.8	2.8	39.0	2.3	44.9	1.4	18.4	-2.3			1.1
54.9	62.6	3.7	14.0	-0.8	South	75.5	1.2	42.7	0.6	50.2	4.7	12.4	-0.8			-0.4
43.9	69.6	2.2	16.4	-3.0	Warley, East	69.4	0.5	35.8	-1.2	49.2	2.1	14.0*	-3.0			-2.9
52.2	68.1	2.0	13.4	0.6	West	70.0	2.2	35.8	2.3	42.6	4.5	15.0	-4.3			0.1
55.4	63.7	2.7	12.9	-1.9	West Bromwich, East	73.2	3.0	40.3	2.9	50.5	-0.3	17.1	-7.4			-0.8
45.2	73.4	1.3	15.5	1.0	West	67.0	3.1	37.2	4.3	41.7	1.6	12.3*	-4.0			2.3
53.4	70.2	2.0	16.8	-0.4	Wolverhampton, North-East†	74.3	4.0	42.1	2.5	48.9	4.2	16.2	-2.9			0.5
49.6	72.4	1.7	16.2	-1.3	South-East	72.5	3.4	33.1	1.2	30.7	3.3	18.0	-5.4			-1.5
61.2	50.1	5.8	12.4	-0.4	South-West	75.5	3.1	50.7	0.1	11.0	2.8	18.6*	-2.9			-1.6
65.8	40.2	5.7	6.6	5.1	*West Sussex, Arundel*	71.2	1.5	61.4	1.8			27.6	-1.9			—

ENGLAND	Car-owners %	Working class %	% with degrees	% Unemployed	Electorate change %	% voting	% change in voting	% Con.	Con. change 1983–87	% Lab.	Lab. change 1983–87	% Alln. (*SDP)	Alln. change 1983–87	% Green	% Other	Swing
Chichester	74.0	38.5	7.7	4.2	4.9	74.4	2.4	61.8	−1.9	7.9	0.7	28.3	0.7	2.0	–	–
Crawley	75.8	47.1	5.5	4.0	1.9	81.9	5.6	49.5	1.5	29.0	2.8	21.5*	−4.3	–	–	−0.7
Horsham	78.1	36.5	7.7	3.2	7.1	72.5	−2.0	63.7	0.8	8.7	0.4	25.4*	−1.5	2.2	–	–
Shoreham	65.6	37.0	5.4	5.0	2.3	77.5	3.8	60.9	−0.8	9.1	1.8	30.0	−1.0	–	–	–
Sussex, Mid	75.4	31.6	8.6	3.0	4.1	77.2	2.4	61.1	−0.3	7.4	1.4	31.5	−0.8	–	–	–
Worthing	58.6	32.9	6.0	6.3	1.6	72.8	1.6	61.7	0.9	9.6	3.8	28.7	−3.9	–	–	–
West Yorkshire,																
Batley & Spen	55.5	54.3	3.9	9.0	0.7	79.0	5.6	43.4	3.9	41.1	3.2	14.3*	−7.3	–	–	0.4
Bradford, North†	44.0	61.3	2.9	14.7	1.6	72.7	2.0	39.5	5.2	42.8	12.0	17.7*	−7.8	–	–	−3.4
South	49.3	59.8	2.8	11.1	0.2	73.7	2.6	40.8	3.5	41.4	3.9	17.8*	−6.8	–	–	−0.2
West	41.5	60.8	4.3	15.4	−0.7	70.2	1.3	36.7	3.8	51.9	12.2	11.4*	−15.7	–	–	−4.2
Calder Valley	56.6	50.2	5.4	7.7	2.9	81.1	2.6	43.5	−0.1	33.4	6.4	23.1	−6.2	–	–	–
Colne Valley†	58.5	53.9	6.0	7.2	0.8	80.1	3.9	36.4	2.5	29.1	3.3	33.4	−6.4	1.1	–	–
Dewsbury†	58.5	52.6	5.3	9.7	1.6	78.8	4.8	41.6	2.3	42.4	7.1	16.0*	−9.4	–	–	−2.4
Elmet	67.7	47.4	5.9	6.4	3.0	79.3	3.8	46.9	−0.4	37.1	5.3	16.0	−4.9	–	–	−2.9
Halifax†	48.6	60.3	3.8	10.4	0.9	77.7	2.6	41.3	0.4	43.4	6.0	15.3*	−6.4	–	1.2	−2.8
Hemsworth	51.4	69.8	3.4	12.8	1.2	75.7	7.1	17.2	−2.4	67.0	7.7	15.8	−5.4	–	–	–
Huddersfield	45.8	61.3	3.7	11.0	−2.6	75.5	4.5	31.4	−1.9	45.9	4.5	21.5*	−3.4	1.2	–	−3.2
Keighley	57.3	51.2	5.9	8.1	3.4	79.4	0.5	45.8	3.2	35.0	−2.0	19.2	−0.6	–	–	2.6
Leeds, Central	31.1	72.8	2.7	17.3	−6.8	64.8	3.1	25.6	2.0	55.6	7.7	17.9*	−8.9	–	–	–
East	41.8	63.5	2.7	15.6	−3.8	70.2	4.0	26.6	−2.8	48.7	5.0	24.7	−1.1	–	0.9	−3.9
North-East	61.4	34.3	9.1	9.7	−0.9	75.3	4.7	45.6	−2.0	25.2	1.5	28.3*	0.2	–	–	–
North-West	59.3	40.3	10.3	7.6	0.3	75.7	4.4	43.5	−3.0	21.7	−0.5	33.5	4.5	0.9	–	0.2
South & Morley	47.7	62.6	2.6	9.7	−0.2	71.6	3.7	34.1	2.3	49.6	3.6	16.3*	−6.0	1.3	–	−0.6
West†	42.3	64.9	3.1	11.4	−1.8	73.3	4.3	23.2	−3.7	43.2	9.2	33.6	−4.8	–	–	–
Normanton	59.0	57.3	4.0	8.1	2.7	74.8	4.4	34.1	0.2	49.5	6.0	16.4*	−6.2	–	–	−2.9
Pontefract & Castleford	51.0	69.4	3.2	12.2	−0.7	73.5	6.0	21.2	−4.6	66.9	9.8	11.3	−5.8	–	0.6	−7.2

	Car-owners %	Working class %	with degrees %	Unemployed %	Electorate change %	% voting	% change in voting	% Con.	Con. change 1983–87	% Lab.	Lab. change 1983–87	Alln. % (SDP*)	Alln. change 1983–87	% Plaid Cymru	% Other	Swing
Pudsey	62.8	45.4	5.7	5.6	1.6	78.0	2.2	45.5	−0.2	20.5	2.7	34.0	−1.8	–	–	–
Shipley	61.2	41.3	7.7	6.6	1.7	79.2	2.2	49.5	−0.2	23.3	1.7	26.3	−1.4	0.9	–	–
Wakefield	56.8	54.2	5.8	9.8	1.7	75.6	6.2	41.3	1.7	46.6	6.2	12.1*	−7.2	–	–	−2.3
Wiltshire, Devizes	75.2	49.7	5.3	5.2	3.4	77.2	2.2	54.8	0.8	17.3	0.5	27.9	−1.0	–	0.6	–
Salisbury	70.6	45.3	5.8	5.4	2.7	75.6	2.8	54.9	1.4	9.5	3.7	35.0*	−5.2	–	–	2.4
Swindon	60.1	59.2	3.6	9.5	12.1	77.8	3.7	43.8	4.7	36.6	−0.1	19.6*	−4.6	–	–	–
Westbury	72.6	49.2	5.0	5.7	5.8	78.2	2.8	51.6	0.2	12.0	2.0	36.4	−1.0	–	–	–
Wiltshire, North	74.7	44.4	5.8	5.3	6.0	79.3	2.8	55.1	2.1	6.8	1.8	38.1	−2.6	–	–	–

WALES	Car-owners %	Working class %	with degrees %	Unemployed %	Electorate change %	% voting	% change in voting	% Con.	Con. change 1983–87	% Lab.	Lab. change 1983–87	Alln. % (SDP*)	Alln. change 1983–87	% Plaid Cymru	% Other	Swing
Clwyd, Alyn & Deeside	70.7	60.6	4.0	9.1	3.6	80.4	2.3	35.0	−2.2	48.6	8.3	15.4*	−6.2	1.0	–	−5.3
Clwyd, North-West	61.3	44.4	5.5	13.5	5.8	75.2	2.1	48.5	−2.4	24.8	8.5	22.7	−6.4	4.0	–	–
South-West†	66.8	49.9	5.1	9.3	4.2	81.1	3.8	33.2	−0.6	35.4	8.0	22.9*	−7.3	8.5	–	–
Delyn	68.5	55.4	5.4	10.8	1.7	82.6	4.7	41.4	−0.2	39.1	9.7	17.0	−8.8	2.5	–	−4.9
Wrexham	65.4	56.9	5.0	9.9	2.8	80.9	3.4	35.6	2.3	43.9	9.6	19.4	−10.3	1.1	–	−3.7
Dyfed, Carmarthen	71.3	35.2	5.3	8.7	2.8	82.9	0.7	27.4	−2.0	35.4	3.8	13.3*	2.3	23.0	0.9°	−2.9
Ceredigion & Pembroke N	72.8	72.8	7.2	9.7	4.3	76.5	−1.2	26.9	−3.0	18.6	4.0	36.6	−5.2	16.2	1.7°	–
Llanelli	59.1	64.6	3.7	10.1	0.0	78.1	2.7	17.2	−2.8	59.1	10.9	13.5	−5.4	10.2	–	−6.9
Pembroke	71.3	49.1	4.4	12.2	3.6	80.8	2.7	41.0	−5.9	31.0	1.7	26.1	5.4	1.9	–	−3.8
Gwent, Blaenau Gwent	48.1	74.2	2.3	12.3	0.1	77.2	0.3	11.5	0.3	75.9	5.9	8.9	−6.2	3.7	–	–
Islwyn	59.0	66.3	2.9	9.5	0.3	80.4	2.7	14.7	0.6	71.3	12.0	9.2*	−13.3	4.8	–	–
Monmouth	74.4	43.4	6.7	7.2	4.2	80.6	1.7	47.5	−1.6	27.7	6.0	24.0*	−4.0	0.8	–	−5.2
Newport, East	60.1	60.4	3.3	11.9	−0.6	80.1	3.5	32.2	−0.9	49.1	9.5	17.6*	−7.9	1.1	–	−3.7
West†	60.3	53.2	5.3	12.9	2.5	81.8	4.3	40.1	2.1	46.1	9.4	13.0	−11.2	0.8	–	–
Torfaen	59.3	65.9	3.9	10.9	2.0	75.6	1.1	19.1	−3.2	58.7	11.4	19.9	−8.4	1.3	1.0°	–

WALES	% voting	% change in voting	% Con.	Con. change 1983-87	% Lab.	Lab. change 1983-87	% Alln. (*SDP†)	Alln. change 1983-87	% Plaid Cymru	% Other	Swing	Electorate change %	% Unemployed	% with degrees	% Working class	% Car-owners
Gwynedd, Caernarfon	78.0	-0.6	21.1	0.1	15.9	-3.5	5.9	-0.9	57.1	—	—	3.4	11.8	5.2	48.6	67.8
Conwy	76.9	0.5	38.7	-3.0	22.3	5.2	31.2	0.4	7.8	—	—	2.5	11.5	6.6	45.1	61.2
Meirionnydd Nant Conwy	82.2	0.9	28.3	-0.2	16.9	1.3	14.8*	-2.4	40.0	—	—	3.9	10.1	6.0	47.3	67.6
Ynys Môn†	81.7	2.0	33.2	-4.2	16.9	-0.1	6.7*	-5.7	43.2	—	-6.4	4.5	12.2	5.6	48.9	71.5
Mid Glamorgan, Bridgend†	80.3	3.3	38.0	-0.4	47.5	12.3	12.2*	-11.1	2.3	—	—	6.4	8.5	6.6	48.7	68.0
Caerphilly	76.5	2.0	19.4	-0.2	58.4	12.8	14.1	-7.1	8.1	—	—	1.1	10.5	4.0	61.5	58.2
Cynon Valley	76.7	3.3	12.2	-2.0	68.9	12.9	12.2*	-8.3	6.7	—	—	-1.3	11.4	3.5	67.3	50.1
Merthyr Tydfil & Rhymney	76.1	3.5	11.9	-0.7	75.3	8.0	8.1	-6.6	4.7	—	—	-2.0	11.2	2.4	69.8	47.7
Ogmore	80.0	3.2	15.0	0.3	69.4	10.2	9.6*	-5.6	4.4	—	—	-0.2	11.7	3.2	69.1	55.0
Pontypridd	76.6	3.9	19.5	-3.4	56.3	10.7	18.9*	-6.9	5.3	1.6	—	0.6	9.5	6.2	55.2	64.2
Rhondda	78.0	1.8	7.6	-0.7	73.3	11.6	8.3*	-8.7	9.0	1.8	—	-2.6	11.4	2.5	71.1	47.0
Powys, Brecon & Radnor‡	84.4	4.3	34.7	-13.5	29.2	4.2	34.8	10.5	1.3	—	—	4.5	7.2	5.7	42.7	72.5
Montgomery	79.4	0.2	38.5	-2.6	10.4	1.9	46.6	3.2	4.5	—	—	6.2	7.3	4.2	42.6	74.5
South Glamorgan, Cardiff C	77.6	5.4	37.1	-4.4	32.3	8.1	29.3	-3.2	1.3	—	—	-1.6	14.7	8.9	40.6	59.2
North	81.0	3.7	45.3	-1.8	26.7	6.7	26.5*	-4.0	1.5	—	—	2.5	6.5	8.1	34.9	67.7
South & Penarth	76.4	5.3	36.5	0.6	46.8	5.5	15.4	-5.5	1.3	—	-2.4	-1.4	12.1	3.8	57.1	50.5
West†	77.8	8.2	36.5	-1.5	45.5	11.9	16.4*	-9.1	1.6	—	-6.7	-2.0	13.2	5.1	52.0	52.4
Vale of Glamorgan	79.3	5.1	46.8	-1.3	34.7	8.9	16.7*	-7.2	1.8	—	-5.1	3.9	9.5	6.3	42.7	68.9
West Glamorgan, Aberavon	77.7	2.1	14.4	-1.9	66.8	8.0	16.0	-4.3	2.8	—	—	-2.2	10.1	2.9	72.7	54.0
Gower	80.7	2.0	34.5	-0.9	46.6	8.6	16.1*	-7.3	2.8	—	-4.7	3.8	7.8	6.6	47.9	70.1
Neath	78.8	2.3	16.1	-1.2	63.4	9.8	14.1*	-7.4	6.4	—	—	0.0	9.7	4.4	64.9	58.1
Swansea, East	75.4	3.9	18.9	-0.9	63.7	9.3	14.8	-6.6	2.6	—	—	-0.1	12.0	2.8	67.4	56.8
West	76.1	2.5	33.0	-3.6	48.6	6.4	15.4	-3.3	2.0	1.0°	-5.0	2.7	13.2	7.0	50.7	56.2

Constituency (SCOTLAND)	Car-owners %	Working class %	% with degrees	% Unemployed	Electorate change %	% voting	% change in voting	% Con.	Con. change 1983–87	% Lab.	Lab. change 1983–87	% Alln. (*SDP)	Alln. change 1983–87	% S.N.P.	% Other	Swing
SCOTLAND	61.9	60.5	3.6	7.3	3.4	77.2	1.4	37.2	-2.4	8.8	1.5	49.2	-1.1	4.8	—	—
Borders, Roxburgh & Berwickshire	61.2	53.8	6.4	6.8	2.2	77.2	-0.6	29.6	0.7	11.4	3.7	49.9	-8.5	9.1	—	—
Tweedale, Ettrick & Lauderdale	57.0	63.8	4.9	12.2	3.0	77.0	1.5	14.9	-3.2	53.7	8.0	10.5*	-6.8	20.9	—	—
Central, Clackmannan	54.9	64.7	4.2	12.6	1.0	75.0	2.6	18.7	-2.3	54.2	6.6	11.7*	-6.8	15.4	—	-4.4
Falkirk, East	53.6	61.7	4.8	12.0	1.7	76.7	2.6	17.4	-3.6	52.6	7.0	12.6	-7.9	17.4	—	-5.3
West	63.1	45.5	8.7	9.3	2.7	79.4	3.7	38.3	-1.7	36.2	8.3	14.8	-9.1	10.7	—	-5.0
Stirling	62.0	58.9	5.3	9.4	3.0	75.6	2.6	41.8	-2.7	25.2	4.3	18.0*	-5.9	14.2	0.8°	—
Dumfries & Galloway, Dumfries	66.4	56.8	5.2	10.7	3.1	76.8	1.0	40.4	-4.3	12.9	1.5	14.6	1.6	31.5	0.6	—
Galloway & Upper Nithsdale	48.7	66.9	3.5	12.6	2.6	76.6	4.6	14.8	-4.0	64.8	13.2	10.5	-9.6	8.9	—	-8.5
Fife Dunfermline, East	60.5	54.0	5.9	9.9	4.1	77.0	3.5	23.1	-6.0	47.1	11.0	21.1*	-5.1	8.7	—	—
West	55.7	65.1	3.8	12.6	3.1	76.2	3.7	16.7	-5.8	53.4	10.3	15.2	-8.2	14.7	—	—
Fife Central	64.8	48.2	9.0	7.3	3.5	76.2	2.6	41.2	-4.9	7.4	0.9	44.8	4.6	6.6	—	—
North-East†	50.2	58.6	5.0	12.7	0.7	76.5	4.7	21.3	-5.0	49.6	9.3	17.4*	-6.9	11.7	—	-7.2
Kirkcaldy	44.1	68.4	4.1	10.9	0.3	69.9	4.9	14.3	-3.8	54.7	7.6	17.8*	-6.9	13.2	—	—
Grampian, Aberdeen North	49.6	47.8	11.2	9.7	9.4	67.1	-1.6	34.8	-4.1	37.7	7.8	20.9*	-5.3	6.6	—	-5.9
South†																
Banff & Buchan†	63.7	57.8	4.4	8.5	2.9	70.8	3.8	38.7	-1.0	7.5	-0.3	9.6*	-5.5	44.2	—	—
Gordon	78.6	47.5	8.9	5.9	12.1	73.7	3.5	31.9	-10.1	11.5	3.0	49.4	5.6	7.2	—	—
Kincardine & Deeside	71.2	47.1	7.7	6.7	6.8	75.2	3.7	40.7	-7.0	15.9	0.7	36.3	7.0	6.5	—	—
Moray†	63.5	59.3	4.9	9.1	-2.3	72.6	1.6	35.0	-4.2	11.3	4.1	10.5	-7.8	43.2	0.6°	—
Highlands, Caithness & Sutherland	63.0	56.8	5.3	10.8	1.3	73.6	-1.9	16.7	-5.9	15.0	0.7	53.6*	1.6	10.3	4.4°(2)	—
Inverness, Nairn & Lochaber	61.3	56.1	6.3	13.3	4.9	70.9	0.4	23.0	-6.8	25.4	11.0	36.8	-9.2	14.8	—	—
Ross, Cromarty & Skye	68.1	57.5	6.3	13.2	8.2	72.7	0.2	19.7	-14.0	19.1	5.2	49.4	10.9	11.8	—	—

SCOTLAND

Constituency	% Car-owners	% Working class	% with degrees	% Unemployed	Electorate change %	% voting	% change in voting	% Con.	Con. change 1983-87	% Lab.	Lab. change 1983-87	% All. (*SDP)	All. change 1983-87	% S.N.P.	% Other	Swing
Lothian, East Lothian	57.6	55.9	5.7	9.4	3.9	78.7	2.5	28.3	−2.5	48.0	4.1	15.5	−5.4	7.3	0.9°	−3.3
Edinburgh, Central†	39.0	42.7	16.5	13.5	4.3	69.0	4.1	34.7	−3.4	40.2	9.1	17.8	−7.8	6.2	1.1°	−6.2
East	37.5	57.4	4.9	13.4	−4.4	74.1	3.7	24.7	−3.9	50.4	5.5	15.4	−5.6	9.5	–	−4.7
Leith	32.9	61.2	6.0	16.2	−0.3	70.9	3.6	22.9	−3.4	49.3	9.6	18.3*	−9.2	9.5	–	–
Pentlands	57.4	40.3	9.5	7.8	−2.0	77.7	4.3	38.3	−0.9	30.0	6.1	24.5*	−4.8	7.2	–	–
South†	49.4	41.4	14.2	9.4	2.1	75.7	4.0	33.8	−2.9	37.7	9.1	22.5*	−6.1	5.1	0.9°	–
West	57.6	38.0	8.8	5.6	1.9	79.4	3.7	37.3	−0.8	22.2	2.0	34.9	−2.2	5.6	0.3	–
Linlithgow	54.3	62.4	4.9	12.1	2.5	77.6	2.4	14.8	−4.3	47.4	2.3	12.6*	−4.4	24.9	–	–
Livingston	59.8	60.9	5.0	11.2	6.2	74.1	2.5	18.7	−5.2	45.6	8.2	19.1	−6.3	16.6	–	–
Midlothian	58.8	57.3	5.2	9.8	0.1	77.2	2.2	18.2	−3.6	48.3	5.5	22.0*	−7.1	10.6	0.9°	–
Orkney & Shetland	68.5	51.4	6.2	7.6	3.2	68.7	0.8	23.3	−2.3	18.7	5.7	41.7	−4.3	14.5	1.8	–
Strathclyde, Argyll & Bute†	57.6	50.8	6.5	11.9	2.5	75.5	2.6	33.5	−5.1	12.1	2.8	37.3	9.8	17.1	–	−7.8
Ayr	59.1	47.8	7.3	10.8	2.2	79.9	3.3	39.4	−3.4	39.1	12.3	14.8	−10.8	6.7	–	−6.0
Carrick Cumnock & Doon Valley	53.3	66.5	3.3	16.2	0.8	75.8	1.6	20.7	−3.4	60.1	8.6	9.6*	−8.3	9.6	–	–
Clydebank & Milngavie	46.4	60.1	5.4	12.2	−1.3	78.9	3.0	15.7	−4.6	56.9	12.1	14.9*	−9.9	12.5	–	−5.6
Clydesdale	60.1	58.7	5.7	10.8	2.3	78.2	1.7	23.5	−4.7	45.3	6.5	16.4*	−5.1	14.8	–	–
Cumbernauld & Kilsyth	54.5	58.5	4.9	12.0	2.8	78.5	2.0	9.0	−4.5	60.0	10.8	11.4*	−8.4	19.6	–	−7.2
Cunninghame, North†	52.0	53.9	5.9	14.1	3.2	78.3	2.6	34.0	−4.7	44.4	9.8	12.1*	−6.0	9.5	–	−5.8
South	49.1	67.1	3.4	15.6	2.7	75.0	1.4	16.3	−4.9	60.8	6.7	11.9	−6.0	11.0	–	−3.2
Dumbarton	53.2	56.0	6.7	12.6	2.8	77.9	2.8	31.7	−0.1	43.0	6.3	13.2*	−9.6	12.1	–	–
East Kilbride	61.8	50.3	5.4	9.4	2.7	79.2	2.2	14.7	−9.6	49.0	11.9	23.7*	−4.2	12.6	–	–
Eastwood	70.8	30.2	9.6	7.0	4.2	79.4	3.2	39.5	−7.1	25.1	5.0	27.2*	−0.3	8.2	–	–
Glasgow, Cathcart	41.9	50.2	6.6	12.5	−3.4	76.4	0.5	22.4	−8.1	52.1	10.7	15.2*	−7.3	10.3	–	−9.4
Central	21.3	67.4	3.9	21.6	−0.2	65.6	2.7	13.0	−5.9	64.5	11.4	10.5	−6.2	10.0	–	−8.7
Garscadden	27.3	73.5	1.7	17.6	−5.2	71.4	2.3	10.7	−4.7	67.7	11.5	9.4*	−8.3	12.2	2.0°(2)	–
Govan	28.5	70.1	3.4	17.9	−2.2	73.4	1.7	11.9	−7.8	64.8	9.9	12.3*	−7.1	10.4	0.6	–

Constituency																
Hillhead†	39.7	44.2	14.5	13.9	1.4	72.4	0.4	14.4	−9.1	42.9	9.5	35.1*	−1.1	6.5	1.1°	–
Maryhill	22.8	72.8	4.0	20.6	1.0	67.5	2.0	9.4	−5.4	66.4	11.3	11.7	−10.5	11.0	1.5°	–
Pollok	33.7	65.8	4.1	18.6	−3.4	71.7	3.4	14.3	−6.2	63.1	10.8	12.0	−5.3	9.6	1.0°	−8.5
Provan	19.5	80.8	1.0	24.3	−8.3	69.1	3.9	7.7	−3.1	72.9	8.5	7.3*	−7.7	12.1	–	–
Rutherglen	37.7	63.7	3.8	15.5	−3.2	77.2	2.1	11.5	−6.5	56.0	7.7	24.4	−3.4	8.1	–	−7.6
Shettleston	30.4	67.6	2.6	17.4	3.2	70.4	2.2	13.3	−5.9	63.6	9.4	10.4	−8.1	12.7	–	–
Springburn	18.1	77.2	1.5	22.4	−3.4	67.5	2.4	8.3	−4.9	73.6	8.9	7.9	−6.2	10.2	–	–
Greenock & Port Glasgow	36.0	73.8	3.0	19.3	−2.8	75.4	1.2	9.6	−0.1	59.7	17.1	17.9	−18.5	8.6	–	–
Hamilton	50.3	58.2	5.2	13.2	1.3	76.9	1.2	14.4	−4.8	48.5	7.2	13.2	−7.0	12.7	–	−5.0
Kilmarnock & Loudoun	54.6	60.5	4.4	11.9	2.0	78.0	2.4	19.6	−5.1	61.0	4.9	13.7*	−9.0	18.2	–	−8.4
Monklands, East	46.5	66.4	3.3	15.5	1.3	74.8	1.8	16.8	−7.0	62.3	9.7	9.3	−6.7	12.9	–	−7.2
West	49.2	60.2	4.6	12.7	1.1	77.3	1.6	15.7	−6.3	66.9	8.1	11.2*	−6.1	10.8	–	–
Motherwell, North	44.9	69.7	3.4	14.4	2.0	77.3	2.3	11.1	−4.5	58.3	9.2	8.0	−6.1	14.0	–	–
South	44.5	66.1	3.1	13.8	−0.1	75.5	2.7	14.5	−5.5	55.5	5.9	11.3*	−6.4	15.3	0.6	–
Paisley North	38.1	62.5	3.9	14.9	−1.9	73.5	4.9	15.8	−5.7	56.2	9.9	15.8*	−7.9	12.9	–	–
South	47.5	60.1	4.6	13.8	−1.7	75.3	2.7	14.7	−6.0		14.7	15.1	−9.0	14.0	–	–
Renfrew West & Inverclyde†	67.4	45.8	8.4	8.5	5.0	80.5	2.4	29.8	−2.9	56.2	9.7	21.4*	−8.2	10.1	–	–
Strathkelvin & Bearsden†	71.8	33.3	10.5	7.0	3.6	82.2	2.8	33.4	−3.1	38.7	12.5	21.4*	−7.3	7.1	–	–
Tayside, Angus East†	59.7	52.9	8.4	10.6	2.9	75.5	2.0	39.0	−5.0	38.1	2.8	7.8*	−3.6	42.4	–	–
Dundee, East†	39.9	61.5	4.9	17.5	−3.1	75.9	2.2	12.9	−2.6	10.8	9.4	4.7	−3.0	40.1	–	–
West	40.6	60.6	4.8	14.5	−1.2	75.4	1.0	18.0	−3.8	42.3	9.9	12.7*	−4.4	15.3	0.7	−6.8
Perth & Kinross	60.0	49.1	7.3	9.4	3.2	74.4	2.1	39.6	−0.6	53.3	5.9	16.9	−7.9	27.6	–	–
Tayside, North	66.5	54.0	6.3	8.6	3.9	74.7	2.1	45.4	−5.7	15.9	3.3	12.9	−6.3	32.9	–	–
Western Isles†	56.5	59.8	4.6	11.8	3.0	70.2	3.7	8.1	−1.5	42.7	12.6	20.7*	14.9	28.5	–	–

Table A1.4 Northern Ireland constituency results, 1987

	% voting	Change in % voting	Unionist parties				% APNI	APNI change 1983-7	Republican parties							% Green
			% OUP	% DUP	% Ind. U.	Unionist change 1983-7			% SDLP	SDLP change 1983-7	% SF	SF change 1983-7	% WP	WP change 1983-7	Republican change 1983-7	
Antrim, East	55.2	-9.7	71.6	–	–	-2.3	25.6	5.7	–	–	–	–	2.8	1.3	-1.5	–
North	68.9	-0.9	–	62.6	–	-15.8	11.3	◇	20.2	6.2	5.8	-0.7	–	–	5.5	–
South	59.1	-6.4	69.8	–	–	-4.1	16.0	4.1	9.9	1.2	4.4	0.2	–	–	-0.0	–
Belfast, East	60.2	-9.8	–	61.9	15.4	-8.2	32.1	8.0	–	–	–	–	4.0	2.9	1.8	–
North	62.3	-7.1	39.0	–	–	-3.9	7.8	-1.3	15.7	1.7	13.7	0.9	8.3	2.6	5.3	–
South	60.3	-9.2	57.8	–	–	-4.4	21.3	-2.7	13.0	4.4	3.1	0.2	4.7	2.4	7.0	–
West	69.1	-5.2	18.7	–	–	7.8	–	–	35.7	11.1	41.2	4.2	4.4	0.2	15.5	–
Down, North	62.8	-3.5	–	–	80.6§	4.3	19.4	-2.7	–	–	–	–	–	–	–	–
South†	79.4	2.7	45.7	–	–	-1.9	1.9	-1.7	47.0	7.8	4.2	-3.8	1.2	-0.5	3.5	–
Fermanagh & S. Tyrone	80.3	-8.3	49.6	–	–	2.0	1.7	–	19.1	2.6	26.4	-8.4	3.2	2.1	-3.7	–
Foyle	69.0	-8.6	–	28.5	–	-1.9	2.6	0.5	48.8	2.8	17.9	-2.4	2.1	1.0	1.4	–
Lagan Valley	64.1	-3.4	70.0	–	–	-6.0	13.8	2.5	6.9	0.5	6.4	2.1	2.9	0.9	3.5	–
Londonderry East	68.7	-7.5	60.5	–	–	-1.2	6.6	2.0	19.2	0.9	11.2	-2.6	1.9	0.3	-1.4	0.6
Newry & Armagh‡	79.2	3.2	37.9	–	–	-2.1	1.3	◇	48.1	11.3	11.8	-9.1	0.9	-1.3	0.9	–
Strangford	57.6	-7.3	75.9	–	–	-2.8	20.3	4.6	–	–	–	–	3.7	◇	-0.6	–
Ulster, Mid-	77.4	-6.9	–	44.2	–	1.0	3.5	0.3	26.2	3.8	23.9	-6.0	2.2	0.8	-1.4	–
Upper Bann	65.6	-6.4	61.5	–	–	-5.8	5.9	◇	20.5	2.6	7.4	-2.0	4.7	-0.7	-0.1	–
Northern Ireland	67.4	-5.4	37.6	11.7	5.3	-2.5	9.9	1.9	21.5	3.6	11.4	-2.1	2.6	0.7	2.3	0.02

Notes:
§ In North Down 45.1% of the vote went to the Independent Unionist incumbent and 35.4% to an Independent Unionist challenger.
◇ No candidate in 1983.
OUP: Official Unionist Party.
DUP: Democratic Unionist Party.
APNI: Alliance Party of Northern Ireland.
SDLP: Social Democratic and Labour Party.
SF: (Provisional) Sinn Fein.
WP: Workers' Party (ex-Official Sinn Fein).

Table A1.5   *Outstanding results, 1987*

10 Highest Turnouts

%
84.4 Brecon & Radnor
83.2 Richmond & Barnes
83.1 Derbyshire West
82.9 Leicestershire North-West
82.9 Carmarthen
82.6 Delyn
82.5 Bury North
82.5 South Ribble
82.3 Taunton
82.2 Meirionnydd Nant Conwy

10 Lowest Turnouts (GB)

%
55.4 Hackney S. & Shoreditch
55.6 Peckham
57.4 Bow & Poplar
57.6 Bethnal Green & Stepney
58.1 Hackney N. & Stoke Newington
58.2 City of London & Westminster S.
60.6 Birmingham Small Heath
63.5 Birmingham Sparkbrook
63.8 Hendon South
63.9 Manchester Central

10 Closest Results

%
0.1 (56) Brecon & Radnor (Lib.)
0.1 (56) Mansfield (Lab.)
0.2 (147) York (Con.)
0.3 (182) Ayr (Con.)
0.4 (205) Portsmouth South (Con.)
0.4 (204) Wolverhampton NE (Con.)
0.5 (180) Dulwich (Con.)
0.5 (279) Wallasey (Con.)
0.6 (309) Bradford South (Lab.)
0.6 (336) Norwich South (Lab.)

10 Alliance Nearest Misses

%
0.4 (205) Portsmouth South (SDP)
1.3 (774) Stockton South (SDP)
1.8 (853) Blyth Valley (SDP)
2.0 (805) Islington South (SDP)
2.5 (1428) Cambridgeshire NE (Lib.)
2.5 (1234) Edinburgh West (Lib.)
2.7 (1412) Bath (SDP)
2.7 (1413) Hereford (Lib.)
3.0 (1677) Colne Valley (Lib.)
3.4 (1840) Hazel Grove (Lib.)

10 Best Other Votes (GB)

%
14.5 Orkney & Shetland (OSM)
3.6 Hartlepool (Ind.)
3.6 Weston-Super-Mare (Green)
3.4 Windsor & Maidenhead (Ind. C.)
3.0 Mansfield (Mod. Lab.)
2.9 Islington North (Green)
2.6 Hackney North (Green)
2.6 Brent East (Ind. Lab.)
2.3 Surrey East (Green)
2.2 Horsham (Green)

10 Best Nationalist Votes

%
57.1 Caernarfon
44.2 Banff & Buchan
43.2 Ynys Môn
43.2 Moray
42.4 Angus East
40.1 Dundee East
40.0 Meirionnydd Nant Conwy
32.9 Tayside North
31.5 Galloway & Upper Nithsdale
28.5 Western Isles

Table A1.6   By-elections, Great Britain, 1983–1987

By-election		Turnout (%)	Con. (%)	Lab. (%)	Alln. (%)	Others (%)	
Penrith & the Borders	1983	73.1	58.8	13.3	27.9	–	
	28.7.83	55.7	46.0	7.4	44.6	(5)	2.0
	1987	77.5	60.3	11.0	28.7	–	
Chesterfield	1983	72.6	32.4	48.0	18.5	–	
	1.3.84	76.9	15.2	46.5	34.7	(7)	3.6
	1987	76.7	25.0	45.5	29.6	–	
Cynon Valley	1983	73.4	14.2	56.0	20.6	(1)	9.3
	3.5.84	65.7	7.4	58.8	19.9	(4)	13.9
	1987	76.7	12.2	68.9	12.2	(1)	6.7
Stafford	1983	76.5	51.2	23.7	24.7	(1)	0.4
	3.5.84	65.6	40.4	27.4	31.8	(1)	0.4
	1987	79.5	51.3	21.2	27.5	–	
Surrey South-West	1983	74.5	59.7	8.1	32.1	–	
	3.5.84	61.7	49.3	6.7	43.4	(3)	0.8
	1987	78.4	59.5	5.6	34.4	(1)	0.5
Portsmouth South	1983	67.3	50.0	22.6	25.4	(2)	2.0
SDP gain	14.6.84	54.5	34.3	26.5	37.6	(6)	1.5
Con. recovery	1987	71.3	43.3	13.0	42.9	–	
Southgate	1983	69.6	58.1	17.9	23.4	(1)	0.7
	13.12.84	50.6	49.6	11.9	35.6	(6)	2.9
	1987	72.6	58.8	18.8	20.9	–	

Brecon & Radnor	1983	80.1	48.2	25.0	24.4	(2) 2.4
SDP gain	4.7.85	79.4	27.7	34.4	35.8	(4) 2.1
	1987	84.4	34.7	29.2	34.8	(1) 1.3
Tyne Bridge	1983	61.5	25.2	56.5	18.3	–
	6.12.85	38.1	11.1	57.8	29.7	(3) 1.4
	1987	63.1	20.6	63.0	16.4	–
Fulham	1983	76.1	46.2	34.0	18.2	(2) 1.5
Lab. gain	10.4.86	70.8	34.9	44.4	18.7	(8) 2.0
Con. recovery	1987	77.1	51.8	36.7	10.4	(1) 1.1
Derbyshire West	1983	77.4	55.9	17.1	27.0	–
	8.5.86	71.9	39.5	19.8	39.4	(2) 1.3
	1987	83.1	53.1	11.7	35.4	–
Ryedale	1983	71.8	59.2	10.3	30.5	–
Lib. gain	8.5.86	67.3	41.3	8.4	50.3	–
Con. recovery	1987	79.2	53.3	8.1	38.6	–
Newcastle-under-Lyme	1983	77.3	36.4	42.0	21.6	–
	17.7.86	62.2	19.0	40.8	38.8	(4) 1.4
	1987	80.8	27.9	40.5	30.9	(1) 0.7
Knowsley North	1983	69.5	20.1	64.5	14.8	(1) 0.6
	13.11.86	57.3	6.3	56.3	34.6	(3) 2.8
	1987	74.2	12.5	69.9	16.2	(1) 1.4
Greenwich	1983	67.7	34.8	38.2	25.1	(3) 1.8
SDP gain	26.2.87	67.3	11.2	33.8	53.0	(5) 2.0
	1987	73.4	23.3	34.9	40.6	(3) 1.3
Truro	1983	79.6	38.1	4.5	57.3	–
	12.3.87	69.9	31.5	7.1	60.4	(2) 0.9)
	1987	79.9	40.8	10.2	49.0	–

Table A1.7 By-elections, Northern Ireland (All 15 took place on 23.1.86)

By-election		Turnout (%)	OUP (%)	DUP (%)	Ind.U. (%)	Alln. (%)	SDLP (%)	SF (%)	WP (%)	Others (%)
Antrim East	1983	64.9	37.4	36.5	–	–	2.7	–	1.5	1.9
	23.1.86	58.9	84.9	–	–	15.1	–	–	–	–
	1987	55.2	71.6	–	–	25.6	–	–	2.8	–
Antrim North	1983	69.0	24.3	54.2	–	–	14.0	6.5	–	1.0
	23.1.86	53.5	–	97.4	–	–	–	–	–	–
	1987	62.8	–	68.7	–	12.4	12.5	6.4	–	2.6
Antrim South	1983	65.5	45.7	28.2	–	11.9	8.7	4.2	1.4	–
	23.1.86	52.2	94.1	–	–	–	–	–	–	5.9
	1987	59.1	69.8	–	–	16.0	9.9	4.4	–	–
Belfast East	1983	70.0	24.8	45.3	–	24.1	1.3	1.8	1.1	1.7
	23.1.86	61.7	–	81.0	–	17.3	–	–	1.7	–
	1987	60.2	–	61.9	–	32.1	–	–	4.0	–
Belfast North	1983	69.4	36.2	19.5	2.7	9.1	14.0	12.9	5.7	–
	23.1.86	50.6	71.5	–	–	16.7	–	–	11.8	–
	1987	62.3	39.0	–	15.4	7.8	15.7	13.7	8.3	–
Belfast South	1983	69.6	50.0	12.2	–	23.9	8.6	3.0	2.3	–
	23.1.86	56.6	71.4	–	–	25.0	–	–	3.6	–
	1987	60.3	57.8	–	–	21.3	13.0	3.1	4.7	–
Down North	1983	66.2	20.5	–	56.1	22.1	1.6	–	–	–
	23.1.86	60.5	–	–	79.2	20.8	–	–	–	–
	1987	62.8	–	–	41.5,35.4*	19.4	–	–	–	–
Down South	1983	76.6	40.3	7.3	–	3.6	39.3	7.9	1.7	–
	23.1.86	73.8	48.4	–	–	–	44.9	5.7	1.0	–
	1987	79.4	45.7	–	–	1.9	47.0	4.2	1.2	–

Constituency	Year									
Fermanagh & South Tyrone	1983	88.6	47.6	–	–	–	16.5	34.8	1.1	–
	23.1.86	80.4	49.7	–	–	–	21.5	27.3	1.5	–
	1987	80.3	49.6	–	–	1.7	19.1	26.4	3.2	–
Lagan Valley	1983	67.5	59.2	16.8	–	11.3	6.4	4.3	2.0	–
	23.1.86	56.7	90.7	–	–	–	–	–	9.3	–
	1987	64.1	70.0	–	–	13.8	6.9	6.4	2.9	–
Londonderry East	1983	76.3	37.9	23.8	–	4.7	18.3	13.8	1.6	–
	23.1.86	47.0	93.9	–	–	–	–	–	–	6.1
	1987	68.7	60.5	–	–	6.6	19.2	11.2	1.9	0.6
Newry & Armagh SDLP gain	1983	76.0	40.0	–	–	–	36.8	20.9	2.3	–
	26.1.86	76.6	40.3	–	–	–	45.5	13.2	1.0	–
	1987	79.2	37.9	–	–	1.3	48.1	11.8	0.9	–
Strangford	1983	64.9	48.8	30.0	—	15.8	4.4	–	–	1.1
	23.1.86	55.1	94.2	–	–	–	–	–	–	5.8
	1987	57.6	75.9	–	–	20.3	–	–	3.7	–
Ulster, Mid-	1983	84.3	13.1	30.0	–	3.2	22.4	29.9	1.4	–
	23.1.86	77.0	–	46.1	–	–	25.3	27.2	1.4	–
	1987	77.4	–	44.2	–	3.5	26.2	23.9	2.2	–
Upper Bann	1983	72.0	56.9	10.4	–	–	17.9	9.4	5.5	–
	26.1.86	57.2	80.8	–	–	–	–	–	19.2	–
	1987	65.6	61.5	–	–	5.9	20.5	7.4	4.7	–

Notes:
OUP: Official Unionist Party.
DUP: Democratic Unionist Party.
Ind. U: Independent Unionist.
SDLP: Social Democratic and Labour Party.
SF: (Provisional) Sinn Fein.
WP: Workers' Party (ex-Official Sinn Fein).
* Amalgamated – 2 candidates stood.

Appendix 2 Analysis
John Curtice and Michael Steed

INTRODUCTION

At first glance the Conservative victory of 1987 mirrors that of 1959. In both elections the party was returned to office for the third time in a row, and with a comfortable majority of around 100. In 1959 the Conservatives had attempted to appeal to a working class supposedly newly embourgeoised by the spread of car-ownership and consumer durables, and in 1987 it had promoted the growth of owner-occupation and share-ownership. After the 1959 election, the question was asked, 'Must Labour Lose?'; the 1987 result raises the same question.

But there are important differences between the two elections. The Conservative predominance in terms of votes in 1987 was much less marked than in 1959 (see Table A1.1). Since 1945, the Conservatives have only won a smaller share of the United Kingdom vote in 1966 and the two elections of 1974. Indeed their share was less than Labour received in 1959 or at any other election between 1945 and 1970. It was the lowest share of the vote won by a Conservative government since 1922.

But at the same time the Conservative lead over Labour was exceptionally large. At 11.5% of the UK votes it was over twice the 1959 margin (5.6%). But for the even greater disaster of 1983, Labour's performance would appear calamitous. Between 1950 and 1979 neither Conservative nor Labour had as much as 55% of the combined Labour and Conservative (two-party) vote; in 1987 the Conservatives succeeded in doing so for the second time running, securing 57.9% of the two-party vote. Despite the 3.2% increase in its share of the overall vote, Labour's percentage was still lower than at any election, bar 1983, since the election of 1931.

The Commons majority of 102 thus both exaggerates the Conservatives' strength and hides Labour's weakness.[1] That Mrs Thatcher's majority in seats was not greater than Mr Macmillan's, despite her much larger voting lead, reflects the decline in the ability of the electoral system to exaggerate the winner's lead in votes into a larger lead in seats.

However, Mrs Thatcher's capacity to retain power by a comfortable majority on a smaller share of the total vote than Mr Macmillan won in 1959 or Mr Heath secured in 1970 reflects the strength of the Liberal/SDP Alliance, which polled 23.1% of the votes cast in Great Britain alone.[2] That figure was, however, a setback compared with 1983, although how serious a reverse is debatable. The Alliance's share of the total vote in 1987 was higher than any post-war Liberal performance, although in comparison with February 1974 (allowing for the seats the Liberals did not fight then) the Alliance polled slightly below the Liberal vote in England and Wales, and only above it in Scotland. The 3.0% drop is on a similar scale to the falls in Liberal support in 1966, 1970, October 1974 and 1979. Those, however, were

316

elections following a period of Labour government and the Liberal vote has always fallen at such an election. Apart from 1935, the Liberal vote has never fallen following a period of Conservative government. Further, the Liberal vote has always increased sharply at a general election which followed a series of good by-election performances such as occurred in the 1983–7 parliament. The Alliance also had reason to expect to improve its vote on the basis of its local election record since 1983, confirmed by the clearly higher level of support in May 1987 than in May 1983. Given that progress, it is more likely that the disappointing Alliance performance reflected the weaknesses of its election campaign rather than any reversal of the 30-year long upward trend in Liberal fortunes.

Table A2.1 summarises the performance of the parties in terms of the change since 1983. It has been argued that in recent years the electorate has become more volatile, and that one way in which that manifested itself was in larger movements of votes between general elections. Yet the swing between Conservative and Labour was lower than at any general election since 1959, except for October 1974. Similarly, the mean change in the Alliance vote was lower than that for the Liberals or the Alliance at any election since 1970. The Pedersen Index (a measure of the overall volatility of the result),[3] at 3.4, was also lower than at any election since 1959 apart from October 1974.[4]

But this picture of relative stability in the national vote covers a pattern of sharp divergences between different parts of Britain. The standard deviation of the two-party swing was as high as between October 1974 and 1979, itself the highest at any post-war pair of elections fought on unchanged boundaries.[5] Meanwhile the Alliance vote continued the Liberal tradition of greater constituency to constituency variation than either the Conservative or Labour vote. The denationalisation of British politics continued apace.

Table A2.1   Measures of change since 1983

Change	Overall	Mean	Median	Standard deviation
Conservative change	−0.2	−0.6	−0.4	3.6
Labour change	+3.2	+3.7	−3.1	3.9
Alliance change	−3.0	−3.2	−3.4	4.2
Total vote swing	−1.7	−2.1	−1.6	3.1
Two-party swing	−2.8	−3.0	−2.5	4.1
Turnout change	+2.9	+2.8	+2.7	1.5

Notes:
Total-vote swing is the change in the Conservative share of the vote plus the change in the Labour share of the vote divided by two; *Two-party swing* is the change in the Conservative share of the votes cast for Conservative and Labour only; figures in the *overall* column are based on the overall votes cast in Great Britain; those in the *mean column* are the average of the results in all 633 constituencies in Great Britain; the *median* is the 317th value in a rank ordering of constituencies.

In this Appendix we describe, and where possible account for, the geographical variation in the movement of the vote since 1983, and assess its implications for our understanding of the British electorate and the operation of the electoral system. We pay particular attention to three issues which aroused interest before and immediately after the election. First, what accounted for the geographical variation in change in support? How far did it reflect a response to differences in economic well-being under the Conservative government, or did its causes lie in longer-term social and political changes which pre-date the policy initiatives of Mrs Thatcher's government? Secondly, we consider to what extent and in what circumstances there was evidence of tactical voting. The possibilities for tactical voting received greater media attention than at any previous election, and there was also some pressure group activity aimed at fostering it. Did this activity have any impact? And finally, how were votes translated into seats? What are the possible implications of the trends evident at this election for the future operation of the electoral system and for the debate about electoral reform?

METHODOLOGY

But before we can proceed to these substantive questions, there is one methodological issue we must face. How are we to measure change in party support? It has previously been the tradition of these appendices to concentrate on changes in the relative standing of the Conservative and Labour parties as measured by two-party swing. There have been two principal reasons for this. First, despite the substantial growth in support for third parties, the Conservative and Labour parties have continued to dominate parliamentary representation in the House of Commons. Most seats changing hands have been between Conservative and Labour, and such transfers are determined by those two parties' relative standing. Secondly, the factors that influence the change in the Conservative and Labour shares of the vote have largely been similar, while those which influence the change in Liberal/Alliance fortunes have been different. The change in the Conservative and Labour share of the vote has mostly been influenced by socio-geographical factors operating across groups of constituencies, while the change in the Liberal/Alliance vote has been influenced more by factors specific to an individual constituency – such as the popularity of an individual candidate, strong local campaigning, or the tactical situation.

Although the first reason still held true in 1987, the second did not. In Table A2.2 we look at the correlation between the change in share of the vote for each pair of parties at three levels – constituency, Euro-constituency[6] and Registrar-General's standard region (with Greater London and the rest of the South-East considered separately). In 1983, when we undertook a similar analysis, we also found that at constituency level the correlation between the change in Conservative and change in Labour share of the vote was less than the correlation of either with the change in the Alliance share of the vote.[7] However, when we looked at a higher level of aggregation such as the standard region, then the correlation between Conservative and Labour performance was strong, while the correlation of either with the Alliance performance was weak. In 1983 the changes in the Conservative and Labour shares of the vote varied systematically together from one part of the country to another in a way that the Alliance performance did not.

Table A2.2   *Correlation between Conservative, Labour and Alliance performance*

Parties	Level of measurement		
	Constituency	Euro-Constituency	Standard region
Conservative and Labour	−0.38	−0.73	−0.85
Conservative and Alliance	−0.37	−0.06	+0.44
Labour and Alliance	−0.59	−0.57	−0.81

Note: All correlations in this and succeeding tables are Pearson product moment correlations.

   But as can be seen from Table A2.2, in 1987 this pattern does not hold. It is true that at higher levels of aggregation the correlation between Conservative and Labour performance is much stronger than at constituency level. There is clearly an important geographical covariation in their performance. Meanwhile, the negative correlation between Conservative and Alliance performance which exists at constituency level does not hold at higher levels of aggregation (indeed at the level of standard regions it is positive – both parties did best in roughly the same regions). But the negative correlation between Labour and Alliance performance is stronger at regional than constituency level. Labour appears to have performed best not only where the Conservatives did badly, but also where the Alliance did.
   Because of this more complex pattern of covariation, swing is not as useful a summary statistic as it has been in previous elections. It will not enable us to capture most of the broad geographical variations in party peformance. The performance of all three parties has to be considered together. Therefore in this appendix we use change in each party's share of the vote as our principal tool in analysing the geographical variation in party support. However, the continued domination of parliamentary representation by the Conservative and Labour parties means that swing is still a simple and useful way of analysing the operation of the electoral system. It is therefore used in that section of this appendix.

THE GEOGRAPHY OF THE CHANGE

Overview

The scale of the geographical variation in the change in each party's share of the vote is immediately apparent from Table A1.2 (p. 284). The electorate did not cast a nationwide verdict. This was particularly true for Labour. In not one of the 24 subregions in Table A1.2 was Labour's recovery close to the national figure of +3.2%. In every one of the 14 subregions in Scotland, Wales and the North of England its vote rose by 4% or more; nowhere in the South and Midlands was the subregional rise above 2.5%. For the Conservatives the pattern was similar, but not identical. A few subregional figures were close to the national one (−0.2%). But whilst the Tory vote increased everywhere in the South and Midlands, except Devon & Cornwall, it fell everywhere else except in West Yorkshire (where the overall Conservative rise can be accounted for by a strong Conservative performance in Bradford). The regional pattern was least consistent for the Alliance (whose performance also varied most within each region), but broadly its vote held up best in the South (actually increasing in Devon & Cornwall) and fell most in Scotland and Wales.

Thus we have clear evidence of a broad division between North/West Britain, consisting of Scotland, Wales and the North of England, in which Labour advanced strongly, and a contrasting area, which we will call South/East Britain, in which the Conservatives were doing better than in 1983. This latter area includes the whole of the South of England and the Midlands except for the Devon & Cornwall subregion which does not fit easily into either of these broad divisions and which we have consequently set aside in the analysis that immediately follows. Table A2.3 sums up the differences between these three divisions of Britain in terms of the average changes in shares of the vote:

Table A2.3   The main regional changes

| Region | Mean change in % of vote 1983–87 | | | No. of seats |
	Con.	Lab.	Alln.	
North/West Britain	−2.7	+6.5	−4.2	(344)
South/East Britain	+1.2	+1.6	−2.5	(273)
Devon & Cornwall	−3.1	+2.6	+0.7	(16)

But the differences in the results in the North/West and the South/East extends well beyond these differences in the level and direction of change. Within each half of Britain the pattern of change was distinctive in two important ways. First, the interrelation between the performance of the three parties differs. Secondly, the social factors that underly the variations in each party's performance are different. We explore these two patterns in turn.

In Table A2.4 we repeat the analysis undertaken in Table A2.2 separately for these two broad regions. With the biggest regional variation removed, this table brings out more clearly one feature evident in Table A2.2, the way that the more variable Alliance vote dominates the pattern of the other parties' performances at constituency level. But when we look at local clusters, the Euro-constituencies, the pattern in the two halves of the country is different. In South/East Britain variation in the Alliance performance

Table A2.4 Correlation between Conservative, Labour and Alliance performance in North/West and South/East Britain

	Level of measurement	
Region/Party	Constituency	Euro-constituency
North/West Britain		
Con. and Lab.	−0.17	−0.47
Con. and Alln.	−0.46	−0.29
Lab. and Alln.	−0.58	−0.59
South/East Britain		
Con. and Lab.	+0.00	+0.08
Con. and Alln.	−0.68	−0.73
Lab. and Alln.	−0.64	−0.67

continues to account for much of the variation in the other two parties'
performances. Indeed, we find a clear relationship between the Conservative
and Alliance performance at this level which was hidden in the national
analysis. But in North/West Britain it is the Labour performance which is
the key to the pattern of movement. The correlation between Conservative
and Alliance performance is clearly weaker than that of either with Labour's.

The contrast suggests an important hypothesis about the behaviour of
former Alliance voters at the 1987 election. This is that while in South/East
Britain those switching from the Alliance generally moved in similar
proportions to Conservative and Labour, in North/West Britain they moved
disproportionately in Labour's direction. The evidence examined here cannot
ultimately prove such a hypothesis; the pitfalls of the ecological fallacy are
too great. But it does suggest an important item for the agenda of survey
research into the election.

But we can explore whether any social or localised geographical influences
can account for the differences in the pattern of intercorrelations in the two
parts of the country. To that end in Table A2.5 we correlate party
performance in the two parts of the country against measures of the social
character of a constituency.

This table does indeed show a further striking difference between the two

Table A2.5 Social correlates of change in party share, 1983–87

Region/Party	% unemployed 1987	% employers & managers	% working class	% skilled workers	% agriculture	% with degree
North/West Britain						
Con.	−0.27	0.04	−0.02	0.06	−0.07	−0.08
Lab.	0.49	−0.52	0.43	0.44	−0.43	−0.24
Alln.	−0.21	0.36	−0.35	−0.43	0.33	0.22
South/East Britain						
Con.	0.01	−0.15	0.12	0.04	−0.18	−0.20
Lab.	0.17	−0.06	0.06	0.02	−0.03	0.00
Alln.	−0.06	0.09	−0.09	−0.10	0.10	0.11

broad regions. In South/East Britain the correlations are either weak or non-existent. The variation in movements between the parties in this area had little to do with the socioeconomic character of constituencies. The same is largely true for the Conservative performance in North/West Britain. But here the variations in both Labour and Alliance performances do correlate systematically with the social character of a constituency, and it is this which helps to account for the relative strength of the Labour/Alliance correlation in that part of the country.

This finding also reinforces our argument that the changes between 1983 and 1987 need to be analysed in more complex terms than swing allows, and that the national figures of change for each party hide very different sets of results in the two parts of Britain. We shall proceed to examine separately the results in each of these two regions, but before doing so we should examine more carefully the precise boundary between them.

All our analysis has been conducted using the standard regional boundaries of the Office of Population Censuses and Surveys (OPCS). They need not identify the exact division between the two parts of the country, but in practice they do so almost precisely, although at a number of points along the boundary there is evidence of a 'transitional zone', an area where the pattern of change lies somewhere between what one would typically expect from the regional averages.

An examination of the constituencies lying along the boundary that separates off the Midlands from the North clearly indicates that this line on the map is indeed a meaningful one. Starting at the North Sea the standard boundary divides a trio of constituencies in South Humberside from another trio in Lincolnshire, which were shifted in 1974 from the Yorkshire & Humberside region to the East Midlands; further south lie the remaining three Lincolnshire constituencies which have always been considered part of the Midlands. The rise in the Labour vote in the first group was 6.0%; in the middle trio 4.3% and in the last three 2.6%.[8] The area of North Lincolnshire seems to have been a transitional zone at this election, just as it has been in administrative history.

Further westwards we find that the psephological border was particularly stark. Labour surged ahead in South Yorkshire, its rise in the metropolitan boroughs which adjoin the Midlands being consistently high (+8.3% in Doncaster, +7.1% in Rotherham and +6.8% in Sheffield). But the Labour vote actually fell in most of the similar mining and industrial constituencies next door in Nottinghamshire and Derbyshire. (See also p. 330).

In the north-west Midlands there is again sign of a transitional belt. In 1979 and 1983, when the North and the Midlands also voted differently, the Potteries tended to go with the North. This time, however, Labour did poorly in North Staffordshire (+0.8%), and also in the adjoining part of Cheshire. However, its performance in Shropshire (+3.9%) was above the Midland average, and brought one of Labour's rare gains in South/East Britain, The Wrekin. Though it is possible to regard Shropshire as part of a Welsh Marches transitional zone, since the Conservatives did poorly both there and in several seats in Hereford and Worcester, the Anglo-Welsh border is clearly a dividing line. In the five Midland seats lying along it, the Labour vote rose +2.8%, but in the five Welsh seats abutting the Midlands

Labour achieved +5.9%. The divide between England and Wales is even more marked when we reach the Severn estuary. In Bristol Labour lost ground, while the Labour vote leaped 8.0% in Cardiff and 9.4% in Newport. Similarly, the Alliance vote dropped only 1.7% in Bristol but 5.4% in Cardiff and 9.6% in Newport.

The clearest example of a transitional zone is in the South-West. The Conservative vote rose in most constituencies in Avon, Wiltshire and Hampshire. But it fell, typically by around 1%, in most of Somerset and Dorset. The six constituencies of south-east Devon had very similar results to those of Dorset and Somerset. Meanwhile, all five Devon seats to the west of Dartmoor and Exmoor saw the Conservative vote plummet (−7.1%). Thus the truly distinctive area of the South-West peninsula is limited to the ten constituencies of the furthest West, while the adjoining constituencies in Devon, Somerset and Dorset form a transitional zone. This is the only case where the administrative boundary clearly does not fit the behavioural one.

Since 1964, whenever there has been a regional pattern to the swing, Devon & Cornwall has behaved as part of the South of England, despite its peripheral position and cultural history giving it something in common with North/West Britain. But as we saw in Table A1.2, at this election the Conservative performance was in line with that in North/West Britain, Labour's more resembled South/East Britain and the Alliance's was different from either. The pattern of variation within the two counties also exhibits a mixture of South/East and North/West Britain characteristics.[9] We remain undecided as to whether at this election it belongs to one of the two broad regions that we have so clearly defined, or to neither.

South/East Britain

We have already seen that the variation in party performance within South/East Britain cannot be generally be accounted for by the particular social character of individual constituencies. So what does explain it? In fact, as Table A1.2 on p. 284 suggests, the broad region divides naturally into two. The Conservative advance was greatest in Greater London and the surrounding ring, named by OPCS the Outer Metropolitan Area (OMA). In these three subregions covering 141 constituencies, which for convenience we shall term the Metropolitan London Area, the Alliance vote also fell consistently, in contrast to the rest of the South. The Labour vote, however, rose slightly and fairly steadily across the whole of South/East Britain.

The line drawn by the census statisticians around the London Metropolitan Area corresponds uncannily with the actual political boundary of 1983–7 changes, most remarkably where it cuts through the middle of counties. Thus, for example, the Conservative performance in both the two northern-most constituencies of Bedfordshire is weaker than in any of the three southern, Metropolitan ones; the Alliance performance was the exact converse. In Essex the OPCS boundary runs between five constituencies furthest from London (Conservative +0.1%; Alliance +0.6%) and the remaining Metropolitan eleven (Conservative +3.6%; Alliance −4.7%).

Kent is divided simply between West Kent and East Kent. The Conservative vote rose in every one of the nine seats in West Kent (+1.5%) and fell in every one within East Kent (−1.6%). Once again the Alliance vote followed the reverse pattern: −1.8% in West Kent and +0.5% in East. Only to the west of London is the political dividing line less sharp, though it is still noticeable. Within the three Thames Valley counties, the Conservative vote rose 1.7% in the Metropolitan constituencies and 0.8% outside that area.

Thus we find in the London Metropolitan Area a precisely defined region, covering nearly twice as many voters as Greater London alone and nearly a quarter of the British electorate. This was the region of Mrs Thatcher's triumph, not the South as a whole or just Greater London, as some commentators immediately after the election suggested. The London effect, as it was called, was not confined to the administrative area of London and did not, as some interpretations suggested, mainly affect Labour. It was the Alliance (despite its achievement in holding on to its Greenwich by-election prize) which did badly in votes, not Labour. Labour lost three seats to the Conservatives, including its only seat (Thurrock) in the Outer Metropolitan Area, due mainly to an exceptional Tory performance rather than an unusually bad Labour one. The Alliance had no seats here that it could lose to the Conservatives but it had targeted several suburban and outer Metropolitan area seats on the basis of the 1983 figures; in all the Conservative majorities rose remorselessly.

We shall look later at whether there was any electoral reaction to the policies of individual left-wing councils (see p. 342), but at this stage we can conclude that the evidence points against a general, London-wide, effect caused by much publicised and controversial Labour policies on such issues as ethnic minority and gay rights. Those who would argue the contrary have to show that but for this Labour would have done better in Greater London than anywhere else in South/East Britain, something that the general pattern of voting makes unlikely.[10] A more likely reason for the general effect across the London Metropolitan Area is the attraction of Thatcherite Conservatism to some 1983 Alliance voters.

However, although so clearly distinct in its behaviour from the rest of South/East Britain, the London Metropolitan Area was not internally homogeneous in its behaviour. There was considerable variation in the Conservative performance within Greater London. The two best Conservative results in Britain, with the vote shooting up by over 10%, were Newham South and Ealing North, while London accounts for two-thirds of the 24 seats in which the Tory vote rose by more than 5%. All but two of these 16 best London votes for Mrs Thatcher were north of the Thames, and the declining personal votes for former SDP MPs can account for the two exceptions (see p. 335). Conversely, the Conservative vote dropped by more than 1% in nine London seats, only four of which can readily be explained by local Alliance strength (for example, Islington South). Four of the remaining five lie south of the Thames. This indeed appears to be part of a more general tendency for the Conservatives to perform better north of the Thames than to the south. For as can be seen from the figures already quoted, the Conservatives did better in the portion of the Outer Metropolitan Area within Essex than in that within Kent, and similarly better in that portion of Essex outside the OMA than in the equivalent part of Kent. In both cases the difference is 2%.

The subregions used in Table A1.2 subdivide the London Metropolitan Area into concentric rings, grouping constituencies in a way which has corresponded well with actual voting behaviour at recent elections. This time these groupings clearly fail to capture the variation we have just illustrated, which appears to be more a matter of contrasts between north and south inside London, or of radial lines of influences extending outwards from the centre. To show this more systematically in Table A2.6 we examine the pattern of variation within Greater London by putting together groups of London boroughs which in practice do fit together at this election.

Table A2.6   The pattern within Greater London

Area	Mean change in % of vote 1987			No. of seats
	Con.	Lab.	Alln.	
North-East	+3.8	−0.7	+2.3	(18)
North-West (Outer)	+4.7	+0.6	−5.1	(18)
North-West (Inner)	+1.3	+2.7	−3.2	(12)
South-West	+2.7	+2.1	−4.4*	(17)
South-East	+0.4	+2.4	−2.2*	(19)

Notes:
* These two Alliance figures are affected by the Croydon North-West and Greenwich by-elections.

North-East: Constituencies in the boroughs of Waltham Forest, Havering, Tower Hamlets, Newham, Redbridge, Barking & Dagenham and Hackney.
North-West (Outer):   Enfield, Barnet, Brent, Harrow, Ealing, Hillingdon.
North-West (Inner):   Islington, Camden, Haringey, Westminster, Kensington & Chelsea, Hammersmith & Fulham.
South-West: Wandsworth, Merton, Croydon, Sutton, Kingston-upon-Thames, Richmond-upon-Thames, Hounslow.
South-East: Lambeth, Southwark, Lewisham, Greenwich, Bromley, Bexley.

The traditional distinction between inner and outer London only appears in a north-westerly direction, where quite good Labour performances in Camden and Westminster contrast with good Conservative ones in Barnet and Brent. Elsewhere the variation fits into radial segments, each extending beyond the Greater London Council (GLC) and even the Metropolitan Area boundry. The most distinctive segments are the North-East, the South-East and the outer North-West.

Within the North-East segment, the constituencies of the East End are the clearest exception to the rule in South/East Britain that a good Conservative performance corresponds with a bad Alliance rather than a bad Labour one. Labour lost ground particularly in its old strongholds of Tower Hamlets and Newham, though it is also likely that the Conservatives were able to mop up the remainder of the former National Front vote there.

But further out, in Dagenham or Ilford, Alliance losses do correspond better with Conservative gains, as we have already seen they do in Essex. Overall, we are probably witnessing here a continuation of the long-term movement to the right in North-East London and the adjoining parts of Essex and Hertfordshire that was so striking at the 1979 election.[11] Included in this area are a number of seats with large numbers of skilled workers such as Basildon, Harlow, Thurrock and Dagenham where the Conservatives did particularly well. But given the strength of Labour's performance amongst constituencies with large numbers of skilled workers in North/West Britain (see Table A2.5 and p. 328), the election results do not support any thesis that there was a nationwide movement of skilled workers towards the Conservatives.

This area of strong Conservative performance does not, however, extend into East Anglia, where the Conservative vote actually fell in most constituencies along the East Coast, although the rest of this region moved in line with the adjoining Midland constituencies. The poor Conservative performance in such east coast port and resort seats as Harwich and Waveney (that is, Lowestoft) may be linked to the Conservative loss of support in East Kent and a number of resort towns along the south coast. But East Kent also fits clearly the pattern of a radial influence; it is the far corner of a block of some 50 contiguous constituencies in South-East London and in Kent, Surrey and Sussex where the Conservative performance was almost everywhere 1 or 2% below the subregional figures shown in Table A1.2.

The contrast between the results in that south-eastern block and the strong Conservative showing in outer North-West London is striking. We have already noted that the fall-off in Conservative performance at the Metropolitan Area boundary is less marked in the Thames Valley. Good Conservative performances seem to radiate outwards along the M1 and M4 corridors to Northamptonshire and the Swindon–Bristol belt. The big rise in the Tory vote in Swindon (+4.7%) may be in part a vote for the new incumbent (see p. 333), but it may also reflect Swindon's rapidly expanding electorate, as it must do in Basingstoke (+4.7%). The Conservative rise in Northamptonshire, another area of expanding electorate, is less sharp at +2.6% but the county stands out as the only one in the Midlands or East Anglia where the Conservatives moved ahead significantly more than Labour.

Across the Midlands and East Anglia as a whole, if we leave aside the transitional zones which we have already discussed, the Conservative and Labour votes moved upwards by a similar modest amount almost everywhere. Apart from Northamptonshire, the only other exceptions are in four cities (Birmingham, Coventry, Leicester and Nottingham), in each of which Labour improved its vote rather more than the Conservatives. There is thus a hint of a divergence between the most urban constituencies and the rest of the region, but there is little consistency in the pattern. The variation within Birmingham and Leicester is particularly marked and the Conservatives did better than Labour in Derby and some of the Black Country boroughs. It is only Coventry that stands out as unambiguously different; the Labour vote rose sharply across the whole city (+5.7%) and the Conservative vote dropped in three out of its four seats (−1.8%).

Apart from an across the board fall in Alliance support, which went down in every county by a figure close to its national drop and which here seems to have favoured the other parties about equally, there was only limited movement of votes in the Midlands and East Anglia, and little pattern in the limited variation. High unemployment could help to account for the scatter of better Labour peformance in urban seats in the East Midlands. But if so, the West Midlands did not follow suit; the Conservatives solitary gain was in the seat, Wolverhampton North-East, with the sixth highest unemployment in that region. Altogether few seats in the Midlands and East Anglia changed hands: the Conservatives gained three (two from Labour and one from the Liberals), and Labour gained five from the Conservatives, four of them in Leicester, Norwich and Nottingham.

This analysis of the vote in South/East Britain leaves us with two principal findings. First, it is location and, particularly, both distance from London and certain lines of communication radiating out from the capital, which accounts for much of the variation in the parties' performances. Within each geographical zone, constituencies of strikingly different social character moved in much the same way. Secondly, urban–rural differences, so marked in recent elections, were barely visible. Indeed far from Labour doing better in the inner cities than in the surrounding suburban and commuting areas (the consistent feature of the previous four elections), London and, to a much lesser extent Bristol, stood out as centres of Conservative advance. Whilst much of the geographical pattern manifest in the 1987 election was a continuation of the trend which started at the 1959 election, this pattern of big cities acting as centres of Conservative advance was a new one.

North/West Britain

As in South/East Britain, so also in North/West Britain there was some clear geographical variation within our broad region. The Conservatives did worse in Scotland than in Wales or the North whilst Labour advanced and the Alliance retreated more in Scotland and Wales than in the North. The differences for each party, around 2%, were not insignificant but were smaller, except for the Alliance, than the gap in behaviour between North/West Britain as a whole and South/East Britain.

Part of the differences between Scotland, Wales and the North was due to the presence of Nationalist parties in Scotland and Wales. Plaid Cymru's share of the Welsh vote dropped slightly from 7.8% to 7.3%, and had therefore little impact on the other parties' overall votes. But there was a clear variation in its performance which had an impact on the variation in the other three parties' shares of the vote within Wales. Its best four increases were clustered in rural West Wales, while its biggest loss (−1.8%) was in Mid-Glamorgan. This was a continuation of the pattern of the Nationalists gaining strength in rural Welsh-speaking Wales and losing it in Anglicised industrial Wales observable at each general election since 1970. It means that Plaid Cymru is now stronger than ever before in Gwynedd, but at the same time is at the lowest level of support it has ever received in the mining valleys of South Wales.

In contrast there was a modest improvement in the Scottish Nationalist vote throughout virtually the whole of Scotland (mean increase of 2.2% in the 71 seats it fought). Only in the Highland subregion and Dundee did it consistently suffer reverses. In one constituency it stood down and supported a candidate from the Orkney and Shetland Movement (OSM), who received the same share of the vote (14.5%) as the Scottish Nationalist Party (SNP) had received in 1983. Overall the SNP took 14.0% of the Scottish vote, or 14.1% if we include the OSM vote, compared with 11.8% in 1983. The nation-wide increase affected the change in the overall share of the vote won by the other parties, but not the variation from constituency to constituency within Scotland. Thus if we allow for the fact that it was achieved against a rising Nationalist vote, Labour's advance in Scotland could be judged as a better performance than the similar figure achieved in Wales.

The case for analysing the voting behaviour of North/West Britain in 1987 as if it were an entity therefore does not rest on any claim that there were no differences between Scotland, Wales and the North. Part of the case is that the internal differences within Scotland and the North, which we discuss below, were an important part of the same locational pattern. But the strongest case for our treatment lies in the consistency of the correlations shown in Tables A2.4 and A2.5. If the equivalent correlations are produced separately for each part of North/West Britain, the same pattern is found in each.

Thus, if we look at geographically contiguous clusters of constituencies, in both Scotland and Wales we find the stronger covariance between the Labour and Alliance performance than between Conservative and Alliance performance. In the North, Merseyside is a deviant case; here the Alliance did well while the Conservative vote plummeted. But if that is excluded the North of England follows the Scottish and Welsh pattern.

Similarly, if we look at the social correlates of change we find convincing evidence of the same phenomenon operating across the whole of North/West Britain. Table A2.5 showed that the most distinctive feature of the whole region was that Labour did best and the Alliance worst in the more working-class constituencies, and especially those with most skilled workers. When we look separately at each part of North/West Britain, we find not only that this statistical link is confirmed each time, but if anything strengthened.

We conclude that the correlation between Labour and Alliance performance and the class character of a constituency is a significant and distinctive pattern common to the whole of North/West Britain. In working-class constituencies, and particularly those with large numbers of skilled workers, irrespective of their location, Labour gained ground most and the Alliance suffered its greatest losses (see Table A2.7).

It is unlikely that we would have found this effect so clearly demonstrated in the analysis of constituency results unless there was a substantially greater movement from the Alliance to Labour amongst individual working-class voters living in Scotland, Wales and the North than among such voters living in the rest of England, or among non-working-class voters in North/West Britain.

Labour's performance was also on average relatively strong in urban constituencies. These are, of course, also disproportionately working-class constituencies, but even if we control for the percentage of skilled workers

Table A2.7   Class and party performance in North/West Britain

| % Skilled workers | Mean change in % of vote since 1983 | | | |
	Con.	Lab.	Alln.	No. of seats
Less than 25%	−3.2	+3.9	−0.9	(64)
25–30%	−2.5	+6.4	−4.3	(63)
30–35%	−2.6	+7.1	−4.9	(83)
Over 35%	−2.4	+8.5	−6.7	(63)

Note:
Skilled workers are measured as the percentage of economically active and retired males in s.e.g. 9 (1981 Census).

in a constituency, the tendency for Labour to do best in the most urban seats, and least well in the most rural ones was still evident.[12] But as Table A2.8 shows, it was not simply true that the more urban the seat, the better Labour did; Labour's performance in mixed constituencies was on average better than in mainly urban ones. Similarly, none of the other parties' performances showed a simple association with the urban/rural character of a seat. This is but a relatively weak echo of the urban/rural variation in party performance at previous elections.

Table A2.8   Urbanness and party performance in North/West Britain

| Urban category | Mean change in % of vote since 1983 | | | |
	Con.	Lab.	Alln.	No. of seats
Very urban	+4.2	−8.8	+5.0	(52)
Mainly urban	+1.2	−5.9	+4.1	(73)
Mixed	+2.3	−7.2	+5.4	(97)
Rural	+3.3	−3.8	+1.4	(51)

Notes:
Very urban: Electorate density (1982 electorate) greater than 24 electors per hectare.
Mainly urban: Electorate density greater than 8 electors per hectare and less than 24 electors per hectare.
Mixed: Electorate density greater than 1.3 electors per hectare and less than 8 persons per hectare.
Rural: Electorate density less than 1.3 electors per hectare.

We also find a hint of a pattern of urban centres of strong Labour and/or weak Conservative performance whose influence stretches out into the surrounding area. Liverpool is the focus of an extraordinary Conservative débâcle: their vote plummeted 11.7% in the city, 7.5% in the adjoining Knowsley district, 3.0% in the remaining nine Merseyside constituencies, 2.4% in the four immediately adjoining Lancashire or Cheshire seats but

by only 0.9% in the rest of North/West England. A strong Labour advance
in Glasgow similarly stretches out into Clydeside. But Edinburgh does not
stand out from the surrounding areas of Lothian and Fife, nor Cardiff from
the rest of industrial South Wales. Labour fared rather better, and the
Conservatives rather worse, in South Yorkshire and Tyne & Wear, than in
the rest of their regions, but Sheffield and Newcastle do not stand out from
the rest of these two metropolitan counties.

Two other features of the variation in party performance in North/West
Britain should also be noted. First, as Table A2.5 shows, there was a
weak tendency for the Conservatives to do less well in seats with high
unemployment. Secondly, the Conservatives tended to do worse the further
a constituency was from London. The heaviest Conservative losses were in
the northern and western parts of Scotland (around −5% or worse in most
constituencies) along with Merseyside. In the south-eastern quarter of
Scotland, together with the area around Tyneside and along the western
coast of Lancashire, a loss of 3 or 4% was typical. In the rest of the North
and throughout Wales the drop in most constituencies was less than 2%
and actual improvements were recorded in some parts of Greater Manchester
and West Yorkshire.

But a couple of areas stand out as exceptions to this pattern. First, the
Conservatives gained ground in five out of the six Cumbria constituencies
(+1.2%), for which there may be different explanations in different parts of
this diverse county, for example, Labour's embarrassment over nuclear
energy in Copeland, which contains Sellafield; the sensitivity of the nuclear
defence issue in Barrow. Secondly, there was a consistently above average
fall in the Conservative vote in South Yorkshire (−3.0%). Given also the
sharpness of the contrast with the results in the adjoining East Midland
mining seats discussed on p. 322, the South Yorkshire results probably reflect
an intensification of Labour loyalties brought about by the local solidarity
for the miners' strike.

A new map or an old one?

At almost every election since 1959 Labour have done better in the North
of Britain than in the South, while the opposite has been true of the
Conservatives. This pattern was particularly marked in 1979 and 1983. The

Table A2.9   *Long-term geographical variation in swing*

Years	South of England	Midlands	North of England	Scotland	Wales
1955–70	+1.7	+3.1	−2.0	−4.8	−1.9
1970–79	+2.5	+0.1	−2.4	−5.3	+5.1
1979–83	+2.4	+1.0	−2.8	−3.7	−0.3
1983–87	+2.3	+1.7	−1.8	−5.3	−2.3
1955–87	+8.9	+5.9	−8.6	−19.1	+0.6

geography of voting changes in 1987 in general terms continues this well-established divergence. In Table A2.9 we fit the 1983–7 movements for Conservative and Labour into the measure (two-party swing) and regions we have previously used to describe this long-term trend.[13] For each area we show the mean deviation from the average national swing during each period.

The cumulative impact of the steady divergence over the last three decades is shown in the bottom row. The Conservative share of the two-party vote in the average Scottish constituency is now nearly 20% below what it would have been if Scotland had moved in line with Britain as a whole: conversely, the Conservative share in the average constituency in Southern England is now about 9% higher than a uniform national trend would have produced. Only in Wales is there no consistent long-term trend.

Thus we should beware of seeing the strikingly varied verdict of the voters in June 1987 as a simple comment on the policies of the last eight years of Conservative government. The divide pre-dates Mrs Thatcher's election as Prime Minister. Only in Cornwall and the western part of Devon was there a reversal of the long-term regional trend. It is true that the annual rate of the divergence, between the swing in the North and the swing in the South has increased in the 1980s. But that acceleration had already started in the 1970s; North and South diverged as much in the nine years up to 1979 as in the 15 years up to 1970. We conclude that a large part of the geography of voting in 1987 must reflect such fundamental changes as the long-term decline of the North's economic base and the social processes, such as middle-class migration, which that has produced.

Indeed, there was less evidence in 1987 than there was in 1983 that the Conservatives did badly where economic problems were locally evident. Then pockets of unemployment stood out sharply on the map of swing, particularly in Birmingham and in the inner area of London.[14] This time that measure of prosperity correlates only (weakly) within North/West Britain and may help to account for the poor Conservative performance in a number of seaside resorts[15] and possibly some urban seats in the East Midlands. Within the London Metropolitan Area there is even a weak positive correlation between unemployment and Conservative performance, that is, here and there the Conservatives did rather well in places with fewer jobs. The best Conservative result, in Newham South, was in one of the London constituencies with the highest unemployment, or indeed worst deprivation on any other measure.[16] Despite the well-known problems of Liverpool, and the Conservative collapse there, Mrs Thatcher's government did not do consistently badly in the inner cities. Her comment on the night of her victory, 'We have got a big job to do in some of those inner cities . . . Politically we must get right back in there, because we want them next time too', was in fact singularly inappropriate in the light of the votes which had just been counted.

For there is one important respect in which this election as a whole bucked the long-term trend. At every election from 1964 to 1983 Labour had done consistently better in the most urban seats and the Conservatives in more rural or mixed areas. This, too, seemed to be caused by inexorable long-term economic and social changes. But such an urban/rural pattern was almost wholly absent in 1987 in South/East Britain, while in North/West Britain it was but weakly and inconsistently present.

There is, however, one nation-wide pattern which may have contributed to the impression that the Conservatives had a particular problem in the cities in 1987. In provincial cities (but not London) the Conservatives fared badly in one or two middle-class divisions. They held Edgbaston and Selly Oak in Birmingham, Bristol West, Cardiff Central and North, Leeds North-East and North-West, Rushcliffe (part of greater Nottingham) and Sheffield Hallam but did poorly in votes in all of them. All these seats possess marked concentrations of the professional middle-class, including particularly University dons and students, as can be seen from the third column of Table A1.3. This pattern also shows up in the results of Cambridge and Oxford and in the weak negative correlation in South/East Britain between Conservative performance and the proportion in the constituency who have a degree (see Table A2.5). This evidence echoes the opinion poll findings during the campaign which showed the Conservatives losing support among the more educated or professional middle-class voters.[17]

But the loss of four other professional middle-class city seats – Edinburgh Central and South, Manchester Withington, and Newcastle Central – created the impression of inner city calamity for the Conservatives. For thereby they lost the last seats they had held in Manchester and Newcastle, adding these names to Liverpool and Glasgow on the roll-call of major cities without a Conservative MP. These four losses were the end-product of the long-term trend which by 1983 had turned them from safe Tory seats[18] into marginals vulnerable to a small pro-Labour swing, together with the behaviour of their local concentrations of the most highly-educated voters. But these mainly middle-class areas are hardly the sort of places conjured up by the term 'inner city'. In inner-city constituencies as a whole, the Conservatives were more successful than at any election since 1959 in ensuring that the change in the share of their vote matched that in the rest of the country.

Another new element in 1987 was that the Alliance performance was part of the geographical pattern. In 1983 the results supported the Alliance boast that it could represent both north and south within Britain; its vote rose as much in Clydeside, Tyneside and South Wales as in the most prosperous parts of Britain. This time its vote moved in a more regional manner than in any of the Liberal Party's ups and downs since the war. It particularly lost support in Labour's northern working-class heartland. One of the hopes of the SDP at the time of its formation was to break Labour's grip on its working-class base, a grip which the Liberals, with only occasional localised exceptions, had failed to challenge effectively. But the setback the Alliance suffered in Labour's heartlands must be regarded as a substantial impediment to any hopes of replacing Labour as the chief opposition to the Conservatives. Yet paradoxically, for reasons we shall come to when we look at tactical voting, its parliamentary representation became more skewed towards North/West Britain. The Alliance emerged from the election with the pre-1981 Liberal party's dependence upon a rural, peripheral and middle-class base.

Thus whilst much of the geography of the changes between 1983 and 1987 was to be expected from the long-term pattern, there are also many signs of a new political map. The reversal of the long-term trend in Devon & Cornwall, together with the pro-Labour tide in Wales, gave a stronger western twist to what had previously seemed a North/South divide. A number of cities, particularly London, Bristol, Glasgow, Liverpool, and indeed Plymouth, appeared to act as centres or poles of their regional trend. The radiating lines of influence from London hint at the importance of changes in transport routes and their effects on relative expansion and decline of different parts of South-East England, and a similar explanation could fit much of the pattern across the whole of Great Britain. Signs of an emerging centre-periphery cleavage, with the Conservatives doing better the closer a constituency to London, as well as a continuation of the core-periphery, North/South, cleavage could be discerned.[19] Yet many details point to cultural or historical differences and defy economic interpretations. The stark contrast between English Bristol and Welsh Cardiff is one example. The complex and subtle pattern of changes in voting between 1983 and 1987 is a challenge to all who wish to understand the shifting sands of British politics.

POLITICAL AND CONSTITUENCY FACTORS

Personal votes

In our analysis of the 1979 election, we argued that there was evidence that the ability of MPs to secure a personal vote had grown. The ability of Labour to limit the swing against it in marginal seats could largely be accounted for by the behaviour of constituencies where a new Labour MP had been elected in February or October 1974 and had done so by defeating an incumbent Conservative MP. Personal votes would be most in evidence in such a situation both because the Conservatives would lose any personal vote held by the former MP, and because Labour would gain from any personal support the new MP had established; in consequence the swing to Labour would be less than elsewhere. Further, the incentive to build up such a personal vote through assiduous constituency service was greatest in marginal seats. We estimated that, on the evidence of that election, an MP's personal vote was worth 750 votes in the average marginal constituency.[20]

At the 1983 election, however, a similar analysis of the performance of Conservative MPs first elected in 1979 failed to show any clear evidence of personal voting. We argued that this was because, given the low level of the Labour vote, their remaining supporters would be more likely to be loyal voters and less subject to such considerations. But at this election, it is again evident that personal votes can be secured in marginal seats.

There were 16 constituencies where a Conservative MP was defending a seat originally secured in 1983 in competition with an incumbent Labour MP[21] and where that former Labour MP was not standing again. There are the circumstances most ripe for new personal voting to be evident. In 11 of them the Conservative majority in 1987 was clearly more than would have been expected given the results in adjoining constituencies. Across all 16 the

Conservatives were 4% further ahead of Labour than would have been expected given their geographical location. This implies that on average newly-incumbent Conservative MPs were able to win the support of 1000 people who would otherwise have voted Labour.

The evidence of personal voting is not confined to these instances. We can identify 38 constituencies where a new Conservative MP was also first elected in 1983 in a Conservative/Labour marginal[22] but where for one reason or another, such as the seat not having been wrested from an incumbent Labour MP, the evidence of personal voting is likely to be harder to discern. Again comparing the result with what could otherwise have been expected given the location of the seat, we can find 14 instances where the Conservatives do relatively well compared with only 11 for Labour. In contrast, amongst 20 marginal seats which were not being defended by new Conservative incumbents Labour did relatively well in eight and the Conservatives only in five. In addition, although we have argued that MPs have the greatest incentive to secure a personal vote in a marginal seat, we can find some evidence that personal voting can occur in seats irrespective of their marginality, for we find that in the 43 seats where incumbent Conservative MPs did not stand for re-election, the Conservative performance was 1% lower than would have been expected on the general pattern of movement.[23]

The political significance of personal voting in marginal constituencies lies, of course, in its potential impact in terms of seats. In 1987 it made only a modest but significant impact in enabling the Conservatives to defend successfully a number of marginal seats in the North of England.[24] There are at least six seats (Hyndburn, Batley & Spen, Bolton North-East, Bury North, Keighley and Darlington) which the Conservatives would have either undoubtedly lost, or would at best seriously struggled to defend, without the strong personal vote which was manifest; in addition there are one or two other cases where it is impossible to be sure exactly how crucial the role of personal voting was.

What the election results undoubtedly confirmed was the importance of personal votes to Liberal and Nationalist support. The most dramatic instance was the Western Isles where Donald Stewart's decision to stand down precipitated a 26% drop in SNP support, the highest change recorded by any party at the election. But there was also a systematic incumbency effect amongst Alliance candidates. Of the 23 Alliance MPs elected in 1983, 20 were standing again. Thirteen of them had been elected for the first time before 1983; the average change in their share of the vote was −2.9%, close to the national norm. But amongst the seven who had first been elected in 1983, the Alliance rose by 1.5% with five of the seven clearly doing better than average. Meanwhile, in the three constituencies where the MP elected in 1983 was not standing again, the Alliance vote fell by an average of 7.5%. Evidently, in those three seats some of the personal support for the previous MP was lost, and indeed two of the seats, Colne Valley and the Isle of Wight were captured by the Conservatives. In contrast, most of the Alliance MPs defending their seats for the first time had succeeded in building up their personal support during their first parliamentary term.

At the 1983 election, many of the SDP MPs who contested constituencies they had won as Conservative or Labour candidates in 1979[25] achieved large increases over the previous Liberal share of the vote, although only four secured re-election. These personal votes for SDP defectors proved to be an ephemeral asset. In nine cases where the SDP defector did not stand again (excluding two where the Alliance vote was divided between Liberal and SDP candidates in 1983), the Alliance vote fell on average by 8.7% and by over 9% in all but two. Of the four defeated defectors who stood again, three fared almost as badly, Jim Wellbeloved in Erith & Crayford losing 9.6% of the vote, Bob Mitchell in Southampton Itchen, 7.9%, and Christopher Brocklebank-Fowler 5.7% in Norfolk North-West. The only candidate to buck the tide was George Cunningham in Islington South, whose vote increased by 2.8%, assisted by a tactical squeeze on the Conservatives in the most marginal Labour/Alliance seat in the country (see further, p. 340).

Tactical voting

The 1983 election result, together with some of the by-election results of the 1983–7 parliament, stimulated greater interest in tactical voting than ever before. It was argued that the Conservatives were only able to win a majority of 144 on just 42% of the vote because the 'opposition' vote was split between Labour and the Alliance. If the 'anti-Thatcher' vote in each Conservative-held constituency could be mobilised behind whichever of the Labour or Alliance candidates could best defeat the Conservative, then Mrs Thatcher could be denied a third overall majority. Clear tactical voting in such by-elections as West Derbyshire and Ryedale suggested the willingness of Labour voters at least to switch to a strong Alliance candidate. These considerations led not only certain newspaper commentators such as Alan Watkins of *The Observer*, and John Lloyd, the editor of the *New Statesman*, to advocate tactical voting, but also to pressure group activity under the banner TV87, who campaigned for anti-Conservative tactical voting (see pp. 97–8).

Tactical voting is not a new phenomenon; it has been clearly evident in some form at every election since 1959.[26] Thus in a number of constituencies, in particular amongst those where the Alliance was already a strong challenger to the Conservatives before 1983, the third party vote had already been squeezed, and much further tactical voting was unlikely. But how successful were the attempts to stimulate more widespread tactical voting?

We can get a first impression from Table A2.10, which analyses the results in the two halves of Britain according to which party was in first place in 1983 and which second. First of all, however, we should note that in Table A2.10, and in the rest of this discussion about tactical voting, certain constituencies are excluded. These are those where either the Scottish or Welsh Nationalists won over 20% of the vote in 1983, thereby creating a distinctive tactical situation, those where an incumbent Alliance MP had been defeated in 1983,[27] and those constituencies where a by-election since 1983 had drastically altered the tactical situation.[28] These seats are dealt with on pp. 339–41 below.

Table A2.10 clearly suggests that some voters were influenced by the tactical situation. On average, in both North/West Britain and South/East

Table A2.10   Tactical situation

| First/Second | Mean change in % of vote 1983–87 | | | No. of seats |
	Con.	Lab.	Alln.	
North/West Britain				
Con./Lab.	−0.7	+6.5	−5.7	(41)
Con./Alln	−2.5	+3.9	−1.4	(49)
Lab./Con.	−2.8	+7.1	−4.9	(99)
South/East Britain				
Con./Lab.	+2.3	+2.5	−4.2	(79)
Con./Alln	+0.6	+1.3	−1.7	(192)
Lab./Con.	+1.7	+1.2	−2.6	(5)

Britain, the Alliance was best able to defend its share of the vote in seats where it started off second to the Conservatives, and least able to do so in Conservative seats where Labour were second. Labour did better in Conservative held seats where it started off second than where it began in third place. The differences are not large but at the margin there does appear to have been some concentration of the 'anti-Thatcher' vote.

But in practice the story is more complicated than this. For example, as Table A2.10 also reveals, not only did Labour do better in Conservative/Labour seats but so also did the Conservatives. Further, the variation in Labour and Alliance performance is more marked in North/West Britain than in South/East Britain. In order to unravel the pattern of anti-Conservative tactical voting we will first of all look in detail at the pattern in Conservative/Alliance seats and then look at Conservative/Labour seats.

The influence of the tactical situation upon the propensity of Labour voters to switch to the Alliance is very clear in Table A2.11. In that table we divide the Conservative/Alliance seats according to how far the Alliance were ahead of the third-placed Labour candidate in 1983. While it is true that this statistic is related to the size of the Conservative majority (the greater the gap between Alliance and Labour, the lower the gap between the Conservatives and the Alliance), it appears that the willingness of Labour voters to defect was dependent more on how hopeless their party's situation was, than on how close the Alliance was to winning. This was particularly evident in the three-party marginals where the lead of both the Conservatives over the Alliance and of the Alliance over Labour was low. Thus in four seats, Clwyd South-West, Strathkelvin & Bearsden, Renfrew West & Inverclyde and Edinburgh South, Labour was able to come through strongly from third place to victory, actually squeezing the Alliance in the process.

While the evidence of tactical voting is clear, it is also apparent that its incidence varies between the two parts of the country. In North/West Britain there is a much stronger relationship between the hopelessness of Labour's position and their supporters willingness to vote tactically than in South/East Britain. In South/East Britain the incidence of new tactical voting was patchy;

Table A2.11   Conservative/Alliance seats

| Alliance lead over Lab. (%) | Mean change in % of vote 1983–87 | | | No. of seats |
	Con.	Lab.	Alln	
North/West Britain				
0–5	−2.5	+6.0	−3.9	(14)
5–10	−2.6	+3.7	−1.1	(15)
10–15	−2.3	+3.6	−0.7	(9)
15–20	−2.5	+2.3	+0.5	(6)
Over 20	−2.7	+0.9	+1.5	(5)
South/East Britain				
0–5	−0.0	+2.3	−2.2	(24)
5–10	+1.9	+0.8	−2.4	(34)
10–15	+0.7	+1.3	−1.7	(39)
15–20	+0.1	+1.2	−1.3	(44)
Over 20	+0.4	+1.2	−1.4	(51)

it tended to occur only where the Alliance had established a strong local government as well as a parliamentary base (for example, Cheltenham, Southend West, Bath and Folkestone). The Alliance was also less successful than were the Liberals in the 1974 and 1979 elections in squeezing Labour systematically in seats where they had secured second place for the first time at the previous election. In contrast, in North/West Britain the pattern of tactical voting was systematic. Of those seats where the Alliance began more than 10% ahead of Labour, there was only one (Clwyd North-West) where the Labour vote showed no sign of being squeezed.

One point we should, however, note is that the differences in tactical situation in the two halves of the country are correlated with the social and geographical variations in performance we have already identified. Those seats in North/West Britain where Labour's position was weakest all had a low proportion of skilled workers. Within South/East Britain Labour's weak third places are mostly outside the London Metropolitan Area. The seats where the Alliance apparently squeezed Labour were therefore ones where they could be expected to do well for reasons other than the tactical situation. But the differences in Table A2.11 are still present even if we take these factors into account. If in North/West Britain we examine the residuals from a regression of skilled workers on the change in Alliance vote, we find they are, on average, positive in Labour's weak seats.[29] Meanwhile, if in South/East Britain we replicate the analysis of Table A2.11 for the London Metropolitan Area and the rest of South/East Britain separately, the existence of a small tactical squeeze in Labour's weak seats is still apparent.

Turning to Conservative/Labour seats we can see from Table A2.12 that the Alliance was squeezed most in those seats where Labour was closest to the Conservatives. The Alliance performance was worse in both parts of the country where the 1983 Conservative majority was less than 15%. But again, the pattern was both stronger and more consistent in North/West Britain than in South/East Britain. There were only 5 seats in North/West Britain where the 1983 Conservative lead over Labour was less than 15% and where the Alliance vote fell by less than 5%:[30] in South/East Britain there were 19 seats. These differences cannot simply be accounted for by the Alliance's generally stronger performance in parts of South/East Britain. As in Conservative/Alliance seats, the Alliance's ability to defend its vote was noticeably better in seats such as Hyndburn, Pendle, Bolton West, Birmingham Yardley and Norwich South, where it had recently done well in local government elections.[31]

Table A2.12   Conservative/Labour seats

	Mean change in % of vote 1983–87			
Con. majority 1983 (%)	*Con.*	*Lab.*	*Alln.*	*No. of seats*
North/West Britain				
Less than 15%	+0.0	+6.4	−6.2	(30)
Over 15%	−2.5	+6.9	−4.4	(11)
South/East Britain				
Less than 15%	+3.2	+2.2	−4.9	(42)
Over 15%	+1.3	+2.8	−3.6	(37)

But if the Alliance was squeezed in Conservative/Labour marginals, who benefited? One of the difficulties faced by the tactical voting campaign was that, in opinion surveys, as many Alliance supporters preferred the Conservatives as their second choice party as did Labour. A squeeze on the Alliance could help the Conservatives as much as Labour. Indeed, Table A2.12 would appear to suggest that the Conservatives were the beneficiaries. It is the Conservatives who do better in Conservative/Labour marginals, not Labour.

Our difficulty here is that we have to attempt to disentangle two possible effects. One is that Alliance voters voted for their second choice party because of the tactical situation. The other is that, in building up personal votes, new Conservative incumbents won over Alliance and/or Labour supporters. As the majority of Conservative/Labour marginals were being defended by new Conservative incumbents, the impact of any tactical switch from Alliance to Labour could have been counteracted by the incumbency effect.

Close examination of the result in each constituency does, however, allow us to draw two important, albeit somewhat tentative, conclusions. First, if we examine the results in the small number of seats where no incumbency effect could be expected to operate and compare them with the rest, we see a striking difference in the balance of advantage. Amongst the seats not being defended by a new Conservative incumbent, and where the Alliance vote fell by more than 5%, there were only two seats where the Conservatives did better than could have been expected given the results in neighbouring seats, but five where Labour did so. In contrast, in those seats where the new Conservative incumbent had defeated a Labour incumbent in 1983 and where the Alliance was squeezed, there were 14 where the Conservatives did better than could have been expected, and only four where Labour did so. It seems likely therefore that Labour were the net beneficiaries of tactical voting by Alliance voters, but in many constituencies this was negated by the incumbency effect. If this conclusion is correct it would suggest that the tactical voting campaign did have an impact upon the behaviour of some Alliance supporters. Certainly, this is the first election since 1964 at which there has been any evidence that a squeeze on the Liberals/Alliance disproportionately favoured Labour.

Secondly, in the same way that tactical switching from Labour to Alliance was more prevalent in North/West Britain than in South/East Britain, so also was switching from Alliance to Labour. Amongst all Conservative/Labour marginals in which the Alliance vote was squeezed, there were nine in South/East Britain where the Conservatives did better than could have been expected, and eight where Labour did so. In North/West Britain the equivalent figures are six and nine. Further, nowhere in North/West Britain did the Conservatives do better than could be expected where they were not the potential beneficiaries of an incumbency effect. North/West Britain exhibited a clear tide of anti-Conservative sentiment. Not only did the Conservative vote fall, but Alliance and Labour voters were much more prepared to switch tactically to whichever candidate was best able to defeat a sitting Conservative MP.

However, the clearest example of tactical voting against the Conservatives lies not in any of the situations we have discussed so far, but in seats where there was potential for an Alliance squeeze on a Nationalist candidate or vice versa. This was most evident in the Scottish seats with a strong SNP vote (more than 20% in 1983). Of the seven such seats defended by Conservatives, the Nationalists started the election ahead of the Alliance in five and behind in two. In the former group the SNP vote rose by 6.5% while the Alliance fell back by 6.2%; by contrast, in the latter the Alliance vote rose by 8.4% while the Nationalist vote fell by 4.4%. Elsewhere in Scotland there was less scope for a tactical squeeze on the SNP because of its low vote in 1983, but it is noticeable that, in the six Conservative seats secured by Labour, the SNP vote only rose by 0.5%.

In rural Wales, Plaid Cymru's performance was also influenced by the tactical situation in Conservative-held constituencies. Their capture of Ynys Môn owed little to any Conservative collapse in the wake of Keith Best's resignation (see p. 196), and more to their success in preventing the Labour vote from increasing and in squeezing the already depleted Alliance vote. The Liberals, meanwhile, managed to squeeze the Plaid Cymru vote in the one constituency (Conwy) where they were the clear challengers to the Conservatives, and there was something of a Nationalist vote left to squeeze.

Although most attention was given during the campaign to the possibility that anti-Conservative tactical voting might bring about the loss of Conservative seats, this was not its only possible role. Tactical voting could also influence the distribution of seats between the opposition parties if Conservative voters switched tactically to the Alliance in seats where their party was third. And indeed the fall in the Conservative vote was clearly greater than in neighbouring constituencies in at least four of the five Alliance/Labour seats (Glasgow Hillhead, Woolwich, Southwark & Bermondsey and Rochdale), and in all five constituencies where the Alliance had been within 10% of Labour in 1983. The one seat where Conservative voters did not switch was Leeds West which was unsuccessfully defended by the left-wing Liberal MP, Michael Meadowcroft.

But although the tactical voting campaign made some impression, its overall impact upon the election result was limited. The Conservative majority was only slightly dented. Just one Labour gain is clearly attributable to tactical voting (Oxford East) while its precise importance is debatable in only two or three other cases. But in the battle between the Conservatives and third parties it was more important. Every one of the seven Alliance and Nationalist gains was at least in part assisted by tactical voting, and without it the Alliance might have lost Montgomery to the Conservatives. It was the greater prevalence of tactical voting in North/West Britain that accounts for the paradox that the Alliance made its only gains (Southport, Fife North-East and Argyll & Bute) in that part of the country where they were doing less well. But its concentration in that part of the country was overall a disadvantage to the Alliance for, as Table A2.11 above indicates, there were far fewer Conservative-held seats in North/West Britain where the Alliance was clearly ahead of Labour (or could benefit from a squeeze on the Nationalists), than in South/East Britain. But even if this had not been the case, the election result suggested that any tactical voting campaign is only likely to have a limited impact upon the distribution of seats. Too few voters are readily prepared to switch their votes in the desired direction at a general election. The Conservatives will only lose their majority in future if there is also an overall change in the distribution of party support.

Of the 16 by-elections held during the 1983–7 parliament, 13 saw a substantial increase in the Alliance vote of 7% or more (see p. 312). What happened in these by-election results clearly affected the parties' general election performance in those seats, though in all but one the Alliance fell back from its 1983 position. But a by-election was more likely to influence the general election result if it had changed the tactical situation. In every seat the Alliance's progress at the by-election had been more at the Conservatives' expense, and the Conservatives' ability to regain their support was noticeably weaker in four seats in which they had consequently slipped to third place (Brecon & Radnor, Greenwich, Chesterfield and Newcastle-under-Lyme), where their vote was still down by an average of 10.3% compared with 1983. In the other nine seats their support was only down by 2.2%. Continued Conservative support enabled the Alliance to retain Greenwich and Brecon & Radnor.

Ironically, in the one seat where the Alliance improved upon its by-election vote, it was to no avail. In Portsmouth South Mike Hancock won a further 5.2% of the vote. He did so by squeezing Labour, whose support was 13.7%

down on the by-election and 9.6% down on the 1983 result. Labour also fell back noticeably in Derbyshire West (−8.1% on the by-election and −5.4% on the general election) which the Alliance had lost by just 100 votes. Elsewhere, where the by-election left Labour voters less reason to switch their support, the apparent Labour squeeze was only 1 or 2%

Ethnic and Left-Wing candidates

A record number of 28 ethnic minority candidates stood for the main parties at this election of which four, three black and one Asian, were elected. All four new MPs, the first ethnic minority MPs elected since 1924, were returned as Labour MPs, and, with 14, Labour had the largest number of such candidates. The results also confirmed the evidence of the 1983 election that Labour ethnic minority candidates do not necessarily suffer from discrimination, while those standing for the Alliance do. But unlike 1983, ethnic minority Conservative candidates were more likely to suffer the same fate as Alliance rather than Labour candidates.

Of the eight black or brown Alliance candidates, all did worse than they should have done. On average their vote fell by 7.7%. The reverse effect can be seen in the eight constituencies which had a black or brown Alliance candidate in 1983, but a white one in 1987. In five of the eight cases the Alliance rose this time, with an average change of −0.4%. The Conservatives only put up three ethnic minority candidates in 1983 and six in 1987, one of whom was standing again for the same seat as in 1983, so the evidence is more limited. But in four of the seats where a new ethnic minority candidate stood, the Conservative share of the vote was 2 or 3% below what would have been anticipated from the results in neighbouring constituencies. However, Nirj Deva in Hammersmith, the first Conservative ethnic minority candidate to stand in a constituency that was even remotely winnable, increased his party's share of the vote (+2.6%) in line with the local movement.

The contrast with Labour candidates' experience is clear. Not that ethnic minority Labour candidates generally did particularly well – 8 of the 13 who were standing in a constituency for the first time (one stood in the same seat as in 1983) did 2% or more worse than could have been expected, given the general geographical pattern of movement, although in three cases, tactical or incumbency effects could well account for the deficit. But the fate of the remaining five showed that Labour candidates need not necessarily suffer discrimination. Indeed, Keith Vaz in Leicester East secured a remarkably good result, gaining a Conservative seat with the third best increase in the Labour vote in South/East Britain. Further, in none of the five seats fought by ethnic minority candidates in 1983, but by white ones in 1987, did Labour's share of the vote recover unusually well.

But amongst those Labour candidates, whose skin colour does appear to have mattered, were two who had achieved widespread publicity for their left-wing views and who had wrested the local Labour nomination from the incumbent MP. In Tottenham, Bernie Grant suffered the largest fall in the Labour share of the vote in the country (−8.4%) (excluding seats where a by-election result affected the Labour vote); comparison with nearby constituencies suggests he polled about 10% less than he should have. Meanwhile, in Hackney North the first female black MP, Diane Abbott, won about 5% less than she should have.

But a similar fate also befell two left-wing white candidates who had also relaced sitting MPs. Thus both Ken Livingstone in Brent East (−4.4%) and Dawn Primarolo in Bristol South (−3.1%) performed poorly. A similar reaction was evident in two other constituencies, Blyth Valley and Mansfield, where, although the sitting Labour MP had retired voluntarily, he attacked his successor for Militant or hard-left associations. In all four cases the Labour underperformance was of a similar scale to that in Hackney North; only the refusal of nearly a fifth of Labour voters in Tottenham to vote for Mr Grant really stands out.

But outside these limited circumstances there is no evidence of a general unwillingness to vote for left-wing Labour candidates. The Alliance's list of 101 allegedly hard-left Labour candidates (see p. 105) actually did better (+4.9%) than their party's national average (+3.7%). Part of that difference is because the Alliance's list consisted of seats held by Labour or on the party's target list, and these were concentrated in North/West Britain. But if we control for that by comparing each candidate's performance with the relevant subregional change shown in Table A1.2, the 101 still bettered their party's performance by 0.7%. Controlling for other factors we have already identified, such as tactical voting or incumbency, can account for this remaining difference. Thus the 39 sitting MPs on the list improved on the Labour subregional change by 1.4%, but 23 selected to replace incumbents did worse, on the same test, by 1.2% But the fact that incumbency stands out in this way while left-wingedness does not, itself speaks eloquently for how little most Labour voters are concerned about where their candidate stands in their party's internal debate.

Indeed, for every individual case that we have quoted of left-wingers doing particularly badly, the Labour left could quote a counter-example. Both Militant MPs, in Coventry South-East and Liverpool Broadgreen, did well. True, they may both have benefited from a generally good Labour performance in those cities. Yet, arguably, Mr Nellist and Mr Fields form a part of Labour's image in those two cities, while in Liverpool the local Labour party's performance reflected its success in mobilising popular support for its hardline tactics in opposing the government. Labour also did notably well (its second best result among the 32 London boroughs) in Lambeth where, as in Liverpool, its councillors were disqualified and surcharged for their delay in setting a rate.

Labour also did fairly well in two other London boroughs, Camden and Islington, where left-wing Labour control is longstanding. But in three other London boroughs where it gained control in 1986 and had been under attack for controversial policies then adopted, Labour did notably badly. Labour's performance in Waltham Forest, where it had introduced a 62% rate increase, was the worst of any borough in London, in Ealing (65% rate increase) the third worst, and in Brent (a well-publicised row over education policies) the fourth worst. In contrast, in the borough where the introduction of controversial right-wing policies has received the most attention, Wandsworth, the Conservatives performed better than anywhere else south of the river. Here a factor of particular importance, particularly in the surprise Conservative gain of Battersea, was the influx of young middle-class couples seeking cheaper housing, an influx encouraged by the local council's policy of large-scale selling of its municipal housing stock.

There is other evidence from outside London which also suggests that the way that people voted at a general election was influenced by their attitude towards their local council. Labour's performance in the local elections in Coventry in May presaged the good result there in June, and the good Conservative performances in Bradford and Cumbria may also have reflected local governments issues. But the relationship is not necessarily a simple one. Voters may not simply be casting a judgement on their local council, but also be influenced by it. The contrast between Labour's success in its well-established left-wing London boroughs and its new ones could imply that, where a controlling party has had a lengthy period in which to explain its policies, it may actually succeed in winning over votes. Further, in a city like London where individuals have considerable freedom to choose where to live in relation to their work, people may actually gravitate towards boroughs whose policies suit their pockets, social interests or political views. If so, we may see further striking borough-level differences in voting behaviour in future. But whatever their precise cause, these apparent local government influences are further testimony to the denationalisation of British politics.

Liberal and SDP candidates

It was widely noted after the election that, overall, Liberal candidates had performed rather better than SDP candidates. While the Alliance vote fell by an average of 2.7% in Liberal-led constituencies, it fell by 3.6% in SDP-led ones. However, there is no consistent evidence that SDP candidates generally did worse than Liberal candidates in constituencies of the same socio-geographical character and tactical situation.[32] Consider, for example, Conservative/Labour marginals. At a first glance there would appear to be a difference in the two parties' performances. The average fall in the SDP vote in South/East Britain was 5.0%, while the Liberal fall was only 4.5%. In North/West Britain the equivalent figures are 6.0% and 4.7%. But this difference can be accounted for by the fact that the Liberals fought more of the seats in which the Alliance (albeit usually Liberal dominated) had recently done well in local government elections, and where Alliance candidates, irrespective of their party label, generally resisted the squeeze on their vote. Indeed, more generally, the difference between the two parties' performances mainly arises from the fact that the SDP fought more of those seats where Alliance candidates, irrespective of their label, did badly, and the Liberals more of those where they did well. The SDP fought considerably more Conservative/Labour marginals (39) than the Liberals (27), while the Liberal party fought 17 of the 20 Conservative/Alliance seats in North/West Britain where the 1983 Alliance lead over Labour had been more than 10%.

Minor parties and candidates

The 1987 election was the worst ever for Independents and the various tiny parties of British politics. The rise in the deposit (see p. 122) reduced the number who stood and in particular was cited as the reason why the National Front did not contest this election. Apart from the Greens, 92 other candidates polled altogether a mere 34 541 votes, an average of 0.8% each. Only five polled over 2%, the best score (3.6%) going to an Independent in Hartlepool; the other four were all rebels from the main parties, including Independent Labour candidates standing in protest against the selection of left-wingers to replace moderate sitting Labour MPs in Brent East and Mansfield. For the first time in their party's history, none of the 19 Communist candidates standing managed even this modest score: their average (0.8%) continued the CPGB's slow decline.

In this gloom for the British political fringe the slight advance achieved by the Greens (formerly the Ecology Party) shines out. Their vote rose by 0.3% in the 52 seats they fought in both 1983 and 1987 and overall this was the largest vote in the party's brief history.

Table A2.13   The Green vote

	1979	1983	1987
No. of candidates	53	108	133
Total vote	39 918	54 299	89 753
Mean vote (%)	1.5	1.0	1.4

Note: In 1983 and 1987 one Green candidate stood in Northern Ireland.

The Greens polled best in the South-West region (1.8%) while their support was only 1% in every region in North/West Britain. But otherwise there was little regional variation in their vote and, after allowing for what there was, none by social type of constituency. The main cause of variation in their support was clearly whether a vote for one of the main parties was seen to matter. In the 12 seats they contested which had been won in 1983 by less than 5%, the Green vote in 1987 averaged 0.9%; in 32 with a 1983 majority between 5% and 15% they scored 1.2%; and in the remaining 89 the Green vote was 1.5%. Indeed their best vote was in a fairly safe Conservative seat, Weston-super-Mare (3.6%), where their support seems to have come particularly at the Conservatives' expense; it was the Conservatives' fourth worst result in South/East Britain, excluding seats where a by-election had been held. The Greens' biggest increase was in a safe Labour seat, Hackney North (+1.2%), where they were probably assisted by dissatisfaction with the local Labour candidate. So long as they are fighting with the handicap of the British electoral system, the Greens would be well advised to concentrate on safe seats.

TURNOUT

Turnout rose by 2.6% to 75.3%, just below the 1979 level but typical of British turnout figures over the last quarter of a century. In sharp contrast to the regional pattern of voting movements, the increased willingness to vote was much the same across the country: in all but one of the 24 subregions listed in Table A1.2, the rise in turnout was between 2.1% and 3.8%. The only exception was the Scottish Highlands (+0.8%). Even when we examine small geographical clusters of constituencies throughout Britain, the rise is almost always close to the national figure: in only one county did turnout rise by more than 5% (South Glamorgan, 5.6%). Overall, the standard deviation of the change in turnout in individual constituencies was only 1.5. This consistency suggest that there was a nationwide cause for the increase in turnout. Perhaps, despite the eventual result, there was significantly greater uncertainty over the outcome of the election than in 1983.

Some such explanation is certainly suggested by the variation that did exist at constituency level. Much of this is clearly the result of changes in the uncertainty of local outcomes. Many marginal seats had, of course, been marginal seats before, but turnout often jumped by three or four points more than it did nationally where boundary change in 1983 had created a new marginal (for example, Batley & Spen) or where there had been an unexpected by-election result since 1983 (for example, Ryedale). Conversely the biggest drop in turnout since 1983 took place in a new safe seat, Preston, which was carved out of what had been for the previous 33 years two classic marginals.

Increased political awareness also produced higher turnout. The clearest example is mining constituencies which used, in the 1950s, to have the highest turnout in the country but where, from 1966 onwards, turnout has been declining at an above-average rate. In 1987 the passions felt on both sides of the dispute amongst the miners over the 1984–5 strike were evident. In the 18 constituencies with over 15% employment in mining,[33] turnout rose 4.4% on average and in the nine with over 20% employment it jumped 5.2% As a result, turnout in mining seats is now once again higher than the national average, even though most are safe seats; turnout in 1987 averaged 76.5% in the 33 constituencies with most mining. It is noteworthy that this rise in voting occurred in both Arthur Scargill's Yorkshire bastion and in the Nottinghamshire stronghold of opposition to his leadership of the strike. Mansfield, the headquarters of the Notts miners, had the third biggest rise in turnout in Britain, whilst Hemsworth and Barnsley East, the two most solidly mining Yorkshire constituencies, lay seventh and fifteenth in that league table.

Local political controversy also probably explains another of the biggest rises in turnout, in Folkestone & Hythe, which is the constituency most affected by the proposed excavation of a Channel Tunnel. The extra voters here seem to have favoured the Alliance. There is evidence that this may be part of a general pattern in South/East Britain, viz., that the Alliance held its ground best when turnout increased most: the change in turnout correlates positively (0.29) with the change in the Alliance vote, and negatively by smaller amounts with both Conservative and Labour change (0.21 and 0.13).

In Britain as a whole turnout rose by 4% on average in the 24 seats where the Alliance vote went up by 5% or more. In contrast, turnout fell or only rose slightly in a number of seats where the Alliance did particularly well in 1983; in the 23 seats won by the Alliance in 1983, turnout rose on average by only 1.3%. This suggests that there was a waning of enthusiasm for the Alliance in some of its stronger areas, which was counterbalanced by the ability of Alliance candidates with a by-election victory, a local issue, or simply a strong campaign behind them, to attract more people to come out and vote.

However, there is no evidence that the Conservatives achieved any consistent advantage over Labour where there was a higher turnout in South/East Britain, or vice versa, or of any relationship between turnout change and party performance in North/West Britain. The million extra people who came out to vote in 1987 can have had almost no effect on the results.

Finally, there is a puzzling feature to turnout change in London. Greater London contributed five out of the 11 biggest drops in turnout, all from just two boroughs; conversely, it contained five out of the 13 biggest rises in turnout, including all of the seats in two boroughs. The overall turnout changes in the London boroughs concerned were:

Barnet	−0.9
Ealing	−0.8
Islington	+7.0
Kingston	+6.8
Westminster	+6.7

We can find no political or social pattern in these figures. This fact, together with the borough-wide, rather than constituency level, character of these deviations suggests that they reflect variations in the quality of the electoral register rather than variations in peoples' willingness to turn out.

Electoral registration is a London borough responsibility, and in a conurbation where multi-occupation and a more rapid turnover in occupancy makes compiling an accurate register more difficult,[34] there is considerable scope for local variations in practice, and thus for changes of practice when new officials take charge of electoral registration departments or local councils initiate new policies. Further, the variations and changes which do occur are more likely to have a significant effect on the proportion of eligible people who get on to the register and on the proportion of names on the register which should not be there. One London borough, Haringey, has recently made an exhaustive effort to improve its register, with the result that the registered electorate of the borough increased by more than a tenth between 1983 and 1987. Its turnout rose by a typical 2.3%, but of the five boroughs we have identified with unusually large rises or falls in turnout, Ealing, where turnout fell, had the second largest increase in electorate, while amongst those boroughs with large increases in turnout, Westminster had by far the biggest drop in electorate and Kingston the biggest drop in Outer London. The change in the official turnout figures in these boroughs must reflect changes in the way the register was compiled, as well as in the true level of participation.

The accuracy of the electoral register not only affects the right of people to vote; it is the basis upon which the parliamentary boundary commissions allocate seats and, internally to each borough, the local government boundary commission determines ward boundaries. It also affects the estimates of population used in the calculation of the rate support grant to local authorities. These striking illustrations of how apparently unreliable the electoral register is, confirms the need for a thorough review of the procedures used in its compilation, particularly in London (see also p. 118).[35]

NORTHERN IRELAND

The election in Northern Ireland was once again an entirely separate event from that in Great Britain. It was also, to a degree unusual even by Ulster standards, a series of distinct local battles for one of the regular province-wide encounters, that between the two Unionist parties, was cancelled. The Official Unionist Party (OUP) and the Democratic Unionist Party (DUP) agreed an electoral pact which gave a free run to each other's sitting MPs. This, like the collective resignation of all Unionist MPs, and the similar pact at the consequent 15 by-elections in January 1986 (shown in Table A1.7 on pp. 314–15), was designed to demonstrate Unionist unity and determination in face of the Anglo-Irish Agreement. A necessary effect of the pact is to rule out any meaningful comparison of the performance of the rival Unionist parties with previous elections; hence in Table A1.4 (p. 310) we only show figures for change since 1983 for all candidates grouped together.

This contributed to a drop in turnout from 72.8% to 67.4%, which was by a small margin the lowest level of turnout in the province since 1966, the last Westminster election before the current outbreak of sectarian strife. Although the tightening of the rules designed to prevent personation may also have reduced recorded turnout, it seems clear that there was a modest level of loyalist abstention. The Unionist share of the vote dropped by 2.5%, while the combined share of the votes for Republican parties (35.5%) was higher than at any previous Westminster election. But the percentage of the electorate voting Republican was, at 23.9%, barely changed from 1983 (24.2%). The equivalent Unionist percentage was, however, 4.8% lower than in 1983.

The importance of turnout to party fortunes is clearly seen if we look at the results in four seats that in some way bucked the general trend. In two seats, Newry & Armagh and South Down, turnout actually rose; these were the only two Unionist/SDLP marginals in this election. Despite this increase in turnout, the Unionist share of the vote fell in these seats also. But in Fermanagh & South Tyrone and Mid-Ulster, the Unionist share of the vote increased, despite a sharp fall in turnout. These were two seats where a previously winning Republican position had been rendered hopeless thanks to a split in the vote. It seems likely that in the first two constituencies

Catholic voters were encouraged by the political situation to turn out and vote, while in the latter two they were similarly discouraged.

But in one constituency, North Down, the Unionist pact did not hold. Although not a member of either the OUP or the DUP, the pact was regarded by the two party leaders as extending to the incumbent unionist MP, James Kilfedder, leader of the Ulster Popular Unionist Party (in practice a personal organisation of local supporters). The local branch of the OUP voted, however, to nominate Robert McCartney, who as the OUP candidate in 1983, had come third behind the Alliance candidate, and who had strongly attacked the Unionist leadership's tactics over the Anglo-Irish Agreement, opposing in particular the policy of abstention from Westminster. The OUP executive expelled both Mr McCartney and the local association, but Mr McCartney was nominated as a 'real Unionist', favouring a policy of closer integration of Northern Ireland politics with that of the mainland under the aegis of the Campaign for Equal Citizenship.[36]

This highly publicised squabble turned North Down, normally the safest and most predictable of seats, into a cockpit of inter-Unionist strife. In a situation unique in recent Westminster elections, the contest in the constituency was dominated by two candidates, neither of whom had the backing of a real party organisation. Yet it was the only contest that gave the Unionist electorate the opportunity to pass judgement on one of the central issues of the day, the Unionist leaders' response to the Anglo-Irish Agreement. For Mr McCartney's stance gave the Unionist electorate in North Down the chance to cast a vote of censure on the Unionist leaders. Mr Kilfedder was re-elected, but by the smallest majority in his career (9.7%), while the rise in Mr McCartney's vote since he last fought the seat (as OUP candidate) was, at 15.1%, the second biggest increase achieved by any candidate in the United Kingdom.

Meanwhile within the Nationalist electorate, an entirely different battle was taking place. In the 1982 Northern Ireland Assembly elections, Sinn Fein had put up candidates for the first time,[37] taking 32% of the votes cast for the three republican parties. At the 1983 Westminister election, following what it claimed as the success of its tactics over the hunger strikes, it advanced this score to 40%, and appeared to be making an effective challenge to the SDLP's claim to speak for the Nationalist community. Elections held subsequent to 1983 had given equivocal signals as to whether the SDLP was holding back Sinn Fein's advance. In the 1984 European parliamentary elections, the Sinn Fein candidate polled exactly the same share of the overall votes cast as his party had in 1983, but his share of the Republican vote sank to 36%. The cause was a peculiarly Northern Irish form of tactical voting, as Catholic Alliance voters switched to the SDLP candidate John Hume, in order to put him well ahead of, and thus put down, Sinn Fein. The 1985 local elections saw Sinn Fein making a big gain in seats (it had not fought them four years earlier), but the SDLP holding its own.

But at the 1986 by-elections there was clear evidence of a reversal of its fortunes. In the four constituencies fought by the two main Republican parties, Sinn Fein's share of the vote fell by an average of 5.1%, while the SDLP's rose by 5.6%. As Table A1.4 shows, the 1987 votes largely confirmed that message. Sinn Fein lost ground; on average its vote was 1.9% lower than in 1983. The Republican vote was shared 60.6% for the SDLP to 32.1% for Sinn Fein, with the rest going to the Workers' Party, which improved its vote a little in most seats. Indeed, in three of the four contested by-election seats, the SDLP extended its 1986 advance. But Sinn Fein's discomfiture was confined to the Catholic areas along the border. In working-class Catholic parts of Belfast, Sinn Fein held its own, and the SDLP signally failed to recapture its former seat in West Belfast, which it had lost in 1983 because its former leader split the moderate Nationalist vote.

The SDLP's success in concentrating the Catholic vote had its greatest impact in Newry & Armagh and South Down. Both were won by Unionists in 1983, thanks to a split in the Republican vote. But the SDLP established a clear lead over Sinn Fein, and won the first of the two seats at the 1986 by-elections. By 1987 Sinn Fein's support had halved in the two constituencies and the Workers' Party was also clearly squeezed. With this transfer (and the apparent increase in Catholic turnout discussed above), the SDLP took both seats, and the Commons career of one of Westminster's most notable figures, Enoch Powell, was brought to an end.

Meanwhile, the Alliance Party of Northern Ireland fought a lone battle across the province for votes from both communities. It, too, was squeezed in the two Unionist/SDLP marginals, and also in North Down. But elsewhere the Alliance vote rose, and its overall share, 9.9%, was the best it had achieved at any sort of election in Northern Ireland since 1979.

Thus the results brought some comfort for each of the two parties, the SDLP and APNI, which had accepted the Anglo-Irish Agreement. The message of dissatisfaction with their leaders among the loyalist electorate expressed in the North Down result, the abstention of some of them and the loss of two seats was clear; the two Unionist parties duly embarked on a re-appraisal of their strategy of opposition to the Agreement. Westminster elections in Northern Ireland only incidentally fulfil the role of choosing 17 members of the House of Commons; they function rather as part of a series of tests which the situation and their supporters impose on Northern Irish parties and politicians. The 1987 election served to bring out more clearly the dilemma facing Ulster Unionism.

THE ELECTORAL SYSTEM

The scale of the Conservative victory, a lead of 157 seats over Labour, and an overall majority in the House of Commons of 102, took most observers by surprise. The main reason for this was that the Conservative lead over Labour in votes (11.8% of the vote in Great Britain) was a little higher than most opinion polls had anticipated, though well within their margin of error. The attempts to translate opinion poll figures, whether from the whole electorate or from varying selections of marginal seats, into the distribution of seats in the House of Commons were also subject to little realised pitfalls. In this section we start by examining how, given the votes cast, the seats should have been distributed if the shift of party fortunes since 1983 had been uniform across constituencies, and then go on to show what factors caused the deviations from that projection which actually occurred. We then turn to longer-term questions about the operation of the electoral system.

Projecting the likely composition of the House of Commons on the basis of an individual constituency result, as has, for example, become habitual to make from by-election rsults, assumes that the changes in party support will be uniform in every constituency across the country or, more realistically, that the variation that does occur will not be systematically correlated with the previous distribution of party support. But projecting the distribution of seats from an opinion poll result involves a further, less well understood assumption, namely, that the variation in the change in party support is not correlated with differences in the sizes of constituency electorates or turnout. If a party does systematically better or worse in seats with smaller electorates and/or lower turnouts, then the change in its share of the vote in the average constituency will not be the same as the change in its share of the overall total vote.

Indeed, as reference back to Table A2.1 shows, there was a significant difference between the mean and the overall change in both the Conservative and the Labour share of the vote. The mean fall in the Conservative vote was higher than the overall, while the mean Labour increase was greater than the overall. This has happened at most recent elections. Labour has tended to perform better in those parts of the country with lower electorates and lower turnouts. Lower turnouts tend to occur in urban areas, and thus the lack of a clear urban/rural divide at this election means that the correlation between turnout and party performance is only weak. While Labour did do slightly better in constituencies with lower turnouts than in those with high ones, the Conservative performance shows no correlation with the level of turnout.[38]

At this election it is the relation between party performance and electorate size which is important. As Table A2.14 shows, Labour's vote increased much more sharply in those constituencies with below average electorates than in those with above average ones. In contrast, while the Conservatives held their support in above-average, sized constituencies, it fell in those of below-average size.

Table A2.14 Change in vote by electorate size

Electorate size	Con.	Lab.	Alln.	No. of seats
Over 20% below average	−3.3	+6.0	−3.1	(57)
Up to 20% below average	−1.0	+5.0	−3.9	(240)
Up to 20% above average	+0.1	+2.6	−2.5	(296)
Over 20% above average	+0.9	+1.5	−2.2	(40)

Note: The average constituency contains 66 496 electors.

This pattern is a clear consequence of the geography of the vote. The average constituency in North/West Britain is smaller than that in South/East Britain. In part this reflects the rules laid down by parliament which ensures the overrepresentation of Scotland (average 1987 electorate: 54 895) and Wales (56 614). But it is also true that, because the rate of population growth is slower in the North of England than elsewhere, by 1987 the average North of England constituency (67 182 electors) was smaller than the average South/East Britain constituency (69 543 electors). Indeed, but for the strength of the Conservative performance in Greater London, where the interpretation of the rules by the Boundary Commission produced a substantial overrepresentation (average 1987 electorate, 60 850), the correlation between party performance and electorate size would have been even greater.

If then we wish to see how far the relationship between seats and votes fitted the expectations of a model of uniform change, it is the mean constituency figures we should use rather than the overall. The latter are distorted by the inequality of electorates. If the country had moved uniformally in line with the mean changes, the Conservatives would have have won 374 seats, Labour 237 and the Alliance and the Nationalists together, 22. The Conservatives thus won just two more seats than could have been expected, but Labour won eight less and the third parties, six more. The deviations came from two sources. First, fewer seats transferred from Conservative to Labour than predicted. Secondly, the third parties' maintained their representation at the Conservatives' expense. These two effects largely cancelled each other out so far at the Conservatives were concerned, but left the balance between the opposition parties less favourable to Labour.

On a uniform shift, 26 seats should have switched from Conservative to Labour.[39] In fact, Labour took only 14 of these. Labour did win eight seats that should not have fallen, but also actually lost five to the Conservatives. Thus, overall, Labour made 17 net gains from the Conservatives, a shortfall of nine, and 25 seats were won by the 'wrong' party – 17 by the Conservatives and eight by Labour. All eight of Labour's unexpected gains were in North/West Britain and 15 of the 17 excess Tory seats were in South/East Britain. It might seem from this that it was the regional variation in party performance which caused the expected seats/votes relationship to break down.

But this is not in fact so. For if we take that variation systematically into account by calculating what would have happened if all seats in South/East Britain had moved in line with the mean changes in that part of the country (shown in Table A2.3 above), while seats in North/West Britain moved in line with their regional average, we find that Labour should have gained 25 Conservative seats (24 in North/West Britain and just one, Leicester South, in South/East Britain), only one less than if the changes were nationally uniform. Contrary to much speculation during the campaign, the regional variation alone would have had no significant outcome on the distribution of seats.

Labour's deficit can, in fact, be accounted for by variations in party performance within North/West Britain. In South/East Britain there was no net transfer of seats (five Labour gains from Conservative were matched by five losses), more or less as the uniform change model predicted. But in North/West Britain, nine Conservative MPs held seats that should have fallen to Labour, while Labour secured only one excess seat. The main reason for these Conservative successes was the incumbency effect. All nine successful defendants were newly elected in 1983, and seven had replaced incumbent Labour MPs. However, as six of the nine were in Cumbria, Greater Manchester or West Yorkshire, where the Conservatives showed some general tendency to do a little better, local variations in party performance may also have played some part.

So far as the excess third party representation is concerned, the systematic tatical voting in North/West Britain was the clear explanation. Altogether on a uniform movement, the Alliance ought to have lost five seats and the Nationalists stayed at four. Three of the Alliance losses should have been to the Conservatives, two to Labour. In the event the Alliance and the Nationalists lost eight seats but (including holding two by-election gains) gained another nine, producing a net gain of one rather than the anticipated loss of five. But all but one of those unexpected gains was from the Conservatives who, overall, suffered a net loss of four seats rather a net gain of three. This deficit of seven seats matches exactly the number of Conservative losses which, as we showed earlier (p. 340), could be ascribed to tactical switching by Labour, Alliance and Nationalist supporters, in favour of the anti-Tory candidate best-placed to defeat the local Conservative.

The lower than expected Alliance loss of seats was also matched by a more favourable distribution of its vote. The Liberal party, and subsequently the Alliance, has long been penalised by the electoral system for the even geographical spread of its vote, but in 1987 its vote was a little more concentrated than in 1983. The standard deviation of the Alliance vote rose from 7.3 to 8.9. In those seats where the Alliance share of the vote was over 30% in 1983, it fell by only 1.5%, whereas in those where it started off with under 25%, the fall was 4.1%. Were this to be the start of a new trend, produced perhaps by a steady growth of tactical voting or the growth of support in one particular part of the country, it could improve the Alliance's ability to convert its popular vote into seats.

However, the Liberals also tended to be more successful in retaining their vote in their stronger areas in October 1974 and 1979, and again this ensured that their drop in popular support was not fully reflected in their tally of seats. Meanwhile, in both February 1974 and 1983, when Liberal/Alliance support was rising, there was a 'plateau' effect whereby the local vote rose least where it started highest, thereby denying victory in several seats that it had hoped to win.[40] The precedents suggest, therefore, that the small bonus of seats won in 1987 is a short-term benefit. If the Alliance (or its successors') vote were to rise again at the next election, then there might well be a repeat of the 'plateau' effect, producing a small shortfall in seats compared with a uniform change model.

Despite the marginal improvement in the Alliance's position, the electoral system still operated in a highly disproportional manner. As measured by the Rose Index of Proportionality[41] (79.1), only the 1983 election has produced a more disproportional result in modern British political history.[42] But what the election result also showed, even more strikingly than did the 1983 result, was that the electoral system does not discriminate against third parties in an even-handed manner. Rather, it showed that those small parties, whose vote is geographically sufficiently concentrated find the system no impediment to securing representation. Thus Plaid Cymru, in winning a third seat on a declining share of the vote, was able to acquire a higher proportion of the UK seats than votes (see Table A2.15) while even the minority community in Northern Ireland was able to secure approximately proportionate representation. Rather, the election again confirmed that the electoral system only discriminates against third parties whose vote is geographically evenly spread. If we exclude the two parties for whom that holds, the SNP and the Alliance, from the calculation of the election result we find that as between the other parties the result is approximately proportional. Indeed, the Rose Index (94.8) exceeds the level of proportionality commonly achieved by many so-called proportional systems.

This effect can also be seen if we calculate the outcome of the 1987 election under a system of proportional representation. Only the Alliance and the SNP would clearly have benefited, with up to 150 and ten MPs respectively; the exact numbers would depend on the precise system used. The two big losers would be the Conservatives with around a hundred and Labour with around twenty-five fewer seats than they actually won.[43]

Table A2.15   Two perspectives on the UK result

| | | | | Excluding Alliance and SNP | |
| | | Seats | Vote | Seats | Vote |
Party	Seats	(%)	(%)	(%)	(%)
Conservative	376	57.9	42.3	60.2	55.6
Labour	229	35.2	30.8	36.6	40.5
Alliance	22	3.4	22.6	–	–
SNP	3	0.5	1.3	–	–
Plaid Cymru	3	0.5	0.4	0.5	0.4
Unionists	13	2.0	1.2	2.1	1.6
Republicans	4	0.6	0.7	0.6	1.0
Others	0	0.0	0.7	0.0	0.9

These findings not only show that the electoral system does not discriminate against all third parties, but also that the system is nearly proportionate in its relative treatment of Conservative and Labour. The Conservative lead over Labour in votes is only modestly exaggerated by the electoral system in the allocation of seats. This is a relatively recent feature of the electoral system. Traditionally it was argued that the system was highly exaggerative because it conformed to a so-called 'cube law', that is, that the ratio of the seats won by the Conservative and Labour parties was the cube of the ratio of their votes. As we have shown elsewhere, the departure from this law has been brought about by the long-term variation in swing. But in our previous analysis of this change we suggested that, should that trend continue, the exaggerative quality of the electoral system could disappear entirely by 1987.[44] Yet Table A2.15 shows that there is still a small exaggerative quality. Given the variation in behaviour again between North and South Britain, why has that not happened?

The exaggerative quality of the electoral system depends upon the geographical variation in Conservative and Labour support. The conditions it needs to satisfy for the cube law to operate can be stated quite simply. The frequency distribution of the division of the Conservative and Labour (two-party) vote should be approximately normal with a standard deviation of 13.7.[45] If the standard deviation is higher than this, and/or the distribution is flatter at the centre than is a normal distribution, then the electoral system will be less exaggerative than the cube law states.

Thus by 1983 the standard deviation had become much larger than required for the cube law to operate – 20.0.[46] Further, the distribution was flatter at the centre than a normal distribution is; this can be measured by the kurtosis which was 1.05 less than that of a normal distribution. Put simply, this means that there were insufficient seats which were marginal between Conservative and Labour for the cube law to operate. Using a definition of marginals that controls for the change in the overall popularity of the parties from one election to another,[47] we find that although there needs to be 180 marginal seats for the cube law to operate, and their number averaged 159 between 1955 and 1970, there were only 80 in 1983. If one appreciates that were only one-tenth of all seats to be marginal (that is, 60–65) the electoral system would lose its exaggerative quality entirely, the fall in the number of marginal seats has clearly been dramatic.

What then happened in 1987? Although the standard deviation of the two-party vote did increase further to 21.4 while the kurtosis barely changed (−1.03), the number of marginal seats at the centre of the distribution did not fall as we had anticipated, but rose slightly to 87. It did so because of the absence of a particular pattern in Conservative and Labour movement we have had cause to remark upon at a number of points already – the lack of a consistent urban/rural pattern. Because, as the Conservatives actually did better than average in a number of southern urban areas such as London and much of the West Midlands conurbation, a significant number of southern urban seats which have at recent elections been moving towards Labour moved in 1987 back towards the Conservatives. This meant that some seats which had previously been 'safe' Labour seats became more marginal. Of the 28 seats which were, on our definition, marginal in 1987 but not in 1983, 14 did so as a consequence of swinging towards the Conservatives in 1987 after having moved towards Labour in 1983. And of these 11 are in South/East Britain, comprising eight in the London Metropolitan Area, two in Birmingham and one in Bristol.[48]

Indeed, it is clear that the future behaviour of urban southern Britain is crucial to the future of British politics. First, if its behaviour in 1987 were to portend a long-term reversal of its relatively slow but clear drift towards Labour, then the limited exaggerative quality which the electoral system still retains will probably persist for a few more elections rather than disappear. To demonstrate this we compared the results of two simulations. In one we projected on to the 1987 result the pattern of swing between 1983 and 1987; in the other we projected on to the 1987 result instead, the pattern of swing between 1979 and 1983, with its clear urban/rural, as well as its North/South variation. Whereas in the former simulation the number of marginal seats was almost unchanged at 86, in the latter it fell back to 72. Thus, the

355

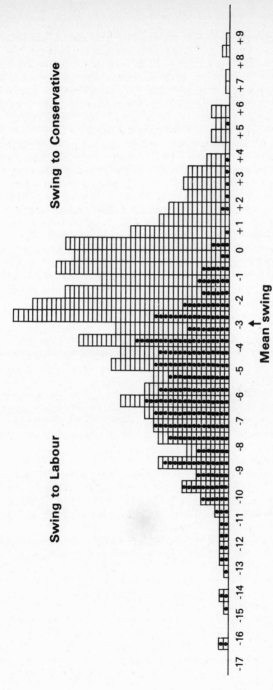

☐ One constituency in South/East Britain or Devon & Cornwall

▥ One constituency in North/West Britain

Figure A2.1 Variations in constituency two-party swing, 1983–87. The extreme cases are not marked (Newham South +12.6, Liverpool Mossley Hill +23.2, Liverpool Broadgreen −20.2, Ross, Cromarty & Skye −20.0, Inverness, Nairn & Lochaber −19.9).

behaviour of London, Birmingham, Bristol and a few other cities is crucial to the future prospects of a continuation of the decline in the exaggerative quality of the electoral system and thus the chances of a hung parliament.

But their behaviour is potentially crucial in a second way. In previous elections, the mixture of urban/rural and North/South patterns in swing produced a division of the country into roughly equal halves, with Labour doing better than average in one-half and the Conservatives in the other.[49] But in the absence of an urban/rural pattern this was not true in 1987. As Table A2.1 above indicated, the change in the Labour vote in the median constituency was lower than the mean, while (to a lesser extent) the opposite was true for the Conservatives. These differences indicate a positive skewness in the frequency distribution of the change in Labour's share of the vote, and a slight negative skewness in the case of the Conservatives. In other words, Labour did particularly well in a minority of constituencies, but below average in a majority. Indeed, the change in Labour's share of the vote was greater than the mean (3.7) in only 275 constituencies and below it in 358.

In Figure A2.1 we illustrate the problem this pattern poses for Labour. The figure shows the number of constituencies with a given level of two-party swing; similar histograms for previous elections can be found in earlier appendices in this series.[50] It shows quite clearly the variation in swing and, given the lack of a clear mode, the absence of any national norm. But it also shows that there are considerably more constituencies where the swing was below the mean (3.0%) than above it.[51] The swing to Labour was concentrated in a relatively small number of constituencies (mostly in North/West Britain), leaving a larger number (mostly in South/East Britain) where the swing was small or non-existent. Labour's difficulty is that its area of substantial advance in 1987, North/West Britain, constitutes only two-fifths of the country. If its support should become increasingly concentrated in that part of the country alone, leaving the Conservatives pre-eminent in South/East Britain, it faces the danger of becoming a permanent minority party. Only if it can reverse the Conservative advance in urban southern Britain does it have any chance of a majority.

The size of Labour's task is shown in table A2.16, which indicates the result in seats for each 1% increase in Labour support at the expense of the Conservatives, assuming that the Alliance and Nationalist parties stay at their 1987 level of support. Labour needs a total-vote swing of 3.9% to deny the Conservatives their overall majority. Their progress in 1987 was so modest that they still need a swing higher than any they have ever achieved since 1945 simply to deny the Conservatives an overall majority. In order to win an overall majority themselves they need a swing of 8.0%.

The table also shows that, even in the absence of any Alliance breakthrough, the range of results that will produce a hung parliament is still substantial. Both Labour and the Conservatives need a majority over their chief rival of 4% to secure an overall majority. Thanks to the decline in its exaggerative quality, the single member plurality electoral system can no longer ensure that an election will produce a single party government backed by an overall majority.

The fact that the lead required by the Conservatives for an overall majority is almost identical to that required by Labour indicates that the electoral

Table A2.16   Uniform swing from 1987 result

Con. (%)	Lab. (%)	Con.	Lab.	Alln.	Nat.	Oth.	Majority
43.3	31.5	376	229	22	6	17	Con. 102
42.3	32.5	365	239	23	6	17	Con. 80
41.3	33.5	356	247	24	6	17	Con. 52
40.3	34.5	335	264	28	6	17	Con. 20
39.4	**35.4**	**326**	**272**	**29**	**6**	**17**	**Con. 2**
39.3	35.5	324	273	30	6	17	None
38.3	36.5	314	285	28	6	17	None
37.4	**37.4**	**303**	**299**	**25**	**6**	**17**	**None**
36.3	38.5	293	309	25	6	17	None
35.3	**39.5**	**273**	**326**	**28**	**6**	**17**	**Lab. 2**
34.3	40.5	258	338	30	7	17	Lab. 26
33.3	41.5	249	346	31	7	17	Lab. 42

system is now almost entirely devoid of bias in its treatment of those two parties. If the two parties had the same share of the vote, the Conservatives would, on a uniform shift, win just 6 more seats than Labour. This arises because the effects of the two main sources of electoral bias cancel each other out. Labour receives a bonus from the fact that the constituencies it wins are smaller than those the Conservatives win. Indeed, the disparity in the size of Labour seats and Conservative-held seats was even greater than in 1983. In the seats won by Labour in 1987 the electorate did not grow between 1983 and 1987, while in Conservative held constituencies it increased by 3.4%. The average Conservative constituency contained 8435 electors more than the average Labour one.[52]

But this Conservative disadvantage is counterbalanced by the fact that the Conservatives distribute their vote more effectively than Labour. The Conservatives waste less votes than Labour in piling up large majorities. Whereas Labour won over 80% of the two-party vote in 71 constituencies (23 more than in 1983), the Conservatives won over 80% in just 19 (6 more than in 1983). Labour's majority exceeds 50% in 22 constituencies, whereas in no Conservative seat is that figure reached.

But while overall Labour may currently be being treated equitably by the electoral system, it does have reason to be concerned about the future. In England at least, the next review of parliamentary constituency boundaries must commence by 1991. The principal purpose of that review will be to make constituency electorates more equal in size. Although part of the reason why Labour seats are smaller than Conservative seats is its greater strength in Scotland and Wales, the review is bound to cost Labour seats. Indeed, on a simple calculation of its possible impact if the review were conducted on the basis of the 1987 electorates, Labour could lose 11 seats, or the equivalent of 1% of the vote.[53] Labour is not only in danger from becoming confined to too narrow a geographical base, but also a diminishing one.

NOTES

1. This figure is based on counting The Speaker as Conservative and including the one Sinn Fein MP with the opposition, even though he was pledged not to take his seat.
2. Herafter, all figures quoted in this appendix are for Great Britain unless otherwise stated. The Northern Ireland results are analysed separately on pp. 347–9.
3. The Pedersen Index is calculated as the sum of the change in each party's share since the previous election (ignoring signs) and dividing by two. See further, M. Pedersen, 'The Dynamics of European Party Systems: Changing Patterns of Electoral Volatility', *European Journal of Political Research*, vol. 7 (1979) pp. 1–27; I. Crewe, 'Introduction: Electoral Change in Western Democracies: A Framework for Analysis' and I. Crewe, 'Great Britain', in I. Crewe and D. Denver (eds), *Electoral Change in Western Democracies* (London: Croom Helm, 1985) pp. 9, 102.
4. But the index figure for that election is affected by the failure of the Liberals to fight all the seats in February 1974, which masks the real level of the fall in the Liberal vote between February and October 1974. If an allowance is made for that, the Pedersen Index rises from 3.0 to about 4.5 – leaving the 1987 election as clearly the least volatile for nearly 30 years.
5. The standard deviations of two-party swing for previous pairs of elections unaffected by boundary changes are: 1955–59, 2.7; 1959–64, 3.1; 1964–66, 2.1; 1966–70, 2.6; Feb.–Oct. 1974, 2.4; Oct. 1974–1979, 4.1.
6. The 78 European parliamentary constituencies are contiguous groupings of about eight Westminster constituencies each. Although most of the groupings are rather artificial, they provide equal-sized clusters of constituencies which are convenient for testing statistically for the presence of factors which are common to adjacent constituencies.
7. J. Curtice and M. Steed, 'Appendix 2: An Analysis of the Voting', in D. Butler and D. Kavanagh, *The British General Election of 1983* (London: Macmillan, 1983) pp. 334–5.
8. As in the rest of this appendix (unless otherwise stated) these are mean rather than overall changes.
9. On the one hand the correlation between Alliance and Conservative performance is stronger than in South/East Britain, making it an extreme example of the pattern of that part of the country, but on the other hand the social correlates of the variation in Labour performance echo closely the pattern of North/West Britain.
10. We would point in particular to the lack of any strong or consistent tendency for Labour to do better in urban areas (see p. 331) and to the signs that there was a centre-periphery cleavage in which the Conservatives did worse, the further a constituency was from London. See p. 329 and p. 330.
11. See J. Curtice and M. Steed, 'An Analysis of the Voting', in D. Butler and D. Kavanagh, *The British General Election of 1979* (London: Macmillan, 1980) pp. 396–9.

12. This remains true even after we exclude those (disporportionately rural) seats where there was evidence of a tactical switch from Labour to the Alliance, that is, those seats won by the Conservatives in 1983 and where the Alliance was more than 10% ahead of Labour (see Table A2.11 below).

13. See J. Curtice and M. Steed, 'Proportionality and Exaggeration in the British Electoral System', *Electoral Studies*, vol. 5 (1986) pp. 209–28; J. Curtice and M. Steed, 'Electoral Change and the Production of Government: The Changing Operation of the Electoral System in the United Kingdom since 1955', *British Journal of Political Science*, vol. 12 (1982) pp. 249–98.

14. See *The British General Election of 1983*, p. 340.

15. The distinctive behaviour of seaside resorts was not confined to South/East Britain. The Conservatives' vote fell by 3% in Conwy (Llandudno) and by 2.4% in Clwyd North-West (Colwyn Bay), their second and third worst performances in North Wales. There was also an above average drop in Blackpool (−2.8%) and in Morecambe & Lunesdale (−3.9%).

16. The constituency is, however, affected by the redevelopment of the London docklands, and the result may have in part reflected local gentrification (see also pp. 342–3).

17. See I. Crewe, 'A New class of Politics', *Guardian*, 15 June 1987; *The Times Higher Education Supplement*, 5 June 1987.

18. Prior to confusing boundary and name changes in 1983, the once safe Tory seat in Edinburgh was Edinburgh North; this was incorporated into Central. In Newcastle the safe Tory seat was North, which has nothing in common with the post-1983 Newcastle North and whose successor constituency was Newcastle Central.

19. For further discussion of the distinction between core–periphery and centre–periphery, see M. Steed, 'The core–periphery dimension of British politics', *Political Geography Quarterly*, vol. 5 (1986) pp. S91–103.

20. *The British General Election of 1979*, pp. 408–10. See also B. Cain, J. Ferejohn and M. Fiorina, *The Personal Vote* (Cambridge, Mass.; Harvard University Press, 1987); B. Cain, 'Blessed Be The Tie that Unbinds: Constituency Work and the Vote Swing in Great Britain', *Political Studies*, vol. 31 (1983) pp. 103–11.

21. Here, incumbent MPs are defined as those MPs whose pre-1983 constituency comprised at least 50% of the new constituency they fought in 1983.

22. A Conservative/Labour marginal is here defined as a seat where Labour were second to the Conservatives in 1983 and where the majority was less than 15%.

23. Spelthorne has been excluded from this calculation because of the impact of the return to the Conservative fold of the vote for Richard Adams, the author of *Watership Down*, who stood as Independent Conservative in 1983.

24. This concentration of the incumbency effect's impact in terms of seats in the North of England does not mean that its impact in terms of votes

was greater there. The incumbency effect could have no impact on the outcome in South/East Britain because, on the regional swing, only one Conservative seat was liable to be lost. Meanwhile, in Scotland and Wales there were few seats where the incumbency effect could have stemmed the stronger anti-Conservative tide.

25. Here we include those SDP MPs standing in a post-1983 constituency of which at least 50% consisted of electors from their old pre-1983 constituency.

26. For a summary of the evidence on tactical voting, see M. Steed, 'The Results Analysed', in D. Butler and D. Kavanagh, *The British General Election of October 1974* (London: Macmillan, 1975) pp. 341–2.

27. These are those seats where an SDP defector was standing in a new constituency of which at least 50% consisted of electors from his old constituency, together with the two by-election gains, Croydon North-West and Crosby, which were unsuccessfully defended.

28. These are the seats which changed hands at a by-election together with two others (Derbyshire West and Penrith & the Border) where the Alliance only narrowly missed victory.

29. We have similarly checked the robustness of the findings in Table A2.12 below by the same method.

30. Further, in two of these cases – Keighley and Bury North – the Alliance vote had already been squeezed in 1983.

31. Thus local government success accounts for the three remaining cases where the Alliance was not squeezed in North/West Britain. In other words, the Alliance was invariably hurt in a North/West Britain two-party marginal unless it had either been squeezed already in 1983 (see note 30), or had recently done well in local elections.

32. There is, however, just a suggestion in the results of a handful of seats with a traditional Liberal vote, and where the party label of the Alliance candidate was different in 1987 from 1983, that a Liberal candidate was more acceptable. This was most evident in Salisbury, which switched from Liberal to SDP, and where the Alliance vote fell by 5.2%, one of the worst Alliance performances in the South-West.

33. These are those constituencies with over 15% employed in energy and water industries as measured by the 1981 Census. Although it includes workers in industries other than coal-mining, this measure does in fact identify concentrations of coal workers.

34. J. Todd and R. Butcher, *Electoral Registration in 1981* (London: Office of Population Censuses and Surveys, 1982).

35. See M. and S. Pinto-Duchinsky, *Voter Registration: Problems and Solutions* (London: Constitutional Reform Centre, 1987).

36. Proceedings to expel Mr McCartney from the OUP, on the grounds of his 'insulting attacks' on the OUP leaders and because the OUP saw the Campaign for Equal Citizenship as encouraging the setting up of rivals to itself, were already in process when the election was called. The local OUP was in fact deeply divided, having decided to nominate him by a vote of 39 to 29 in an executive committee of 190.

37. This, of course, is only true of Provisional Sinn Fein. Official Sinn Fein, now constituted as the Workers' Party, has previously fought elections.

38. In those constituencies where turnout was between 65% and 70%, the Labour share of the vote rose by 5.3%; in those where it was over 80%, it increased by only 3.1%. The equivalent Conservative figures were −0.4 and −0.2. In the handful of constituencies where turnout was below 65%, the Conservatives actually did better than average (+2.1%), reflecting their performance in London.

39. If the calculation is made on two-party swing rather than total-vote swing, the figure is only slightly different (27).

40. See Curtice and Steed, 'An Analysis of the Voting', 1983, pp. 347–8.

41. The Rose Index is the sum of the absolute differences between the percentage of votes won by each party and its percentage of the seats, divided by two. See R. Rose, 'Elections and Electoral Systems: Choices and Alternatives', in V. Bogdanor and D. Butler (eds), *Democracy and Elections: Electoral Systems and their Political Consequences* (London: Cambridge University Press, 1983).

42. The commentary in this paragraph, and Table A2.15, refers to the United Kingdom, not just Great Britain.

43. See M. Steed, 'The 1987 UK results under differing electoral systems' *Electoral Studies* 1988 for the number of seats proportional representation might have yielded.

44. See Curtice and Steed, 'Electoral Choice'; Curtice and Steed, 'Proportionality and Exaggeration', pp. 216–18.

45. For further discussion see G. Gudgin and P. Taylor, *Seats, Votes and the Spatial Organisation of Elections* (London: Pion, 1979).

46. For further details see Curtice and Steed, 'Proportionality and Exaggeration', p. 214. Seats won by third parties are excluded from this calculation.

47. Marginal seats are defined as those seats in which, on a 50:50 division of the two-party vote nationally, the Conservative two-party lead over Labour, or vice versa, would be less than 10%. Seats won by third parties are excluded.

48. The three seats in North/West Britain are all cases where the incumbency effect operated. They might therefore be expected to revert to their long-term trend at the next election.

49. Indeed, in 1983 Labour did better than average in slightly over half the constituencies. See Curtice and Steed, 'An Analysis of the Voting', 1983, pp. 337–8.

50. See M. Steed, 'The Results Analysed', in D. Butler and A. King, *The British General Election of 1964* (London: Macmillan, 1965) p. 352; M. Steed, 'An Analysis of The Results', in D. Butler and A. King, *The British General Election of 1966* (London: Macmillan, 1966) p. 276; M. Steed, 'The Results Analysed', in D. Butler and M. Pinto-Duschinsky, *The British General Election of 1970* (London: Macmillan, 1971) p. 399; Curtice and Steed, 'An Analysis of The Results', 1979, p. 395; Curtice and Steed, 'An Analysis of The Results', 1983, p. 337.

51. The two-party swing to Labour was less than the average in 354 cases and above it in 279.

52. This source of bias to Labour is further exaggerated by the fact that

turnout is on average lower in Labour-held seats (73.3%) than in Conservative held ones (76.6%).

53. We have simply identified how many seats would have to be switched from Labour to Conservative to achieve a position where the size of the electorate in the average Labour seat is as identical as possible to that in the average Conservative seat, the calculation being undertaken separately for Scotland, Wales, Greater London and England outside Greater London.

Bibliography

A select list of books and articles relating to elections and parties published since 1983.

Books

Adeney, M. and Lloyd, J., *The Miners' Strike, 1984–85* (London, 1986).
Anwar, M., *Race and Politics* (London, 1986).
Berrington, H. (ed.), *Change in British Politics* (London, 1984).
Butler, D. and Jowett, P., *Party Strategies in Britain* (the 1984 Euro-elections) (London, 1985).
Butler, D. and Kavanagh, D., *The British General Election of 1983* (London, 1984).
Cain, B., Ferejohn, J. and Fiorina, M., *The Personal Vote* (Cambridge, Mass., 1987).
Cockerell, M., Hennessy, P. and Walker, D., *Sources Close to the Prime Minister* (London, 1985).
Cole, J., *The Thatcher years* (London, 1987).
Crewe, I. and Denver, D. (eds), *Electoral Change in Western Democracies* (London, 1985).
Crewe, I. and Harrop, M. (eds), *Political Communications: the 1983 Election Campaign* (Cambridge, 1986).
Crick, M., *Scargill and the Miners* (Harmondsworth, 1985).
Crick, M., *The March of Militant* (Harmondsworth, 1986).
Dunleavy, P. and Husbands, C., *British Democracy at the Crossroads: Voting and Party Competition in the 1980's* (London, 1985).
Financial Times, *The Thatcher Years* (London, 1987).
Franklin, M., *The Decline of Class Voting in Britain* (Oxford, 1984).
Goodhart, D. and Wintour, P., *Eddie Shah and the Newspaper Revolution* (London, 1986).
Goodman, G., *The Miners' Strike* (London, 1985).
Gould, B., *Socialism and Freedom* (London, 1985).
Hain, P., *Proportional Misrepresentation: The Case Against PR in Britain* (Aldershot, 1986).
Harris, R., *The Making of Neil Kinnock* (London, 1984).
Heath, A., Jowell, R. and Curtice, J., *How Britain Votes* (Oxford, 1985).
Heffer, E., *Labour's Future – Socialist or SDP Mark Two?* (London, 1986).
Hetherington, A., *News, Newspapers and Television* (Basingstoke, 1985).
Himmelweit, H. *et al.*, *How Voters Decide* (Open University, 1985).
Hollingsworth, M., *The Press and Political Dissent* (London, 1986).
Jenkins, S., *Market for Glory: Fleet Street Ownership in the Twentieth Century* (London, 1986).
Johnston, R., *The Geography of English Politics: The 1983 General Election* (Beckenham, 1985).

Jones, B. and Keating, M., *Labour and the British State* (Oxford, 1985).

Jowell, R. *et al.* (eds), *British Social Attitudes: the 1986 Report* (Aldershot, 1987).

Kavanagh, D., *Thatcherism and British Politics: The End of Consensus?* (London, 1986).

Keegan, W., *Mrs Thatcher's Economic Experiment* (Harmondsworth, 1985).

King, A. (ed.), *The British Prime Minister* (London, 1985).

Kinnock, N., *Making Our Way* (Oxford, 1986).

Layton-Henry, Z. and Rich, P. B. (eds), *Race, Government and Politics in Britain* (London, 1986).

Leapman, M., *Kinnock* (London, 1987).

McAllister, I. and Rose, R., *The Nationwide Competition for Votes: The 1983 British General Election* (London, 1984).

McNay, I. and Ozga, J., *Policy-making in Education: The Breakdown of Consensus* (Harmondsworth, 1986).

Melvern, L., *The End of the Street* (London, 1986).

MORI, *British Public Opinion: General Election 1987* (London, 1987).

Mughan, A., *Party and Participation in British Elections* (London, 1986).

Owen, D., *David Owen Speaking Personally to Kenneth Harris* (London, 1987).

Penniman, H. and Ranney, A. (eds), *Britain at the Polls 1983: A Study of the General Election* (Duke University Press, 1985).

Pinto-Duschinsky, M. and Pinto-Duschinsky, S., *Voter Registration: Problems and Solutions* (London: Constitutional Reform Centre, 1987).

Porter, H., *Lies, Damned Lies, and Some Exclusives* (London, 1984).

Prior, J., *A Balance of Power* (London, 1986).

Pym, F., *The Politics of Consent* (London, 1985).

Reece, G., *Voter Representation: A Study of the British Electoral System and its Consequences* (Conservative Action for Electoral Reform, 1985).

Riddell, P., *The Thatcher Government* (Oxford, 1985).

Robertson, D., *Class and the British Electorate* (Oxford, 1984).

Rose, R., *Do Parties Make a Difference?* 2nd edn (London, 1984).

Rose, R. and McAllister, I., *Voters Begin to Choose* (London, 1986).

Scarborough, E., *Political Ideology and Voting: an Explanatory Study* (Oxford, 1986).

Seldon, A. (ed.), *The New Right Enlightenment* (London, 1985).

Steed, M. and Curtice, J., *One in Four, an examination of the Alliance Performance* (Hebden Bridge, Yorkshire: Association of Liberal Councillors).

Steel, D., *Partners in one Nation: A New View of Britain 2000* (London, 1985).

The Times Guide to the House of Commons, 1987 (London, 1987).

Todd, J. and Eldridge, J., *Electoral Registration in Inner City Areas 1983–4* (HMSO, 1987).

Tyler, R., *Campaign: The Selling of the Prime Minister* (London, 1987).

Waller, R., *The Almanac of British Politics* (London, 1987).

Walters, A., *Britain's Economic Renaissance* (London, 1985).

Wilsher, P. *et al.*, *Strike: Thatcher, Scargill and The Miners* (London, 1985).

Wilson, D., *Battle for Power* (London, 1987).

Worcester, R. (ed.), *Political Opinion Polling: An International Review* (London, 1983).
Young, H. and Sloman, A., *The Thatcher Phenomenon* (London, 1986).

Articles

Alderman, G., 'London Jews and the 1987 General Election', *Jewish Quarterly*, Sept. 1987.
Barton, T. and Dring, H., 'The Social and Attitudinal Profile of SDP Activists: Note on a Survey of the 1982 Council for Social Democracy', *Political Studies*, 1986.
Bulpitt, J., 'The Thatcher Statecraft', *Political Studies*, 1985.
Clarke, H. D. *et al.*, 'Politics, Economics and Party Popularity in Britain, 1979–83', *Electoral Studies*, 1986.
Contemporary Record, October 1987. Special issue on Thatcher and Thatcherism.
Crewe, I., 'The Electorate: Partisan dealignment ten years on', in Berrington, H. (ed.), *Change in British Politics* (London, 1984).
Crewe, I., 'Can Labour Rise Again?', *Social Studies Review*, 1985.
Crewe, I., 'The Campaign Confusion', *New Society*, 8 May 1987.
Curtice, J. and Steed, M., 'Proportionality and Exaggeration in the British Electoral System', *Electoral Studies*, vol. 5 (1983) pp. 209–28.
Denver, D., 'Predicting the next British Election (or not, as the case may be)', *Parliamentary Affairs*, 1987.
Dunleavy, P., 'Class Dealignment Revisited', *West European Politics*, 1987.
Flanagan, S. C. and Dalton, R. J., 'Parties under Stress', *West European Politics*, 1984.
Franklin, M., 'How the Decline of Class Voting opened the way to Radical Change in British Politics', *British Journal of Political Science*, 1984.
Franklin, M., 'Assessing the Rise of Issue Voting in British Elections since 1964', *Electoral Studies*, 1985.
Franklin, M. and Page, E., 'A Critique of the Consumption Cleavage Approach in British Voting Studies', *Political Studies*, 1984.
Graetz, B. and McAllister, I., 'Party Leaders and Election Outcomes in Britain', *Comparative Political Studies*, 1987.
Grant, D., 'Unions and Political Funds Ballots', *Parliamentary Affairs*, 1987.
Harrop, M. and Rudd, C., 'Can Labour Recover?', *Political Quarterly*, 1983.
House of Commons, Fourth Report from the Defence Committee session 1985/6: Westland plc: The Government's Decision-Making (HMSO:1).
Heath, A., 'Comment on Dennis Kavanagh's "How we vote now"', *Electoral Studies*, 1986.
Heath, A., Jowell, R. and Curtice, J., 'Understanding Electoral Change in Britain', *Parliamentary Affairs*, 1986.
Heath, A., Jowell, R. and Curtice, J., 'Trendless Fluctuations: A Reply to Crewe', *Political Studies*, 1987.
Hennessy. P., 'Helicopter Crashes into Cabinet: Prime Minister and Constitution Hurt', *Journal of Law and Society*, 1986.
Hennessy, P., 'Michael Heseltine, Mottram's Law and the Efficiency of Cabinet Government', *Political Quarterly*, 1986.

Hirst, P., 'The Issues at Stake in Coalition Politics', *Political Quarterly*, 1986.

Huhne, C., 'The Economics of a Coalition Government', *Political Quarterly*, 1986.

Inglehart, R. and Rabier, J.-R., 'Political Realignment in Advanced Industrial Society: From Class-based Politics to Quality-of-Life Politics', *Government and Opposition*, 1986.

Johnston, R. and Taylor, P., 'Political Geography: A Politics of Places Within Places', *Parliamentary Affairs*, 1986.

Judge, K. *et al.*, 'Public opinion and the Privatisation of Welfare', *Journal of Social Policy*, 1983.

Kavanagh, D., 'Whatever Happened to Consensus Politics?', *Political Studies*, 1985.

Kavanagh, D., 'Power in British Political Parties. Iron Law or Special Pleading?', *West European Politics*, 1985.

Kavanagh, D., 'How we Vote now', *Electoral Studies*, 1986.

Kavanagh, D., 'Margaret Thatcher: A Study in Prime Ministerial Style', Strathclyde Occasional Paper, 1986.

Kavanagh, D., 'The Rise of Thatcher and Thatcherism', *Social Studies Review*, 1988.

Kelley, J. and McAllister, I., 'Social Context and Electoral Behaviour in Britain', *American Political Science Review*, 1985.

Kelley, J. and McAllister, I., 'The Decline of Class Revisited: Class and Party in England, 1964–79', *American Political Science Review*, 1985.

Kimber, J., 'The Ideological Position and Electoral Appeal of the Labour Party Candidates: an Analysis of Labour's Performance at the 1983 General Election', *British Journal of Political Science*, 1987.

Levy, R., 'The Search for a Rational Strategy: the SNP and Devolution, 1974–9', *Political Studies*, 1986.

McAllister, I., 'Housing Tenure and Party Choice in Australia, Britain and the U.S.', *British Journal of Political Science*, 1984.

McAllister, I., 'Campaign Effects and Electoral Outcomes in Britain, 1979 and 1983', *Public Opinion Quarterly*, 1985.

McAllister, I. and Kelley, J., 'Party Identification and Political Socialisation – a note on Australia and Britain', *European Journal of Political Research*, 1985.

McAllister, I. and Mughan, A., 'Differential Turnout and Party Advantage in British General Elections, 1964–83', *Electoral Studies*, 1986.

Maguire, M., 'Is there still persistence? Electoral change in Western Europe, 1948–78', in Daalder, H. and Mair, P. (eds), *West European Party Systems: Continuity and Change* (London, 1983).

Messina, A., 'Ethnic Minority Representation and Party Competition in Britain: the Case of Ealing Borough', *Political Studies*, 1987.

Mitchell, A., 'Taking it Personally', *New Society*, 5 June 1987.

Muller, W., Tagg, J. and Britto, K., 'Partnership and Party Preference in Government and Opposition: The Mid-term Perspective', *Political Studies*, 1986.

Norpoth, H., 'The Falklands War and Government Popularity in Britain: Rally without Consequence or Surge without Decline', *Electoral Studies*, 1987.

Norris, P., 'Conservative Attitudes in Recent British Elections: An Emerging Gender Gap?', *Political Studies*, 1986.

Oliver, D. and Austin, R., 'The Westland Affair', *Parliamentary Affairs*, 1987.

Payne, C., Brown, P. and Hanna, V., 'By-election Exit Polls', *Electoral Studies*, 1986.

Pinkney, R., 'Dealignment, Realignment or Just Alignment? A Mid-term Report', *Parliamentary Affairs*, 1986.

Pinto-Duschinsky, M., 'British Political Funding, 1979–93', *Parliamentary Affairs* (1985).

Rasmussen, J., 'Who Gets Hung in a Hung Parliament?: A Game Theory of the 1987–88 British General Election', *British Journal of Political Science*, 1986.

Rasmussen, J., 'Constitutional aspects of Government Formation in a Hung Parliament', *Parliamentary Affairs*, 1987.

Richards, P., 'The Choice of Government in a Three-Party System', *Political Quarterly*, 1986.

Roberts, H., 'Sound Stupidity: The British Party System and the Northern Ireland Question', *British Journal of Political Science*, 1987.

Rose, R., 'Opinion Polls as a Feedback Mechanism', University of Strathclyde, Occasional Paper, 1983.

Rudig, W. and Lowe, P. D., 'The "withered" Greening of British Politics: A Study of the Ecology Party', *Political Studies*, 1986.

Scarborough, E., 'The British Electorate Twenty Years on: Electoral Change and Election surveys', *British Journal of Political Science*, 1987.

Steed, M., 'The Core – Periphery Dimension of British Politics', *Political Geography Quarterly* (1986).

Studlar, D. and McAllister, I., 'Protest and Survive? Alliance Support in the 1983 British General Election', *Political Studies*, 1987.

Swaddle, K., 'Doorstep Electioneering: An Exploration of the Constituency Canvass', *Electoral Studies*, April 1988.

Vallance, E., 'Women Candidates in the 1983 General Election', *Parliamentary Affairs*, vol. 37, no. 3, Summer 1984, pp. 301–9.

Whiteley, P., 'Predicting the Labour Vote in 1983: Social Background versus Subjective Evaluations', *Political Studies*, 1986.

Williams, P., 'Party Realignment in the U.S. and Britain', *British Journal of Political Science*, 1985.

Index

368

McAllister, I., 73n
McAlpine, Lord, 26, 35, 38, 109
MacArthur, B., 188n
McCartney, I., 192, 210n
McCartney, R., 230, 348, 360n
Macfarlane, N., 219
McGiven, A., 78
McGoldrick, Maureen, 56
MacGregor, I., 11
MacGregor, J., 70, 106
McGuire, M., 192, 207n
McKie, D., 181
McLoughlin, P., 200, 210n
McNair-Wilson, M., 210n
McNair-Wilson, P., 210n
Macmillan, H., 5, 20, 30, 109
Maidstone, 198
Mail on Sunday, 174, 193
Makerfield, 192
Manchester, 272, 352
Mandelson, P., 51, 59–61, 89, 90, 250, 255
Manifestos, Con., 39–45, 101, 172–3; Lab., 69–72, 101–2, 257; Alln., 82–4, 101
Mansfield, 342, 344, 345
Maps, 120, 121
Marginal polls, 128–9
Market Research Society (MRS), 126
Marplan, *see* Opinion Polls
Marshall, E., 209n
Mass Observation, 155, 178
Matt Reese & Associates, 78
Matthews, Lord, 164
Mattinson, Deborah, 63, 64, 73n, 138n
Maxwell, R., 12, 118, 163, 175, 176
Maynard, Joan, 53
Maze Prison, 15
Meacher, M., 48, 53, 70, 73n
Meadowcroft, M., 79, 340
Meetings, 215–16, 244–5
Mellish, R., 208n
Melvern, L., 188n
Mergers, 19
Meyer, Sir A., 196
Michie, Ray, 198
Mid-Ulster, 347
Militant Tendency, 16, 52, 53, 56, 57, 72, 171, 208n, 210n, 342
Millan, B., 200
Millar, Sir R., 34, 44, 92, 108
Miners, 11–12, 52, 56, 322, 330, 345
Mitchell, A., 210n, 237n
Mitchell, R., 335

Mitterrand, F., 14
Monday Club, 31
Monetarism, 5
Montgomery, 340
Montgomery, Sir F., 209n
Moore, J., 40, 156
Moran, M., 210n
Morecambe & Lunesdale, 359
MORI, *see* Opinion Polls
Morris, J., 54, 200
Morrison, C., 210n
Morrison, H., 59
Morrison, P., 25, 38, 122n, 210n
Mortimer, Jim, 49
Mortimer, John, 63
Moscow, 42, 45, 69, 249
Murdoch, R., 12, 55, 105, 163
Murphy, C., 196
Murray, L., 12

National Association of Local Government Officers (NALGO), 122n
National Graphical Association (NGA), 54, 105, 220
National Front, 99, 325
National Health Service (NHS), 5, 16, 30, 67, 107, 112, 141, 146, 155, 158, 219
National Liberal Club, 90
National Opinion Polls (NOP), *see* Opinion Polls
National Union of Mineworkers (NUM), 11, 52, 203
National Union of Railwaymen (NUR), 203
Nationalists, 95, 272, 335
Nellist, D., 210n, 219, 342
Neuberger, H., 50
New Socialist, 58
New Society, 176
New Statesman, 58, 97, 176
New Zealand, 271
Newby, R., 78, 80, 122n
Newcastle, 272, 359n
Newcastle Central, 332
Newcastle-Under-Lyme, 340
Newham, 325
Newham North West, 57, 199, 235
Newham South, 324, 331
Newport, 323
Newry & Armagh, 8, 235, 347
News International, 163

Yardley, 338
Yarm Hospital, 150
Ynys Mon, 196, 229, 339
Yorkshire Post, 175
Yorkshire TV, 150
Young & Rubicam, (Y & R), 32, 35, 36,
42, 108, 135–6, 250–1
Young, H., 242

Young of Dartington, Lord, 97
Young of Graffham, Lord, in 1983–7, 28,
31, 35, 39–40, 42, 44; in campaign,
107, 109, 122n; assessed, 241, 250–1
Younger, G., 21, 103

Zia, President, 221